A BLOOD-DIMMED TIDE

A BLOOD-DIMMED TIDE

Dispatches

from the

Middle East

AMOS ELON

Columbia
University
Press
New York

Columbia University Press
Publishers Since 1893
New York   Chichester, West Sussex
Copyright © 1997 Amos Elon
Library of Congress Cataloging-in-Publication Data
Elon, Amos.
    A blood–dimmed tide : dispatches from the Middle East / Amos Elon.
        p.   cm.
    Includes bibliographical references and index.
    ISBN 0–231–10742–0 (cloth)
    1. Israel—Politics and government.   2. Israel–Arab War, 1967—
Influence.   3. Intifada, 1987–   4. Shalom akhshav (Organization :
Israel)   5. Jewish–Arab relations—1973–   I. Title.
DS126.5.E41948   1997
956.9405—dc21   96–48966
                                                          CIP

⊛

Casebound editions of Columbia University Press books are printed on permanent and
durable acid-free paper.
Printed in the United States of America
c 10 9 8 7 6 5 4 3 2 1

Chapter 1 appeared in *Commentary* Magazine, August 1967
Chapter 2 appeared in *Encounter* Magazine, December 1967
Chapter 3 appeared in *The New York Times Book Review*, January 16, 1979
Chapter 4 appeared in *Ha'aretz*, August 6, 1981
Chapter 5 appeared in *Ha'aretz*, February 10, 1979
Chapter 6 first appeared in Amos Elon, *Flight Into Egypt* (New York: Doubleday, 1980)
Chapter 7 appeared in *The New Yorker*, July 29, 1985
Chapter 8 appeared in *The New Yorker*, July 27, 1987
Chapter 9 appeared in *The New York Review of Books*, April 14, 1988
Chapter 10 appeared in *The New Yorker*, Februrary 13, 1989
Chapter 11 appeared in *The New Yorker*, April 23, 1990
Chapter 12 appeared in *The New Yorker*, July 18, 1988
Chapter 13 appeared in *The New Yorker*, December 12, 1990
Chapter 14 appeared in *The New Yorker*, April 1, 1991
Chapter 15 appeared in *The New York Review of Books*, August 12, 1993
Chapter 16 appeared in *The New Yorker*, December 20, 1993
Chapter 17 appeared in *The New York Review of Books*, April 12, 1994
Chapter 18 appeared in *The New York Review of Books*, October 7, 1993
Chapter 19 appeared in *The New York Review of Books*, April 6, 1995
Chapter 20 appeared in *The New York Review of Books*, September 22, 1994
Chapter 21 appeared in *The New York Review of Books*, December 21, 1995

For Bob Silvers, a prince among editors

CONTENTS

A BLOOD-DIMMED TIDE

Introduction

This Introduction is written in the aftermath of the 1996 elections, and the fall of Shimon Peres's Labor government. It was a government that had signed a historic accord with the Palestinians (for which had received the Nobel Prize) and a peace treaty with Jordan and had brought about an economic boom unprecedented in the history of the country, but was nevertheless narrowly defeated by a coalition of right-wing nationalists and religious fundamentalists led by Benjamin ("Bibi") Netanyahu. The last article in this book was written in 1996 after the assassination of Yitzhak Rabin.

Like most men, Netanyahu wanted peace but did not know or did not want the things that make for peace. He pledged to be a better patriot, a better "Zionist" than Peres. Unlike Peres, he did not offer to surrender territories occupied by Israel in the 1967 war in return for peace. He offered peace for peace. It remains to be seen if the peace process can be advanced by such rhetoric alone and by the flexing of muscles. Netanyahu may not remain true to *all* his hardline campaign promises. Yet, at the very least, his rise to power heralded an interruption in—and possibly the end of—the peace process launched with so much hopeful fanfare by the previous government. As a potential peacemaker, Netanyahu's difficulties were considerable. If he made concessions to the Arabs in order to make peace, he risked losing the support of his right-wing party and his religious coalition partners. If he satisfied his party and his coalition partners he risked losing the peace.

If 1967 had been a miraculously victorious year for Israelis, by 1996 they were a bitterly divided nation. Between these melancholy dates fall the events discussed in these pieces. They reflect a drama not only political but also human and often tragic. It is a story of wars won and peace opportunities missed—by both sides. First the Arab states missed them. Later, as some Arab states gradually came to recognize the need for peace, Israel missed its opportunities. Then again the Arabs and the Palestinians missed theirs. These days, the Arabs and the Palestinians again seem ready for peace, or perhaps are tired of war, but Netanyahu is less anxious to compromise that his predecessor had been. It is this terrible disynchrony between the two sies that leads some people to conclude that the problem may be intractable. Abba Eban once observed that it wasn't true that governments are constitutionally incapable of arriving at the right decision; it is just that they do so only as a last resort. Will Israelis and Palestinians ever do so simultaneously? And until that moment arrives, how many more casualties will fall? How many more widows and orphans will weep, how many more resources will be wasted?

The dispatches, arranged in this book as separate chapters, are for the most part reproduced as they appeared. They reflect one observer's view of the trials, errors, opportunities, and disasters of those stormy years. The victory of 1967 had given Israel the bargaining chips it had lacked before. But instead of opening a way for peace, Israel's stunning victory in war merely closed too many leading political minds. Few things can be as debilitating, intellectually, as a great victory. "Nothing except a battle lost can be half so melancholy as a battle won," Wellington wrote from the field of Waterloo.

The painful irony of this early denouement overshadows the events described in these pieces. Their recurrent theme is the search—mostly in vain, sometimes partly successful—for the peaceful solution of a conflict that has continued for nearly a century. The bitter debate over it has divided the experts for as long as most of us can remember. Underlying it was the tragedy of an ideology commonly known as Zionism. The tragedy reached its high point, ironically, at a time when Zionism, as *originally* conceived by its founders, seemed to have successfully achieved most of its purposes. Yet in its current interpretation by nationalist hardliners and religious fundamentalists, this century-old ideology has for some time been a stumbling block on the way to peace. It remains to be seen if a democracy, an open society, can co-exist with a "state-ideology" (especially in its recent re-interpretation). When religion is seen primarily as a quest for identity it comes at the expense of its other, higher, purposes—charity and compassion. In the final analysis, as Karl Kraus warned, "every ideology gravitates toward war."

❊

The first Zionists, in the 1880s and 1890s, ignored the presence of another people in the land they hoped to repossess after an absence of almost two millennia. The political imagination, like the imagination of the explorer, often invents its own geography. The early settlers did not consider the country "empty" as did some Zionists abroad. Yet even if there were people living in the country the settlers saw that it was populated only very sparsely. They believed they were operating in a political void.

They were fervently, at considerable human and material cost, promoting their own national renaissance but remained blind to the possibility that the Palestinians might entertain similar hopes. It is always difficult for one people to "understand" the nationalism of another. Hindsight makes all this sound unbelievable today. The fact is that there was little evidence of Arab nationalism before 1908, and none at all of a specific Arab-Palestinian variety. Before 1918 few Zionists ever contemplated the possibility that Arabs and Jews might one day clash in bloody battle as Germans and French did over Alsace-Lorraine, or as Greek-Orthodox Serbs, Catholic Croats and Muslim Bosnians still do in the former Yugoslavia. The few early settlers who paid attention to the Palestinian population assumed that their arrival would inevitably raise living standards among all; the sparse native population would assimilate among the Jews and become their closest ally. They were inveterate diarists and polemicists. It was said about them that never was so much polemic written by so few men and women in so short a time about so many political and social issues. The problem posed by the presence of Arabs in the Land was not one of these issues.

With characteristic optimism (and sarcasm), Theodor Herzl, the founder of modern Zionism, assured his successor David Wolfsohn that Zionism would eventually triumph, but added, a few weeks before his death in 1904: "Don't commit any follies *while* I am dead!" At that early stage, "Zionism" was not yet endowed with the supernatural qualities as it has today in the eyes of certain religious fundamentalists. It was simply a fancier term for "Jewish nationalism." Like other European nationalisms of the time—the nationalism of the Czechs, the Italians, or the Poles—Zionism was a child of the Enlightenment and the ideas of the French Revolution, the Declaration of the Rights of Man, and the need to separate church and state. Its aim was to provide persecuted Jews with a safe haven, recognized in international law, a National Home.

It was after the Six Day War of 1967 that this view of Zionism, as a secular political movement was first seriously challenged by expansionist revisionist right-wingers and by religious fundamentalists. The former believed that might was right. In the eyes of the latter, "Zionism" was a messianic idea, a meta-political task. The great victory of 1967 was, in their eyes, a miraculous event charged with divine meaning. It heralded the Coming of the Messiah, the End of Days, and the beginning of Redemption. The hard core of the Jewish settlers in the occupied West Bank after 1967 came from this community of believers.

There was no shortage of follies after Herzl's death, nor of critics to point them out. The early innocence of the first settlers and of their Zionist supporters abroad abruptly ended early in the 1920s following the first civic disturbances in Palestine. This was a rude awakening. For the first time, arguments proliferated on how to achieve peace and reconciliation. To meet the Arabs of Palestine halfway, David Ben-Gurion in 1924 favored a bi-national state. The Zionists, he insisted, "have no right whatsoever to deprive a single Arab child, even if through this deprivation we shall realize our aims." There is no reason to doubt the sincerity of his sentiment at that time. Others proposed limits on Jewish immigration. All such compromise solutions, including several schemes to partition the country, were rejected by the Arabs. In 1936 the Palestinians launched an open rebellion.

Hannah Arendt, in the mid-1940s, went further than most critics and declared the entire enterprise a tragic miscarriage. According to Arendt, this was so because of the failure to achieve a peaceful modus vivendi in Palestine between Arabs and Jews. She attributed the responsibility for this failure almost exclusively to the Jews. Jacob L. Talmon, another prominent historian of nationalism, pondered the same question. Like Arendt, he was disturbed by the seemingly irresistible move to all-out war but became confirmed in the grim conclusion that although in detail, in style, and in tone, the Jews might have acted more wisely and more tactfully, it would not have made much difference in the final analysis. The same could not be said about the Arabs, Talmon thought. By adopting an attitude of absolute and total intransigence, the Arabs had reduced the Jews' alternatives to two: Either give up their aspirations—this would have seemed quite unthinkable in those years, immediately after the Nazi Holocaust— or build the National Home in the face of Arab opposition. Since no give-and-take was possible and even such modest forms of Zionism as limited immigration and limited settlement invariably met with maximum Arab resistance, there was no choice, Talmon wrote, but to aim for maximum results with maximum strength.

❋

Half a century has since passed. Many people today may find those arguments of limited interest. Israel's hundred year old existential struggle seems over, or almost over. Israel is said to be the strongest, most effective military power between France and India. For some years now, it has been in possession of a nuclear deterrent and of sophisticated intermediate-range delivery missiles. It has become a regional mini-power in alliance with the United States and powerful other allies in Europe and the Near East.

The strategic balance has changed. The Middle East is no longer contested by outside powers as it had been for the last two centuries—England v. Germany or France, more recently the United States v. the Soviet Union. Two (older) regional powers, Turkey and Iran, are trying to step into the resultant vacuum. In this new regional power game Israel's strategic position has improved. The collapse of the Soviet Union deprived its worst enemies of the political support and war arsenals of a superpower. There are still clashes and setbacks but the general trend has been fairly steady for some time. Its highlights were Israel's peace treaties with Egypt and Jordan, the end of the Arab boycott, and Israel's new diplomatic contacts with the Gulf states and with Morocco and Tunisia. Even under the new right-wing Israeli government, the remaining issue with Syria is no longer one of existential "principle," as it had been during the first decades of the Jewish state when, in Syrian eyes, it was overloaded with seemingly insurmountable metaphysical, psychological, and conceptual problems. The remaining issues with Syria are the more "normal" problems of neighboring states: borders and water resources.

The Palestinian issue is more complicated. It touches the heart of the conflict and deeply ingrained myths. Rabin and Peres were reconciled with the idea that the Palestinians would eventually establish their own independent state. This cannot, at least not yet, be said of the administration headed by Netanyahu. Perhaps it never will be. It was Rabin and Peres's strategic understanding with the Palestinian Liberation Organization in Oslo in 1993 that had opened the doors to peace with Jordan and to diplomatic contacts with Arab countries from Morocco to the Gulf. If Netanyahu puts this understanding in jeopardy, Israel's new relations with Jordan and other Arab states will be in jeopardy too.

Netanyahu promised to honor the 1993 agreement between Israel and the PLO in which, after decades of mutual demonization, the two recognized each other and vowed to resolve their differences in peace. Netanyahu may or may not keep this (and other) campaign promises. But if he does not, the Palestinians will not dissolve into thin air. He must confront this problem politically: all attempts to "resolve" it militarily have failed in the past. In this sense, it is fair to say that *in the long run* the peace process remains irreversible.

There are still terror attacks, as there are elsewhere in the world. Terrorism is painful but it does not pose the strategic, or existential threat comparable to that presented in the past by the extreme hostility of the neighboring Arab states. For the first time since 1948, most Arab governments (and the new autonomous Palestinian Authority) are ready to fight terror jointly with Israel. (Freud remarked that it was easier to establish bonds of love between two parties if there is a third they can both hate). Most Arab governments, and the new Palestinian Authority headed by Arafat, feel seriously threatened by Islamic fundamentalists.

On both sides of the great chasm that has divided Israel and its Arab neighbors for almost a century, passions are cooling. New generations are at work searching for reconciling formulas. This is not to say that they have found all. They have found a *few*.

❀

In the past, Arab rejection had been total. It went so far as to decry the simplest human contacts between individuals. Threats were hair-raising. At times, they bordered on the genocidal. Among those Israelis who witnessed or fought in one of the Arab-Israeli wars—there were at least five full sized wars and endless skirmishes in between—many are still overwhelmed by memories of those days, and by their fears. The fears are real, as was shown by the narrow defeat of the Peres government. Years of conflict have left large sediments of hatred, paranoia, brutality, dehumanization, and tribalism. Many Israelis still find it emotionally difficult to adapt to the new realities. Even as Israel gains in power, many still genuinely feel (or are manipulated to feel) vulnerable and weak. The past may be a lengthening shadow, but the Nazi Holocaust remains a national trauma. Some have argued in recent years that it is time to begin curing the wound instead of only administering to it. Thus far, this advice has not been followed. Memory has often been crudely politicized (as when the late Menahem Begin compared Arafat to Hitler). As in the former Yugoslavia, "history" is worshipped as a goddess and it is often difficult to distinguish between memory and propaganda.

Israelis are still at the mercy of blind forces. As they witness some of the more harrowing mindless acts of violence by suicide terrorists, the parallels to Bosnia or Northern Ireland easily come to mind: It is that same confluence of blind forces, political demagogy and ethnic hatreds, that same explosive mixture of nationalism and religion. In William Butler Yeats's well-known lines

> The blood-dimmed tide is loosed, and everywhere
> the ceremony of innocence is drowned;
> the best lack all conviction, while the worst
> are full of passionate intensity.

❋

The tide is not yet dammed. Muslims worshipping in a mosque are massacred by a doctor, an observant orthodox Jew. Buses full of innocent Israeli passengers are blown up in central Tel-Aviv and Jerusalem. Cities in northern Israel are shelled by Islamic terrorists across the Lebanese frontier. Nor do Israel's massive, indiscriminate retaliation attacks across the Lebanese border—often launched for reasons, mostly, of domestic politics—restore peace along that border. Protract a mistake long enough and the worst warnings become self-fulfilling.

Those who witness these events, and certainly those who pay their human or material price, will continue to argue the pros and cons, as Arendt and Talmon did forty years ago. Wherever a great upheaval in human affairs has taken place there will be people who go on asking: Could it have been achieved at a lower price? What were the alternatives? How real were those alternatives in the minds of those who rejected, ignored or simply could not grasp them? What opportunities for making peace were there between Israel and the Arabs after 1948? After 1967? Or 1973? Were there none? Which, if any, were missed by conscious design, ignorance, or miscalculation?

❋

Of miscalculation, there was no lack on either side. The worst miscalculation of the Palestinians was most probably their failure to accept the "full autonomy," (full "national" autonomy!), offered them in 1978 at Camp David, within the framework of the U.S.-sponsored Egyptian-Israeli peace treaty. It was offered as an interim solution, pending new negotiations and possibly a referendum on the final status after only five years. This was twenty years ago! If the Palestinians had accepted that interim plan, if they hadn't made war on it, I think it is fair to say that by now they would have had an independent Palestinian state side-by-side with Israel. It would have come about by the sheer dynamic of events and the specific political and cultural situation. The thirteen American colonies started out with very much less. The offer of "full autonomy" was made before the powerful rise of Islamic fundamentalism, and before the massive influx of militant Israeli settlers into the occupied West Bank and Gaza Strip. A couple of years ago I asked Yassir Arafat why he had rejected that offer. "Wouldn't you have had an independent state by now?" He answered pointedly: "For your information, nothing was offered personally to *me*" (see "A Visit with Arafat," p. 000).

On the Israeli side, which is my main concern in this book, I would name two equally disastrous miscalculations or delusions. Before I list them let me remind the reader that they were committed by a traumatized people only twenty or twenty-five years after, possibly, the worst disaster to hit an ethnic or religious group in modern history. The first miscalculation was the delusion that dominated Israeli military opinion in the aftermath of the lightening victory of 1967, that in the foreseeable future the Arabs would have no real military option.

The second was the conviction that the national aspirations of the Palestinians could safely be overlooked. Golda Meir, a Laborite, made the well known autistic comment: "Who are the Palestinians? I am a Palestinian!" I once asked Moshe Dayan "Can you really ignore their wish for national self-determination ?" "Why see a problem where there is none," he answered. Like so many top people in today's world, Dayan was a hedonist, accustomed to viewing the Middle East from his helicopter. "What is the West Bank?," he said. "At the very most, five or six small townships." They would cause no problems if treated fairly and humanely.

Later on, during the years of the *intifada*, all parties of the governing Grand Coalition, including Rabin and Peres and, of course prime minister Yitzhak Shamir and housing minister Ariel Sharon, equally shared in the delusion, that in an open democratic society such as Israel's, a national uprising by stone-throwing Palestinian youths could be crushed by force. Rabin and Peres later changed their minds (See "The Peacemakers," p. 000). In his heart of hearts, Netanyahu perhaps still believes that it can be done. In the past, it just couldn't be done. Not by breaking bones, as Rabin tried early in the intifada, not by expelling hundreds of militants, nor by placing more than ten percent of the adult male Palestinian population in military prisons and detention camps (see "From the Uprising," pp. 000). Harsh prison terms merely produced more fanaticism. The detention camps were political schools where the new generation of Palestinian leaders was formed that now fill leading posts in the new Palestinian Authority and National Council. Heavy casualties were inflicted on the insurgents, including many children, but to no avail. When feelings supplant rational thought in international relations they become the substructure of brutality. Unlike most colonial enterprises in this century, the Israeli occupation regime on the West Bank, in Gaza and the Golan Heights never generated among the local elites even a modicum of political or cultural collaboration. The only collaborators were paid spies and turncoats.

Another Israeli miscalculation was the attempt to pre-empt Egyptian, Palestinian, and Syrian peace options by massively settling the occupied Sinai Peninsula, the Gaza Strip, the West Bank, and Golan Heights. The settlements, in the nearly unanimous opinion of military experts, did not add to Israel's security (on the contrary, during the 1973 Yom Kippur War they constituted an additional security burden). By promoting the settlements Israel manacled its own hands; the more settlers there were, lured by heavily subsidized housing, the larger the national lobby opposing all territorial concessions. Furthermore, billions were invested by several Labor governments in the occupied Sinai, only to be written off in 1979, when the settlers were uprooted and that territory was returned to Egypt in exchange for peace. Many many more billions will be written off, I am afraid, and tens of thousands of more Israeli settlers will lose their homes, their livelihoods, and illusions, as Israel withdraws from much of the West Bank and the Golan Heights in exchange for peace and coexistence with Syria and the independent Palestinian entity, as is likely sooner or later.

Peace, at least with Egypt and Jordan, we now know, was a practical possibility from as early as 1970–1971. It is true that immediately after the Six Day War the Arab coalition at Khartoum proclaimed their famous "three No's": "No negotiations, no recognition, and no peace with Israel." But this rigid position soon changed, at least in Egypt and Jordan. In 1971, U.N. mediator Gunnar Jarring addressed identical notes to the governments of Israel and Egypt. He asked Egypt whether it was ready to conclude a peace treaty if Israel withdrew from occupied Egyptian territory. And he asked Israel whether it was ready to withdraw if Egypt made peace with it. Egypt's answer was yes. Israel's answer was no. Israel's declared position at that time was that the occupation of Sinai (as far down the peninsula as Sharm-el- Sheikh) without peace was preferable to peace without Sharm-el-Sheikh. United States policy was equivocal at best. Prior to the Yom Kippur War of 1973, United States efforts to reconcile Israelis and Arabs were half-hearted. It has been argued that during the Vietnam war, the United States was happy to have its Israeli client in the Middle East humiliating the clients of the Soviet Union. Israeli troops were stationed alongside the blocked Suez Canal. There was no American national interest in reopening the Canal; on the contrary, as long as Soviet supply ships heading for North Vietnam had to sail around Africa, the U.S. may have been interested in keeping the Canal blocked.

The price for peace was the evacuation of territory occupied in the 1967 war. A succession of Israeli governments was in no mood to relinquish any. Sinai was finally relinquished by the Begin government in 1979 in the expectation that this would grant Israel a free hand on the West Bank and on the Golan Heights. This too proved to be an entirely vain hope. How many lives could have been saved in two bloody wars, and during the intifada, if peace had been concluded earlier? How much human energy was wasted for more than a generation on shortsighted settlement programs? How many false hopes were generated only to be crushed into cynicism, or still worse, religious fanaticism and violence? What could have been achieved if the billions poured into the shifting sands of Sinai, the Golan Heights, and the West Bank, had been spent on more useful causes?

These are iffy questions, of course. Some historians often refuse to address them. They believe that the lessons of history must be deduced from what has actually happened, not from what might have happened. And yet these are precisely the questions that make it so worth while to study history. They are not only clever hindsight. They also continue to crop up relentlessly as national archives are opened. The answers, of course, offer only tentative hypotheses. But such hypotheses are, in a sense, necessary too. We go to archives not only to find out what happened but also to see if the alternatives were real in the eyes of those who rejected or overlooked or could not grasp them.

The best was never attainable. The worst might have been avoided. Only if we look at events in the light of these alternatives can our history claim to be objective and more than just useless, often bad, prose. Things did not happen only out of so-called "necessity," as a sequence written in the stars. They happened in the aftermath of the lightning victory in 1967 over three Arab states. The Six Days it took to win that astounding victory—only two decades after the Holocaust!—assumed the near mythic quality of the Six Days of Creation. Things happened after that great victory, decisions were made or not made, as a result of particular human traits, preferences, acci-

dents and other events that in themselves were not, so to speak, "necessary." It might have been otherwise.

❊

I raise these iffy questions because they are important. And because,
despite the miscalculations and their high human and material cost, as
movements of national liberation usually go, traditional Zionism has, by
and large, been a success, or a relative success. The success should not color
judgment. I am not saying, as the Hegelians might, that history is the
Ultimate Day of Judgment, leaving the final verdict to Success. I'd rather
stick to Kant and insist on the autonomy of men and women, and on their
capacity to act independently of things and of events as they are, or have
come into being, for whatever reason.

If Zionism is considered not as a theology (which it was for Rabin's
assassin) but as the secular liberation movement it originally was, it has
been at least a relative success. It was recently beginning to achieve so
many of its original aims that one might say that as an ideology, it has out-
lived its usefulness. Hence the recent talk in Israel of "post-Zionism." The
attempt to give Jews a territory, a national homeland where, for better or
for worse, they would be able to exercise a measure of political control over
their own fate, has been successful. Such control they had lacked over the
centuries, wherever they lived. Whether free or locked into ghettos they
had always been dependent on shifting moods of tolerance and persecu-
tion—nowhere as much as in Nazi-occupied Europe during the Second
World War.

The recent talk of "Post-Zionism" has nothing to do with the current
"postmodern" discourse. It reflects a conviction that the Zionist revolution
has achieved its aim, as well as a growing desire to move away from an
"official Jewish ideology," especially since a fifth of its citizens are Arab. It
reflects a desire to move ahead to a more Western, more pluralistic, less
"ideological" form of patriotism and of citizenship. It is also a reaction to
the increasingly religious use of the older term by the religious and fundamentalist Israeli right. One of the earliest exponents of post-Zionism was
Menahem Brinker, a professor of philosophy at the Hebrew University of
Jerusalem. In 1981 he published an essay entitled "After Zionism." But the
first self-styled "post-Zionist" was in fact Israel's first prime minister,
David Ben-Gurion, who claimed in 1951 that there was no further need for
"Zionism" since an independent state had been established in which the
majority of citizens were Jews. This, after all, had been the aim.

Thirty years after Ben-Gurion, Brinker went further. He argued that not only had the state been established; even the maximalist task the "Zionists" had set themselves was being realized: the ingathering into Israel of the majority of the Jewish people. Brinker based his statement on the spread of Jewish assimilation in Europe and America. For this reason, Brinker argued, Zionism would soon be "over." Israel would enter a "post-Zionist" age. He was not making a value judgment about assimilation. He was observing a reality.

Leading Jewish thinkers now often decry the spread of assimilation in America and in Europe as a disaster, even (at the risk of dwarfing Nazi crimes) as "another shoah," another Holocaust. And yet Herzl and some of the other early Zionists would have hailed assimilation as a welcome byproduct of the Enlightenment. Zionism itself had grown out of this future-oriented source. It is true that an acute nostalgia for the past was inherent in all romantic and nationalist thought. But in its essence Zionism was a new beginning rather than the sudden politicization of an ancient religious bond.

Zionism was a risorgimento for Jews. Theologically, it was the great Jewish heresy of the nineteenth century. The religious establishment was vehemently opposed to it. Herzl spoke of the need to establish a National Home (not necessarily in Palestine) recognized in international law, for those Jews, who were "unable or unwilling to assimilate." The original formula was later narrowed to Palestine and refined to embrace the revival of Hebrew and a secular Jewish or Hebrew culture. These limited aims have certainly been achieved. Most early Zionists would have been content with considerably less. Still later the declared aim of Zionism was to bring about the "repatriation" to Israel of the majority of the Jews of the world. With almost five million Jews living in Israel today also this aim should not be far off. A close reading of official statistics, and of the conflicting definitions of what constitutes being a Jew today, may suggest that it has already been accomplished.

Zionism was part of the final wave of liberal European nationalism. At its cradle stood men as diverse as Fourier, Kropotkin, Herder, Mazzini, Herzen, Tolstoy—apostles of socialism, nationalism, and populism—together with their lesser known Jewish counterparts, disciples and interpreters, Moses Hess, Leon Pinsker, Ben Yehuda, Ber Borochov, and A. D. Gordon. It was perhaps more European than Jewish. In one of his letters to Hannah Arendt, the German Zionist leader Kurt Blumenfeld claimed that Zionism was "Europe's gift to its Jews." The early Zionists were acutely aware of this. They were, of course, of that pure species of revolutionaries who lived in their own world of radiant expectations. They endorsed radically different subtexts. The leftists looked forward to a just society. The rightists postulated the rebirth of the so-called "Muscle Jew." All upheld the need for assimilation on a *collective* basis: to become like other people and peoples.

Assimilation did not mean that one ceased being oneself. It did not mean slavishly abandoning one's historical or ethnic identity. Assimilation meant abandoning the uniquely religious identity Jews had insisted on during the Middle Ages. It meant exchanging the absolute singularity of "A People that dwelleth alone" for the more relative difference that existed between, say, Frenchmen and Germans, or Italians and Danes. In this sense the early Zionists (and the secular majority of Israel today) were following in the footsteps of Spinoza. He too had rebelled against the old totality, complaining in the *Tractatus* that for Jews religion was still the quasi-political law of a phantom state: those observing rabbinic law were said to be "patriots" and those who didn't were "traitors." This is what the Zionists meant when they called for the Jewish people to become a more "normal" people, a "people like all other peoples." In this too they were successful, perhaps too successful.

❋

Israelis have, of course, never been as wonderful or as dreadful as they were sometimes described. They were the first predominantly Western people whose birth as a nation and formative years suffered from a near total exposure to the modern mass media. The process of history-making in the old-new land was so encumbered by the manufacture of stereotypes that it was often difficult to disentangle fact from fiction. Years after Leon Uris's novel *Exodus* made the transition from book to movie with all of its two-dimensional characters fully intact, many continued to see Israel as a place where potential Einsteins and Freuds were playing chess in corner coffeehouses, and others—when they were not draining swamps—were dancing the horah and making the desert bloom. After the Six Day War some of the stereotype reversed. David grew into Goliath. The hero was now the ruthless oppressor. It was still a cliché, however, and it hardened over the years as Palestinian resistance mounted against the continued occupation of the West Bank and Gaza. In a recent issue, a popular American news magazine coupled two clichés in describing Israel as the land of "money and brains." I wish this were true. Nevertheless, Israel's true achievements are considerable:

- Despite half a century of near-permanent war, during which time the military prerogative was deemed paramount, democracy was preserved—as was a truly remarkable freedom of consciousness. Fifty years ago this was far from certain. Hannah Arendt was not alone in assuming that no democracy could survive where the military effort tied up so many human and material resources. But it did survive and with it came an astounding degree of openness, with few attempts by Israelis to hide faults from themselves and from others.

- An ancient language was rekindled from the ashes. Witness the remarkable flowering in recent years in Israel of the arts, poetry, theater, music and literature. The best of this literature, from the Nobel laureate S. Y. Agnon down to Amos Oz, A. B. Yehoshua, Yoram Kaniuk and David Grossman, in our own time, has been devoted to the exposure of the dark underside of "Zionism," the gap, often half-tragic and half-comic, between what one had hoped for and what was achieved.

- A mass of frightened, demoralized refugees—was reconstructed and given a name, an identity. They were harassed by men and women who believed, not without reason, that without a country of your own, you have neither voice, nor right, nor admission into the fellowship of peoples, you are, in Leon Pinsker's words, the "bastards of humanity."

- After decades of austerity—a thriving economy, at least in recent years, with little unemployment, growth rates surpassed only by those of South-East Asia and an annual per capita Gross National Product approaching England's.

- Thanks to recent waves of immigration from the former Soviet Union, Israel's population has finally achieved a critical mass.

- Finally, the beginnings of something like peace. It is not a sentimental or happy ending to a sad story of bloodshed and seemingly endless war. Peace is not being made as in some old Russian novel, where after long and bloody struggles, enemies fall into one another's arms and kisses are exchanged on faces bathed in tears. The ending is messy and cantankerous and not yet complete. There are heated exchanges in smoke-filled rooms; and expletives are uttered on both sides. But the process, at least until very recently, has kept moving forward because, in the eyes of both sides, every possible alternative was seen as being much worse.

This, too, is new. For decades, the consensus of so-called responsible opinion was that the situation was not "ripe" for peace. It was always either too soon or too late. War followed war. After each act, as in a Shakespearean tragedy, the sides exchanged poisoned swords. The stage was littered with corpses. After the third or fourth act, many felt like saying "Wait a minute, where is the catharsis in this tragedy?" There never was a catharsis. Parents felt that their children were given them on loan. The disorienting abstractions of national and international political rhetoric produced a kind of fatalism, a kind of numbness. Strategic thinking in the Arab countries was paralyzed by a mixture of fear and disdain, and in Israel by an antiquated and dangerous notion of "secure borders"—antiquated, because it ignored the changing nature of modern weapons-technology, and dangerous, because it echoed that most lethal of nineteenth-century European myths when no border was ever considered secure unless it made the other side feel so insecure that the next war was inevitable.

A theology of conflict evolved on this basis. In Arab eyes Israel was seen as the vanguard of Western imperialism. The Israeli theology of conflict postulated the existence of an ingrained, peculiarly Arab form of anti-Semitism. Behind every Arab or Palestinian they saw an SS man. Nasser was "Hitler on the Nile." The conflict was unlikely to be resolved because of its allegedly unique existential nature and for a variety of other reasons—psychological, conceptual, and religious. This too was eventually disproved, first with Egypt, later with Morocco and Tunisia, then Jordan, and most recently with some of the leading Gulf States.

Add to this, *the beginning*, at least, of the cure of the root-cause: the slow, hesitant beginning of reconciliation and territorial compromise with the Palestinians. Until a short time ago this too was thought to be quite impossible. It was thought to be a zero sum game. Years of indiscriminate terror had made all compromise improbable and unacceptable. Terror on the one hand, and the de-facto annexation and settlement of the West Bank and Gaza on the other, were thought to have left such sediments of hatred and tribalism as to become self-perpetuating. And yet, this bleak view slowly began to change. The popular support for the peace process among Palestinians has grown dramatically during the past two or three years.

It is interesting to reflect on the deeper reasons for this sea change. The collapse of the Soviet Union and the end of the cold war is often mentioned as one of the factors. To the extent that the Arab-Israel conflict actually served, for a while, as a war-by-proxy between the two superpowers, this sounds convincing. The superpowers certainly found opportunities here to test the efficacy of their latest weapons under real battle conditions. But this is not the only reason, or even the major one. The basic change on the Israeli side—the recognition that the Palestinians also have a case—was not a victory of "Jewish ethics" over right-wing crypto-fascist Likud thinking, as Peres suggested last year. Nor was it, in the words of Arafat, who echoed a well-known phrase by De Gaulle, a "peace of the brave." It was a peace of the tired.

In the century-old Palestinian-Israeli conflict, exhaustion was the great peacemaker. Two national movements clashed for almost a century over the same piece of real estate. On both sides, leaders finally came around to realizing, *simultaneously*, that the only practical way out of this quandary was to divide it. In the past this had never happened simultaneously on both sides. There were times when the Jews favored partition (perhaps because they were weak) but the Palestinians were opposed (because they thought they were strong).

In the 1980s, the PLO slowly worked its way through to a recognition of Israel and to accepting a Palestinian state on less than a third of the contested territory. In Israel, a government was in power that regarded the repartitioning of the country as absolute anathema. Today, Netanyahu and his allies may be convinced that Israel is again strong enough to claim the entire country. If he does, he will cause another war. But if, as he claims, he also hopes to make peace he will discover that he can't square the circle. In less than four months after his election, Netanyahu has pushed Israel back into the black hole of history. He has caused a deep crisis with Egypt and Jordan, and an even deeper crisis with the Palestinians. He seems willing to grant them only a dozen or so Bantustan-style enclaves on the West Bank, surrounded by ever-growing Israeli settlement areas.

In Israel, meanwhile, the former underclass of immigrants from Arab countries is undergoing a further process of social change. They have, in the past, tended to vote for Likud. With growing prosperity, many are adopting middle-class attitudes. They are still politically conservative. By and large, they dislike Arabs. But many now agree that the occupied territories—and the settlers—are a burden. Like other Israelis, they are joining the consumer society. Like most Israelis they don't visit the territories. On holiday seasons they travel, en masse, on charter flights to Turkey (there were twenty-six flights a day from Tel Aviv to Antalia, in southern Turkey, during last year's Passover week). It does not mean that they have become "doves" or believers in what Peres had been calling "The New Middle East." It means that they want to begin to enjoy life.

If many continue to vote Likud, as they did in 1996, they will not necessarily do so as "hawks." In principle, the struggle, which had endured for thirty years, between Israeli hawks and Israeli doves is over. The idea that land must be traded for peace has won out. Even Netanyahu promises to respect the Oslo accords if the PLO will do likewise. Will he send the army to reoccupy the autonomous Palestinian regions in the Gaza Strip and the West Bank that were evacuated by Israel in 1994–1995? Not likely. Likud has, in a way, accepted the principle of re-partition. The Oslo agreement enables both sides, at least until 1999, to haggle over the details. Let us hope the new right-wing government will not go back on its promise to respect the Oslo agreement. Let us hope Netanyahu wishes only to extract more reciprocity and better terms.

✳

A successful settlement with the Palestinians will lend new urgency to constitutional and other crucial questions affecting the political system, civil liberties, and the general quality of Israeli life. The self-centered, conformist features that often marked Israeli society over the years could disappear. During the years of struggle, siege, and isolation, there was perhaps no other way. But anyone who would now try to reimpose the tribal values of years past would provoke a cultural revolution. The Israeli Supreme Court might likely prevent it. During the past decade the court has considerably widened its dual role: legislative review and restrictive actions against government by way of *order nisi* suit. In an *order nisi* suit plaintiffs are able to force the government to desist from acting in a certain way, or to act more in keeping with existing laws or constitutional guarantees.

People will ask with renewed fervor: What kind of society, what kind of state is this? A Jewish state, where Muslims and Christians are formally equal but where, practically (and sometimes legally) Jews, are more equal than others? Is Israel going to be a liberal Western society, secular, democratic, and pluralistic? Many will look with envy to the United States where patriotism is focused on the Constitution, naturalization is conferred by a judge in a court of law, identity is defined politically and is based not on history, culture, race, religion, nationality, or language but on law. In the past, most immigrants to Israel have not felt strongly about all this. Many came from hate-infested regions in Eastern Europe where religion and nationality were closely linked, and civic societies and citizenship, in the Western sense of that term, were unknown.

A young generation growing up in relatively prosperous times of peace—or near-peace—might alter attitudes beyond recognition. Most of the pioneer ethos has disappeared. The pioneers' dream of a free Commonwealth of Labor has not materialized beyond a mixed economy of state, corporate, and private initiative. The ideal of university men and women plowing fields and workers discussing philosophy has succumbed to the demands of a modern, differentiated, increasingly high-tech economy. There will be renewed pressure, I think, to separate synagogue and state. The first step would be to allow religious pluralism not only for Christians and Muslims but also for Jews: an end to the monopoly on all matters of personal status now invested in the orthodox rabbinate.

The pretense that Israel is not the state of its citizen but "belongs" to all Jews wherever they are will also come under attack. I say "pretense" because nobody has ever suggested that non-Israeli Jews be given the vote. Its only concrete meaning is the Law of Return that guarantees every Jew automatic citizenship upon arrival in the country. This too is likely to come under criticism as undemocratic and discriminatory in a country where twenty percent of the population are non-Jewish. If the task that the Zionists had set themselves is about to be accomplished, it could be argued that as a form of "affirmative action" the Law of Return has become redundant. The current reading of that law poses serious problems anyway. The immigrant absorption minister warned in 1995 that unless the law is revised, eight or ten million people in remote African and Asians countries calling themselves Jews may qualify for repatriation and automatic citizenship: Up to two million Falashmora in Ethiopia, some four million in Burma and India, and many others. The country is already as crowded as Holland and Singapore. It is running out of space, clean air, and water. Prime real estate in Tel Aviv is already worth twice as much, per square meter, as in Beverly Hills.

What all these concerns have in common is a preoccupation with human rights and quality of life. Not surprisingly, much of the opposition to change comes from the fundamentalist orthodox parties represented in the Israeli Knesset. They have consistently voted against every civil rights bill presented to the Israeli parliament. From that same political and cultural background also comes the most principled, vehement—even violent—opposition to the peace process. Rabin's murder was a "religious" murder. It was committed with the monstrous innocence of a true believer by a man who was convinced he was acting with rabbinic authority. He was trained in an elite yeshiva by well-known rabbis and as far as he was concerned he pulled the trigger for them.

During the first ten or twenty years of the state, the orthodox parties concerned themselves mostly with the maintainance of an orthodox monopoly on all matters of personal status, from the cradle to the grave. In the Six Day War these parties became radicalized. They no longer insisted only that trains and buses not run on the sabbath or that the army serve kosher food to its soldiers. After 1967 they demanded that foreign and security policy also conform with their reading of *halacha*. Their idea of Israel was not a political or territorial but a theological concept. They saw the state as an instrument for the coming of the messiah. (The hassidim of Lubawitsch claimed they already heard his footsteps). What many of them now call Zionism is not what most Israelis still see in it, or have seen in the past: a holy war, a Jewish jihad which will be over only in the End of Days. David Flusser, the great historian of religion at the Hebrew University of Jerusalem, warned a few days after Rabin's murder that we could be witnessing one of the deepest crises of orthodox Judaism since the days of Sabbatai Zevi. "Ancient religions are reawakening (both in Israel and in the Arab countries)" he said. "But behold, they are vampires. It's really high time," he added, "for God to intervene."

During the years of struggle, the contrasts between the orthodox community and the rest of the population were often swept under the carpet for reasons of national unity and political expediency. In times of peace, they are bound to break out again. The early Zionists had never foreseen this. Theodor Herzl wrote that in the future state the rabbis would be strictly confined to their synagogues just as the military would be restricted to their barracks. He was right about the latter but tragically wrong about the former. The first president, Chaim Weizmann, was more realistic. In his memoirs he expressed great concern over the expanding political role of the rabbis. Shaul Tchernichovsky, poet of the Hebrew revival early in this century, assumed that the difference might be unbridgeable. He wrote:

> Between us there's an abysmal deep
> Deep enough to howl, deep enough to weep.

The abyss may be deep but it should be manageable under the rule of law. The politicized orthodox and ultra-orthodox community has recently increased its representation in parliament. But under the new electoral law, its power is limited by the new office of a powerful directly-elected prime minister. Immigration from Russia continues to be largely secular. Separation of synagogue and state will not happen overnight. Certainly not in my lifetime. Perhaps in that of our children. Will they be more immune than my generation has been to the lure of simplicities generated by the complexities of our times ? Will they insist on living in an open society, without an official state ideology, whatever name you give it, religious or political? In a state, reconciled, at long last, not just in practice, but in theory too, with the diversity of its own population and with the diversity and plurality of the Jewish condition elsewhere in the modern world?.

Amos Elon
Jerusalem, November 1996

1

War

For us, it all began on Independence Day, May 15, 1967. It was a late spring day in Jerusalem. At the Municipal Stadium, the sun shone brightly on a festive, select crowd—chosen by electric computer, for equity's sake, from a list of Jerusalem taxpayers. Present at this official celebration of Israel's nineteenth birthday was Prime Minister Levi Eshkol, flanked by his Chief of Staff—General Yitzhak Rabin—cabinet members, and the few members of the diplomatic corps who recognize Jerusalem as Israel's capital city. Conspicuously absent was former Prime Minister David Ben-Gurion, who two days earlier had viciously attacked the Eshkol government for bowing to Western pressure by agreeing not to hold a full-size parade in the divided city. In fact, the whole show—a modified military, display—was commonly referred to as "Eshkol's mini-parade."

Flags fluttered in the wind. Infantry and light armored units, carefully selected to comply with armistice regulations prohibiting artillery and other heavy equipment in the Jerusalem area, rumbled past to the gay sounds of an old Austro-Hungarian marching song, played by a ribbon-bedecked military band. As the mini-parade drew to a close, a fleet of jeeps carrying service banners passed the grandstand. It was at this moment that a few persons in the crowd noticed the Prime Minister lean over to his saluting Chief of Staff and whisper something in his ear. No one could then know that this act marked the beginning of the intense drama that was to unfold in the next few weeks.

Eshkol had asked General Rabin to meet with him at his home immediately after the parade for an urgent consultation. Rabin just nodded. Moments earlier, he, too, sitting in his grandstand seat, had received an upsetting message from army intelligence. The report stated that two Egyptian armored divisions were moving in the Sinai desert, in the direction of the Israeli border, and that Nasser's deputy, Field Marshal Amar, had visited advance headquarters in Sinai that very morning. Coupled with this intelligence was the fact that Radio Cairo had announced on the same morning that Egyptian Chief of Staff Fawzi had met with Syrian military leaders to "coordinate joint military action." The radio had added that Egypt was prepared at any moment "to fight Israel in order to restore the Palestinian homeland, stolen by the imperialists, to its rightful owners."

For the moment, however, this report did not generate great alarm. At their meeting later in the day, Rabin and Eshkol agreed that President Nasser was undoubtedly engaged in yet another one of his extravagant propaganda moves. The United Nations Emergency Force was still stationed along the Sinai borders and in the Gaza Strip as a buffer against any Egyptian action. There was, in addition, no abrupt change in Israeli intelligence estimates of Arab forces: Nasser—with much of his army committed in Yemen—was clearly neither willing nor ready to wage war at this particular time. British and American intelligence strongly corroborated this judgment. It was not until a week later, when the Egyptian military buildup was reaching its peak and the Straits of Tiran were closed, that officials began to wonder whether Israeli and Western intelligence experts had not talked themselves into a comfortable fairy tale. A top government expert reportedly lamented then to a full staff meeting, "I was mistaken, I was mistaken, I was mistaken. . . ."

On May 15, however, such doubts had yet to rise to the surface. The general feeling that Nasser was only engaging in a propaganda move was strengthened by the fact that Egyptian troop convoys on their way to Sinai had been circuitously routed through Cairo, where they were paraded almost under the windows of Western embassies and hailed by masses of civilians waving flags and banners. One banner reportedly saluted Egypt's glorious army now on its way to a quick annihilation of the Zionists; another proclaimed, "This week in Tel Aviv!" Nevertheless, despite the ominous overtones of Europe in the summer of 1914, most Israeli observers thought of this as one gigantic propaganda stunt, designed to reassure Syria and other Arab states that Nasser's Egypt, though in its eleventh year of uneasy coexistence with Israel, was still in the forefront of the Holy Arab War against "imperialism and its Zionist lackeys." "Nasser is bluffing," said one highly-placed Foreign Office official, "we must do likewise." Few people at that early stage paused to think that if fighting were indeed to break out, it would not be the first time in history that actual war resulted from mutual bluffing and shows of force.

As Independence Day celebrations went on throughout Israel, Prime Minister Eshkol continued to meet with his top advisers. After Rabin came Foreign Affairs Adviser Yaacov Herzog, and Foreign Minister Abba Eban. Together they decided on a wait-and-see course, and meanwhile to consult with friendly powers, notably the United States. That afternoon, the annual Bible Quiz was held in Jerusalem and Eshkol presented the awards. In the evening he was guest of honor at a party for servicemen and their families that was held at an air force base. But he met a second time with General Rabin later that night, and they decided it would be wise to call up a few reserve units, particularly from the air force, and to accelerate the delivery of vital military equipment that had been ordered but not yet received. "I don't think anything will happen." the Prime Minister reportedly told a friend, and added—as is his custom—in Yiddish. "*ober sicher iz sicher*" ["There's no harm in being sure"]. The next day, the cabinet met and approved these measures, though most members agreed they were only a safeguard.

So began three weeks of nervewracking waiting, a period that was quickly nicknamed "The Phony War." Pressures mounted slowly. On May 16, the morning after Independence Day, newspapers made no mention of the impending crisis. *Ha'aretz*, Israel's leading independent daily, headlined, "Two Hundred Thousand Watch Parade Through Jerusalem"; a single editorial discussed recent changes in the British administration of Aden. In *Davar*, the newspaper of the ruling Mapai party, Ben-Gurion published another scathing attack on the Eshkol government for not holding a full-scale military parade. Another paper discussed internal Mapai dissension, still another editorialized on a recent conflict between a cabinet minister and the chief of Israel's police.

But by the following day, May 17, the newspapers had caught up. *Ha'aretz* led with "Egyptian Army Movements to Sinai Seen as Show of Force to Pressure Israel," and its editorial discussed how "Egypt encourages Syria." An uneasiness began to set in. What could Nasser be up to? Some observers in Israel offered answers to this question. Israeli leaders had been making particularly strong statements at patriotic rallies both before and on Independence Day, all warning Syria against the continuation of terrorist attacks by Syria-based El Fatah Palestine Freedom Fighters on Israeli settlements and roads. Perhaps this had indeed given the Syrians, and their Soviet patrons, the erroneous impression that Israel was about to march on Damascus in order to topple the present regime. Many Israelis felt that the Soviet Union, anxious to preserve a leftist regime almost as dear to it as Castro's Cuba (as one Soviet leader told visiting Minister of Labor Yigal Allon in Moscow later that week), had asked Egypt to frighten Israel into inaction in Syria by staging a big military show in Sinai (and then calling in Western television teams to photograph it). There was a dissenting minority view, however, which held that the Soviet Union was deliberately aiming to open a new East-West front in order to strengthen its bargaining position in Vietnam.

Meanwhile, one dramatic event quickly followed another. On May 17, Nasser ordered the United Nations Emergency Force out of its positions in the Gaza Strip. On May 18, the United Nations responded by ordering the removal of all of its troops from Egypt. What might have happened if U Thant had refused to comply, or had limited the UN withdrawal to the troops in Gaza while maintaining those in Sinai and along the Straits of Tiran, is a question undoubtedly to be debated by historians for years to come. It is not likely to be settled.

Had Nasser deliberately planned all this? Had he thought it all out in advance, carefully effecting, step by step, a grand design? Did he actually assume the time was ripe for a final reckoning with Israel? Or was he making up his mind as he went along, grasping the opportunity handed to him by U Thant, then going further to call what he must have thought was Israel's bluff? Perhaps he had taken seriously the long and intense personal campaign led by Ben-Gurion and the Rafi party against the leadership of Levi Eshkol, the constant insinuations that Eshkol was weak, indecisive, even guilty, in Ben-Gurion's words, of an unspecified horrendous "failing" in vital defense matters. Could it be that Nasser thought all this was true? Israel, moreover, was in its sixth month of a grave economic crisis and was paralyzed militarily. Did Nasser think it possible to execute a tremendous political victory by closing the Straits of Tiran without Israel lifting a finger to stop him? Could he have thought that after the dismissal of the UNEF troops and the successful blocking of the Gulf of Aqaba, *fedayeen* attacks against Israel could again be launched as in 1956, but this time with impunity? Unless Nasser himself speaks up, we will never really know what lay behind his actions.

By Monday, May 22, at any rate, the first visible effects of the crisis began to be seen. Life in Tel Aviv was still fairly normal, but partial mobilization had already left it a town of women, children, and middle-aged men. From this bustling, vivacious, normally swinging city of crowded sidewalk cafes, lively discotheques, and bars, the young men had suddenly vanished. Nor was Tel Aviv alone in this atmosphere of sudden emptiness. All over the country young men were being called up, some by telephone, others by cable or personal message. That evening, Eshkol played host at a state dinner for the Prime Minister of Finland, who had arrived the week before and was now going through all the pomp of an official visit—planned months before and now determinedly unfolding as though nothing was amiss—complete with visits to chicken farms, social institutions, and museums. At dinner, the possibility of war was scarcely discussed. Eshkol stayed up late, entertaining his guests with old Jewish tales. It was long past midnight when he went to bed.

At four o'clock in the morning, his telephone rang. It was General Rabin, informing him that the expected had come to pass. Nasser had ordered the Straits of Titan closed to all ships headed for Israel. Within an hour the Prime Minister was on his way to army headquarters in Tel Aviv.

It was now that the most terrible of apprehension began to make itself felt: an awareness that war was "inevitable," and that men were now reduced to being the slaves, rather than the masters, of events. In *Ha'aretz*, Avraham Schweitzer, a journalist sympathetic to Rafi and long opposed to the Eshkol government, with a venom that had been typical of Israeli politics in recent months, called for war against Egypt before it was too late, before Nasser had a chance to complete the movement of his troops into Sinai.

Thus, whether Nasser actually wanted war or not, the danger point had been reached. The machinery of war began to gain control over men, like robots overpowering their masters. Few observers now thought that Nasser would or could turn back. Too many words had been spoken, too many soldiers had moved into position. Israelis have always lived reconciled to the idea of war. Now it was here. The country, under a pleasant spring sun, the fields abloom with wild flowers, the pretty girls in miniskirts and gaily printed cotton dresses filling the sidewalk cafes, was somberly, stoically waiting for war, as if for the impending visit of a tedious, meddling mother-in-law. Some said, fatalistically, that maybe the price for Israel's existence was a periodic bloodletting, as regular as income tax. There was little hysteria, but the fear was considerable among civilians—the wives and oldsters left behind in seemingly indefensible cities. Stocks of food were ample, but markets were soon cleaned of staples by those who remembered the last war. Most Israelis, however, refused to hoard under any circumstances.

Watching the entire Middle East move inexorably closer to war, drawn as a magnet toward a calamity in which thousands must die and whole cities go up in flames, one could feel only despair, and a disgust tempered only by disbelief in the absurdity of the situation. Not a few of the men in uniform shared this feeling of absurdity, as they awaited the cataclysm in hastily prepared field positions throughout the Negev desert. I spent most of that week with the army in the south. The vast emptiness of the desert had been turned into a gigantic waiting-room, a movie-set ready to go. The expanse had suddenly been populated by masses of uniformed men. Soldiers in green fatigues lay alongside mud-camouflaged tanks and armored half-tracks, in the hot, ankle-deep dust, waiting. Camouflage nets were perched like tents over tanks and trucks. A vast army spread out across the desert, folded into the sides of rock mountains, waiting, brushing off thousands upon thousands of flies. Some were regular conscripts, serving their thirty months of national service. The majority were reservists; just yesterday their units had existed only on paper, or in a card index. Today they were out and active, a coiled spring suddenly released. A clerk from Tel Aviv operated the wireless set; a baker from Haifa cleaned the release mechanism of a jeep-mounted recoilless rifle; a mechanic, a college boy, and a kibbutznik waited in their Centurion tank, snatching catnaps when they could. A salesman from a Tel Aviv supermarket opened tins of goulash, made in Brazil and marked "kosher," and poured the contents into a huge pot. From the mobile van office came the clatter of typewriters. Inside, two young women soldiers typed out intelligence reports and orders. Two other women, who had worked all night, were napping on an inflated rubber mattress spread out under the wheels of the van. All four— in their early twenties—had recently completed their military service, but were now back with the reserves. Three of them had been recently married. One said she had been called three days before her husband.

A brigade commander, called at his law firm by telephone, had brought his private secretary and chauffeur along with him, and within ninety minutes was busy getting his brigade out of the card index and into the field. The brigadier noted that, for some inexplicable reason, more reservists had shown up than were actually in the files. One sixty-three-year-old, who had served twenty-five years ago in the British army, also came down and insisted that he be taken along. "*Dachilak!*" exclaimed the Brigadier (in the Hebrew equivalent of "*For Christ's Sake!*"), "*Dachilak,* I can't take you along. I haven't anything for you to do." The man insisted and the Brigadier gave in. "Okay, I'll take you if you bring a jeep." The next day, the old man showed up with a jeep rented from Hertz. Now he too was sitting under the hot desert sun, next to a mobile field kitchen, waiting.

In the meantime, back in Jerusalem, Foreign Minister Eban was pleading for patience. He felt that the United States must be given a fair chance to honor its 1957 commitment to keep the Straits of Tiran open to Israeli shipping. As the cabinet divided into the proverbial hawks and doves (with Eshkol reportedly a hawk), Eban anxiously requested to be allowed first of all to exhaust all diplomatic opportunities. Eban reportedly held the view that any future military action by Israel would more likely be condoned by the outside world if diplomacy were first given a chance to work. In this he was eventually proven correct, but the decision to delay was actually less the result of international diplomatic considerations than of indecisiveness within the cabinet itself. Though confident of eventual victory, Israel's political and military leaders could not overlook the appalling toll it would undoubtedly take in human lives and property. This war, they felt, would hardly be the same as the walkover of 1956, when Britain and France had bombed Egyptian airfields and maintained an effective air umbrella over Israel's cities. This time, the hinterland would not remain untouched: thousands would die in battle, and cities like Tel Aviv and Haifa, without adequate air shelter, could be devastatingly attacked from the air.

As Eban continued to plead for time, and then took off on a much-criticized visit to Paris, London, and Washington, the cabinet met in marathon sessions lasting for days on end to debate the pros and cons of military action. With Egyptian troop concentrations in the Sinai growing ominously every day, it now became clear that even if the United States were to send a warship through the blockaded Straits, Israel would still be faced with the threat of close to 100,000 Egyptian troops in Sinai, and some 800 tanks.

Eban returned from Washington with an apparent promise of diplomatic action by the United States and other maritime powers, to be followed, *in extremis*, by the dispatch of an allied armada through the Straits. Nothing, presumably, was to be done about the Egyptian troops in Sinai. Criticism of the Foreign Minister became more severe, even within his own party. Most of his critics thought it unlikely that the United States would take any active role, but even if a ship were sent, this would in no way solve the growing Egyptian menace in Sinai. There were cries for Eban's resignation as well as nasty insinuations, never proved, that he had "misled" the cabinet on the true outcome of his talks with President de Gaulle and President Johnson.

Nevertheless, Eban's policy of restraint, supported by powerful factions within the cabinet, would probably have prevailed, were it not for the sudden eruption of a long-simmering crisis of confidence in Prime Minister Eshkol himself. The resentment felt by hawks and doves alike at Eshkol's failure to provide firm leadership was the culmination of a long-brewing dissatisfaction inside his own party as well as outside of it (among the members of the National Religious party, a partner to the government coalition). The crisis was brought to a head by Eshkol himself, in a most unfortunate, badly prepared, apparently unrehearsed, half incoherent, stammered short radio address to the nation. In his statement, Eshkol announced that the blockade of Tiran was an act of aggression and that Israel's army was ready, if necessary, to take action. His message was clear and uncontroversial; his delivery was disastrous. It raised grave doubts throughout the country, and in particular among members of the armed forces lying in their field positions. All over Israel, people began to feel that the nation's security must be placed in firmer hands.

I was with a tank regiment that evening, on a dusty desert plain south of Beersheba, listening to the Prime Minister's faltering voice on a transistor radio. We were lying on blankets spread out in the dust under a camouflaged Centurion tank. We were not the only ones listening. This time Israel's reservists—unlike in past wars—had joined their units carrying transistor radios in their knapsacks. All over the vast fields of the Negev, where armored and mobile infantry units had taken up positions, men listened to the radio. After Eshkol's address, there was a feeling of severe frustration among the troops. "Our real problem is not Nasser, but the Second Aliyah," one officer aptly commented, referring to that generation of early pioneers—the age group of Coolidge or Ramsay MacDonald—who still hold power as they have for forty years among Israel's Jews.

The cries for strong leadership now became a unified chant throughout the country. And the strong man most clamored for—in speeches, letters-to-the-editor, and paid advertisements—was ex-General Moshe Dayan. Eshkol, so the demand went, must relinquish his second role as Defense Minister to the war hero of 1956, victor of Sinai, now a leader of the Rafi opposition.

Despite fears and internal wrangling within Mapai, Dayan was finally swept into office by two completely unrelated events: a demonstration of Tel Aviv housewives, and demands by the normally apolitical National Religious bloc within the cabinet coalition. The Mapai Secretariat was meeting for the umpteenth time when the housewives appeared under the window angrily chanting, "We Want Dayan," and tired, harried party dignitaries nervously counted many more heads below than the seventy-five that were actually there. The seemingly spontaneous demonstration had been organized by Rafi ladies, but shocked Mapai members were effectively impressed. Coupled with this in the end was the demand by the National Religious party that the major opposition blocs be included in the government as an absolute necessity. Religious party members of the cabinet were doves; they pressed to gain time for America's efforts to save Israeli interests without war. They actually felt that General Dayan would oppose the war, in agreement with his mentor Ben-Gurion, who at that time was advising National Religious cabinet ministers that Israel was not ready for war, but must dig in and wait until it gained active military support from a friendly power. At that time Dayan did nothing to contradict this assumption; nor did he, in talks with politicians and newsmen, commit himself to any single course of action. His advice to all who asked was to play it cool.

His appointment on June 2—after long political bickering—was greeted with relief. The most docile doves hoped that the mere appointment of Dayan would frighten Nasser into backing away from a confrontation. There was no time even for a swearing-in ceremony, Dayan's appointment was only confirmed two days later when the Knesset met. But he went to work immediately in a subterranean war-room in Tel Aviv.

Dayan held his first press conference the following day. The vastly swelled press corps now numbered more than 250 foreign newsmen. Calmly, even brightly, he answered and evaded all questions, stating that the time was not ripe for war, it was both too late and too early. Diplomatic means must first be exhausted, he deadpanned, but if war should come, Israel would fight alone. There was neither a desire nor a need for American or British boys to die in battle for Israel. We would be sure to win, he said smilingly. The feeling swept across the country that Israel was in for another period of waiting.

Two days later, at 7:50 A.M. the air raid sirens began to wail through Tel Aviv, and then through the entire country. There was considerable confusion. Some sirens were sounding an all-clear while others were just beginning the alert. There were few shelters in Tel Aviv; even those persons who had managed to pile a few sandbags in entrance halls or had dug trenches in their gardens did not bother to seek shelter. Automobiles, in the early morning rush to downtown offices, continued uncertainly along their way. Citizens scanning the skies could see only a KLM passenger jet leaving on a normal run from Tel Aviv, apparently having just taken off from nearby Lydda. No, it was undoubtedly a test, a false alarm, a small incident like several that had occurred over the past few days.

The announcement on the 8 o'clock news was terse: "The Israeli army spokesman announces that air and armored battles have been taking place since the early hours of the morning following an enemy move toward Israel." Then, total mobilization began by radio. Reserve units were called up over the radio by their code names: "Lovers of Zion," "Good Dish," "Lily of the Valley." Meeting-points were also relayed by code. In Tel Aviv, people went about their jobs solemnly, not talking much. It was no time for talk. By nightfall most of the houses were blacked out; car headlights were painted black, windows were taped, and shelters readied for occupancy. Few knew that within two hours of the beginning of the war the entire Egyptian air force had been virtually destroyed, for the most part on the ground; nor that a few hours after Syria and Jordan had joined in, their air forces too lay in ruin. It was not until late Monday night that Army headquarters confirmed the almost incredible fact that Israel had gained full control of the skies; it was this feat that determined the outcome of the battle from the very beginning.

That afternoon, a few hours after Israeli armored columns had begun to push into Sinai, I joined the Southern Front Commander, General Yeshayahu Gavish, in a military helicopter flying south to the advance command position of General Avraham Yaffe, commander of one of the three advancing armored columns. Just over the Sinai border we suddenly saw, through the open door of the Sikorsky helicopter, a collection of camouflaged transport lorries, jeeps, and armored half-tracks. Were it not for the forest of wireless antennas sticking up from the yellow nets, it might have been an encampment of Bedouins.

The helicopter landed in a cloud of dust. Out jumped General Gavish, bareheaded but wearing dark goggles against the sun and dust, a tall, uncommonly goodlooking man, born forty-four years ago in a Tel Aviv slum to a cartman who has since become general manager of a Tel Aviv trucking company. Gavish brushed some dust from his pants and proceeded to a consultation with Yaffe in his war-room, a hastily constructed enclosure protected by nets slung between two trucks. Maps were unfolded, positions marked by colored pencils. Some fifteen minutes later Gavish returned to his helicopter and took off. I stayed on. The sun was just setting over Sinai, and soon it was pitch black, except for the dim light emerging from the folds of the tents. From the south, rolling over the darkened hills, came the thunder of cannon fire.

I was told to dump my sleeping bag and rucksack on the back seat of a jeep. In General Yaffe's war-room, huge maps were tacked onto wooden boards, haphazardly leaning against canvas sheets. Past and future Israeli moves were plotted in blue ink, enemy positions and movements were marked in red. A group of staff officers continued to mark the maps, or talked on the radiophone. As the night wore on, we watched the first stage of the battle that was to end just ninety-two hours later with a cable from General Gavish to the Chief of Staff: "Am happy to inform you that our forces are stationed along the banks of the Suez Canal. The entire Sinai Peninsula is in our hands."

That first Monday night, the short, bloody battle of Rafiah—a town south of the Gaza Strip—was already over. An armored column headed by General Israel Tal was moving on to begin wiping up last-ditch pockets in El Arish, an important supply depot enroute to the Suez Canal, on the Sinai shore of the Mediterranean. Further south, in his war-room near the crossing point of Nitzana, General Yaffe was perched on a wooden stool , talking by wireless to his units a few miles ahead. Yaffe is a large man in his early fifties, heavy-set and portly, with broad, sympathetic features and the goodnatured, warm sense of humor that mark many men of his proportions. To most Israelis he is known less as a military commander than as the head of the National Parks Commission, a dedicated conservationist who has taught Israelis not to pick wild flowers, and who spends much of his time lecturing high-school students on the importance of preserving pockets of wildlife in the midst of a country threatened by urban conglomerations. Here in the desert he was a reservist general, just as a week earlier most of his men had been busdrivers, farmers, shopkeepers, or unemployed individuals queuing up for the dole. Their job was to break through central Sinai and reach the southern part of the Canal at a point between the city of Suez and the Bitter Lakes.

The Egyptians relied on Russian manuals. Their defenses were in depth: long lines of trenches feeding into well-situated concrete bunkers, and dug-in tanks surrounded by barbed wire entanglements extending six to nine miles. They had some two hundred Russian tanks, including T-55's which are about the latest word in tank design, complete with infra-red equipment for night fighting, long-range guns, and special armor plating that can take a great deal of punishment. These tanks, in short supply even in Russia, have not yet been provided to most of Russia's Warsaw Pact allies. In addition to the tanks there were SU-100 mobile cannons, enormous steel monsters transported on tank-like, steel-plated vehicles, and capable of both intensive fire and quick maneuverability.

The battle lasted the entire night. Commanding the Israeli forces was a veteran officer(Israeli censorship prohibits the mention of any names other than those of a few top-ranking officers) whose brigade was responsible for destroying more Egyptian armor than any other. He too was a reservist, barely two weeks back in uniform; in civilian life, ironically enough, he is general manager of a business corporation called "Shalom, Inc." The brigadier's voice, growing more and more hoarse, came through every few minutes over the radiophone in the war-room to report both successes and failures. Again and again he begged for air support, but Yaffe refused, saying he was certain they could make it without it. Later on, the brigadier finally did get air cover. "Be sure you mark yourselves carefully," Yaffe called into the microphone. "I don't want our planes mopping you up."

Then came the calls for helicopters to evacuate the wounded. Fuel and water were parachuted to the troops. At dawn the Egyptian positions between Bir Lachfan and El Arish were still holding. Then the Israel air force arrived and the long lines of trenches and tanks dug in alongside the hills turned into a sea of fire. An hour later some fighting still continued, but the battle had been decided.

General Yaffe had spent the night by his maps and radiophones, and, except for a short half hour after midnight, had had no rest. Adina, his secretary at the National Parks Commission, a woman in her late twenties who had gone to war with her boss, handed him a hot cup of tea. Tired, but relaxed, his thick, paternal voice emerged hoarsely between sips. "I'd like very much to be in Nasser's headquarters now. What can he do? He's got quite a problem on his hands." Then he rose heavily from his uncomfortable seat, stretched a bit, watched with fascination the magnificent sunrise over Sinai, and walked off to shave.

Soon afterward, a helicopter flew in to take him forward to the front at Bir Lachfan. We flew over the sand at a height of about thirty feet. Through the open slide-door Yaffe followed the line of advance his troops had taken the day before. "Their first line of defense is obviously broken," Yaffe said. He assumed the Egyptians would maintain a second, even stronger line of defense further south, around Djebl-Libne, in order to block further Israeli advances toward the Canal. At that early stage, on Tuesday morning, it was impossible to know, or even to conceive of the possibility, that from now on the battle would turn into a hot, almost nonstop pursuit, a chase at speeds unheard of in the history of armored warfare. Below us, rear supply units could already be seen establishing themselves on the barren dunes. White parachutes, used only a short while ago to drop fuel and water for the advancing units, lay spread out on the sand like sails drying on a beach. We landed outside of Bir Lachfan, some fifty miles inside Sinai, alongside a tank regiment.

Yaffe climbed into his Advance Command Position, an armored half-track sent ahead the night before. It was a specially built vehicle, unarmed except for one machine gun, but equipped with complicated wireless sets that enabled instant voice communication both with GHQ in Beersheba or Tel Aviv and with his own units in the fields nearby—a mobile headquarters, able to move with the troops. Forward, some six feet above the driver, where normal armored half-tracks are equipped with light guns, there was a wooden, slightly inclined board covered with maps under a cellophane cover, and behind it a broad, padded, rotating armchair. Yaffe settled into this seat, his broad figure towering above the vehicle, his right hand clutching a microphone. We scrambled in behind him.

We started moving north toward El Arish at great speed. Heading toward us from the north were General's Tal's units, the other arm of the pincer movement. Suddenly we stopped short. On a low hill to our left, some twenty Israeli tanks were poised like infantry horses, spitting fire. Clouds of black smoke gathered along the road ahead of us. Through loudspeakers attached to Yaffe's seat came the echoes of battle. "Fire northeast . . . fire north . . . ten Egyptian tanks engaged, four directly hit, the others seem to be abandoned. . . ." We started moving forward again through thick smoke, dust, and the sickening smell of burning flesh. A few miles further on, at a road junction littered with burning Egyptian tanks, we had a dramatic meeting with the forces of General Tal, who had pushed south from El Arish. Dozens of soldiers jumped from their tanks and armored cars for quick embraces and victory hugs. Smoking remnants of Egyptian fortifications were visible on both sides of the road, spreading for miles out into the hills. Trenches and blown-out concrete bunkers, trucks, and dug-in tanks burned like torches in the sand. Corpses, hundreds of them, were spread out in the sand, some charcoaled, others just blackened, their arms spread out on the sand in gestures of horrifying helplessness. An Israeli helicopter came in to pick up the wounded. Some of the engines in the abandoned Egyptian vehicles were still running. The faces of the corpses that filled the shallow ditch next to the road were twisted in the frightened grimace of sudden death. A buzzing army of hungry desert flies settled over torn limbs covered with slowly congealing blood.

Yaffe's column now turned around and started rolling south again, this time toward Djebl-Libne. It was 1:20 P.M. on Tuesday, June 6. By now the Egyptian army was withdrawing at top speed to the Suez Canal. Egyptian army communications had broken down to the extent that some orders were being broadcast over Radio Cairo. Our task was now to rout and destroy as many Egyptian units as possible. A big chase began. It was to last for the next three days, interrupted only for brief spells to refuel. We moved south at twenty-five miles an hour. The air force had preceded us like a broom of fire; there were burning tanks everywhere, and Egyptian uniforms, hurriedly cast off, lying about in the fields. Fleeing Egyptian soldiers had thrown them off, hoping to be taken for civilians. And shoes—tens, hundreds of shoes, cast off when their owners, broken as soldiers, had turned into frightened men and tried to escape into the dry hills—barefoot, in their underwear, bareheaded, and without water. Wandering through the desert toward the Canal, still some hundred miles away, they were doomed to die of hunger, or thirst, or sunstroke, unless they came back to surrender.

Later that evening we watched a tank battle at Djebl-Libne from a nearby hill, much as Napoleon at Dresden in the famous painting. As we watched, someone tuned his transistor radio to Radio Cairo's Hebrew broadcast. "Israeli soldiers, you are fools," came the pronouncement in heavy, guttural, ungrammatical Hebrew. "We have lured you to the desert so we can destroy your hinterland at our ease. . . . we still haven't used our secret missiles. . . . O Israeli fools, our soldiers will beat you; they are courageous, yes courageous, even too courageous. . . ." A little later, the voice added, "Soldiers of Israel, where is your Prime Minister Levi Eshkol now? He is enjoying himself with his young wife Miriam in the air raid shelter . . . our heroic air force has reduced Tel Aviv to dust ... we have taken 4,026 prisoners so far. . . . O foolish Israeli soldiers, we'll catch your one-eyed General Dayan and take out his other eye."

Next day, and the day after, the pursuit continued over roads littered with the burning of abandoned remnants of the Egyptian army. We encountered our first prisoners of war, lining the road, hands bent over their heads. For the most part, they were dark-skinned, undernourished, emaciated frightened *fellahin* from the Nile valley. They were ordered to wait alongside the road for rear units to come and fetch them. They said their officers had abandoned them, driving away in their cars. Early one morning, south of Djebl-Libne, we captured an Egyptian colonel, the commander of an artillery brigade. Moments later, a jeepload of soldiers seized Major General Salah-a-Din Mohammed Yakum, who claimed he belonged to the Army Accounting Inspectorate in Cairo, since Monday on a routine inspection visit to Sinai. General Yaffe asked him: "Why are we fighting? Let us be frank, General! What is the sense in all this, when you have so much territory and we so little?"

"I am a soldier, carrying out orders," General Yakum answered. "And we aren't fighting this war for ourselves but for the people of Palestine whose land you have robbed." Later, I asked the captured colonel how he felt about Nasser now. "No, no!" he exclaimed. "Nasser has not let us down. It is true we have been beaten twice. But this is war. Sometimes you win and sometimes you lose."

Another captured general had been wounded in the leg. He was carried on a stretcher to field headquarters, where a young woman soldier brought him some tea. A doctor was called to his tent before he was evacuated north by plane. Inestimably more bitter was the fate of wounded Egyptians of less exalted The Egyptian wounded lay everywhere along the road, under collapsed or abandoned vehicles, and among corpses in the sands, trying to attract attention with the little strength they had left. Above their torn and bloody bodies, their faces were terrible to look at. Even worse was the feeling that one was powerless to do anything for them at the moment. At this early stage, as the army was rushing to prevent the escape of the Egyptian army through passes leading to the Canal, it was impossible to render any useful assistance. Some Israeli soldiers jumped from their trucks and left their own water bottles beside their wounded enemies. By the time the rear guard moved up, with its ambulances, field hospitals, and military police, it was often too late.

It was difficult, too, to assemble the unwounded prisoners who gathered alongside the advancing columns and to arrange for their dispatch to camps in the north. Everything had happened too fast, much ahead of schedule. Those who were captured within a day's walk to the Canal were disarmed and told to swim across. It happened more than once that they were fired on by their own compatriots as they scrambled ashore.

They were leaving behind them in the desert an immense array of equipment—some of it ruined, but much of it abandoned, unused. It was as though children had been given a complicated electronic computer to play with. Doubtless, these men were also obeying an ancient, healthy, peasant instinct—seen in many stupid wars—prompting them to quit the fight and try to survive. Even in the heat of battle, and despite heavy losses to Israel, one was filled with compassion at the sight of these poor wretches, who looked like nothing so much as characters in an anti-war play by Bertolt Brecht. Their bitter fate must be reckoned as part of the crime committed by Nasser against his own people. By their rules of military strategy they should have been the victors. Egyptian troops were trained and equipped by the Russians down to the last and finest detail, superior to the Israelis in all but the human element. What failed was less the army than the social structure of Egypt, which collapsed under the stress, despite—or perhaps because of—fourteen years of "Arabism" and socialist doctrine. Western and Israeli intelligence experts had been partially right after all: Nasser, even if willing, was not ready for war.

❋

No one had as yet counted the captured equipment. It appeared that more than half the Egyptian armor had been captured intact or hit. Lying in the desert were Russian T-34, T-54, and T-55 tanks, some brand new and without a scratch, straight from the factory; there were amphibious tanks and cannons of all sorts, some with their barrels still protected against the dust by airtight plastic covers. Large parts of Sinai looked like enormous junkyards. The biggest single area of devastation was the Mitla Pass, leading from central Sinai to the Canal. We drove through it a few hours after its capture and saw a valley of death, littered with hundreds of corpses and burning tanks and trucks in clouds of smoke and touched by the sweet smell of burning human flesh.

On Friday morning we began our final descent toward Suez. Here too the remains of battle were to be seen along the blown-up road. Then the mountains parted like a curtain, ahead of us lay the Canal, shimmering in the distance like a silver knife. On our right were the Bitter Lakes; on the left, the southern Canal. Over on the other side, there were trees, and a few isolated houses. On this side, only the desert. Israeli soldiers lay on the bank, under their tanks and trucks (there was no other shade) unmindful of occasional snipers, exhausted, their faces unshaven for three days and covered with dust, grease, and carbon. Some had fallen into their first exhausted sleep in sixty hours. After a while they gathered together—still sitting or lying down—under the road sign, "Ismailia-Suez." General Yaffe stood, addressing them. "I am sorry I can't talk very well," he said hoarsely, his voice almost inaudible from fatigue and the layers of dust covering his vocal cords. "But actions are more important. Anybody who wants to destroy us now knows he'll pay dearly. It's been said that we're turning lazy, soft, that we care for nothing. But there's apparently something that ties us to this land. You are civilians who suddenly put on uniforms and you beat the aggressor. I can only cheer you all and thank you for everything you did."

Then he saluted the tired men who sat or lay before him on the incline of the small hill. The soldiers—at first—did not respond; they remained prone. Then someone started to shout: "*Kefak Hey,* for he's a jolly good fellow!" Everyone joined in.

As the cease-fire finally went into effect on Saturday, June 10 an eerie silence descended over the desert. Occasionally it was broken by shots fired from across the narrow canal at Israeli vehicles moving along the east bank. That afternoon I drove back north, bouncing in the back seat of a jeep, back again through all the debris of the war and straight across Central Sinai to Beersheba. Israeli army salvagers were beginning to clean up the ruins that lay directly on the road. Huge supply convoys heading south were held up at mountain passes and road junctions in hopeless traffic jams. Military police were collecting POW's in busses and trucks. We crossed the border at Nitzana, which less than a week before had been the front-line command headquarters. It was an odd feeling to approach warning signs in Hebrew reading "Attention! Mines, Frontier Ahead"—from behind. I reached Jerusalem late that night. The city was ablaze, and few signs of the shelling it had sustained were immediately obvious. The blackout had been abolished three nights before. Jerusalem was a city changed beyond recognition. While we had been racing toward Suez, Israeli troops had seized the Old City and the entire West Bank of the Jordan River, and had pushed King Hussein back into his ancestral desert kingdom on the East Bank, first granted to his grandfather as an emirate by Winston Churchill following the First World War. For nineteen years the Old City, with its religious and historic monuments, had been like the other side of the moon; now it was suddenly open.

Syria, too, had toppled. Israeli troops, who quickly moved north following the fierce and terrible battle of the Old City, had conquered the steep mountain ridges from which Syrian artillery had for years been shelling the Israeli settlements lying below.

There was an air of euphoria in Jerusalem that night. "I can't believe it, I can't believe it" was on everybody's lips. Newspapers, the next day, envisioned the Messiah walking behind advancing Israeli tanks. There was much genuine jubilation, a great deal of apprehension about the future, and not a little doubletalk as well. Officials and newspapers began to speak of the "liberation" of Jericho, El Arish, and Kuneitra in Syria. It was a victory notable for its lack of hate, but marked by a more than a trace of arrogance. Only a few days after the Old City fell to Israel, David Ben-Gurion publicly demanded the razing of the Old City walls because they had been constructed not by Jewish hands but by Ottoman sultans in the fifteenth and sixteenth centuries—a statement prompting *Ha'aretz* to headline its lead editorial "The Barbarians Are Coming." Ben-Gurion was wildly cheered by a select Rafi audience in Jerusalem. Members of the right-wing Herut party called for the annexation of the West Bank with no civil rights for the million Arabs who live there—a Middle Eastern Rhodesia. Others proposed a puppet-state on the West Bank, surrounded by Israeli territory, a kind of Bechuanaland for Arabs.

An ominous case in point was the Wailing Wall, where action followed immediately upon the heels of victory. Two days after the conquest, bulldozers moved in to destroy some thirty or forty old houses inhabited by some two hundred Palestinians facing the ancient Wailing Wall, creating an enormous parade ground in front of what had for hundreds of years been a place of intimate and solemn prayer. It is not certain who ordered this rash act of destruction at the site holiest to Jews everywhere. "It just happened. It just grew of itself," those directly involved explained. "We had to clear space for the masses expected at Shavuoth." Others justified the act by saying the houses that were removed had been an ugly slum and a disgrace to the Wall. Mayor Teddy Kollek of Jerusalem wholeheartedly supported the deed. One angry interviewer, Herbert Pundik of *Davar*, told the mayor bluntly he felt it an outrage to turn a place where prayers have been offered up for hundreds of years into a "vast, noisy Piazza del Popolo." Mr. Kollek disagreed. "It was the best thing we did and it's good we did it immediately." In a vein characteristic of the new feeling, he added, "The old place had a *galut* (Diaspora) character; it was a place for wailing. Perhaps this made sense in the past. It isn't what we want in the future."

Whether the time for "wailing" and intimate prayer is now over for all time is a matter for conjecture. As the days wore on, Israelis settled down to consider what had been achieved and what had not. In less than a week Israeli forces had beaten three Arab armies to the ground and found themselves in possession of enormous territories many times the size of the state. From the moment of cease-fire it was clear that winning the war had been hard but winning the peace would prove even harder. Some talked of setting up a semi-autonomous Arab state, under Israeli tutelage, on the West Bank. Others, like members of the right-wing Herut party, were in favor of clearcut annexation. Still others held out the hope that King Hussein would settle for peace in exchange for the occupied West Bank territories minus Jerusalem. And almost everyone agreed that the time was ripe for a settlement of the Palestine Arab refugee problem, especially since most of the refugees now inhabited lands occupied by Israel. Whatever the eventual fate of the occupied territories, it was felt that any workable plan would have to be accompanied by a solution of the refugee problem. Necessary now was imagination and initiative in high places, farsighted statesmanship, and the generosity of wise victors, lest the potential fruits of this victory be lost as they were in 1948 and 1956.

2

Conquerors

Israel's leaders are sitting on their laurels as uneasily as on a heap of ants. As a result of the six-day earthquake, everything has changed here radically—parties, populations, national opinions, military strategy, the facts of economic life. But little happens. Much seems ready for movement yet official action remains slow, spasmodic, and limited in scope. Cabinet sessions—in Israel always long and wordy affairs, dedicated less to decision-making than to the art of thinking out loud—have never been as lengthy or as frequent. At no time have there been as many ministerial committees, subcommittees, brain trusts, action groups. On a Sunday in August 1967 the Cabinet went into a session that continued—with breaks only for food and sleep—until the following Wednesday. The subject under discussion: what to do with occupied Jordanian territories.

Various proposals for action—as well as inaction—were discussed, but in the end nothing was decided. Meanwhile, in the occupied areas themselves, policy—which is likely to have a more than medium-range political and economic effect—is in the often contradictory hands of (politically motivated) civil servants and army officers. One disappointed cabinet member commented: "Israel now resembles an enormously powerful machine with a stuck gear-box."

There are various reasons for this delay. One is obvious and very human. The men of Jerusalem, now discussing the momentous consequences of a war they did not want, simply were psychologically unprepared for what happened. Victory has, in a way, stupefied them; their imagination falters under its weight. Exhausted by success, Israel's ageing power-elite seems paralyzed by a sense of crushing responsibility. How great this responsibility is, they are only now beginning to realize. The occupied areas, notably the former Jordanian West Bank, a traditional hotbed of violent nationalism populated by some 950,000 Arabs, at times seems like a crocodile that one has received on one's birthday; one does not know whether to flush it down the toilet as soon as possible, to put it up more or less permanently in the bathtub, or to display it behind protective glass in the living room.

Israel, which has always had "more history than geography," now suddenly has both. It controls 90,000 square kilometers instead of the 20,000 it held before the war; its armies are entrenched on the east bank of the Suez Canal; they are forty-five kilometers from Amman, fifty from Damascus and a hundred from Cairo. Before June 6 the Jordanian army was within shooting range of Tel-Aviv. The annexation of Old Jerusalem and its environment has opened vast, undreamt-of possibilities in tourism; the seizure of Egypt's oil fields in Sinai might render this country, at least temporarily, self-sufficient in oil, and open possibilities for export as well.

But the overriding desire, at least of most cabinet members, is for peace and not for territories; this hope has not yet been crushed by continued Arab intransigence. Ministers realize they are no longer discussing some industrial credit or tax increase that can be undone at will at year's end, but an issue that is likely to decide the fate of this country for generations. And so they hesitate.

A second reason for the government's slow motion is that the twenty-one-man "National Coalition" hastily slapped together on the eve of war is still no empty phrase; it is supported by practically the entire Knesset. There is a widespread desire to arrive at decisions not by majority vote, but by consent. Divisions within the cabinet come on the basis of personal rather than party policy. There are serious differences among Dayan, Allon, Eban, Shapira, Begin, and Eshkol; at this stage none of them is ready to impose his view by a simple majority vote.

A third reason seems no less important. "We know how to fight and win a war," a columnist on one of the local papers wrote recently, "but we don't yet know how to decide." Government decisionmaking techniques here have often been described as outmoded, suitable more for the early days of Zionist colonization than for running the affairs of a modern, highly complex state. While there was planning for war, there has been little, if any, planning for peace; though, based on army estimates, government had had good reasons to believe in victory, nobody had thought of what to do with any of the territories certain to be occupied. All planning was purely military. There is still no policy planning apparatus, either in the government or in the universities, to parallel the most effective one run by the army. The political system here is Government by Committee, but the absence of an effective chairman is widely felt. The events preceding this last war, culminating in General Dayan's entry into the cabinet on the wave of a near-hysterical popularity, gave a supreme expression to the crisis of leadership in Israel. Dayan's appointment reassured public opinion. But the crisis of leadership continues. Prime Minister Eshkol, still sulking and annoyed with his own party for wresting the Defense Ministry from his hands on the eve of victory, unwittingly defined his own position when he remarked, partly in jest and partly in bitter seriousness, that he now was "a Minister without Portfolio."

In Jerusalem, as elsewhere, it was felt immediately after the war that the likeliest Arab partner for an early settlement with Israel would be King Hussein of Jordan. Of all Arab rulers, he had suffered the worst defeat; he had lost almost half his population, a third of his national income and half of all agricultural production. It was felt that while Egypt and Syria could sit it out, lick their wounds, cure them with further Soviet medicine, Jordan could not. Moreover, the "courageous young king" had always been known as the most moderate of Arab rulers, more open to reasonable counsel than others, and dependent on the good will of the West as well. Had he not anxiously been trying to stop Syrian-trained infiltrators from using his territory as a base for terrorist attacks on Israeli settlements? Had not his grandfather "almost signed" a formal peace treaty with Israel prior to his assassination in 1951?

In an interview a few days after the war, General Dayan was asked about peace talks with the Arabs. His laconic answer was: "We are waiting for them to ring us up." Months have since passed. Hussein has not yet telephoned Dayan, nor have any other Arab leaders; and it is becoming increasingly questionable that they ever will. On Allenby Bridge, spanning the River Jordan a few miles from Jericho, there have been a number of meetings between Israeli and Jordanian representatives, but on purely technical matters only, such as the restoration of the damaged bridge or the repatriation of refugees. As far as such things can be ascertained there have been no other discussions and no political feelers have been put out by the Jordanians, except on one occasion through an unidentified third party; judging from what Prime Minister Eshkol recently told an interviewer about this feeler it does not appear to have been serious. Nor has there been much Israeli encouragement, if indeed such encouragement could help break the stalemate. Some observers argue that there is no longer anything in it for Hussein that would make it worthwhile for him to risk his head; the annexation by Israel of Jerusalem and its environment and certain border rectifications in the Jordan Valley and the coastal plain would leave him at best with poor pasture land inhabited by restive people long opposed to his regime.

In their present mood of victory, most Israelis are not too bothered by such arguments, nor has there been anything in what the Arabs have said or done to encourage a different line. Both sides have thus been pushing each other to positions hardly more negotiable than before. Hussein has been calling on West Bank Arabs to revolt against their Israeli overlords. Dayan has been taking an increasingly inflexible position. When Rudolf Augstein, publisher of the German news-magazine *Der Spiegel,* asked General Dayan how he hoped to achieve peace, the following account of his conversation with the General was recorded:

DAYAN: By standing firm as iron, wherever we are now standing, until the Arabs care to consent.

AUGSTEIN: Then it's only King Hussein who is likely to qualify as a partner in negotiations. But he isn't strong enough to agree to Dayan's conditions.

DAYAN: In this case let them find themselves another king.

AUGSTEIN: But Jordan as a country may not be strong enough to agree to peace on Dayan's conditions.

DAYAN: In this case let them find themselves another country.

AUGSTEIN: Under these circumstances, it is hard to hope for peace soon.

DAYAN: That's probably right.

The tone of Dayan's answers may reflect his personality alone; the feeling behind them is characteristic of a much wider circle—a circle deeply pessimistic about the chances for peace and highly suspicious of any possible treaty with the Arabs (if such a treaty should ever come about). Their case is difficult to refute. Dozens of "pacts," "fraternal agreements," and "unions" among themselves have been signed by the Arabs during the past twenty years; few have lasted. "They are worthless scraps of paper," one younger Cabinet minister commented recently, "we would be mad to rely solely on them." In the months following the war, there has thus been a growing tendency here to insist on far-reaching territorial changes— notably the permanent stationing of Israeli troops along the River Jordan, by the Straits of Tiran, and on the Syrian heights overlooking Israel's northern settlements—as the basis of any accord with Jordan, Egypt, or Syria. When Chief of Staff Yitzhak Rabin announced on June 5 that Israeli forces would soon shift the scene of battle from Israel to Arab territory, Prime Minister Eshkol immediately added that Israel did not seek territorial gain. Except for Old Jerusalem, this is still the official government policy, at least verbally. But even as moderate a man as Foreign Minister Abba Eban recently said that any peace conference would serve first to negotiate a "new map" of the area. How this map should look is the subject of many a heated discussion, both within the Cabinet (where no decision has yet been reached) and out of it, at political meetings and in the press. Leading Cabinet ministers, speaking "in a private capacity" have already spelled out their views in some detail. Loudest among them are Defense Minister Dayan and Labor Minister Yigal Allon, both "Sabras" and at 52 and 49 years respectively, the two youngest members of the Cabinet. Both are considered serious candidates to succeed Eshkol, which is perhaps one reason why they have been engaged recently in a race to declare more and more patches of occupied territory to be "inseparable parts of Israel's ancient heritage."

Originally, General Dayan had supported a loose confederation between Israel and the West and East Banks of Jordan (apparently under King Hussein) in exchange for a peace treaty and adequate security guarantees. Shortly afterward he supported the idea of an independent Palestinian state under Israeli tutelage. By July 1967 he was recorded as saying that the Gaza Strip was part of Israel; this, though recorded on tape, was later denied, but nevertheless caused a good deal of annoyance within the Cabinet. In August, General Dayan told a party political rally that Israel must never return to her former borders. He quoted David Ben-Gurion who said once that the borders of 1948 were a cause "to lament for generations" because they did not include the West Bank. The borders of 1948, said Dayan, had been part of the reason the Arabs had attempted three times to conquer Israel. What Israel needs for peace, he said, is not only an Arab recognition but the "space and borders" that will no longer tempt the enemy to attack. The 1948 borders were no "borders of peace"; those of 1967 are. Here is an opportunity, said Dayan, rare in the lives of nations, to revise borders, and Israel must not miss it.

Dayan drew a distinction between the various captured territories. Sinai, Suez, and the Syrian Heights are "dear to our hearts," but he would not compare them with the "cradle of our history, in Hebron, Shilo and Anathot." Those who appreciate the special link between the people of the Bible and the Book of the Bible, he said, must also recognize that there is a "Land of the Bible." Its heart was the precincts of the Judges, of Abraham, Isaac and Jacob, in Jericho, Jerusalem, and along the banks of the Jordan. He told his wildly applauding audience that these were not political plans, but something much more powerful—"the dream of a nation come true." Dayan admitted the present Arab population of East Jerusalem, Nablus, or Hebron did not want to live under Israeli rule, but, he added, Israel was not here "because the Arabs wanted it." If what they wanted had come to pass, Arabs would now be sitting in Tel-Aviv and all of Israel's cities would lie in ruin.

A few days prior to Dayan's speech, Labor Minister Allon had expounded some of his views and proposals in an address to the National Federation of his Kibbutz movement. His proposals, though couched in terms less extravagant in their appeal to national and religious sentiment, amounted to almost the same. Allon suggested the annexation of the entire Jordan Valley, from south of the Lake of Galilee down to the Dead Sea—an area currently only sparsely populated—as well as the heavily populated area between Jerusalem and Hebron. This would put both Bethlehem and Hebron within Israel's borders. The single remaining enclave, that of Samaria, populated by some 400,000 Arabs, would be granted independence, in close political, economic, and military liaison with Israel. Allon went on to suggest the immediate establishment of Jewish agricultural settlements throughout the annexed areas, and especially on the barren hills along the winding River Jordan, as strategic and political bulwarks toward a hostile East.

Allon did not ignore the problem of the refugees, and suggested that Israel proceed immediately to resettle the hundreds of thousands of Arabs homeless since the 1948 war who are now for the first time under Israeli control. This was not an opportunity to be missed, he said, both from humanitarian and political considerations. If Israel could start with an imaginative, well-planned, and generous resettlement scheme, Allon was sure large-scale international aid would be forthcoming. It was possible, according to Allon, to settle some of the refugees on former Egyptian territory, in northern Sinai near El Arish, an area rich in water that was early in this century discussed (between the Zionist movement and the British government) as a possible Jewish national home. Others might be settled in an independent enclave of Samaria. Still others should be encouraged, with generous monetary grants, to emigrate to Canada, Australia, New Zealand, or Brazil, each of whom have stated their readiness to receive some of the refugees as their contribution toward a lasting Middle East settlement.(A few days after Dayan's speech, Allon was quoted as being affronted by the Dayan declaration that Israel's historical borders took in only the West Bank. According to Allon, Biblical borders also included Sinai and the Syrian Heights. And so the contest continued.)

While none of these proposals has as yet been adopted by the Cabinet as a whole, the trend of governmental opinion is definitely moving in that direction. The feeling grows that Israel, which is in need of peace, can live without it. There is even a rationale behind "non-peace" and one was recently offered by Professor G. Baer (Deputy Head of the Institute of Islam Studies at Jerusalem University). Writing in *Ha'aretz*, Baer said that tension and danger serve a useful role in the crystallization of a new nation, "giving it backbone and unity." Some ministers, notably those of the left-wing Mapam, the National Religious Front, the Independent Liberals, and the Old Guard of Mapai led by Abba Eban and Education Minister Zalman Aranne, would still prefer a settlement with Hussein. But even one of them recently said in conversation that "should the unexpected happen and Hussein telephone Dayan, it might embarrass us awfully. . . ."

The government has been appearing increasingly as a prisoner of public opinion. This in turn has been fed by the "private statements" of some leading government figures and by a press that is by and large opposed to the return of any territory whatsoever, especially that of the West Bank. Along with the popular afternoon press, Allon's organ *Lamerchav,* and of course right-wing Herut's *Hayom,* have become to some degree protagonists of *"Eretz Israel Hashlema"* (the Greater Israel Movement).

❋

The Army of reservists has given way to the Army of tourists in the occupied areas. The ancient towns of Hebron, Bethlehem, Jericho, and Nablus in the last half-year have been stormed by tens of thousands of Israelis, with their wives and children, crowding the churches and mosques, climbing the ramparts, causing fantastic traffic jams, exploring the picturesque bazaars, where they quickly buy up English jams, Japanese smoked oysters, and plastic toys from Red China. Judging simply from the size of the crowds, an Arab could have easily gained the impression that there were at least ten million Israelis. At first, the authorities frowned upon this onslaught, and tried to limit it by an elaborate system of permits. But Israel is not only a state, it is also a *mishpoche*: with just about everyone having a relative, friend, or friend's relative near enough to the permit-issuing offices, the system of permits quickly broke down. Mass tourism to the Gaza Strip, to Northern Sinai, and to the ancient cities and breathtakingly beautiful landscapes of Samaria, Jericho, or Hebron, has since exercised a political effect of some significance. To the recent immigrant, the shortened bus route he now takes from Tiberias to Jerusalem via the *new* (but really old) direct route through Nablus has become a fact of life. To him it has become unthinkable that he must return to the longer, roundabout way through the coastal plain that was the only way prior to the war. One understands the practical reasoning of this; there are emotional factors, however, that seem to play an even more important part. The emotional factor appears to possess such primeval force that one may well ask whether any government would dare to oppose it.

The territory of Israel prior to the Six Day War, though rich in Roman, Byzantine, Nabatean, and Crusader ruins, actually had very few historical monuments testifying to the Jewish past here. The old territory never embraced the ancient territory of the Hebrews—who were people of the Hills—but rather that of their plainland enemies, the Philistines, as well as the Edomites' Negev and "Galilee of the Gentiles." The Six Day War has suddenly confronted Israel with its history. Its cradle was not in Tel-Aviv, as Davan put it, but in the Hills of Judea, at Hebron and Jericho, at Anathot, the birthplace of Isaiah, and in the shades of the mighty ramparts surrounding these ancient city of David, in its alleys and pools and above all on Mount Moriah—now the precinct of two great Mosques. Here David placed the Tabernacle and Herod the Great built his temple, of which only the Wailing Wall remains. The sight of these ancient remnants, sparse as they are, has nevertheless fired the imagination of people to an extent that even the "Canaanites," an esoteric group which has always been in favor of shedding Jewish traditions to assimilate with the Arabs, have been described as feeling that some of their best friends are Jews. Avowed Atheists have been making moving and pious statements about the sanctity of the Wailing Wall.

The daily press has been filled recently with maps of Joshua's, Solomon's, and Herod's conquests on both sides of the Jordan, and with argumentative articles proclaiming Israel's right to the whole of Palestine, irrespective of the wishes of its present 950,000 Arab inhabitants. These Palestinians would of course not be molested, but they must expect to live quietly in a Jewish State, because the whole of Palestine is the legal heritage of the Jews. The founders of Zionism had hoped that Palestine could serve as a national home for both Jews and Arabs. But this now seemed to many a hopeless dream, fit only for cranks and political non-realists. While this, in view of recent events, may be the sad truth, it is still difficult to agree with exhortations published in the press such as that by Mr. Aharon Amir, a leading publisher and poet, who wrote that Israelis must overcome what he called the "complex" of partition (of Palestine), to him the unnatural complex of those who cannot think of the country as it was meant to be—a single entity. In a lonely, but correct, response, Dov Bar-Nir argued in Mapam's *Al Hamishmar* that since two legitimate national movements had clashed over Palestine, its partition, far from being a "complex," was in effect the only just and moral solution. Why, he wrote, undo it now?

With the sword in one hand and the Bible in the other, some of the more fervent have argued that deeds contracted in the Late Bronze Age are the legal and moral basis for present claims, whether for real-estate or political control in general. One example given was the traditional burial cave (now a Mosque) of Abraham, Isaac, Jacob, and their wives at Hebron. The cave was not only conquered by Caleb of Yephune around 2000 B.C., and again by General Dayan in June 1967 (this is the argument of Israeli Minister of Religious Affairs, Dr. Zerah Wahrhaftig), but it was also "purchased" by Abraham from Ephron the Hittite, and modern Israel holds the title. The same was true now, he said, of the site of the Temple in Jerusalem, after Mecca and Medina, Islam's holiest place. Israel, Dr. Wahrhaftig announced, has the legal right to destroy the present (and most beautiful) Dome of the Rock in order to rebuild the temple; but "it will not exercise this right" because according to the Halacha the third Temple can be built only by God. "I am thus extremely happy," said Wahrhaftig, "that we shall so evade a nasty conflict with the Moslems."

Even so moderate and serious a man as Professor J. Praver of the University of Jerusalem in a symposium organized by the mass-circulation tabloid *Maariv* came up with the astounding statement that although many peoples in history had held Jerusalem, the Jews alone succeeded in "striking roots" there.

A new somewhat animistic cult of holy place has sprung up, actively propagated by the Ministry of Religious Affairs and the Chief Chaplain of the Army, and still spreading, as "authentic" Biblical sites and graves of prophets and famous rabbis are being "discovered" almost daily in the newly occupied territories (in late October 1967 the official count was more than 300 new "discoveries," including the allegedly authentic graves of relatively minor biblical figures such as Avner ben Ner, King Saul's Chief of Staff, or the prophet Nathan). The Minister of Religious Affairs issued an angry official announcement criticizing Professor Yigael Yadin, the well-known archaeologist, who said that in his opinion Abraham, Isaac, and Jacob are probably not buried in the Machpela Cave in Hebron. The tombs there were probably those of some Arab sheiks, Yadin thought. Some old stones, of whatever origin, have become subjects of adoration bordering on fetishism. While reminiscent in many ways of Catholic practice—the cherishing of bits of the cross, or the handkerchief or footprint of Jesus—a new element was here being introduced into the traditionally abstract character of Jewish religious worship. At the Wailing Wall, a whole densely populated quarter has been razed overnight and its inhabitants moved elsewhere, to make way for tens of thousands of visitors. To judge by sounds and sights alone, the Wailing Wall is paralleling the mass-gatherings in Southern Italy following a "miracle."

The poet-publisher Amir has called on Israel to face "the intellectual and moral challenge of the new borders of victory"—there to establish the Greater Israel which would stand firm, persevere, and impose its will in the face of pressure even from all the world's powers.

Amir tried to reassure those of his readers who might have some concern over a possible Arab majority by 1990 in a united country. Majorities, he wrote, do not necessarily count; after all, the ancient Romans never had a numerical majority in their empire, nor do the Russians today in the Soviet Union. Israel, says Mr. Amir, "has a Manifest Destiny" to become the dominant power in the Near East, through exploiting her present military superiority and through becoming the patron power of all political, ethnic, or religious minorities in the area, from the Maronites of Lebanon to the Kurds in Iraq and the Copts in Egypt. Another leading poet who has recently entered the discussion is Nathan Altermann, perhaps Israel's finest lyricist and through his political essays long known as "the conscience" of the Israeli labor movement. He, too, is for annexing the West Bank. Returning the West Bank to Jordan, he says, even in exchange for a peace treaty, would be another "Munich." A Munich is possible not only between one nation and another but also "between a nation and its history," between an individual's present and his sense of belonging to a past.

❊

The Israeli occupation regime on the West Bank has been marked on the one hand by a humanity and generosity rarely evinced by occupation armies, and on the other hand by growing civil unrest and unwillingness (e.g., by Palestinian teachers) to cooperate with Israel. The distinguished political columnist of *Yediot Aharonot*, Erel Ginai, has suggested that there is "only one safe way to get the Arabs on the West Bank to collaborate with Israel, and that is to impress it on their consciousness that Israel has absolutely no intention to evacuate the territory inhabited by them."

Another poet and regular political commentator, Haim Guri, writing in the daily *Lamerchav*, felt that there was no need to worry about the possibility of the Arab population gaining a majority through natural increase by the end of this century as long as there was continued mass immigration by Jews into *Eretz Israel Hashlema* (Greater Israel). If for one reason or another there will be no such mass immigration from the West, Mr. Guri suggested issuing an "Appeal to the Gentiles"—Norwegians, Dutchmen, Danes, Mexicans, Frenchmen, and Italians—who might be, he wrote, more open to Israel's message than the Jews of the Diaspora.

> Let us tell them: Come and partake in the wonderful adventure of building Eretz Israel.... We will share everything with them. We will give them our pretty daughters for wives and their dark or light-skinned women will find men here worthy of the name. We will make it easy for them to convert to Judaism, and those who will not want to convert can live here as a sympathetic minority of Christians or Atheists, tied to us in heart and soul, as citizens.

Since the war, a curious reversal of roles traditionally played by "intellectuals" and "power elites" has taken place here, indeed has become a characteristic of the country. In Israel, as elsewhere, intellectuals, poets, novelists, et al., have often criticized real or apparent governmental excesses. Here, as elsewhere, the intellectual community has tried to serve as a corrective to what was or seemed illiberal or overnationalistic in governmental policies. Since the war, intellectuals and liberals have been in the forefront of a vociferous campaign for holding on to the "liberated areas," while many of the traditional hawks within the government and army have counselled moderation, peace with the neighboring states being more important in their eyes than the acquisition of new territories. One senior army officer recently referred to Israel's conquering poets, saying: "They frighten me, these intellectuals and poets.... It is strange: if I were intoxicated with victory, that would be bad but natural. But they...?"

How characteristic is all this talk of the climate of opinion in the country as a whole? Some observers dismiss much of it as marginal and unim-

portant. Others are less sure. Explaining why he was opposed to the annexation of the West Bank as well as to the establishment of a puppet-state
there, Professor J. L. Talmon of the Hebrew University recently wrote:
"The example of other nations fills me with the fear of lurking dangers to
the moral texture, mental balance and spiritual values of a master race."
Some of the letters and articles recently appearing in the Israeli press could
serve as first illustrations to what Talmon must have had in mind: some
protest the "excessive humanitarianism" of the authorities in the occupied
areas, others demand to reintroduce the death penalty. There was the offer
by one reader of a popular afternoon paper to serve as hangman, or the
announcement by Eytan Livny (former Chief of Operations of the *Irgun
Zvai Leumi*) that "hundreds of former *Irgunists* are ready to help deal with
hostile populations."

Others feel that most Israelis are at heart realists, who will not be swept
off their feet by foggy poets and emotional rabbis who travel about the
occupied territories sounding their *shofars* like Joshua's army outside the
walls of Jericho. (The Army Chief Chaplain, Brigadier General Rabbi
Shlomo Goren, who previously had descended on Mount Sinai by helicopter, blowing his *shofar,* caused a good deal of embarrassment to the government and as much anxiety to the Arabs of Jerusalem, by entering on
Tisha Ba'Av the enclave of the holy mosques on Mount Moriah and holding a public prayer there. He planned to conduct to hold regular prayer services there and announced plans to build a synagogue in one corner of the
mosque courtyard; but government pressure has prevailed upon him to
cancel those plans—at least temporarily. His demonstration unnecessarily
lent further weight to an Arab obsession dating from the days of the earliest Zionist settlers: that the Jews are bent upon razing the mosques to
rebuild their temple.)

It was argued that given the right kind of political leadership a considerable majority of Israel would stand the test and prefer peace more than
territories and security more than ancient sites. At year's end, hardly anyone expected to be put to such a test. There was nothing to suggest that the
Arabs were ready for settlement. Deadlock was in the air.

3

Dayan

This gloomy, lonely, gifted man—too cunning, too admired, too hated, too ambiguous, too glamorous, too extravagant, too famous—who has played a leading role in Israeli life for thirty years. This paradox of charm and jaundiced pessimism, sheer courage and bleak despondency. This homebred Talleyrand who has served all the political regimes of the last thirty years save one, left wing as well as right and center, always landing on his feet, and sometimes on other people's toes.

This millionaire—in real estate, antiquities and book royalties—who came out of the austere world of the early pioneers, the first child born in the first kibbutz. Sullen, introverted, impatient with his fellow mortals. Too easily bored. "Charismatic" in a country in which that designation, in the eyes of many, is a compliment. Feline, artful, a notorious womanizer, yet probably without a single close friend: incapable of companionship among equals. Emotionally blocked, estranged from his sons as he himself had been from his father. A lover of power, money, good food, fast cars and all manner of creature comforts. Acquisitive.

At bottom, perhaps, a hedonist. In a word, rather human. Soldier, author, statesman, occasional poet. Lucky. Another man would not have managed as rapid and successful a political comeback after the bloody fiasco of the

Yom Kippur War (1973), when he was spat on in the streets by war widows and forced to resign, virtually to withdraw from public life.

A compulsive collector. His antiquities collection is one of the world's largest and richest private hoards of ancient Near Eastern artifacts—assembled partly through illicit excavations. No public prosecutor has ever dared to file charges, although his private digs have often been savagely criticized in the press.

Immune to all complaints. The darling of the foreign electronic media, favorite star of all the Barbara Walterses, in the eyes of millions on five continents he continues to symbolize the new Jew, the sabra, an ancient people's newfound vitality in modern times. Yet in the intimacy of his home he lives in a morbid décor of burial urns, funeral plaques, death offerings, and sarcophaguses, which he has extracted from countless catacombs and ancient burial grounds throughout Israel and the occupied territories.

Eros and Thanatos in the den of power? Robert Posen, the Israeli poet, had Dayan in mind when he wrote in March 1973 "After the Shooting Down of the Libyan Passenger Plane":

bony worms are my fingers
they dig and dig
in ancient tombs.
Along the walls of my house
hollow and silent
the shrines of my Covenant glance hauntingly
my member explores
the dark cavities of the women
the men my eye calls up
torn wide open and awesome
the words of my mouth keep shifting
for with ruses I make my wars
but my sealed lips
spell your true judgment.

Ever since he shed his uniform in 1957 and entered politics, Moshe Dayan embarrasses, infuriates, confuses, fascinates the public. He is the mysterious Cyclops of Israeli politics.

A fierce war god? A maker of peace? He is the first senior Israeli politician whose roots are not in Eastern Europe, but in the Near East. Golda Meir disparagingly, despairingly referred to him behind his back as "that Arab." In a disappointingly shallow, tedious autobiography he hid his inner face in a sea of official documents. The autobiography was published on the ruins of his public career in the aftermath of the Yom Kippur War.

At that low point Lord Weidenfeld, the English publisher, came to him with a new idea. Write another book, he said, on archeology, on the geography of the Bible—from your own personal viewpoint. It was 1975. The decision was facilitated by a six-figure advance and his newly acquired free time. It would have turned out to be an interesting project even had Dayan not so unexpectedly returned to power in 1977 as one of the architects of peace. The manuscript was handed in in May 1977, a few days before Dayan joined Menachem Begin's cabinet as Foreign Minister.

The finished product *(Living with the Bible* [New York: Morrow, 1979]) has now reached the book stores. Its sleek décor (a *coffee*-table album of photographs in saccharine colors and nondescript black and white) is misleading. The name is trite. You live with a woman, or a poodle; no one "lives with" the Bible. Yet despite the packaging, this is not the synthetic product of a shrewd bar mitzvah gift manufacturer who mated a good ghost-writer with a famous, selling name. The bookshop stalls are full of those. The late Golda Meir contributed hardly a line to her recent book of memoirs, which were written, as is now well known, by Rinna Samuel, who also wrote Yigal Allon's *David's Shield.* Even Abba Eban did not write all of his *My People* but took on Neal Kozodoy, an editor of *Commentary* magazine. There is very little doubt that Dayan wrote this particular book himself.

His style, character, and personality are clearly embedded in its spare, almost primitive text. It is full of strange charm and, at times, is curiously naive. The interesting thing is that in these 232 pages (mostly pictures) there emerges a more intimate portrait of the man than in the 767 pages (Hebrew version) of his autobiography.

This is an intimate love story. The account of a complex, at times dark, illicit affair, a crime of passion, an obsession runs through this spare, bony text of landscape descriptions, childhood anecdotes, and paraphrased Biblical tales: love of country, passionate collecting. Dayan makes love to the sights, the topography, the weather, the sun and wind, the fauna and flora, the rocks and thistles and antiquities of the Holy Land. Especially the land. If he has loved not wisely, he has loved too well. He has risked his life in archeological excavations more often, it would seem, than in war. When in 1969, a burial cave he was digging up near Tel-Aviv collapsed upon him, had it not been for a boy who saw him enter, he might well have perished in the mud among the Stone Age shards and artifacts he so cherishes.

Dayan's love of Israel is not abstract, it is concrete and sensual. It does not grow out of books or the sound of Biblical names—as in the case of

many Zionists—but out of a link with the land on which he trod as a barefoot child. It is also the patriotism of one who has often observed his land
from the cockpit of a helicopter. There is in our day and age a select brand
of man to whom it is given, as it were, to view creation in one glance, like
an Aristotelian god, and Dayan is one of them. The privilege produces a
very special distortion of the political optic, an arrogance of power. In the
cockpit of a helicopter, away from normal constrictions of space and speed,
you play God. You are far away from traffic jams, cops, and parking meters.
There is a tendency to see order where there is chaos. From this lofty perch
Dayan sees only "one land," the Land of Israel "bounded in the east by the
River Jordan and in the west by the Great Sea, crowned in the North by
Mount Hermon, sealed in the South by the parched wilderness."

He does not see the messy fact of two nations, Israeli and Palestinian,
one occupied, one free, distinctly divided into separate zones of residence
and bitterly at war with each other, precisely because the Palestinian will
not see all of it as Israel's land, and Yasir Arafat sees all of it as his.

Yet Dayan's patriotism is also that of a fellah. He seems to know all about
the domestication of camels, about sheep and old-fashioned plows and hoes
and pitchforks and the habits of mules and donkeys in the fields and the
planting seasons and the proper humidity of soils prior to seeding. When he
purchases an old artifact he insists that the dealer first take him to the cave
in which it was found. He must touch before he knows whether he loves.

Few men have sounded as moving a love song to the physical land of
Israel as he does in this odd book, not since the poets of the Hebrew revival,
under the iron sky of the Ukraine, sang of a land they had never seen, its
trees, its birds, flowers, rivers, crags, and hills. A pleasing song, it sweeps the
reader along with a sweet, enticing tune. One so tempting, in fact, that—politics apart—for a moment one forgets that this is the memoir of a grave-rob-
ber, who frankly tells us of his hair-raising adventures in the fields and gul-
lies and shelves and deserts and mountains, where he has been conducting
his clandestine excavations for almost forty years. As in an old Humphrey
Bogart movie, where the villain is cast in the role of a sympathetic safe-
cracker, we end up by falling in love with him.

Dayan is known as an able digger. He is said to have worked for ten
hours in the rain in a deep ditch, digging. He is attacked by "disgusting"
leeches, contracts cave fever, catches a bad cold. But the "Philistine swan-
shaped jar" he finds in the end, near Ashdod, "warmed my heart." He
rarely comes home from a dig without some interesting find. He is said to
have a sixth sense. Professor Benjamin Mazar of the department of archeology of the Hebrew University has said about Dayan that with his one eye

he sees more than ten professional archeologists. He knows where to dig. He has also built up, through the years, a network of tipsters—tractor drivers, building contractors, army scouts, and public-works officials—who come to him with news of promising sites. They plow up his finds for him and transport them to his suburban home near Tel-Aviv.

And yet Dayan is not truly an archeologist. He is a collector. Freud regarded compulsive collecting as an infantile urge in man. Archaeologists almost never collect their artifacts. Israel's best-known archaeologists, Yigael Yadin or Mazar, collect briar pipes or books. Mazar books. A brief passage in this book describes Dayan's arduous foot journey through a wadi in the Sinai to the site of some marvelous Egyptian rock inscriptions and reliefs discovered in the nineteenth century by the great archeologist Sir Flinders Petrie. He writes: "I offered silent thanks to Petrie for having left them there. In a museum they would just be part of a collection of ancient artifacts. Here they were reality itself—not mute witness of what had happened, but the events themselves, with the seal of the Pharaoh marking his control of the quarries and mines and access highways." Yet Dayan's house and garden in Zahala are filled to the brim with similar reliefs and inscriptions, and from this area itself. He has dragged them there—sometimes by army helicopter—from all parts of Israel and the occupied territories. They are not "reality itself" but mere objects amassed in the home of a rich, powerful and resourceful man. Nowhere in this otherwise candid book is this contradiction resolved, not even the beginning of an effort to explain it.

"My parents who came from another country," Dayan writes, "sought to make the Israel of their imagination drawn from the Bible their physical homeland. In somewhat the reverse way, I sought to give my real and tangible homeland the added dimension of historical depth."

It is at once fascinating and discouraging to see how Dayan does just that. The main influence, he tells us, was his school-teacher in the little village of Nahalal, where he grew up, a man named Meshulam Halevi. Halevi, he says (in the English version) "invested [the tales of the Bible] with a sense of present reality." In the Hebrew original he says that Halevi "invested" the schoolboys of Nahalal with the Bible. The verb *hinchil* he uses is the same one used nowadays to "invest" the occupied territories with Jewish settlements.

Dayan's reading of the Bible is selective. It is a pagan Bible of wild barbaric tribes, sweeping out of the desert to conquer the land of Canaan. His Bible begins with Abraham and ends with David. Joshua and Saul are his heroes, the prophet Samuel merely a moralizing bore. Isaiah, Jeremiah, and

Ezekiel are never mentioned in this book—nor are any other of the great prophets. In Dayan's Bible there are only wily nomads and gloomy kings and bloody warriors. There are no ethics, no psalms, nor any of the moral precepts of the Mosaic code.

Hence the sudden transitions in this book from Samson to Dayan himself, and the crude comparisons between the exodus from Egypt and the crossing of the Suez Canal by General Arik Sharon's commandos in 1973. ("Not until 3,300 years later did the children of Israel return to Goshen; during the 1973 war.") He relates Moses to David Ben-Gurion, the patriarch Abraham to Dayan's own father, the Philistines of the eleventh century B.C. to the Egyptians of today; between the tribes of Gad and Menashe who settled in Transjordan and the paratroopers of the Israeli army. Such a selective, "topically" dramatized Bible leads at best to a Dayan. At worst it leads to the Jewish Defense League, or to the nationalist-religionists and squatters of Gush Emunim. All of this, amid descriptions of landscapes, historical sites and gorgeous beasts and plants and birds and flowers.

The love of Zion that burns in the pages of this strange text is not the kind that inspired the early Zionists. The Jewish poets and populists of Eastern Europe who founded modern Zionism in the latter part of the nineteenth century were fired by the dream of redemption in a new and just society. They loved Jews. Dayan loves the land. He does not seem, in this book at least, to love its inhabitants, except perhaps the Bedouin, the shepherds, and fellahin, who remind him of the ancient Hebrew barbarian and who follow wooden plows in remote villages of the West Bank. They are likely to greet his arrival with cries of "your excellency" or "o wazir!" He often descends on such isolated scenes of Biblical allure from the sky, as it were, like a Homeric god, to mix briefly with mortals.

Dayan records with relish one such occasion. An old Bedouin shepherd told him: "All the evils of the world come from heaven. All the blessings from the government."

To such a declaration Dayan could not remain impassive. He asked for evidence: "Look, o wazir, sickness comes from the Lord, and the doctors are provided by the government. Not so? Wars are arranged in heaven [it was shortly after the 1956 Sinai campaign], and peace is made by the government. Not so? Now, this year, drought has come from heaven, but we shall receive compensation from the government, shan't we?"

Dayan adds: "My heart naturally swelled with pride. . . . I of course agreed with every word he uttered, and a beatific expression lit his face. That evening he would tell his companions in his tent that the Minister of Agriculture had confirmed the grant of drought compensation to their tribe."

Dayan loves these chance encounters in remote mountain regions and in the desert. They never seem to take place in Israel proper, only in the occupied territories. Even more than the historical land of Israel, he loves the occupied Sinai Peninsula, a strange and wonderful land, "from the golden velvet of the sand dunes in the north to the crimson rocks and red coral at its southern tip."

Here the heart knows no limitations of time and space, it is "a wide open expanse without barrier . . . whenever I travel westwards from El Arish . . . I feel as if I were given wings." The Bedouin are "wild and free." They taught him that to survive one must know "how to walk between the raindrops."

As a soldier, negotiator, politician, he seems to have learned this lesson well. He ran for the present Knesset on the Labor Party list. He quit that party after it lost the 1977 elections, in order to serve the victorious Begin as his Foreign Minister. Ever since, he has been a "one-man faction" in the Knesset. Machiavelli would have found in Dayan a man to his liking. He is the only man in Israeli politics who seems to get away with everything. Golda Meir said about him: "I just don't understand it. I just don't understand how he does it."

The late Finance Minister Pinchas Sapir once remarked: "If I snatched a kiss from a grown-up woman in a dark corridor, it would mean the end of my political career," but if Dayan "raped a minor on a busy street corner," he would somehow induce the crowd to cheer him for it." Golda Meir said he was a kind of *Sonnenkind*, "altogether too lucky." Things always came his way easily, or so it seemed. He made war, he made peace, he made books. The curious matrix of his mind has never been as clearly exposed as in this latest one. A terrible simplicity of purpose is coupled throughout by a tragic sense of life. He is the armed colonizer, coming, as it were, unabashedly with the sword, claiming his inspiration in a book.

"I don't believe in pagan images," he says, speaking of the brazen idols the biblical Rachel had taken with her from her father's house when she married Jacob, "but I believe in the power of belief, in the comfort that faith can bring." It is not God, nor the Jewish religion Dayan talks about, but the secular religion of nationalism.

Dayan's "faith" is in the Jewish people, its link with this land. Faith, he says, is the "serenity in the face of a child who falls asleep with a tattered teddy bear clasped in its arms."

Elsewhere, he goes so far as to say that God is where young people rally to the call of a great inspired leader, in this instance, Ben-Gurion. You don't have to take his kind of theology as seriously as that of Louis Finkelstein, or Kirkegaard, or Barth. But it does say something about the makeup of this particular political mind.

"The future borders of Israel have been my closest concern since the establishment of the state," he writes. One might expect him to cite Clausewitz on this score, or theorists of modern weapons technology, but he sees the problem as akin to that faced in the early Iron Age by King David: If the frontiers enclose only the territory of Jewish settlements, they do not give Israel the security she needs against hostile neighbors. "David's kingdom solved this problem by subduing the surrounding hostile neighbors. Edom, Moab, Ammon, and Assyria." Elsewhere he says that the relations between Israel and Egypt in our own days remind him "somewhat of Pharaonic times." He gives this interpretation to President Anwar el-Sadat's decision to make peace with Israel: Sadat came to seek peace because in the "Yom Kippur War Egypt was defeated, and it ended with Israel's forces being closer to Cairo than in the previous wars. Sadat learned something from this. He nullified his alliance with Russia, sought closer relations with the United States and announced that he favored peace."

Years ago there was a teacher at the Hebrew University, Professor Ernst Simon, a close friend of Martin Buber, who used to say: "We are forced unfortunately to shed blood. But for god's sake, let us at least not shed ink as well." Yes, even when it produces such gorgeous, telling Rorschach blobs.

4

End of an Affair

The feelings elicited here by Moshe Dayan's sudden death exemplify once again that in this raw, unfinished society, so prone to fits of temper and to finding consolations in illusions of all kinds, Dayan's public career was a cultic phenomenon, not necessarily a political one.

David Ben-Gurion, the principal founder of this republic, never evoked similar sentiments in his lifetime and was never so lauded upon his death as Dayan was, in terms borrowed from religion ("saviour," "prophet"), mythology ("phoenix," "demigod") or the bedroom ("perfect womanizer"). The people respected Ben Gurion but were attached to Dayan in a passionate affair, complex, a little morbid occasionally, enigmatic at all times.

Nathan Altermann, perhaps the finest Hebrew lyricist of the past fifty years, writing in 1958, was one of the first to recognize the aesthetic roots of the Dayan cult. "The people loved in you their Land- of-Israel/ shining in your face like the light of dawn."

The Dayan cult was sensual, like that of a pop-star. His sex appeal worked on men no less than on women, perhaps more. Many loved in Dayan their own darker egos, themselves, or an illusion of themselves.

The cult that surrounded him home at home spread abroad after his lightening victory in the Six Day war. A former Wehrmacht general announced that Field Marshal Rommel would have done likewise if only he had been allowed to have his way. For a time, Dayan was probably the world's best known Jew since Jesus Christ. This was possible only in the age of television where the process of making history is often mistaken with the process of making images.

In Dayan's case, powerful stereotypes combined to produce the romantic image of a New Jew, a blond, un-Jewish, Goyish Jew, the facial features—Ukrainian, the eye hard and firm, the heart cruel, the soul poetic, with a sub-machine gun in one hand and a bible in the other. A similar combination of violence and soulfulness, propaganda and sexual suggestion, western efficiency and eastern mystery produced in its time the saga of Lawrence of Arabia.

Why, of all people, did this happen to Dayan? Several local generals were able over the years to play a role in Israeli politics. None became such a superstar. Dayan represented a new, locally bred, locally oriented generation of hardened, morally disillusioned younger men, self-reliant, asking no man for sympathy and with little of their own to give. His lifestyle was hedonistic. Fast cars, profitable investments in real estate, innumerable mistresses, and one of the world's richest private hoards of archaeological antiquities attested to the variety of his tastes and talents, as well as to his cavalier disregard of accepted bourgeois norms, laws, and fellow human beings. Many of the antique *objets* that filled his large house and garden outside Tel-Aviv he had dug up himself in violation of the laws, but no inspector of archaeology ever dared to call him to order, let alone file criminal charges against him. Dayan was stern and harsh to others; himself he coddled. A slim and good looking man, women found him irresistible. The thin sensuous lips cut a diagonal frown across his smooth, oval, sunburnt boyish face. Dayan was the Rudolf Valentino of Zionism.

He conformed to a somber ideal of perfection not untypical of the modern world. Amos Oz, in his short story "Late Love," described the daydream of an aging Zionist pioneer: at the head of an armored column Dayan advances into the Ukraine to avenge the tsarist pogroms. "[There he stands] dressed in stained battle clothes, calm, tall and terrible. He accepts the capitulation papers from the hands of the Governor General of Kishinev. Church-bells are ringing. . . ."

The hallucination well reflects those wishful dreams that have seen Zionism as the great "retaliation act" of the post Holocaust generation. The quintessential sabra, Dayan was said to be free of the "sensibilities" and "complexes" of the Jews of the diaspora. Many were entrapped by his charm, rare in this country of rough-edged machos. He could turn his charm on and off like a lamp. Still others saw something poetic in the apparent contradictions that frequently marked this man, who had been a soldier since the age of sixteen and who knew despair but never, apparently, fear. He was the kind of existential hero whom Camus described always looking down an abyss—without fear but also without hope.

In the Yom Kippur war Dayan defeated himself. He had to resign because of his arrogant underestimation of the Arabs, his failure to foresee and prepare for that war. His career after the war highlighted the limitations of aesthetics in politics. Golda Meir and Menachem Begin effectively neutralized him. His dramatic switch of allegiance from Labor to Likud—the readiness to serve as Begin's foreign minister—merely increased his political isolation. He resigned two years later without ever explaining why. He founded his own party, which garnered barely two percent of the votes in the elections. Many accumulating factors contributed to this political defeat—the most fascinating, and perhaps also the most foreseeable defeat in the political history of this country. He never fought for his ideas. A fatalistic streak prevented him from doing so, perhaps also a certain self-indulgence in his character, which was softer than most people thought. He wanted to govern but not to assume responsibility. He was cunning and shrewd. But in the last resort he had no true sense of politics and of history.

There were far too many shifts and turns in his political career, never enough clarity; too many ruses, too few loyalties; too much improvisation, too little long-range planning. When, after his resignation, he said that his conscience was clean, Abba Eban remarked: "Anything stays clean if you don't put it to use." Of all the legends rampant about Dayan, the most unfounded was the legend about the alleged clarity of his strategic thinking. He hid his intentions, whatever they were, in a thick fog of elliptical formulations and ambivalent terms. He was the mysterious cyclops of Israeli politics. His admirers often compared him to De Gaulle. De Gaulle too surrounded himself in fogs and mysteries yet through them every child could recognize a grand design: de-colonization in Algeria, a new Europe. What was Dayan's grand design? His contribution to the peace process with Egypt was considerable. But who can say with any degree of certitude what his "grand design" was, vis-à-vis the Palestinians—who are our principal adversary and the root cause of all Arab-Israeli wars? Did he have a strategy? In 1956, as Army Chief of Staff, he pushed Ben-Gurion into the the military adventure of the Suez war in collusion with two dying empires, England and France. What did he hope to achieve for Israel politically at that time? As Minister of Defense in 1967 he led Israel into war with Egypt, Syria, and Jordan without any clear idea about what he hoped to achieve politically. Peace or territorial aggrandizement? He never realized that he could have one or the other, but not both.

Everything he did was improvised from one day to the next. People trapped by his charms hardly noticed it. Israel was never so blinded to reality, so dizzy and irrational as it was between 1967 and 1973, Dayan's years in power, when peace could be had with Egypt and Jordan (and perhaps with the Palestinians as well) in return for withdrawal to the pre-war lines. Charisma is always irrational, as is religion. Democratic rule depends on power as well—on the forcing of one's will on others, by such or other means of seduction. It's a question of proportion . "Greater than the shame of suffering a defeat by the hands of a great nation is the shame of nation entrapped by one man" (Lassalle).

5

Far City in the Fog

Fogs hang in the stony mountain valleys, as often at this time of year in the early morning hours. Little stone houses, olive trees, and vineyards float in the grey vapors. The narrow road from Bethlehem to Hebron winds through the hills. Visibility is difficult. Traffic is sparse and slow. A few miles before Hebron an army roadblock stops all vehicles. Soldiers in wet heavy overcoats carefully pick through the contents of a small delivery truck; they are searching for hidden weapons. The Arab driver is waiting by the roadside. A young soldier glances at our faces and at our Israeli license plates and impatiently waves us on.

"Drive on, drive on!"

"Say, how do you know whose face is who?"

"It's simple," he snaps back. "Those who have Jewish eyes, we know immediately they are Arabs." The crack sounds rehearsed, too quick and too mechanical. Others must have posed this question before. We drive on past a half dozen Palestinian cars waiting in line to be checked.

On the outskirts of Hebron, with rain coming down in thin sheets from the cloud-corded sky, the fog lifts. Minarets and domed stone houses come into view. A road sign in Arabic and English: *Welcome to Hebron*. Then another sign, in Hebrew only: *Welcome to Kiryat Arba*. Kiryat Arba is the new Jewish settlement outside the old city of Hebron, established by right-wing squatters one night after the 1967 war, ostensibly against the wishes of the Israeli government at that time but soon afterward endorsed by the same government and showered with heavy subsidies and cheap loans and broadened over the hilltops on land expropriated from its Arab owners (ostensibly for "security" reasons).

The left turn off toward Kiryat Arba is a new four-lane highway that circles the old city of Hebron through the hills on the east. After a mile or so the road reaches the edge of a broad valley covered with vineyards. The massive block of concrete that is Kiryat Arba rises on the steep hill. At first sight, the stark mass of prefabricated, square, squat, reinforced-concrete apartment houses, strikes you dumb with its ugliness. The place is surrounded by barbed-wire fences, armed guards, searchlights on high poles, and prefabricated fiberglass watch towers. Even one accustomed to other dreary new housing estates on the outskirts of Jerusalem would likely be appalled by the sight. It is hard and bleak, its architecture somewhere between the Maginot line and a concentration camp. (Pier Paolo Pasolini, on a recent visit to Israel, was quoted as saying that only Jewish masochists would reconstruct in their own country the architecture of the Nazi concentration camp.)

The outlines of Kiryat Arba are sharp and angular, heavy and vertical, alien and brutal in this landscape of soft, undulating hills, which we once called "biblical" and pretended to love, of small farmhouses in rose-colored, handhewn stone, olive trees and almonds, and terraced, plowed brown earth, and flocks of sheep and vineyards. Eleven years have passed since a rabbi named Moshe Levinger and his followers of the right-wing Greater Israel Movement first arrived at the Hebron Park Hotel posing as Swiss tourists wishing only to hold a Passover seder service at the hotel, and then refused to leave until the army agreed to house them temporarily in an army barrack, pending their request for a permanent settlement outside Hebron. The official historian of Kiryat Arba, Moshe Mayefsky, in a government-subsidized booklet published in 1976, compared Levinger's ruse to the "acquisition" of the Cave of the Machpelah by the patriarch Abraham (Genesis 23:9–16). Just as Abraham paid the cave owner its full price, Mayefsky writes, so the squatters paid the hotelier $1.00 a night per room (seventy cents for each additional folding bed), in keeping with the Talmudic saying, "The deeds of the fathers are a model for the sons."

"The uniqueness of Hebron," Mayefsky writes, "is in its spiritual essence, rooted in the dawn of our national history. The acquisition of the Land of Israel in its practical sense, first took place here." The first Hebrew, he informs us, came to Hebron in the late Bronze Age, eight hundred years before King David. They acquired the Machpelah for four hundred shekels of silver, as is recorded in the Holy Book. With this title in one hand, and a submachine gun in the other, the militants and activists of the Greater Israel Movement have been pushing their way in here for more than a decade, first without, then with the tacit, and now with the active support of the Israeli government. They are a mixed lot of secular settlers and ultra-orthodox disciples of a fanatic rabbi named Yehuda Zvi Kook of Jerusalem—sometimes described as Israel's own Khomeini—who has proclaimed that the Kingdom of God is now being established throughout the Land of Israel by the bayonets of the Israeli army.

There are also a few dozen new immigrants from Russia and America here and a handful of German and French converts from Catholicism. One recent settler is a rabbi named Meir Kahane, head of the Jewish Defense League of New York, who, after a stint as informer for the FBI and a series of bloody clashes with blacks in the Williamsburg area of Brooklyn, has recently moved his theater of operations to Hebron. Kahane rents a subsidized three-room flat in Kiryat Arba for forty-eight dollars a month. The housewarming party he gave last month was covered by the press. He used the occasion to deliver a fiery sermon on the theme "Oh God, Throw Thy Wrath Upon the Goyim Who Deny Thy Name." The meaning of this, he said, was that all the Arabs in the Land must be deported. "Otherwise," he added, "we shall become like Northern Ireland."

❋

At the entrance to Kiryat Arba, an armed guard stops the car and asks to see ID cards. Beyond the barbed-wire gate, the road rises steeply into a densely built-up area. There are very few people about. How many are living here today? Nobody knows exactly. There are conflicting claims of 850 government-built apartments, according to one version, 550 are actually occupied, the rest vacant. Others say only 400 are occupied. A year ago, the housing ministry officially estimated the population to be 1,800 souls. No doubt there are many more here now. At least 100 apartments have been sold or rented recently to commuters who work in Jerusalem, where housing is not subsidized as heavily as it is here and flats sell and rent for five times as much. Jerusalem is about forty minutes away by car. There is a small industrial park in Kiryat Arba which employs about a hundred workers, two-thirds of whom are Arabs from neighboring Hebron. Some say as many as 70 percent of all working residents of Kiryat Arba commute daily to Jerusalem.

Kiryat Arba has served as model and source of inspiration for the many official, semi-official, unofficial, or wild Jewish settlements in the occupied territories in the past decade. The pattern has often been imitated. The four basic stages first successfully carried out here have been:

1. *A fact is established.* Squatters arrive surreptitiously on the scene, ostensibly against strict orders of the area military governor, but aided nevertheless—openly or obliquely—by individual officers and powerful politicians within or outside of the government coalition.
2. *Compromise.* The squatters agree to vacate whatever spot they have occupied. They are settled "temporarily" in an adjacent military compound "until review of their case by the authorities." They continue to be financially supported by nameless benefactors in Israel and abroad. Some commute daily to work in a nearby Israeli city. Arguments and squabbles, some violent, persist between the settlers and the army over the construction of permanent structures within the closed compound, first for schools or kindergarten, then for housing and small industries. The military authorities invariably give in. Meanwhile in Jerusalem, political pressures intensify to make the temporary permanent.
3. *Closure.* The government, which first claimed to oppose the settlement, now gives in to these pressures. A large tract of land near the original squatting site is first "closed" and then legally "seized" under the still prevailing British Emergency Regulations which, when they were first promulgated by the British mandatory government, were decried by the Jewish leadership as "Nazi laws." The reason given for the seizure is "public security." At this stage the land is not yet officially expropriated; therefore its Arab owners are not yet entitled to compensation. Later on, when compensation is being offered (it is usually very meager), the legal owners usually refuse to accept it. The tract is fenced in and bulldozed, usually by the army.
4. *Building.* Land seized for "security" reasons is turned over to the housing ministry, which begins to build apartment houses and lays the ground for an industrial park to give employment to the residents. The building workers are usually local Arabs. The settlers move into their new homes. Government grants and inexpensive long-term loans help to establish a few small workshops.

Each of these four stages is always accompanied by furious public outrage, accusations, and counter-accusations. Often the settlers clash with the police, or with the local Arabs; their violence is regularly justified by claims of "high idealism." In the absence of a clear government policy on settling the occupied territories (at least until Begin's rise to power in 1977), it was never easy at one stage to foresee the next with any degree of certainty. In retrospect, it seems that Kiryat Arba—and similar Jewish settlements in the territories where hundreds of millions of taxpayer money have so far been invested—was established, like the British empire, "in a fit of absent-mindedness."

The first formal decision, by the dovish Levi Eshkol government in 1968, allowing the Park Hotel squatters to settle "temporarily" in the military governors's compound in Hebron, stipulated government aid only for the establishment of a "rabbinical seminary" somewhere in ancient Hebron, where such seminaries had existed until 1929. The government resolution stated explicitly that this was by no means a permission "to build a Jewish city (or suburb) in Hebron," nor to "establish a factory or workshops."

Privately, Eshkol and some of his colleagues, including Moshe Dayan, referred to the Park Hotel squatters as "religious nuts" and "crazy fanatics." It was thought unlikely that many would remain in the discomfort of a military barrack, lacking housing and means of livelihood. Most government ministers were convinced that Kiryat Arba would be a temporary affair that would serve "to keep the right wing quiet." Politicians always pretend they can foresee and even program the future. But politics in this country is never a set piece but rather a commedia dell'arte, or better a sad farce, in which the actors are continuously improvising on the text. In the case of Kiryat Arba, the actors long ago threw away the text completely.

❋

The actors: One principal actor in Kiryat Arba is Eliakim Haetzni, 54. In 1953, as a law student at Jerusalem University, he founded a club of "citizen-vigilantes," to combat "public corruption." His style of mudslinging without adequate proof caused a great public controversy. Haetzni's semiclandestine operation faltered after a while following a sensational libel suit. He became a successful Tel-Aviv lawyer and bought himself a fine house in a garden suburb. During the 1967 war, he experienced, he says, "an electric shock," that "changed my entire life." Ever since, he admits, "I am running amok."

"Zionism is a grand adventure," he cries. "A marvelous trapeze act!" A secular man, Haetzni joined with orthodox Moshe Levinger in 1968, during Levinger's first "squat" at the Hebron Park Hotel. Haetzni became Levinger's legal adviser. In 1971, he leased his villa near Tel-Aviv, liquidated his Tel-Aviv law practice, and moved to Kiryat Arba. "Eighty percent of my time is now devoted to fighting the peace agreement with Egypt and the autonomy plan for Palestinians. It's all a question of feeling," he says. "Don't think it's only brains! What do you think we are doing in this country in the first place. . . . It's all based on feelings. . . . I can't explain them. For me they are simply beautiful, like the St. Matthew Passion." As he speaks, a strange light flickers in his eyes, and he clutches and unclutches his hands in short nervous movements. He does not really talk. He gives speeches as he paces back and forth in his small book-lined living room.

In 1954, he was still animated, he says, by the dream of "a small Israel, a miniature state perfect in every way, with flower pots in every window, like Switzerland." He now knows that even if that dream had been fulfilled the people of Israel would not have found its salvation. "What?! You think Jews can be content to simply construct another Sweden here and become drunkards? Not on your life!" Haetzni prefers another form of intoxication, "much more glorious," he says. In the small pre-1967 Israel, "I was miserable." In the new Greater Israel, with Kiryat Arba as its centerpiece, "I am a deliriously happy man." He is still vehemently secular but believes in the national mission as defined by the more extreme among the orthodox. He is a secular Khomeini. He reminds one of French integralists of the nineteenth century, the fathers of European fascism, who believed not in God but in Catholicism quintessentially expressing the Glory of France.

"The Land is *here*, in Kiryat Arba, not in Tel-Aviv!" he cries, and rushes back from the window to his armchair under a large crude oil painting of a King David playing the harp. "Secure borders? Baloney! Kiryat Arba does not exist to defend Tel-Aviv from Arab attack, but the other way round. Tel-Aviv exists to protect Kiryat Arba. We have not built Kiryat Arba for security reasons. Nor for peace. But to realize Zionism. That's it. Full stop. Period."

Haetzni claims that the Arabs of Hebron "warmly welcome our presence here." He is convinced of this. "The Arabs simply cannot understand the demented minds of some self-hating Jews who insist that we not do what all healthy peoples would be doing here, what they themselves would have done if they were in our shoes. Instead, by limiting our presence here, we act as our own worst enemies. Worst enemies, do you hear me?! That's it. Full stop. Period."

True, there is scarcely any human contact between the settlers and the Arabs of Hebron, he admits. Why? "Well, there's been some narrow-mindedness among us here lately. We too have our fanatics." There has been a falling out recently between Haetzni and Levinger. Haetzni has threatened to create an independent Jewish militia in Hebron—similar to the Christian militias in Lebanon—to fight autonomy plans for Arab Hebron. "Yes, sir, we are going to patrol Arab Hebron. We will not permit an Arab autonomy there. I can do better than the Christian militias in Lebanon." Levinger is embarrassed by these threats. It is odd to hear one fanatic call another fanatic a fanatic.

❊

Fanatics: At sunset every day, about two dozen Jewish men begin evening prayers in the great Arab mosque of Hebron, the Haram al-Khalil. The mosque is built around what has traditionally been regarded as the tombs of Abraham, Isaac, Jacob, and their spouses, and has been a Muslim shrine since the seventh century. Two dozen praying Jews huddle around a great stone block, said to be set directly over the tomb of Rebecca, wife of Isaac. The stone is only a few steps away from the richly decorated Muslim *minbar* where at this same moment about thirty Muslims crouch in prayer on dark Persian carpets. The two groups eye each other warily. Surrounding the huge stone block where the Jews are praying, a dozen or so Israeli soldiers wearing battle fatigues and armed with submachine guns stand in a circle. An officer briefs a distant command post through his little walkie-talkie.

Jewish and Muslim prayers alternate in a curious cacophony. The Jews cry, "Lord of Hosts, how beloved is Thy dwelling." Their fervor echoes through the vaulted chamber. The Muslims, a few steps away, will not be outcried in their own mosque. Their cries ring forth, drowning out those of the Jews. "Allah, the Merciful, the Only. . . ." The soldiers stand frozen between them. After the prayers, the Jews say "amen" and withdraw to an adjacent hall now called "Tent of Abraham and Sarah." It is a Muslim chapel built 500 years ago that was expropriated from the Muslims a few years ago and refurbished as a synagogue. Torah scrolls are now permanently housed here, under the rich Muslim decor. In the main hall of the Mosque, behind, the Muslims continue in their prayer. The soldiers have withdrawn. "The prayers were simultaneous." I make this remark rather offhandedly to one of the rabbinical students gathering in the smaller room. "Did you say prayer? They weren't really praying," he answers. "Just quoting a text. To annoy us."

"Let them bark," says another.

"But they were kneeling," I say, "and touching the carpet with their foreheads by the *minrab* in the mosque."

"What mosque?" says the first scholar, sharply. "There is no mosque here. This is a synagogue and it is ours."

Now a slim man, dressed in an old raincoat, approaches through a side door. He marches straight through the praying Muslims in the main hall. This is Moshe Levinger. Everyone in Israel has seen him a hundred times on television, picketing the prime minister's office or shaking hands with generals and politicians, speaking at demonstrations and being dragged away by policemen pulling at his hands and feet. He walks up to the south wall, where two old Muslim ladies are kneeling on the carpet within the section proscribed as only for women. Levinger stops about three steps away from them.

The women wave frantically to make him go away. A soldier walks up to him. "This is the women's section," he says, timidly. "They don't want you to be here." The rabbi's face remains unmoved. His eyes narrow, searching for something beyond the carved wooden screen. Then he turns his head and says, "They don't want us in this country in the first place," and he slowly walks away.

Later on I ask him whether, as an ordained rabbi, he has any contact with the Muslim priests who officiate in this shrine, for which he has so often claimed at least equal rights.

"No, I have never talked to them."

"Why not?"

"You must not talk to the Ishmaelites." Levinger never says Muslims, or Arabs. he always says Ishamaelites. "No, on no account, there must be no negotiation with them. We are in power here. We must decide. We mustn't talk. They threw us out of here once." (This was in the third century.) "If necessary we must throw them out now."

"Why?"

"To put an end to this disgrace. Jews are in an inferior position here."

"Why inferior?"

"The Machpelah is ours. Let there be at least parity."

"You don't mind officiating in a Muslim mosque?"

"No. Maimonides determined that Islam is not pagan, like Christianity. If there had been a crucifix here, it would have been a different matter."

Levinger speaks slowly, as though bored by a well-rehearsed text. His skin is marked by a terrible pallor. He turns to go. A group of Arabs is walking toward him. They look through him as though he were transparent. Only the blind beggar by the gate with his long white stick turns his dead eyes toward Levinger as he passes by and murmurs mechanically, "Welcome, welcome."

The mosque over the cave of Machpelah is, I think, the only house of worship in any civilized country where, at least since the fifteenth century, one faith has been forced to move aside and make room for another. This was achieved by force through a military occupation that prides itself on being one of the most liberal in the world. It is true that Jews and Christians had been forbidden to enter the mosque before 1967. The Israeli military rescinded this senseless restriction after the occupation of Hebron in 1967, and then also enforced the conversion of the mosque at least partially into an orthodox Jewish synagogue. As far as archaeological records go, the Machpelah, although built partly on the foundations of a massive first-century Herodian structure, has never been a synagogue. The claim that Jewish tombs exist underneath has often been challenged, most recently by archaeologist Yigael Yadin, now Israel's deputy prime minister. Yadin said in 1967 that the tombs were more likely those of a few Arab sheiks.

Until recently Jews were permitted to hold services only in two side chapels. In February, the army, at Levinger's behest, forced the opening of the mosque's main hall to Jewish prayer. Shortly before, Defense Minister Ezer Weizman had warned Levinger that further clashes within the mosque could incite anti-Jewish riots in Iran. Weizman eventually gave in. The skirmishes inside the Cave, according to Levinger, result only from the "weakness" of the military government. That weakness is abused by "Ishmaelite provocateurs." He keeps repeating the word, "Ishmaelites," with an expression of holy disdain. The novelist A. B. Yehoshua recently wondered what it is about Jews that brings out the madness in others.

❋

The actors: Haetzni stands by the military security fence around Kiryat Arba which the settlers recently have pulled down in various places. He points at one such breach: "We don't want to be locked in a ghetto."

"If you didn't want to live in a ghetto, why did you come here? The Hebronites don't want you here on the land you took away from them."

"Not true. Only a sick Jewish mind could conceive such a thought."

"Isn't this a security fence?"

"I'm not against security, but the army cannot dictate to me the size of Kiryat Arba. For your information, there will soon be fifty thousand people here!" He gestures broadly, his arm sweeping across the landscape. "You see that far mountain over there? It will be ours. And that one too. And also this."

The settlers have changed the names of the mountains in this region. Jebel Ja'abra is now Har Ha'avot. (Mountain of the Founding Fathers.)

Other mountains have been named after Jacob, Isaac, and Abraham. Jebel Jalass is now Har Eretz Israel HaShlema (Mountain of the Greater Israel.) From there is a magnificent view all the way down to the northern Negev and the outskirts of Beersheba Haetzni: "The whole thing isn't as big as many think. It's *gornischt,* (in Yiddish, *nothing*) a joke!"

❋

Snobbery of the absolute: Moshe Levinger does not immediately respond to one's questions. His eyes continually roam about in space, searching. After about half a minute, he says, "What was that you asked?"

"Do you favor giving Arabs within Greater Israel the vote?"

Levinger says it is very hard to answer this question "directly." It is "too complicated, you see." He pauses again. "I agree the Arabs were also made in God's image. The trouble is, they're opposed to this being a *Jewish* state. Therefore, the Jewishness of this state must take precedence in value over their being created in the divine image. . . . Democracy must be subordinated to Israel's national and religious purposes. Do they grant civil rights to thieves and robbers in the United States?

❋

Levinger is forty-three, a native of Jerusalem. His father, a physician, came from Munich in 1934. A man of medium stature, his face is gaunt, sickly, the muscular neck veined, the lips fleshy, pale, and slightly hared. The eyes, a greyish-blue, bloodshot. The teeth are cigarette stained and flawed. The nose is red and flat. This extraordinary man, whose odd voice and looks would under normal circumstances be counterproductive in a public figure, has made this country jump for years and has successfully manipulated every Israeli administration since 1968. What is the secret of his power?

He is one of the chief ideologues of the Greater Israel Movement. He has established Kiryat Arba against the express wishes of the government. Could he have been as successful without the overt and covert aid of some members of the previous governments, or that of anonymous officers within the military regime? Undoubtedly he would not have. Levinger proved himself a master of manipulating them. He forced himself upon the public scene, invoking a "truth" which even those who don't share it tend to "respect" as something "idealistic." He has been arrested, freed, arrested again for public disorders; he has been tried, acquitted, arrested once more and freed again. Since his success in Kiryat Arba he has spearheaded a dozen other initially illegal settlements in the occupied territories.

Levinger has staged something like a miniature "cultural revolution" in this country. Its political consequences have been wide, and, in creating faits accomplis that may make a future peace treaty impossible, may well prove in the end disastrous.

His ideas have descended like butterfly nets on all too many people here. With his ersatz Zionism, which many regard as something uplifting spiritually, he has penetrated the moral void in the souls of many Israelis. Against the demoralizing background of the previous Labor regime, infested as it was by scandal and dissension, he projected a new violent ideal which, in some circles, produced a kind of catharsis. He supplies a religious ideology for armed settlers as they force their way into an Arab town. He would never have reached this pinnacle if the humane, moderate ideals of practical Zionism, the Zionism of Weizmann and Ben-Gurion that built Israeli society, had not slowly withered away after the 1967 Six Day War. Even before Menachem Begin's rise to power, Levinger and his men had infiltrated enough settlers into the occupied West Bank to make any meaningful territorial compromise there difficult. Levinger and his followers invoke the name of a distant biblical past. Theirs is the democracy of the dead, an arrogant oligarchy that denies the living the right to determine their fate and the right finally to live in peace with their Arab neighbors.

The shallow technocrats and careerists who have governed the Labor party here in the past few years are furious as they watch Levinger emulate the gestures of their past, pioneering age. They are missing the point when they accuse Levinger of being "unserious" as a pioneer, or when they ask how many potential settlers has he got, anyway? There are more people in Kiryat Arba alone than in all the legitimate security settlements established by the Labor government along the Jordan River of the West Bank.

Yitzhak Ben Aharon, the old Labor leader, was right when he said of Levinger not long ago at a Labor party caucus: "He confronts us with an *idea* for which we have not yet found a persuasive answer." He could have quoted W. B. Yeats's lines:

"The best lack all conviction, while the worst
Are full of passionate intensity."

❋

The democracy of the dead: Sarah and Baruch Nachshon have lived in Kiryat Arba for eleven years. When their four-month-old infant died suddenly two years ago, they took the dead body into their own hands, quite literally, and staged a macabre demonstration. The purpose was, as they put it, to force the government's hand. Until that time, the government had been most anxious to keep Jews and Palestinians in Hebron as separate as possible. To avoid possible friction, Jews were not allowed to bury their dead in the ancient Jewish cemetery in Hebron proper, a cemetery which has not been used since the Arab riots of 1929. For this reason, a new Jewish burial ground had been prepared next to Kiryat Arba.

The infant had died in a Jerusalem hospital. Mrs. Nachshon smuggled the corpse out of the hospital without a death certificate. She put it in the back seat of her car and drove back to Hebron. Meanwhile, settlers broke into the old, disused cemetery in the heart of the Arab town and dug a grave.

The army got wind of what was to come. Some 200 soldiers awaited Mrs. Nachshon on the outskirts of the town, along with some 300 Kiryat Arba settlers. The scene was set for an ugly confrontation. An army officer informed the mother that he was under orders to prevent her from entering the Arab town; she had no right to bury her child there. It had to be buried in the new cemetery, he said, citing the appropriate paragraphs in the military code that gave him the right to enforce this decision.

For two hours, while the dead infant lay on the back seat of the Nachshons' car, the two sides argued. At one point, Mrs. Nachshon, crying that what she had done was in the interest of Greater Israel, tried to force the dead infant's body through a line of embarrassed soldiers. She was made to withdraw only at gunpoint. The corpse was taken in and out of the car. Meanwhile, politicians in Jerusalem were negotiating with the army chief of staff, to enable Mrs. Nachshon to have her way. At dusk, the authorities gave in.

Ever since I first heard this story, with all its violent morbidity, from her husband himself, I can't get it out of my mind. What dark guilt feelings resided within this unfortunate woman who turned the corpse of her child into a political flag? What was she compensating? What was she trying to prove to herself and to others? It is inconceivable that only so-called "political" motives played a role in this drama. There is something raw, barbaric, fearsome in it, reminiscent of Greek mythology. This woman, like Antigone, will stop at nothing.

Haetzni says that the incident with the child's corpse moved him "to tears of joy." The sick have a charisma of their own. Haetzni has recently been to Sharm el-Sheikh in the occupied Egyptian Sinai peninsula where he asked the Jewish settlers if they have a cemetery. The answer was no. "In this case you are lost," Haetzni told them. "You have no roots."

❋

How can one understand this orgy of passions that combines frustration with desire, nationalism with fundamentalism, religion with a cult of tombs, fetishism with Maimonides? The Cave of the Machpelah is the only putative Jewish burial place in this country that serves as a regular synagogue, a combination that Maimonides would have considered unacceptable. As one becomes acquainted with members of this strange community, the more tempting it becomes to look for explanations beyond the commonplace religious and political. Haetzni says, "Sovereignty is like a woman. Do you share your wife with someone else?" Many of those who come to worship their God on these dead stones speak of faith but actually mean power. They constantly say "This place is ours, not theirs," "we conquered it," "we won the war, not they."

❋

Frustrations: W. D., a tall, slim looking young man, has been a resident of Kiryat Arba for four years. As a thirteen-year-old boy in the West German city of Hamm, he says, he began his search for the "real" God. His father had been a Nazi judge. He was a sensitive, intelligent, well brought up German boy, who grew in the philo-Semitic atmosphere prevailing in West Germany in the late sixties. His search for the "real" God did not lead him immediately to Judaism. For a time, he was chanting "Ho Chi Minh" in chorus with other leftist youngsters. Then he turned to Buddhism, but discarded it after a while. The Christianity of his parents seemed unconvincing, he says. "What isn't logical cannot be true."

On the first of January 1972, he remembers, he began to meticulously observe the canonic 613 laws of Jewish behavior, the *Mitzvoth*. In June of that year, he rode his bicycle to Brindisi in Italy, where he embarked on a boat to Israel. His parents had granted him a year to "find himself." Six months later he was formally converted to Judaism by the Haifa rabbinical court, and became an Israeli citizen under the Law of the Return. At this stage, he discovered, he says, that Judaism is a "national religion." He had not expected this. In West Germany he had been rather against nationalism. But "God has commanded us to liberate and settle the whole of the Land of Israel and not to return a single inch to those who are outside the faith." Today W. D. is a nationalist Jew no less fervent than Haetzni and Levinger. "In Judaism," he explains, "things are different."

He joined the Israeli army and served his term in the tank corps, then settled in Kiryat Arba. He is not the only convert in Kiryat Arba. There are a dozen others. What is fascinating about this bright young man is that he has not simply converted to Judaism (out of motives one can never know), not only migrated to Israel and become an Israeli, but also, in an interesting mix of Talmudic reasoning with German *Grundlichkeit,* has tried to "think" Judaism through to its ultimate consequence.

Ironically, he has arrived at something reminiscent of his origins: a notion of supra-moral choseness, his new Volk realizes a higher morality—he calls it a divine command—in pursuit of a national task, at the expense of another Volk. Its justice or injustice does not interest this young yeshiva student. In international relations there is no morality, he says, there is only force. Might is right, he exclaims. "Otherwise, what right did we have to hang Eichmann? When Eichmann was strong, he killed Jews. Then the Jews were strong and killed him." There is no logical difference between Nazi law and Israeli law, he says, only an emotional difference. "The strong is entitled to do what he wants."

Coming from under a *yarmulka,* such words sound almost as ominous as from under a black SS kepi. One Volk. One religion. One rabbi . . . Yehuda Kook. W. D. says he would follow Rabbi Kook through fire and brimstone. Israel is not just powerful, she also realizes the will of God. The task of man on earth is to please his Creator. W. D. is fully intent on doing so. He will oppose with all his might Palestinian autonomy in Hebron, for it is "forbidden to hand over Jewish property to a goy." To prevent it, it is even allowed "to violate the holy Sabbath."

W. D. recently married a Jewish woman from Jerusalem, of Iraqi origin. He lives with his wife in a one-room flat. The walls are lined with volumes of the Talmud and Mishnah, alongside *The Revolt* by Menachem Begin and a large map of the Greater Israel. The ashtray on his desk is made of empty rifle cartridges. Behind a thick concordance sits *Der Prozess* in a German paperback. "Ah, Kafka!" W. D. says, "Hero of my youth!" He no longer reads German, he says; he is a student at the Atereth Talmud (Crown of the Talmud) yeshiva in downtown Hebron. He attends daily, from the early morning hours until late at night "except when they mobilize us for national purposes," for example, demonstrations in Jerusalem or to lend support to squatters elsewhere in the occupied territories.

The day after our talk, which lasted many hours, W. D. called me to ask that his full name not be mentioned in print. If only he had said that publication of his name would invade his privacy, or that it was no one's business that he is a German who converted! But this was not how he justified his request. He said that his name must not be published "for reasons of state security."

The explanation brings us back to the original question which is so hard to answer in any ordinary political or religious context.

❋

The settlers in Kiryat Arba claim there is in Hebron today "true coexistence" between Arabs and Jews. The coexistence of which they speak, it seems to me, is rather that between a rider and his horse. Its sole guarantee at the moment is the presence of a sizeable army. Coexistence in the Cave of the Machpelah today means that Jews are able to pray in the mosque alongside Muslims, who, I am afraid, do not slaughter the intruders only because dozens of heavily armed guards stand above them in their shrine.

When will be the next progrom here? Who will be its victims? Every Arab I talk to speaks of unceasing "provocation" by the settlers. Undoubtedly these Arabs cannot be the same Arabs that Haetzni or Nachshon speaks with. Nachshon says he knows mostly shepherds in the field. W. D. says he knows only one Arab in Hebron, his shoemaker. Levinger doesn't talk to Ishmaelites on principle.

Officers in the military administration of Hebron do not share the self-confidence displayed by the settlers behind their barbed-wire fence. The ancient hates and passions, fears and myths that flow through every sewer here and on occasion burst forth in words and bloody deeds, reek in the city's atmosphere and point to the future.

Only mystics or fools can mistake it. In the best case there could be a pluralist state, but it would be neither democratic nor secular. In the worst case, the West Bank under permanent Israeli control would be another Northern Ireland, or Lebanon. It is possible to believe in miracles. The wind blows a piece of paper into the air, but that does not alter the law of gravity. A great visionary often quoted by the people of Kiryat Arba, because they misunderstand him, wrote, "Only lunatics, or the ignorant, reject the laws of nature."—Theodor Herzl.

6

Flight into Egypt

So near a country, and yet so far. As near to Israel, where I live, as Holland is to Belgium, or New Hampshire to Maine. Yet for thirty-one years, my entire adult life, it has been like the other side of the moon—unknown, a menace, distant and dark. Suddenly one morning, in the glare, the dust and rattle of a stifling hot workday, the moon turns on its axis. The dark side comes into view. A passenger plane departs from Tel-Aviv airport and lands peacefully in Cairo seventy-five minutes later.

How I happen to be on this plane is another story. It was mainly as the result of outlandish exertions that may suggest in odd detail the stranger whole that has kept Arabs and Israelis light-years apart for as long as most of us can remember. Transatlantic telephone calls at all hours of the night, letters, telegrams, negotiations with an Egyptian ambassador in a Western capital. He was a friendly man who wanted very much to be helpful. For many months he came back with some such answer as "I suggested to Cairo that they allow you in. Cairo says the moment is not opportune"; perhaps next week will be more "appropriate." Or the one after. But it never was. Various well-wishers and middlemen intervened. This, too, led nowhere. In Egypt a decision on such a matter, which to some people may seem minor, appeared to be vested in the highest authorities of the state, some said in the President himself. And as the Egyptian-Israeli peace negotiations dragged on, from better to worse and back again to better, and the two parties litigated endlessly over euphemisms, commas, and semicolons, whenever President Sadat was angry with Prime Minister Begin it seemed as though he were taking it out on me. I was becoming rather paranoic in the process.

Finally, the ambassador telephoned. It may well have been the first time that an Egyptian ambassador placed a direct call to Jerusalem, Israel. He said that if I would be able to get on this very special plane carrying security men and technicians to Cairo to prepare for the Israeli Prime Minister's two-day visit, as well as a number of newspapermen (who would, however, be required to leave after two days), he would make the arrangements for me to stay on.

Well, I am finally on my way, and that's what matters, I tell myself; although with a splitting headache, bleary eyes (we were told to be at the airport at 4 A.M.), and a sore throat from smoking too many cigarettes, going at long last into Egypt. The very phrase echoes Genesis.

Not that I haven't been there already, so to speak. A few years ago I traveled through some of the remoter parts, but in a rather inappropriate manner, or disguise, in a uniform. How different this is, I tell myself, as I fasten my seat belt and mentally brace myself for shocks of recognition and discovery. In retrospect I think I was a bit smug. *Recognition* was certainly the wrong word. It implied the process of identifying something previously known and forgotten—or perhaps suppressed.

Even our departure is rather anxious. We almost do not get off the ground at Tel-Aviv. Some of the airport personnel have suddenly walked off the job, demanding a 30 percent rise in pay. When we finally take off, after a considerable delay, the route we must take is long and circuitous. The peace treaty between Israel and Egypt is only three days old. It has not yet been ratified by the Egyptian and Israeli legislatures. The ratification will be merely a formality, but we are still, theoretically, at war. The passport control officer at the airport explained this to me very carefully as he read through my travel documents slowly, page by page; he was searching for the special stamp: *Valid for Egypt.* I had raced off to get that stamp yesterday afternoon from a reluctant, highly suspicious bureaucrat who officiates in a dingy little office in Tel-Aviv. It was there that the headache that is plaguing me now began.

"Do you realize we have no embassy in Cairo?" he asked.

"Yes, I do."

"Do you fully realize what that means?"

"Of course."

"Don't dismiss it lightly."

"I do not."

"If you encounter some trouble there is nowhere you can turn."

"Yes, I know. But I don't expect to run into any."

"You might!"

"Why?"

"Because it is enemy territory."

"Is it still?"

"Technically, yes. If there is trouble, there is only one thing to do," he added.

"What's that?"

"Get yourself as fast as you can to the American embassy."

"Okay. Can I have my stamp now?"

"And don't flaunt your Israeli passport. Keep it wrapped away somewhere."

"I must show it at the hotel, mustn't I?"

"I suppose you must. But make sure it's really the concierge you are showing it to."

"I will. May I have my stamp now? Please!"

"Above all, don't talk to any strangers!"

"How's that?"

"You heard me. No strangers. It's the first rule! Do you understand?"

"Yes, I do."

"Plunk. Down went the stamp. I took my leave."

I

The plane flies out first over the Mediterranean, then turns back south of Cyprus toward the Nile Delta. We are flying by a circuitous route because there is as yet no recognized air corridor between Israel and Egypt. The direct route over the old battlefields would have taken us only forty-five minutes.

Still, as we come in through the haze toward the bleak coastline, I reflect that thirty-one years in seventy-five minutes is not all that bad. I peer out at the sand dunes and swamps below and my mouth is suddenly dry with excitement and I grip my seat even though the flight is smooth. It is hard to imagine a greater distance than that which has separated Israelis from Egyptians until now. Proust, who was an expert on the great voids that separate humans from one another, said in *Cities of the Plain* that distances are only the relation of space to time and vary with that relation; yet both are outside of human control. In thirty-one years of war the hostility was total, the distance in human terms so vast it was almost metaphysical. "He seems so near, and yet so far," Tennyson wrote in 1833, a calmer time. Anyway, he was referring to a lover. In romantic literature, lovers were always appealing to the gods to annihilate time and space, and they usually failed. In the same poem, Tennyson wrote:

> I have not seen. I will not see
> Vienna; rather dream that there,
> A treble darkness, Evil haunts
> The birth, the bridal; friend from friend
> Is oftener parted, fathers bend
> Above more graves.

We are flying in fairly low. Here now, just over the coastline, is a large cemetery. It might be the outskirts of Port Said. A line of corrugated tin roofs alongside a desert road. There is the Suez Canal, a narrow strip of green embedded in the sand. And beyond it, the Sinai desert, under a film of mist. I remember some ten years ago lying in a ditch somewhere down there trying to discern faint and floating images on this side of the Canal through a pair of binoculars, while, all around, the vast lunar expanse exploded in shellfire. From the air the desert looks flat, with hardly an undulation; it stretches far out to the eastern horizon. Nothing but sand, or so it seems. Over these arid dunes two generations of Egyptians and Israelis have bled one another since 1948. In the far distance I notice a line of palm trees; other than that, nothing.

The stewards are now moving through the cabin, serving champagne. The three security men across the aisle refuse the proffered plastic cups. Ever since we boarded the plane they have been trying to look inconspicuous in their almost identical blue blazers. In the two seats next to me, an English television news star and his cameraman are sipping their drinks calmly. For them the unfolding process of Egyptian-Israeli reconciliation in the past year must have turned by now from drama to melodrama to the schmaltziest soap opera of the decade. I can understand that they are beginning to be bored.

In the seats behind us, the Israeli newspapermen seem tense and irritable. Sick jokes have been flying about the cabin for some time. "We should have taken the quick route—like the Phantom jets, ha, ha." More jokes in the same tone. They are indications less of bad taste, I tell myself, than of nervous tension and fear of the unknown. One of the Israelis—I have known him for years—lives in Jerusalem on a street called Conquerors of the Mitla Pass. Mitla Pass was the site of a famous battle in 1967 where the Egyptians suffered perhaps the worst loss of the war: the abandoned tanks and shoes and burned-out carcasses of steel have symbolized for Egyptians their most humiliating defeat in modern history. Such names were given to streets in many Israeli cities after the lightning victory of 1967. There is nothing uniquely Israeli in this custom. Many European cities are filled with similar manifestations of military glory. I had a friend in Athens who lived on Basil the Bulgar Slayer Street, and I once asked him what he gave as his home address whenever he landed at Sofia airport, where his business took him quite frequently. "Oh, they don't mind," he said. "It happened over a thousand years ago."

But here everything is still raw: on their side, the memory of a very recent humiliation; on this side, the pain and suspicion. I am grateful, suddenly, for the innocuous Jerusalem address I shall be able to present in a moment to the passport control officer at Cairo airport—I live on Diskin Street, named for nothing more incriminating than a nineteenth-century rabbi.

Someone asks, "You think this treaty is more than a scrap of paper?"

"It's too early to tell."

"I'm certain it's only that."

"Why are you so sure?"

"Don't be naïve. What do you know about Arabs?"

"Not much," I admit.

"You don't know a thing about their m-e-n-t-a-l-i-t-y! I don't trust them."

"I find I must."

"Peace is the lies people tell one another between wars."

The steward is proffering his tray of champagne.

"No, thank you."

"It's free!"

"I'd rather have a glass of water."

"You don't want water. You want champagne."

"No, thank you."

"Don't you like champagne?" El Al stewards are often a little overbearing.

"Okay. Thank you."

"So why didn't you say so before!"

Through the window, still nothing but sand. The champagne is cool and fizzy. The plastic cup is cracked. The grayish dunes are the color of a dirty burlap sack. They shroud the debris of untold numbers of tanks and armored troop carriers, rusting in the sand, and the charred bones of those who burned in them. Ashes and scrap metal of politics. Eighty thousand Egyptians and Israelis are said to have perished on these dunes over the past thirty years. Some say a hundred thousand. No one knows the exact figure. If the dead could come back, would there have been peace sooner?

"Have a croissant with your drink."

"Thank you."

The plane dips a little from side to side. The pilot assures us through the loudspeaker that we are not tipsy; he does this with the rudders, he says, on purpose, to celebrate the occasion. More drinks are served. The pilot's humor is also on the black side.

"The last time I saw this view," he announces, "was from the cockpit of a bomber. . . . We are approaching Cairo, where the temperature is. . . . On behalf of El Al Israel Airlines and the crew . . . we hope you have enjoyed this flight ... and to be able to serve you again . . . hmm, just as soon as they let us . . . on regular scheduled flights along this route."

We are crossing a line of deep green. The Nile Delta, dense as a beehive. Thirty-one years ago, almost to the day, the prominent Egyptian statesman Azzam Pasha predicted a bloodbath against the Jews more terrible, he promised, than that perpetrated by Tamerlane. In the Tel-Aviv newspaper that I hold on my lap I read that President Sadat, who flew home to Cairo yesterday from the peace ceremony in Washington, once again has hailed the "power of love," which, he said, "overcometh everything, solveth every problem. . . . Where there was hatred we are sowing the seeds of love." Love, love. Nothing but love out of Cairo these days. Sadat has been talking like this for months. He is in love, he says, with God and mankind, and with all "Israeli mothers." He thinks of mothers as his main allies, in Israel and in Egypt. Statesmanship, he said the other day, was the "rule of love." I recoil a little at this endless talk of love. We are conditioned to resist such rhetoric, even from our own wives. Are we too cynical? Freud said, "In the final analysis we must begin to love, simply to avoid becoming sick."

The newspaper also reports that Egypt now has a new national anthem; it was played yesterday at the airport in honor of the President's return. It is their third anthem in the past twenty-six years. The first was the old royal anthem sung to the tune of the march from Verdi's *Aida*.

The text of the second was:
O my weapon,
I yearn for you
For the battle, be on guard!

Keen always to say,
I am ready for war.

The latest anthem reads:

My land! My land!
To you I give
My love and heart.
Egypt, mother of the universe,
You are my goal, my hope.
On all mankind your Nile bestows its blessings.

The tune is also new. The rank of honorary general, I read, has been conferred upon Mohammed Abdul Wahhab, the composer. I decide to take this
as a good omen, reminiscent of the recent news out of Melbourne that the
Australians voted to make the old song "Waltzing Matilda" their national
anthem instead of "God Save the Queen"—"send her victorious, happy
and glorious." By all means let us have more waltzing Matildas everywhere, less victories and glory.

The pyramids are just coming into view. They seem rather flat from this
height, dusty and yellow against the surrounding dusty yellow of the
desert. Then Giza, and the islands in the Nile, a bit unreal, like mirages of
Tahiti in the midst of so much sand and dust, with emerald-green lawns
and palm trees, and polo fields and whitewashed hotels. Farther on, the skyscrapers protrude from under the haze. The rest of the city is buried in a
cloud of pollution. The plane touches down and comes to a stop. We file out
by the rear door, dazed by the light and heat, tense, smiling a little sheep-
ishly, hesitant. And quite obviously wondering if this is real after so many
years or just "a dreadful quiet worser far than arms, an interval of peace."
Damn those phrases, I think. It is so hot, so goddamned hot. The pilot just
said it was thirty-eight degrees Celsius in the shade. "They're putting the
heat on, especially for us." We step out on the burning tarmac; the blaze
seeps through the thin soles of my shoes. A hot wind blows and strikes me
near-dumb.

There are no customs controls. No forms to fill out. As soon as we step
down from the plane we are whisked away in tourist buses that have been
waiting on the tarmac. The airport is still decorated with the flags and banners of yesterday's grand reception for President Sadat. Everything seems
a bit worse for wear in the strong wind. Portraits of Sadat are hanging
everywhere, on airplane hangars and fences and lampposts, and an espe-

cially huge one that drapes all the way down from the roof of the white-washed VIP reception pavilion. HERO OF PEACE. SOLDIER OF PEACE. WELCOME HOME. We drive out by a side gate. There are few people about. A million Cairenes are said to have pressed against these fences yesterday, chanting, "Sadat, *ya* Sadat. We sacrifice ourselves for you."

The few people visible now, airport workers mostly, it would seem, in blue overalls or long peasant galabias, are waving with their hands and calling "Salaam," "Shalom." And yet to a bystander I imagine we might seem rather like prisoners of war being led off to an internment camp. We travel at breakneck speed through red lights and stop signs. Two roaring police motorcycles precede us. They wave aside the oncoming traffic and sound their sirens. We are followed by a truckload of armed soldiers. We race down the broad avenues of Heliopolis, the ancient City of the Sun where Plato and Herodotus went to school with the priests of pharaonic Egypt, now a suburb of Cairo. The avenues are lined with gaudy villas and barefoot children wallowing in the sand. We pass gingerbread towers and grotesque statues, and gateposts and remains of gardens that may once have been green but are now yellow and grey with neglect and buried in dust. There are surprisingly few trees. Though this is a built-up area, the overwhelming impression, as at the airport just now, is *sand*. Yellow sand everywhere, between the houses and, in broad patches, on broken-up sidewalks and roads, as though the desert were sneaking back through the asphalt to reclaim the works of man. In the glare of high noon the few people about turn and stare after us. We pass a wretched slum of mud houses and tin shacks huddled alongside the road behind billboards advertising American cigarettes and Kuwait Airlines. The man sitting next to me mutters under his breath, "Look at the wretched poverty. It reminds me of the drive into Delhi."

But for all the obvious wretchedness I see, I can't help feeling good to be here at last, to sense life on the other side. I feel a little guilty, however, and say, "Wearing galabias doesn't necessarily mean they are wretched. We also have our poor."

"Not such poverty," he says. I can't argue that. We turn into a side street and follow it for about a mile. There is nothing but empty desert on both sides of the road; and at some distance, the long monotonous facade of a public housing development. We arrive at an iron gate guarded by armed police. As we enter, the landscape changes abruptly. We drive through a green tunnel of trees, past well-tended lawns and tennis courts, and bridle paths for horses. A blue swimming pool. Rose beds. A sprawling four-story C-shaped building, a white and gold facade in mock English Regency.

Wrought-iron tables, painted white, shaded by red-and-blue-striped parasols. And not a soul to be seen other than soldiers, hundreds of soldiers in steel helmets and heavy black winter uniforms, notwithstanding the great heat. All are carrying submachine guns mounted with bayonets. The blades flash in the sun. A banner is stretched across the road. It bids us "Welcome to Hotel al-Salaam, Cabaret, Sports Club." The hotel is the finest, newest in Cairo, we hear. It has only just opened, and in the nick of time to be named in such an appropriate manner. The doorman is the first civilian we have seen since we entered the gates, although he too is resplendent in a red uniform with gold epaulets. We enter a spacious lobby. The floor, smooth and shiny, is of Italian marble. We stop under a huge crystal chandelier.

"Welcome, welcome to Egypt, dear gentlemen," calls out Mr. Sherif Akhmad as he comes forward to greet us. This may not be his real, or his full, name; it later turns out that he is a colonel in the Egyptian State Security Service, *Mukhabarat*. He is a thickset man, broad-faced, in a double-breasted blue suit, all smiles and handshakes and warm solicitations and good wishes. He tells us we may under *no* circumstances go by ourselves into Cairo proper. Not without an armed escort, that is, which he will be ready to supply at all times. We are the only guests in the hotel, he says. All others were cleared out this morning in honor of our arrival and in order to provide us real comfort. Good grief, I think with a sinking heart. This is going to be one hell of a trip. 'How far away are we from the downtown area?"

"Ten miles or so."

"Oh."

There are brand-new automatic telephones everywhere—as well as color television sets—but the telephone lines to Cairo appear to be out at this moment. It seems impossible to call anybody in the city, or elsewhere in the world.

"What happened? For how long have the lines been out?"

"Oh, for some months."

The contingent of newspapermen is on the verge of hysteria. I go up to my room to unpack my things. From the window I am able to observe the double line of armed sentries that surrounds the hotel, apparently on all sides. The sentries, spaced a few yards from one another, are standing motionless in the heat. From the window they look like black candles. I see only their felted backs. All are facing away from the hotel toward the encircling barbed-wire fence. What terrible dangers loom out there in the bare stretch of sand toward Heliopolis, where the phoenix, I remember, is said to have come to die on a pyre of aromatic woods, only to be reborn? A certain feeling of claustrophobia is building up. We seem like prominent hostages, put up by a benevolent pharaoh in a luxury hotel.

The ominous presence of so many security forces was misleading, of course. A short while later I manage to sneak out of al-Salaam with little difficulty, although with some trepidation. I place myself in the hands of an old friend of mine who writes for the French newspaper *Le Matin*. He is a big, burly fellow who knows a trick or two, and he speaks Arabic fluently, with a distinct Egyptian accent. We simply walk up to the gate. He points at me and casually tells the sentry, "He's okay, too. Let him through." In retrospect, as I write, I am no longer sure we really tricked them. I rather think the sentry may have been too embarrassed to call our bluff and shame us by exposure.

But at the time, I remember, we marched quickly down the deserted road with a certain sense of achievement. A few hundred yards farther on we caught a bus to Cairo. The bus was nearly full. It rolled down the main artery toward the downtown area, leaving in its wake a long trail of diesel smoke. There were no free seats. We stood in the forward section.

"Where are you from?" the driver asked. "American? Ingliz?"

"Israel," we said in casual tones, and near-pandemonium erupted. The driver brought the bus to an abrupt stop.

"No!" he cried in Arabic. "You must be joking!"

We said we were not.

The driver turned around to the other passengers. "Did you hear that? They say they are from Israel!"

A few passengers pushed forward in the aisle, crying, "Welcome! Welcome!" The driver said, "Israel very good. Egypt very good. Peace very good."

Meanwhile a line of stalled cars had formed behind us, sounding their horns. The driver put his head out of the window. "There are people from Israel here! Real people!" The other drivers passed the message along, craning their necks to get a better view. I don't think I have ever felt so conspicuous. All around us in the bus people were saying, "*Mabrouk, mabrouk.* Peace very good."

An elderly gentleman in a panama hat shook my hand and said, "Do you know Mr. Levi from Alexandria? He went to Israel twenty years ago."

I was sorry, I didn't. The driver finally shifted gears and started up again. We were slowly heading toward the main city square, Midan al-Tahrir (Tahrir Square), on the banks of the Nile. At first there was not too much traffic. But as we moved toward the center, gradually we became aware of the enormous size of the city, then—more stunning—the sheer mass that populates it. At one stop a great crowd was waiting for the bus. When we finally moved on, a cluster of people hung on to the door outside. A few climbed up the ladder in the back to sit on the luggage racks atop.

The human mass: The population of Cairo has increased fourfold over the past thirty-five years. In the early evening hours the streets of this enormous city, which are always packed, fill even more. The congestion, always great, increases to a point where one wonders if it can ever straighten out again. One thinks of Ezekiel: "Son of man, wail for the *multitude* of Egypt." I have never in my life seen such crowds. Almost everywhere I go, I find myself in a thick swarm, moving slowly in concert along the narrow sidewalks. A dark sun hangs in a foggy sky of dust and soot. The air is heavy and humid.

In the hazy light the city looks even more dense and congested. In the 1940s 2.5 million people lived here. Today there are almost 10 million. The entire population of Israel could fit into a single district of Cairo.

But these are merely figures. Other cities have quadrupled their population during similar periods of time. What makes Cairo so overwhelming is the fact that the city's infrastructure has grown by only a fraction. The resulting chaos is evident everywhere: in the sad state of the public sewers, the overloaded telephone network, the water shortage, the periodic breakdowns in electricity, the public schools that operate on two, sometimes three, shifts a day. The high rate of illiteracy (70 percent) has remained virtually steady over the past thirty years despite an enormous growth in school facilities and in the number of trained teachers. Huge slum areas have crept into empty spaces, including cemeteries and mosques.

In 1948, before the outbreak of the first Arab-Israeli war, the average population density in Cairo was 11,704 people per square kilometer (about 27,000 per square mile). In 1966, just before the Six-Day War, that figure had risen to 20,549 (50,000 per square mile). The density today is said to be close to 40,000 per square kilometer (100,000 per square mile). In one particular slum area (Bab al-Sharia), the present population is 1.3 million—approximately 4 people on every 3 square yards—as high, I suspect, as anything in India.

Anis Mansour, the influential Egyptian editor said to be a close friend of President Sadat, wrote after the President's dramatic journey to Jerusalem: "Who is against the war? The soldiers themselves! The war has embittered everyone's life. The war has denied them home, street, and livelihood. Whoever reaches for the telephone and does not get a free line, or opens the faucet and the water does not run, or stands in the street for hours and waits for the bus which does not arrive, and when it does there is no space on it, not even on the steps; every young man who does not find work, and if he finds work finds no home, and if he finds a home cannot pay the rent, and so he cannot marry and contemplates emigration—all of these do not want war. None of them is in need of any philosophy to curse their fate. They curse those who took the riches of Egypt and all her resources and spent them on armaments and endless wars. They curse those [Arabs] for whom we fought and who are themselves getting richer and richer all the time. No, we must put a stop to the flow of gold and blood."

And yet I notice that the same Anis Mansour wrote in a recent issue of the mass-circulation magazine *October*, of which he is editor: "Give [the Jews] a chance and they will prove what beasts they can be. . . . What are they doing throughout the world? Smuggling drugs, running cabarets, and engaging in white slave traffic." I have been told that in the past Mansur frequently wrote in this vein. All the terrible deeds of the Jews, however, do not militate against peace. On the contrary, in this week's *October* Mansur vigorously supports the peace treaty. "Egypt is doing nothing radical," he writes; "it merely follows in the footsteps of the Prophet Muhammad, who also made peace with the enemies of Islam. Peace will bring affluence. The crusade for prosperity is on its way!"

Throughout the city, an overwhelming presence of police and militiamen. Not one policeman here and there, but groups of ten or twenty, heavily armed; and motorcycle patrols in fours and sixes. On Midan al-Tahrir, the great square built on the spot where the British army barracks once stood, some twenty or thirty thousand people are waiting for the suburban buses to take them home. Nearby, on the river esplanade, by the doors of the huge television building, a few soldiers are barricaded behind sandbags. The dense human stream flows around them as if they were stranded on an island: poor people in rags, peasants in wide robes, city people in fine double-breasted suits. I can imagine a similar congestion in Tokyo, or Bombay; many foreigners compare Cairo to Calcutta. But I wonder if one finds in any of these cities the same eerie quiet. Bismarck somewhere spoke of the "fanaticism of calm." My first reaction to it is a kind of fear. I know where that fear comes from. Then I tell myself that I must not succumb to generalizations. Westerners often see the East as either treacherously profound or touchingly simple.

There is a quality of grace and affability in daily life here that I have rarely seen elsewhere. Despite the terrible congestion, few seem to push, or kick, or raise their voice. The pace seems leisurely and slow. The encounter with the enormous human mass that surrounds me almost everywhere produces a first very powerful impression. It stuns me. And I cannot help remembering the scenes on television in 1967, of this very same crowd, running amok in these same streets on the eye of the Six Day War, screaming for blood.

I don't think I have ever experienced anything of the kind. It has partly to do, of course, with the thrill of being in a heretofore forbidden place. The origins of this thrill are obvious. They are partly sensuous. In the past thirty years none of us could come here, not for money or fine words, nor by the force of arms. And yet with not a single exception the Egyptians I meet are warm and hospitable and kind, and many of them say, "Welcome, welcome!" and "It's good that it is over." But unlike those Arabs in the occupied territories after the Six-Day War, they don't say "Welcome" to an Israeli because they are afraid and politic, but out of free will, or perhaps from fatigue.

Another thing strikes me, which I have never encountered before. I would call it the weight of time. It comes from the curious meeting here of the visible and the remembered. The past is more sensuous, more palpable in Cairo even than in Jerusalem, where I live. In Jerusalem the distant past also survives in stones, but they are mostly fragments and bits of pieces here and there of walls and foundations carefully dug up, cleaned, and marked to produce an illusion of the whole. I now realize that time is a less abstract notion than we think. In Israel we have the Book. It does not evoke a sense of time nearly so strikingly sensuous as does a perfectly preserved burial chamber five thousand years old with brilliantly colored frescoes on its walls.

The pyramids are more or less intact. Those of Giza are visible from the upper floors of many buildings in Cairo. The even more ancient step pyramid of Saqqara—one of the earliest known examples of human architecture—is less than half an hour away from the city's main square. It is not merely the constant talk one hears here of six or seven thousand years of uninterrupted history, but a syndrome produced by a combination of the tangible and the recollected. Unlike the stunning impact of the unending human mass, it comes upon one gradually, and then one is hopelessly caught up in it. I look over the rooftops at the pyramids, and down at the garbage on the street below. The dust rises in spirals. The sickle of a new moon hangs in the sky, still thin, and sharply pointed as a dagger. A great banner is spread across the wide avenue. It shows Sadat, dressed in the uniform of a field marshal, and with a golden scepter in his hand not unlike that of the boy-king in his sarcophagus in the Egyptian Museum of Antiquities. The inscription under Sadat's picture reads: "Why peace? Well, what did we get from war?" I am told that this is the refrain of a current popular song.

The singer is Mohammed Nuch, one of the best known in Egypt. He specializes in folk music. Nuch is a broad-shouldered, heavily built man in his early fifties. His grey hair is combed back over a large forehead. The eyes are a raven black. He wears a wide, tailor-made galabia with delicate embroidery. His records, he says, are sold in tens of thousands of copies. During the Yom Kippur War—here they call it the October War—he entertained the soldiers in the dugouts. His winning smile comes quickly and spreads across the wide, olive-skinned face. "No, no. I didn't sing war songs. I sang patriotic songs," he says. "Songs of love. Love for this poor land I sang to them."

Mr. Nuch is standing in the lobby of an old Cairo art theater, where his new musical is being rehearsed. The name of the play is *Love in a Box*. It is an attack, says Mr. Nuch, on Nasser's *Mukhabarat*, which used to kidnap Egyptian opposition figures from Europe—an Israeli agent was once kidnapped in the same way—and ship them back to Egypt drugged and packed in a box. Why *LOVE in a Box?* Very simple, explains Nuch in his ringing tenor voice. Love is freedom. We are trying to say that freedom cannot be drugged or packed away in boxes.

"We have been singing only PEACE songs since 1976," says Nuch. I am not sure how to take him. There is an Arab proverb: When the calf is thrown, the knives begin to fall. Everyone gets in on the killing. Is the opposite true as well? If the calf were resurrected, would all get in on the feeding? Mr. Nuch is altogether too trendy for my taste.

But then he tells me that he has lost three brothers in three wars: one in 1956, another in 1967, a third in the 1973 war. The fourth now works as his drummer. We sip black tea with mint from small elongated glasses. Then he plays me one of his records. His voice is soft and comes with a slight, low growl.

I taxi back to the hotel close to midnight, straining in the dim light to decipher the headlines in tomorrow's *Al Akhbar* and *Al Ahram*, wondering if ever two nations have made peace that knew so little of each other. The streets are bright with PEACE slogans and pictures of Sadat. They are still thronged with people. Words have formed the only bridge between us until now, a fragile, narrow bridge, which only the specialists bothered to traverse. I notice a back-page item in one of the newspapers, which reports that Professor Shimon Shamir's book *Egypt Under Sadat* has been translated into Arabic and will soon be published in Cairo by *Al Maaref.*

Shamir is a professor at the University of Tel-Aviv. His book—an analysis of the great changes in Egypt after Nasser—was published in Hebrew more than a year ago. Shamir is one of the few area specialists in Israel who has been correctly gauging the mood of Egypt over the past seven years, saying that Egypt under Sadat was striving for peace with Israel, at least as one possible option, unlike Nasser's Egypt, which had been almost totally committed to war. How many of us have read that book, I reflect as we drive through the night? I myself read it only a week ago, in a bit of a hurry.

And what can Egyptians read about us? Almost nothing, I understand, except what is available in propagandistic tracts. For years we have lived apart from one another, or yet locked in a deadly embrace like two ferocious snakes. The peculiar nature of the relationship made any contact between us mutually destructive. The popular images on both sides were distorted. Behind every Israeli soldier, Egyptians saw a French foreign legionnaire or an English colonialist. Behind every Egyptian soldier, Israelis saw an SS man bent on genocide. We have lived for years in a world of demons and devils. As Nasser called Ben-Gurion "the worst war criminal of the century," so many Israelis called Nasser, and after him Sadat, a "Hitler on the Nile." Nasser announced that Israel's very existence was an act of aggression. Ben-Gurion claimed he sought nothing but peace, but in 1956 joined the British and French military expedition against Egypt. The hostility of Egyptians toward Israelis was not solely political. As the years went by, it was elevated to the rank of ideology and faith. Israelis—and Jews—became symbols of an abomination that must be destroyed, if need be, in a Holy War, as the Crusaders' kingdom had been. A school of anti-Semitic hate literature developed in Egypt as the years went by. It assumed such proportions that when I last saw a representative selection of anti-Semitic books published in Egypt by state-owned publishing houses, they occupied a long shelf in the library of a friend of mine in Jerusalem, the orientalist Yehoshafat Harkabi. I had seen Professor Harkabi over the years grow grey, then white-haired, in the painful process of collecting, reading, and annotating that filth. Harkabi's collection includes several Egyptian reprints, in Arabic, of the *Protocols of the Elders of Zion*, described in one translation as a "secret speech by Herzl at the Zionist congress." Nasser, on one occasion, himself recommended the *Protocols* to an Indian visitor. "It is important that you read it," Nasser said. "I will give you a copy. It proves beyond all doubt that three hundred Zionists, each knowing the others, control the fate of the European continent and elect their successors from among themselves." The remark can be found in the official collection of *Nasser's Speeches and Press Interviews** issued by a Cairo state-owned publishing house, as were the *Protocols* (Cairo, 1958), p. 402.

Other examples in Harkabi's collection: "The Jewish God is not content with animal sacrifices. To placate him, human sacrifices are necessary.

Hence the Jewish custom of slaughtering infants and sucking their blood to mix it with unleavened bread at Passover."

"Jesus told us who they were. Muhammad warned us against them. God cursed them and destroyed their land."

The clear "aim" of the Zionists is to establish Jewish control over the entire world, "through the corruption of morals, financial speculation, the spreading of meanness everywhere, the destruction of religion, and finally through the use of murder as a means to achieve their goal." (Hassan Sabri al-Khuli, Nasser's "personal representative," in a lecture to the troops, published by Supreme Headquarters of the Egyptian Armed Force [Cairo, 1965].)

Where is this al-Khuli now, I wonder? I have asked Mussa Sabry, editor in chief of *Al Akhbar,* whom I visited earlier this evening in his office, if he knew. He said he did not know. Mr. Sabry is a witty, urbane, soft-spoken man, slightly bent over, with an easy and gracious manner. I liked him immediately. His office is lined with books in three languages. By his desk, on a side table, he keeps a pile of recent Jerusalem *Posts.* He reads the *Post* daily, he said, and with "considerable pleasure. I have for years." We must meet one another in a spirit of love and understanding, Mr. Sabry said. We had a very good talk. And yet I have been told by a man who visited Sabry here less than a year ago that on the walls of his office there still hung, in 1978, a few caricatures from Arab newspapers which, in style and in graphic detail, looked as though they had been inspired by the cartoons of Jews in Hitler's *Der Stürmer.*

As we sat chatting pleasantly in his office, I noticed that the cartoons were no longer there. Only pictures of Sadat, and one of Nasser in his familiar pose, the strong chin resolutely pushed out.

Yes, there was some anti-Semitic literature some years ago, said Mr. Sabry. He himself had never read any of those books. But yes, they existed. He urged me not to attach too great an importance to them, however. They had been the byproduct of war, not its cause, he said, a form of "war racism." I asked him what he meant by this.

"Oh, similar to the propaganda directed against the Japanese in America after the attack on Pearl Harbor." Anti-Semitism was not indigenous to Egypt, he thought. Both images and slogans were imported from Europe. It was a form of foreign aid, like—here Mr. Sabry smiled, a bit mischievously, I thought—like nationalism, which was also brought in from the outside.

An interesting thought, I said, hoping to sound a bit ironic. Unfortunately, the fine distinction between genuine racism and "war racism" does not cut much ice with the survivors of the Nazi Holocaust. Mr. Sabry readily granted this point. But anti-Semitic propaganda, he went on to say, never really made any headway here, not even in Nasser's day. And by now it was as good as forgotten.

Egypt and Israel will live in peace, Mr. Sabry said. He was sure of that. He spoke warmly about Israel, which he had visited together with Sadat in 1977. There would soon be cultural and economic exchanges between the two nations, as between Jews and Muslims in the Middle Ages. We could learn a great deal from each other. If both sides conducted themselves wisely, a new era would dawn, a golden age. He described it so ably, so convincingly, with such warmth, I simply could not bring myself to ask him what happened to the caricatures that had hung on his wall six months before.

But then I am here in Cairo—not in Tel-Aviv—tense and self-conscious, grateful for the hospitality I receive and engulfed in friendliness wherever I go, wanting desperately to believe that it really is all over; aware also of the stupidities and mistakes on the Israeli side over the years that helped whip up Egyptian hostility to a point where it began to feed on itself and become almost autistic. Is that self-perpetuating circle broken now? I have read somewhere that ultimate reality can be perceived only intuitively, by an act of the will and the affections. I am surrounded here in Cairo by a new reality, or so I hope. I sharpen my intuitions to it and pray that I am not misled. I sense that in Israel the intuition of most people is fed by different surroundings. Mussa Sabry said that in Egypt 99 percent of the population overwhelmingly supported the peace treaty: only some people in Sadat's government still wondered whether Egypt had made the right move. Within the government, Sabry said, there was still a strong suspicion of Israel's motives and a fear of being "betrayed" by Begin.

In Israel, when I left for Egypt, the opposite seemed true. The government appeared sure it had done the right thing at the right time. The public was still filled with suspicions that bordered on neurosis. This difference between Israel and Egypt is not difficult to understand. It comes from the contrast between a parliamentary democracy and an authoritarian state. Democracies do not easily go to war. When they do they tend to imbue the contest with a final, apocalyptic quality. When I left Israel there was little of the unrestrained enthusiasm for the peace treaty I notice almost everywhere since my arrival among the Egyptian masses. In Israel there was rather a strange, sour atmosphere of boundless suspicion and concern. When the moment finally arrived for which Israelis had been praying and waiting for decades—peace with the largest, most powerful Arab country— it came almost as an anticlimax. The peace negotiations had dragged on for too long, in the worst possible bazaar style, with frightful howls and gri-

maces all around and exquisite gestures of rejection and disdain. The negotiations had gone through too many downs, when everything had seemed
lost, and ups that nobody believed in any longer. Until the last moment we
were none of us certain whether we were about to cross the Rubicon, or
whether we had just been fishing in it. The bargain was finally sealed in the
ludicrous show-business atmosphere of a major Hollywood event.

What a strange sight it had been when Prime Minister Begin left Tel-
Aviv airport for the peace-signing ceremony in Washington! I remember
watching the scene on television. It was gloomy. Only Begin smiled
broadly, but with a bit of strain, I thought. The long line of well-wishers
gathered at the airport treated him with restraint and consideration—as
though they were sending him off to a funeral. "We build Jerusalem like
men mounting the gallows," the poet Sh. Shalom once wrote, summing up
in one memorable line the mixed moods of irony and enthusiasm that
marked many a generation of Zionist pioneers.

The Israeli newspapers that morning—Friday, March 23—had been
dark with misgivings. Aharon Megged, a fine novelist, wrote that his heart
trembled "with sorrow" at the thought of Israel's losing Mount Sinai, sorrow also at the abandonment of "the desert—to the wind, the sun and the
dead," an astonishing remark considering that Sinai is inhabited by some
fifty thousand Bedouin. The Egyptians had already announced plans to
resettle an additional two hundred thousand Egyptians on reclaimed areas
in the Sinai made fertile by piped-in Nile water.

"Where in the history of nations has such a thing been heard?" wrote
Megged. "After victories, not defeats?" He criticized Foreign Minister
Dayan for having declared the peace treaty "a very good thing." He,
Megged, saw very little good in it: nor did he understand how people could
toast the peace and say *"L'chayim."* "How can anyone be happy when the
heart trembles with sorrow?"

Haim Gouri, another well-known author, published a similar paeon to the
lost desert, which he addressed in the imperative, as though bidding good-
bye to a woman writhing at his feet, whom he caresses with tears in his eyes
for the last time in his life. "Farewell, Sinai. Farewell, great expanse of land
extending out to the horizon. Farewell, ancient memories." I wondered at
that remark. Did Gouri mean to lose his memories now? Apparently, yes.
"Farewell, ancient memories, memories of the Exodus from Egypt and
receiving of the Torah [on Mount Sinai]." I gathered from this that Gouri
had no further intention of celebrating Passover. "The Sinai wilderness," he
continued wistfully, had been dear to us "from the earliest dawn of this
nation." I am sure he checked that fact somewhere; I find no reference to it

anywhere. "Farewell, magic, silent coral coasts [of the Red Sea]. Farewell."
Gouri expressed a concern that the Egyptians would now think that won-
drous land "is really theirs, not ours."

I mention such articles here as examples not only of a strident, militant
nationalism—a minority mood—but of the general confusion and concern
and weariness generated by decades of uncertainty and war. Many people
simply could not bring themselves to believe that the kind of Egyptians
whom, as it says in Exodus 14:13, "ye have seen . . . ye shall see them again
no more for ever." Others were looking for bargains. "The Archie Bunkers
of Israel," the novelist Amos Oz said, "would like to have peace without
paying for it." The twelve years of occupation had accustomed people to its
material gains. They had forgotten how it had come about in the first place.

Few in Israel before 1967 had made any claims to sovereignty over the
Sinai Peninsula. When Israel conquered the desert on June 5, 1967, Moshe
Dayan announced that we had "no territorial aims." The territory was held
as a mortgage—to be released in exchange for peace. The appetite for it had
come later. Too many people had grown used, for too long, to the state of
permanent war. It was difficult to shake oneself loose.

An incident that took place in a Jerusalem high school, a few days before
I left for Cairo, struck me as characteristic. The peace treaty was due to be
signed in Washington on March 26, a Monday. The pupils of the two upper
grades of that school serve as junior air raid wardens. They were told, in all
seriousness, by the chief warden, that war was likely to break out on the
following day, Tuesday. They were given coded signals, which, in the case of
emergency, would be broadcast on the radio. When they heard these signals, they were told, they should rush to their posts and help people get to
the shelters.

On the day the treaty was signed, prices on the Tel-Aviv Stock Exchange
fell sharply, as though life were imitating Brechtian fiction. "The Messiah,"
according to an old Jewish saying, "comes in rags."

The newspapers reported that on that Monday an old man had come to
the Western Wall with a note to stick between the ancient stones. The note
was inscribed: "Please, dear G-d, let this last for longer than one night." It
reminded me of an exchange in Brecht's *Mother Courage:*

The Priest: "Now we are in God's hand."
Mother Courage: "I do hope that things aren't as far gone as that!"

They were not, but many had difficulty in sleeping well that night.

7

A Blood-Dimmed Tide

In a three-room apartment overlooking the hills on the western outskirts of Jerusalem, an old man sits alone in half-darkness behind closed shutters. He avidly reads the daily newspapers and listens to the radio news. He rarely speaks to anybody, other than on the telephone. He receives very few visitors. He is Menachem Begin, the former Prime Minister of Israel. He has hardly ever been seen on his large terrace—which, by a weird coincidence, overlooks the remains of the former Arab village of Deir Yassin. During the war of 1948, Deir Yassin was the site of an infamous massacre for which Begin, as leader of the Israeli terrorist group Irgun Zvai Leumi, has been held responsible—an accusation that his political enemies have never allowed him to forget.

Even before his abrupt midterm resignation, in September of 1983, Menachem Begin had disappeared from the public eye. For nearly two years now, he has lived in self-imposed house arrest—a hermit content with his cell, a political Marabout. He has been seen leaving his house only twice—to attend a memorial service for his late wife, and to undergo an operation on his prostate gland at a local hospital. He did not bother to vote in last year's general election, nor was he willing at that time to issue a public statement endorsing his own Likud Party. He has never given a reason for his resignation, except the very personal one, not very satisfying in a parliamentary democracy, of *"Ayni yachol,"* meaning "I cannot." He has never explained why.

The few recent photographs of Begin that have appeared in newspapers have shocked many of those who knew him in his prime, seven years ago, as one of the peacemakers at Camp David. The face seems sallow now, and haggard, the frame skeletal. The voice, once so firm and fierce, is now said to be thick, halting; the eyes glassy. Many Israelis see Menachem Begin's collapse as a Greek tragedy, and others see it as merely evocative of some tale of revolting putrescence by Gabriel Garcia Marquez. There is still much speculation on the "real" reasons behind it—speculation that ranges from the sentimental to the medical. Some of Mr. Begin's former associates refer to the death of his wife, Aliza, in November 1982, as the main cause of his emotional crisis. Others insist that he resigned in remorse over the disastrous war in Lebanon. Hell, it has been said, is truth seen too late.

According to this theory, he feels guilt for the more than 650 Israeli dead and 3,800 wounded so far in the Lebanese adventure—many of the latter invalids for life. Still others are convinced that Begin was felled not by history but by pathology. Although the doctors have pronounced him in reasonably good health, despite a stroke and two heart attacks, there had been a persistent rumor here for years that he was suffering from the effects of heavy medication and from frequent manic-depressive states, characterized by violent ups of excessive mental exaltation and downs of dejection, passivity, and lack of initiative. Sabbatai Zevi, the seventeenth-century "false messiah," according to his biographer, the late Professor Gershom Scholem, was also a manic depressive. Be this as it may, Begin's recent fate has been marked by a nightmarish quality of logic. Whatever the reasons for his breakdown, it was symptomatic of the moral agony, the political failure, the economic muddle, and the military crisis that terminated his six-year rule: a nation demoralized, divided against itself as never before in its history; a futile, costly, still unfinished war in Lebanon; a tottering peace with Egypt; and a worthless currency, three-digit inflation, and an economy that even his own Minister of Finance warned was on the verge of bankruptcy, what with zero growth, dangerously depleted reserves, and a foreign indebtedness of $21.5 billion—the highest, per capita, in the world, and more than double what it was when Begin assumed office.

❋

Shimon Peres, the Labor Party leader who stepped in last fall to pick up the
pieces, is a sixty-one-year-old technocrat and former Minister of Defense.
As a very young man, he had been the boy wonder of the Israeli bureaucracy, and, at the age of thirty, David Ben-Gurion's chief aide, the architect
of Israel's weapons industry, and the "father" of the atomic bomb that
Israel has at least the capability to produce. He became Prime Minister in
the sobering aftermath of the general election of July 1984. For most
Israelis, this was the most crucial and at the same time the most frustrating general election in the country's history. The results did not herald any
turning point but merely highlighted the inner disruption by producing
deadlock and stalemate between the two major political blocs—the nationalist Likud, under Begin's successor, Yitzhak Shamir, and what is known as
the Alignment, composed of centrist and left-of-center labor parties, under
Peres. The two blocs, so different in tone and political ideology, captured
between them the bulk of the Knesset's 120 seats, but each was weaker
than before. Neither had enough seats to form a government of its own.
Each maneuvered frantically, and in the end successfully, to block the possibility of the other's building a narrow majority by getting help from one
of the fragmented extremes of the political spectrum. A new election
would have very likely produced similar results. The solution found was a
Tweedledum-Tweedledee government of "national unity," with alternating Prime Ministers—first Peres for two years, then Shamir until the next
general election, in 1988. The idea of a national coalition was not new. It
had been proposed by Shamir before the election, and had been rejected by
Peres as a prescription for national paralysis. But afterward, in the prevailing hangover atmosphere, Peres began to view the proposition in a different light. Before the election, he had been much maligned by his opponents
as "unpatriotic." His main task, as he began to see it, was to "legitimize"
Labor once again in the eyes of an increasingly nationalistic, increasingly
right-wing electorate, and to restore himself personally as a leader by
national consensus. Public opinion, by and large, favored the grand coalition. It would have the support of at least three-quarters of the Knesset. It
might usher in electoral reform, which had not been possible under any
previous government. It could be the first in Israel's history not debilitat-
ingly dependent for its majority on minute ethnic or ultra-Orthodox reli-
gious-fundamentalist pressure groups. And, finally, a grand coalition was
seen as the only way to address the country's two most urgent tasks: to

shore up the faltering economy and to end the war in Lebanon. Labor, by restraining the unions it controls, would make possible the far-reaching economic reforms necessary to improve the balance of trade and reduce three-digit inflation. In return, Likud, which was politically identified with, if not held responsible for, the war in Lebanon, would agree to a quick withdrawal of Israeli troops there.

But things have turned out differently. No sooner was Peres's twin government formed than the two parties began to prepare, politically, for its dissolution by once more courting the potential good will of the splinter parties. There was no more talk of electoral reform and much speculation about holding an early election before the end of Peres's two-year term. The new government remained bitterly divided on the issue of Lebanon. Nor has Peres been able to restrain the unions as he had hoped. At first, he seemed to have succeeded in scoring a temporary, partial victory against inflation. In December, prices rose by only 3.7 percent. (Previous monthly rises had been as high as 24 percent.) After that, however, prices once more began to rise sharply (by an annual rate of 299 percent in the first six months of this year), because an artificial price freeze that had been imposed in December was not accompanied by large enough budget cuts and because the government continued to print billions of shekels and pour them into the economy to prevent large-scale unemployment.

Throughout these months, Mr. Peres has held on to his office with a kind of grim, grinding resolution. Some still wonder why he had been so anxious to assume the responsibilities of government at this difficult juncture. Most economists insisted that there was little chance of curing the economy without taking some very unpopular measures, which would most probably bring on huge unemployment. The withdrawal from Lebanon, planned to be completed by this summer, almost inevitably raised the risk that Shiite and Palestinian terrorists, who have bedevilled the Israeli army of occupation, would follow it across the frontier into Israel proper. Once again, northern Israel would be exposed to artillery bombardment and terrorist incursion from Lebanon. Which party would be held responsible, politically, for this? Likud, which had started the war in the first place, or Labor, which, in trying to trim the losses, was bringing the troops back across the border? I heard a man tell Shimon Peres the other day that it might have been politically more opportune for Labor to let Likud preside over the unpopular remedial measures. Peres responded, "Yes, probably, but it would not have been very patriotic."

Peres is not what is commonly called a charismatic leader. His appearances on television have always been somewhat awkward. He has on occasion described himself as an "unreasonably optimistic" man. "I am built like that. I am capable of becoming almost intoxicated by the potential of things," he has said. On matters of defense he was known in the past as a hawk. He moved leftward during the years in opposition to Begin's government. In the Prime Minister's office, he has surrounded himself with young aides in their early thirties, most of them sympathizers of the dovish Peace Now movement. They have helped to give him the sober, statesman-like image of one who has taken upon himself an almost impossibly difficult task while remaining a man of compromise and moderation. But in a country mired in recent years of disappointment, so bitterly divided, so emotionally charged by high-pitched discourse, the Prime Minister's consistent pursuit of consensus has inevitably exposed him to charges of indecisiveness and lack of clear leadership. The economy, which in the year since Peres came into office has gone from bad to worse, is a main case in point; there have been others. The most recent was the affair of the hijacking to Beirut of a TWA plane, on a scheduled flight from Athens to Rome, by Shiite fanatics who demanded the release of some seven hundred Lebanese, mostly Shiites, still held without charges in an Israeli prison. There was no reason to delay the prisoners' release for so long and thus sour relations with the United States, especially since they were supposed to be set free anyway, as Yoel Marcus, a leading columnist, wrote in the independent daily *Ha'aretz* (331 have since been released).

Since his first day in office, Peres has been looking for his main chance—for the great message, the event, the breakthrough that will lend momentum to his leadership, much as Anwar Sadat's visit to Jerusalem did to Begin's during his first year in office. He has not yet found it. In January, under the harrowing impact of more and more casualties among the young conscripts patrolling Lebanese towns and highways on search-and-destroy missions, he persuaded his Cabinet to begin the withdrawal from Lebanon despite the great risk. Most Likud ministers, including alternate Prime Minister Yitzhak Shamir, were against withdrawal, but two of them crossed party lines to give Peres the majority he needed. In February, he welcomed a proposal from Egypt's President Hosni Mubarak for direct peace talks between Israel, Jordan, and the Palestinians. But whether this was the great breakthrough he had been seeking, and probably secretly working for, remained to be seen. The way in which he welcomed the proposal as "constructive," despite fears that it might bring the PLO in through the back door or break his coalition, or both, was characteristic. He once told an interviewer that for him "style" was not just a matter of technique but a quality of "vision." He has been very attentive to style and tone. He told another interviewer that he would very much like to fulfill a request made to him by Sadat at one of their meetings. "Please," Sadat had said, according to Peres, "above all, be generous in your public expressions." Since his rise to power, the general tone here toward the world at large, and especially toward the Arab countries—so strident before—has become more amiable. But so far Peres has not been successful in his efforts to improve relations with Egypt, which have been poisoned by Israel's invasion of Lebanon, by Egypt's desire to reingratiate itself with the Arab world, and by a bizarre controversy over a hotel and beach club on a few acres of sand at Taba, near Eilat, at the head of the Gulf of Aqaba.

By mutual agreement, the disposition of Taba was left open after the 1979 peace treaty. Some of the Prime Minister's advisers have been telling him in recent months that Israel's case in the Taba dispute, from the point of view of international law, is not very sound, and he has leaned toward submitting the problem to international arbitration if mediation should prove unsuccessful, as the two governments had previously agreed to do. But this proposal has been vetoed as "defeatist" by Shamir. Peres is reported to have told Shamir, "We are not gangsters. We shall not steal Taba in the dark of night. Taba is not that important, and it is not Jerusalem the Golden." But Shamir has continued to be obdurate on this issue. Perhaps he feels the Likud's diehards, led by Ariel Sharon, breathing down his neck. More likely, as a recent editorial in the Jerusalem *Post* suggested, Shamir became persuaded, after due consideration, "that any binding settlement of the Taba dispute must be resisted for precisely the reason it is favored by Mr. Peres: Because it could spell progress not only on normalization but, through it, on the entire Arab-Israeli peace front." Peres's first year in office has led some people to wonder whether he had not been right, after all, when, in the summer of 1984, he rejected Shamir's offer of a grand coalition as a prescription for national paralysis.

Shamir has similarly vetoed Peres's long-standing plan to approach King Hussein of Jordan with a generous offer of territorial compromise or of a sharing of power on the occupied West Bank. Before the election, Peres was heard to say privately that he was prepared to return "the bulk of the West Bank" to Jordan. When he was asked about the Israelis in the settlements planted in those areas by previous governments, he said, on one occasion, that they would simply have to be content to live under Jordanian rule. Under the circumstances, this was tantamount to saying that the settlements would be dismantled. In 1982, he publicly welcomed President Reagan's peace initiative (self-government for the Palestinians in association with Jordan), which the Begin government had dismissed outright as totally unacceptable. Peres has not repeated such statements, for fear of breaking up his coalition. Some of his aides, however, have been saying that if only King Hussein and the more moderate Palestinians would come forward for peace talks with Israel, as Anwar Sadat did in 1977 and as Hosni Mubarak was now proposing that they do, the entire political situation here could change. Some Likud deputies would bolt the government, with cries of "treason." Others might support it. Talks with Jordan could begin. New elections might be called. Peres could win on a "Let's talk peace" platform.

"I am not worried," Moshe Katzav, the Minister of Labor and Social Welfare and a leading Likud hawk, was quoted in February as saying—a little too glibly, perhaps. "I fully rely on the little king. He is not ready for peace. He will enable us to maintain [the coalition] at least until it is Shamir's turn to become Prime Minister."

❀

Peres has recently been speaking of a new era in Israeli politics, but many still live in the old one. A lot of people here—perhaps excluding the zealots of the far right—seem to be tired. The tiredness may be the result of their having lived for so long—for some, an entire lifetime—in what seems an interminable emergency. Or it may be a result of this country's being so overextended, both emotionally and physically. There was a time when it was said that Israel had too much history and too little territory. Since 1967, the opposite has been true. The strains are showing. Perhaps the weariness comes also from exaggerated dreams and expectations. Classical Zionism pursued a utopian dream of redemption. Like every ism, it produced wild hopes, which were followed by a reaction of cynicism and despair. The early Zionists were not content to found a nation-state like all others. They looked forward to a safe haven for Jews and a new paradise as well: a kingdom of saints; a new world, purged of suffering and sin. Only much later did they remember that in the Jewish tradition even Eden was never a peaceful place but, rather, a celestial cage soon rent with fear, conflict, arrogance, and lies. Perhaps it is only now that Israelis are beginning to awaken from what was so long and so lovingly called the Zionist Dream. When the early Zionists made the decision to "go political," they did not consider the possibility that to the age-old difficulty of being a Jew would be added the perhaps greater difficulty of surviving as a ministate in a very disturbed part of the world.

In consequence, one senses a kind of metal fatigue now attacking the body politic. It invites both rational and irrational treatment. General

Ariel Sharon's continuing—some say growing—mass following is contributing to the latter. So are the emergence of a Jewish terrorist underground and the rise of two new ultra-right-wing parties—General Rafael Eitan's Tehiya (Awakening) and Meir Kahane's Kach. The two have so preyed upon current fears and hatreds and prejudices that unless the wolves in the Middle East suddenly dwell with the lambs, and the lions eat straw like the oxen, it will be very difficult in the future to contain those parties. Tehiya, which won five seats in the election, nearly doubled its representation in the new Knesset, and became the third-largest party. The ultra-right wing has gained the support, partly tacit, partly open and vocal, of an important segment within the Orthodox rabbinical establishment. In the trial of a group of confessed Jewish terrorists in Jerusalem District Court, the distinguished heads of two state-supported Orthodox *yeshivot* as well as one former Chief Rabbi of Israel have been cited as having secretly given the terrorists moral encouragement to commit mass murders. One was said to have hailed the terrorists who planned to blow up the Dome of the Rock, the Muslim shrine on the Temple Mount, in Jerusalem, as saints doing the work of God. Another was said to have been eager to participate in a terrorist attack upon innocent Arab bus passengers. More seriously, the alternate Prime Minister, Mr. Shamir, has been in the forefront of prominent Likud and religious politicians calling upon the President of the Republic to pardon the terrorists because their crimes (which included booby-trapping the motorcars of three West Bank Arab mayors—one lost his legs, another had a foot amputated as a result) were motivated, in his words, by patriotism and love of the Land of Israel. Meir Kahane has openly called upon the country to recognize the terrorists as national heroes.

It may be, as some argue, that Meir Kahane's mind is one of the more underdeveloped parts of the Middle East, as it previously was of Brooklyn, but he, too, has considerably improved his standing in the polls since his surprise capture of a seat in the current Knesset. If an election were held today, the American-born rabbi and founder of the Brooklyn-based Jewish Defense League would win twice as many votes as he did last July. His platform is openly racist. (The Arabs, he says, multiply "like so many dogs;" they must be expelled before they "poison" Israel's Jewish character. Arab men caught sleeping with Jewish women should be "castrated." The Muslim mosques in Jerusalem should be dismantled, because, after all, "there is no synagogue in Mecca.") He used the media to build his movement in New York in the 1960s, and his skill at exploiting the Israeli press has been matched only by his contempt for it, as quotations from him testify: "I'll take care, when I come to power, of Arab dogs and Jewish traitors in the newspapers." "I am not a democrat; I am a Jew." "I'm going to drive this country crazy, and the press will cover every step." When a Jewish terrorist shot a missile at a crowded Arab bus in the heart of Jerusalem, the terrorist (soon apprehended by the police) was praised by Kahane with the words "Blessed be the hands that performed this act."

Still more serious is the continuing shift of young voters toward the extreme right. Had the country as a whole voted as the soldiers did in the last election, Likud, with the small Tehiya Party and its allies among the ultra-Orthodox fundamentalists, might have won a comfortable margin in the Knesset. According to a poll commissioned by the Van Leer Jerusalem Foundation (a privately financed research institute), as many as 40 percent of secondary-school pupils claim that they support the views of Rabbi Kahane's party (the percentage in the religiously Orthodox schools was said to be higher). Another poll by the same foundation showed that only a third of the fifteen-to-eighteen-year-old youngsters interviewed displayed "consistent democratic tendencies" (i.e., endorsed the existing governmental system). The remainder were more or less totalitarian in their attitudes, especially toward their Arab fellow-citizens. Some 44 percent favored legislation to prohibit criticism of the government's foreign and defense policies; 42 percent favored curtailing the civil rights of non-Jewish citizens; 37 percent favored curtailing the rights of Christians; 47 percent felt that Muslims should not attain senior positions in government service; 60 percent said that Arabs should not be entitled to full civil rights. Not only did 38 percent say they supported Jewish terrorist underground organizations but 9 percent said they were, as individuals, ready to join such an organization.

The report created a stir. The Ministry of Education decreed special classes in all schools to "deepen democratic consciousness" among schoolchildren. Shlomo Hillel, the Speaker of the Knesset, invited some thirty university professors, teachers, and writers to form a new Public Council for Democracy. At the council's first—and, so far, only—session, Professor Yonatan Shapiro, a sociologist at Tel-Aviv University, argued that the problem might not be one of age, as most people suppose, but of structure. There was a clear correlation, he said, between nondemocratic attitudes in Israel proper and attitudes toward the occupied territories and their inhabitants, and between such attitudes and Orthodoxy in religion: the incidence of nondemocratic attitudes is said to be invariably greater among the religionists pressing for a theocratic state or among those in favor of annexing the occupied territories.

❋

The late Moshe Dayan, on the strength of a visit to Vietnam in 1966, used to warn Israeli generals against wars that could not be ended. "They are the worst," he said. "Worse than those you lose." Today, many are wiser after the event, and place the blame for Israel's unfinished Lebanese campaign on Begin's alleged naïveté and on the brutality and bellicose lack of realism of Ariel Sharon. But the fact is that in the beginning the war had been a bipartisan cause. The Labor Party, too, with few exceptions, was in favor of the invasion. A handful of Labor deputies abstained from the vote in the Knesset, and only one, Yossi Sarid, spoke out openly against the war; he and the others were sharply criticized by their own party as lacking the minimal amount of patriotic solidarity. One Labor deputy, a veteran of twenty-five years in politics, now says bitterly that the most important lesson he has learned is that when the entire establishment is united on a move—as was the case here—it is almost inevitably wrong. Major General Moshe Levy, the present chief of staff of the Israeli Army, gloomily announced on television that he now knows "*much more* about Lebanon than three years ago"—a courageous but deeply disconcerting admission, as Hedda Boshes, a critic for *Ha'aretz*, wrote the next morning. General Levy, after all, had been deputy chief of staff when the war began.

Wars, of course, always begin in confusion, as in a thick fog or in a cheap waterfront bar. What hurts so much now is the more general realization that in Lebanon Israeli power has for the first time lost its credibility. Israelis love to philosophize about "power." To a certain extent this was always part and parcel of the Zionist ethos. Zionism proposed to give defenseless ghetto Jews, previously dependent upon shifting moods of tolerance among non-Jewish rulers, a measure of power to determine their own fate. And now has come the great power paradox of the Lebanese war. As Abba Eban said recently, "Military power is a very odd thing. When it sheds its defensive role [in a country like Israel], it displays a curious impotence."

It is generally agreed that the war aims of Sharon, if not necessarily of Begin, had been twofold: first, to drive Yasir Arafat and the PLO out of Lebanon, in order to free Galilee from terrorist incursion and weaken the Palestinians enough politically to give Israel a free hand on the West Bank and in the Gaza Strip; and, second, to drive the Syrians out of southern Lebanon and Beirut and help set up a new, Christian-dominated government there, under the Gemayel clan and the Phalange, which had been armed and trained by Israel. In June of 1982, Begin, overjoyed at the rapid advance on Beirut and the smooth dismantling of the PLO infrastructure in the south, spoke of an imminent peace treaty with Lebanon and ecstatically echoed the Book of Judges: "The land will have rest for forty years."

And yet almost from the beginning almost everything went wrong. Power did not grow out of the barrels of Sharon's guns. His main political aims were not achieved. The Lebanese Christians ended up weaker politically than they had been before the war. Bashir Gemayel, and, after his assassination, his brother Amin Gemayel became President, but both refused to make peace with Israel. The Syrian Air Force was crushed, but Syria's President Hafez Assad emerged as the real master of Lebanon. The PLO was driven out, but in its place on Israel's northern border emerged a fundamentalist Shiite Muslim enemy, more lethal than the PLO had ever been. The sudden rise of Shiite power in Lebanon now breeds fears in Israel that all of southern Lebanon, as far north as Beirut, may soon emerge as a bastion of Muslim fanatics controlled by ferocious Iranian ayatollahs, with consequences for Israeli security in the Galilee too awful even to contemplate at this stage. But such may well be one of the unforeseen consequences of Begin's war in Lebanon, which catapulted the Shiites of that country to the political forefront. Moreover, the experience of Lebanon, where Shiite guerrillas made life unbearably difficult for the Israeli Army, was bound to have an impact on the Palestinians, too, particularly on the West Bank. In southern Lebanon, the Shiites have shown that it is indeed possible to *compel* Israeli troops to withdraw from occupied territories if only you kill a sufficiently large number of them. If the Shiites had not thrown hand grenades at Israeli soldiers, the soldiers would undoubtedly not have withdrawn. In the post-Holocaust generation, Israeli attitudes toward power have consistently been complex, and sometimes neurotic. But in Lebanon, it appears, Israelis had failed, at least at first, to make the needed distinction between power and violence. One Israeli writer compared Israel's war in Lebanon to a game of chess in which all the pieces had reached the edge of the board and fallen off.

In June, the evacuation of Israeli forces from Lebanon was officially declared "completed." Unofficially, it continued in a 5-to-15-kilometer-wide security zone from Mt. Hermon to the Mediterranean Sea northeast and west of Metulla, the northernmost town in Israel. Metulla sits astride the Lebanese border. Its streets are lined with old eucalyptus trees. A tourist shop that only a year ago was doing a brisk business in T-shirts inscribed with entwined flags of Israel and Lebanon and the usual crosses and Stars of David carved of olivewood with little thermometers attached is now boarded up. The border station has recently been widened. A big sign facing the Lebanese side says, "Soldier! You Are Entering Israel Territory. Unload Your Gun."

The station has been freshly painted white and looks neat. When a truckload of soldiers comes along amid the flat calm and crosses back into Israel, a sudden, quite deafening noise breaks the quiet. The soldiers shout in chorus, stamp their feet, and beat the seats with their mess tins, and the driver bleats his horn. The military policemen on duty at the crossing point wave them on. They are said to be used to such scenes. As I observed on a recent visit before the completion of the last stage of withdrawal, the latent hysteria suggests something like a psychodrama. The soldiers were behaving as though they had just escaped a natural disaster. There were cries of "We're through!" and "I'll never go back!" A high-ranking officer stood nearby. He commented that nothing like it had ever been seen in the Israeli Army, so well known for and so proud of its high morale. This is the first war that so many men in the Army, including those in its top echelons, have considered futile or wrong. Nor was the human toll limited to those who fell under enemy fire. Twenty-one servicemen committed suicide while on active duty in Lebanon, ten during the past year alone, as Defense Minister Yitzhak Rabin told the Knesset recently. In the past two years, 143 regular servicemen and reservists have been sent to jail for refusing to serve in Lebanon. Dr. Ruth Linn, a social researcher at Haifa University, notes in a soon-to-be published study that most of the refusers belong to combat units and are college graduates; their average age is thirty-one. According to Dr. Linn, the real number of refusers is "very much higher" than 143, for many were quietly released or posted elsewhere—not to Lebanon—by sympathetic company commanders. A fifth of those who refused are said to be officers.

The way soldiers here speak these days is new as well. "This cynicism, this bitter sense of futility over the sheer waste of human lives—was this the way U.S. soldiers spoke in Vietnam?" a writer in *Ha'aretz* asked recently. A well-known poet, Yitzhak Laor, author of "Ballad of the Stupid Soldier," itself a landmark unprecedented in Hebrew poetry, is one of the contributors to a recent book called *Fighting and Killing Without End*. Nearly every leading Israeli poet is represented in the volume, which was issued in 1983 by the distinguished Ha'Kibbutz Ha'Meuchad publishing house. Laor spoke for a small but not insignificant minority when he wrote in one poem that at this time "the real courage is to look at war from afar, perhaps on television."

❀

Across the Lebanese border, the main road from Israel twists along for several kilometers before it forks, leading into the Christian towns of Kelia and

Marj Uyun, on the right, now held by the Israeli-controlled Christian militia of General Antoine Lahad (the so-called SLA, or South Lebanese Army),
and, on the left, to large Shiite villages on both sides of the Litani River. In
1982, Israeli troops were welcomed there by the Shiites as liberators from
the PLO, and were showered with rice and flowers. But as the Israeli occupation continued into 1983 and 1984, cutting the Shiites off from their markets and from their political and religious leaders in Beirut, relations
between Israelis and Shiites deteriorated. By the summer of 1984, Amal, the
main Shiite militia, led by the ostensibly moderate Nabih Berri, was waging open war against Israeli troops wherever and whenever it could. Hardly
a day passed without Army contingents being fired upon from behind roadside bushes, or hitting a land mine, or being the target of a hand grenade
hurled from a balcony.

When I drove with an Israeli Army escort through parts of southern
Lebanon recently, it was raining, but the sun dipped through the clouds and
sparkled in the bushes. Israelis are allowed to travel these roads only in
armed convoys. Everyone is required to wear a bulletproof vest. Two loaded
guns must always point outward from open windows of each car. The wind
slashed cold rain against the faces of the soldiers. Here every turn in the
road could open you to a barrage of automatic fire, every pickup truck might
be that of a Shiite suicide driver, every passing Mercedes sedan might shoot
a missile at you. Religion is the abiding, murderous factor in this particular
heart of darkness. Shiite and Sunni Muslims, Druze, Maronites, and Greek
Catholics have been at one another's throats since the beginning of the
Lebanese civil war. With so many armed sects and clans, and so much fighting among them, it has been difficult in recent years to speak of politics
here, or of issues. There have been only fears and hatreds, and many of the
latter now focus on the Israeli occupiers. Even the Christians have become
eager to disengage; their involvement with Israel has left them weakened in
the Lebanese power game. "You have not brought us luck," a Christian
militia commander from Sidon told me. Only some of the more militant
Maronites still favor a continued Israeli presence in Lebanon. Outside an
ancient church in Kelia, a Maronite priest took my arm firmly and cried,
"We Maronites have been waiting since the twelfth century!" Upon closer
questioning, it transpired that he meant since the Battle of Hattin, which
marked the beginning of the fall of the Crusader kingdom of Jerusalem.
"Israel will help us. Israel must help us to help itself," he said. "Jerusalem
will be theirs, Lebanon ours. *Beau Liban, pauvre Liban!* It must be ours
once more."

"All of Lebanon?" I asked.

"Of course! Forty years ago, the Jews were a minority, too, in Palestine. *Mais ils étaient courageux.* Now they control it all. If the Jews withdraw, the Muslims will slaughter us first and then they will cross the border to slaughter the Jews."

In the next village, a Shiite businessman, seated in a vast formal room with two dozen gilded, embroidered armchairs lining its four walls, had coffee poured for us from silver pots into cups of the thinnest porcelain as we chatted. He complained that the Israeli occupation had lasted far too long. The Israelis had turned their former friends into enemies, he said. Businesses had been ruined. Innocent citizens were paying for acts perpetrated by a few outsiders. The Israelis were foolish to rely on their Maronite mercenaries. The minute the Israelis left, the Maronites would betray them. "I say to them, 'Take care, *Messieurs les Israéliens.* Why, even Danny Chamoun' [the head of one of the Maronite militias] sold the PLO the arms given to him by the Israelis.' "

A high-ranking Israeli Army officer whom I met in his Lebanese headquarters said that the longer Israeli troops remained in Lebanon, even as mere advisers to the SLA within the so-called security zone, the more radicalized the Shiites would become and the greater the chances would grow that Shiite and Palestinian terror squads would penetrate south into Israel after the withdrawal. "But the politicians don't want to listen," he went on. "They have to justify the original mistake that got us into this mess in the first place."

One opinion and the next one contradicting it, but before one hears any of them one drives through the strange ghost city that has sprung up north of Metulla since 1982, on the Lebanese side of the Israel security fence—a conglomeration of residential and commercial buildings that were abandoned even before they were finished, shops that were never opened, gas stations for cars that have never arrived, and the reinforced-concrete skeleton of a five-story hotel and another of a gambling casino. The casino was meant, said the contractor who was building it until about a year ago, to bring together gamblers from Saudi Arabia and from Israel. Yes, he had thought there would be peace and an open border, like that between Switzerland and France. No, he was not yet completely discouraged. To walk through the gaping holes in the casino's walls or over the shaky scaffolding of the half-finished and already crumbling building, crows circling overhead, is to arrive at a situation that is very Lebanese—a situation where the ground under your feet is never solid, and no judgment is firm enough so that it cannot collapse overnight into its opposite. The contractor was an amiable middle-aged man, slim, nervous, all bones and muscles and smiles and gladsome energy. His automobile, a black Mercedes with Swiss license plates, was parked outside the casino. He said he had invested a few hundred thousand dollars in the enterprise. "*C'est fini?*" he asked us, snapping his brown-stained fingers. He lit a new cigarette from the burning stub of the last. As a Lebanese, he explained, he had little chance of dying of lung cancer. He said he was sorry he had never found an Israeli partner for his casino. He had been looking hard for one. Many Lebanese would have come to play.

We asked him if he could be sure of that.

"Absolutely, yes!" he cried. "In Lebanon, everybody is a gambler. It's in our nature. I, too, am a gambler." Then he cited a Lebanese proverb: "God gave the Garden of Eden to those who are mad."

❈

Galloping inflation has recently made the Israeli economy look precariously like that of certain Latin-American countries. Three-digit inflation turns businessmen into gamblers, and consumers into Don Quixotes fighting—mostly in vain—the windmills of daily price rises. The consumer almost always suffers. He pays tomorrow's prices with today's income. Salaried employees invest most of their paychecks in black-market dollars, or buy in sprees during the first week of the month in order to protect themselves against the inevitable price rises of the second week. Bank computers arrive at the limits of their technical capacities because they cannot handle figures of more than fifteen digits. Four percent of the GNP is said to be spent to protect the remaining 96 percent from being undermined by inflation. These are only some of the external aspects of a malaise that affects much more than monetary values. It touches most citizens here more directly than the Arab-Israeli conflict does.

The war in Lebanon is said to have cost Israel three and a half billion dollars so far, and to be still costing a considerable sum each day for the maintenance of the Christian SLA and its Israeli "advisers." But defense expenditure is by no means the sole reason for the hyperinflation. The others are growing foreign indebtedness; the printing of money on a vast scale to compensate for insufficient or diminishing returns from taxes; the spiralling effect of automatic indexation that links wages to whatever average increase in prices is announced each month by the Central Bureau of Statistics; the constant rise until 1984, under an essentially populist government, of real income, despite zero growth; and the relatively high cost of services and of production, caused by overemployment and inefficiency.

Still, the main cause, almost everyone here agrees, has been the enormous expenditure on defense. It amounted to some $6.5 billion dollars in 1984, or roughly a quarter of the GNP (compared with 7 percent in the United States, 4 percent in most European NATO countries, and 1 percent in Japan). A good way to visualize this burden in rough financial and human terms is to imagine maintaining a military power the size of that in France on the resources of Luxembourg. Professor Haim Barkai of the Hebrew University in Jerusalem, recently argued that "if West Germany had the same percentage of men under arms as Israel, its standing army would total four million"—instead of 450,000, which is the largest European force in NATO. He went on to say, "The United States would have 14 million men under arms, more than it did in the Second World War. In effect, for at least ten years we have maintained an armed force of a size that is characteristic of a full war." Even following the peace treaty with Egypt, in 1979, the defense budget continued to grow, although at a slower rate. While some Israeli governments have tried, none has ever managed to cut the defense budget, except the government of Ben-Gurion, who in 1952 ignored a threat of resignation by his Army chief of staff and sliced 18 percent from a budget of $32 million. Ben-Gurion's successors have lived under the trauma of too many wars. And they have not had the self-assurance to tell generals, as Ben-Gurion did, that a stable economy is as important to national security as arms and manpower are.

"I don't want another Yom Kippur War," Peres was reported to have told Treasury advisers in January, when they urged serious cuts in the defense expenditure. Peres has instead applied himself to reducing civilian expenditures by $2 billion, a difficult—or, according to some observers, impossible—task, since more than half of the national budget of $24 billion is untouchable. (Some $13.5 billion goes either to defense or to the servicing of loans.) Food subsidies, public works, old-age pensions, and health and education services have already been slashed. Heavy new taxes have been imposed on already highly taxed imports and foreign travel. A small European car—a Fiat 127—now costs more than $11,000, of which more than $7,000 is taxes. Each time they go abroad, Israelis now pay a flat departure tax of $300, a 20-percent tax on the price of the airplane ticket, and a charge of 15 percent on a travel allowance of $800. Nevertheless, foreign-currency reserves have steadily declined by some $140 million each month since October. This June, reserves dropped to the $2 billion mark, considered the absolute minimum. Were it not for the probable approval by the United States of more than a billion dollars in special aid (over and above close to $3 billion already approved), the country's international credit standing might be seriously harmed. Bankers and economists have been wondering whether it is possible to achieve real progress by administrative means only, without structural changes, defense-budget cuts, and drastic devaluation—all of which would, of course, mean large-scale unemployment.

Peres has so far rejected all such bold measures. Increased unemployment is another taboo that no government has dared to risk violating since 1965, and the jobless rate is currently being maintained at a relatively low 4 to 6 percent. Peres has been strongly warning against both devaluation and unemployment, and has been saying that it is naïve and childish to think that inflation can be ended with a stroke. Difficult decisions are necessary, he has admitted, but can be made only "by joint agreement between management and labor." He has expressed hope for increased United States aid. Gad Ya'acobi, his Minister of Economic Coordination and one of his oldest, most loyal political lieutenants, has warned him not to take this for granted, and Ya'acobi has somberly suggested that few societies have thus far survived an inflation such as Israel's without succumbing to one form or another of totalitarianism.

✺

During this time of almost invariably bad news, the sudden influx of Ethiopian Jews has come as a welcome morale booster—as a reminder that in some areas this country is not yet like all others. Few others would have gone to such trouble at home and abroad to import 14,000 destitute Africans, many of them illiterate, at a time of economic crisis. The announcement that thousands of Jews were being rescued by secret airlift from the horrors of famine in Ethiopia and the hardships of the Marxist Mengistu regime was met with a satisfaction rare in its near-unanimity. The rescue mission—quickly nicknamed Operation Moses—gave Israel its first good press notices abroad in the past few years. For many Israelis, Operation Moses brought back for a moment the heady atmosphere of Entebbe. For some, it must have brought back as well something of the lost innocence and romance of the early years of Zionism. Israel, after all, was intended by its founders to be a haven for persecuted Jews, not the policeman of Lebanon, fighting Muslim fundamentalists, or of Nablus, quelling riots by Palestinian students.

The simple faith of the Ethiopians touched many a heart. "It is impossible not to love them," a doctor at one of the hospitals was reported as saying. He may have meant that they were not like most other Israelis today.

Stepping off the airplane, still dressed in the burlap rags in which they had walked hundreds of kilometers from Gonder, in northern Ethiopia, to Gedaref, in the Sudan, and looking skeletal, even famished, some of the new arrivals resembled the survivors of Nazi concentration camps after the Second World War.

Although there are bigots in Israel, as there are in other countries, the black Jews from Ethiopia have been received with unusual warmth. They were welcomed as members of the Jewish *people* rather than of the Jewish *faith*. The only serious objection to their immigration has come from Orthodox rabbis who insist that their Judaism is "incomplete," since it is based on Old Testament teachings alone, and not on latter-day Talmudic law. The newcomers from Ethiopia have so far rejected, as "unjust and degrading," demands by the Chief Rabbinate that they submit to conversion rites that include symbolic circumcisions, carried out by drawing a drop of blood from the tip of each man's penis. By and large, popular opinion has been on the side of the Ethiopians, but the controversy was far from being over this summer. Most young Ethiopians continue to refuse to undergo conversion rites, and the Rabbinate refuses to marry them, a serious predicament in a country where there is still only rabbinical marriage. Last week, the newcomers from Ethiopia were demonstrating in the streets against their treatment by the Rabbinate. Their resentment was dismissed—too slickly perhaps, in view of the circumstances—by Arye Dulzin, chairman of the Jewish Agency, which is responsible for their absorption, as the result of "Communist indoctrination" in Mengistu-controlled Ethiopia.

The lesson has not gone unobserved. "The newcomers have exposed to us once again some of the darker, inhumane aspects of Orthodox rabbinical custom," Gideon Samet, a well-known columnist, noted. Immigration to Israel was at a low 18,766 people last year, according to official figures; if it had not been for the sudden influx of the Ethiopian Jews, it would have reached an all-time low. The new immigrants, Samet added, "have taught us something about ourselves—more precisely, perhaps, they help us once again to entertain our illusions." By July, the public euphoria over the rescue of the Ethiopian Jews was over. The government was struggling, with little apparent success, to put the economy in order. The prevailing mood of bitterness and sarcasm, if not near-despair, was expressed by Yoel Marcus, in *Ha'aretz*, who wrote in June that "the will-power of this people is simply astounding. Nobody gave the Jewish state a chance, and nevertheless we established it. Everybody said we will not be able to withstand the assault of seven Arab countries, but we withstood them [and survived]. . . .

Everybody said that if Likud gets into power they will make a war; notwithstanding this warning, we voted Likud into power, and they made a war. Now everybody is saying that the Israelis have decided to commit suicide. You better trust their willpower; there's no force on earth that will stop them."

8

Jerusalem Blues

A few years ago, Peter Ustinov announced that he would never salute a flag before he knew who was holding it. This is still a minority attitude, but in one important sense modern democracies already live in a post-nationalist era. Even in the relatively young nation of Israel, few people seem nowadays to be in the mood for unreflective national celebration. The celebration, in 1987, of Israel's thirty-ninth Independence Day, which came shortly before the twentieth anniversary of the Six-Day War, is a case in point. In this exuberant country, there is usually no dearth of loud-talking generals and journalists and flag-waving politicians, especially on Independence Day. But veteran observers this year could not remember a more subdued Independence Day or one highlighted by so much political divisiveness. In former years, the celebrations were marked by displays of national unity in the face of outside threats, which have usually been ample. This year, there was not even a semblance of unity: doves and hawks, and secular and religious groups, were at one another's throats as never before in the country's short history. The consensus on making war or making peace was broken. For the first time since 1948, one of the two major political blocs, the Labor Party, was insisting that peace—or, at least, peace talks—with Jordan and with moderate Palestinian nationalists was a distinct possibility; the other, Likud, was saying that this was at best a dangerous illusion and at worst something close to treason. Labor regarded Jordan's readiness to attend an international peace conference with Israel, to be sponsored by the five permanent members of the United Nations Security Council, as a historic breakthrough, an unprecedented opportunity that should not be missed. Likud vehemently opposed the possibility out of fear that the great powers, especially Russia and China, would put pressure upon Israel to relinquish territories occupied in 1967. The pre-1967 borders were "Auschwitz borders," Likud leaders claimed; Israel would never return to them.

In 1984, the two parties, each short of an absolute majority in the Knesset but between them holding the bulk of its 120 seats, formed an uneasy National Unity government with alternating Prime Ministers. This government has successfully presided over the withdrawal of Israeli troops from Lebanon and has trimmed three-digit annual inflation down to a more manageable level. The two parties, for all their disagreements on other important issues, had in the past been able to stand united at least on issues of war and peace: in 1979 on making peace with Egypt, in 1982 on making war in Lebanon. (Although Labor was in the opposition in 1982, the Party voted almost enthusiastically in favor of the Lebanon invasion. Doubts came only later, when things began to go badly for Israel and the casualty rate mounted.) Until this year outside threats were judged more or less similarly by the two parties. Now, for the first time in memory, this is not so. In the past, any differences that might have emerged between the parties on ways to deal with outside threats were essentially tactical; this year, they are strategic. The Labor Party, led by the mercurial Shimon Peres, a hawk turned dove in recent years, is intent on breaking the deadlock with Jordan and the Palestinians, in the belief that failure to do so would lead to another war; Likud believes that the territorial status quo can go on indefinitely.

Independence Day speakers this year reflected the polarization and the resultant somber public mood. Some, hardened by the fears and uncertainties of forty years of war and rejection by the Arabs, or by old-fashioned national resolve, believed there was little, if anything, Israel could do to placate the Arabs; Arabs and Palestinians would eventually reconcile themselves to an Israel with its present frontiers. But when, as always on Independence Day, the 1948 Israeli Declaration of Independence was recited over the air ("In the land of Israel the Jewish people first arose. . . . Exiled, the people remained faithful to it in all the lands of their dispersion") it must have occurred to some Israelis that the Palestinians, too, had first arisen in this country, and that they, too, remembered it in all the lands of their dispersion. If there was now an "unprecedented" possibility, as

Peres claimed, of discussing peace with a Jordanian-Palestinian delegation, and perhaps even of making peace on the basis of a territorial compromise, to miss it would be a tragedy.

The mass media, too, reflected a curious, and perhaps significant, shift in public sensibilities and interests. On previous anniversaries of the Six-Day War, the media tended, by and large, to highlight the grave dangers Israel had faced in 1967 and the triumphant victory that dispersed those dangers with lightning speed. But this year television and newspapers were filled with harrowing reports of repression on the West Bank and in the Gaza Strip. For years, the convention had been to refer to the West Bank obliquely as the "administered" territories, or, covetously, as Judea and Samaria; on this anniversary of the Six-Day War, the term "occupation" suddenly appeared again. It was a term that only leftist and Peace Now activists would have used in the past.

Earlier this year, Abba Eban, the grand old man of Israeli diplomacy and the chairman of the Knesset Foreign Relations and Defense Committee, surprised a group of Jewish intellectuals from the United States by saying at a conference in Jerusalem that Israel had never been more *secure* against external menace than it was today, or more *vulnerable* to domestic folly. The statement was the more remarkable because Eban had until the 1970s been the most brilliant Israeli or Jewish articulator of the opposite view. His current reasoning, which he also expounded in a recent article in the Jewish-American magazine *Tikkun*, was that the "American-Soviet balance creates an international environment favorable to Israel's stability." No Arab army today posed a serious threat to Israel. There was formal peace with Egypt, which had "removed itself in its own interest from the cycle of recurrent wars." With Jordan there existed a state of de-facto peace, with borders open to trade and tourism. Iraq was weak, and busy in a war with Iran and was likely to remain so for the foreseeable future. Syria, the only country still actively belligerent, was effectively checked by the deterrent power of the Israeli Army. True, Eban said, there was the serious problem of Palestinian terror, but terrorists are a threat to individual Israeli lives, not to Israel's existence. Under these conditions, Eban maintained, "the darkest shadow hanging over Israel comes from within itself."

"Most tragedies in history are self-inflicted," Eban warned. The grave danger facing Israel was its own impulse to incorporate the West Bank and the Gaza Strip, with their 1.3 million rebellious Palestinians, into the State of Israel. The stupendous folly of doing so against the express wishes of the Palestinians—"1,300,000 members of a foreign nation owing no devotion to our flag, our faith, our tongue, our name or our national vision"—would cause a "structural defect" within the Israeli body politic which it might not be able to survive, at least as a civilized society or a democracy. If, Eban continued, we were to hear that the United States wanted to annex ninety million rebellious Russians, or that the Netherlands had decided to incorporate four million unwilling Germans into Dutch society—some of them engaged in terrorist activity supported by powerful neighboring states— we would assume that the governments of those countries lacked good sense. In Israel there was still a major political party that continued to support the permanent incorporation of the West Bank and Gaza. The leader of that party was currently Prime Minister, and there were friends of Israel in foreign countries who supported this position. They continued to speak of annexation as though it were a "serious" option. It cannot be, Eban insisted, unless Israel is ready to cease being a Jewish state or a democracy, or both. It was astonishing, he said, to find so many American Jews, ostensible friends of Israel, seeming so indifferent to Israel's remaining a democracy, or even becoming, for all practical purposes, an apartheid state. (By 2000, an estimated 4.5 million Jews will face 3.5 million disenfranchised Arabs.) "The idea of exercising permanent rule over a foreign nation can only be defended by an ideology and rhetoric of self-worship and exclusiveness that are incompatible with the ethical legacy of prophetic Judaism and classical Zionism." A conscious return to those legacies, leading to the repartition of Palestine between the two nationalities that have been contending for it since the beginning of this century, might now, finally, lead to a historical compromise between them, and—with luck or United States help—to peace.

❀

Some of those same fears and hopes—though he has seen fit (for allegedly tactical reasons) not to articulate them publicly so far—are generally thought to have motivated Shimon Peres in his active pursuit since 1984 of some diplomatic breakthrough with Jordan and with moderate Palestinians on the West Bank and in the Gaza Strip. As Defense Minister in the government of Yitzhak Rabin until 1977, he was a hawk. As leader of the Labor opposition to the right-wing government of Menachem Begin, he moved to the left. Both in and out of office, he surrounded himself with young aides openly sympathetic to the dovish extra-parliamentarian Peace Now movement. From September of 1984 until October of 1986, as Prime Minister of the Tweedledum-Tweedledee government of National Unity, and, after 1986, as Vice Prime Minister and Foreign Affairs Minister under the right-wing Likud leader Yitzhak Shamir, Peres sent peace feelers and secret emissaries to Jordan, and messages to intermediaries in third countries, notably in Morocco, Egypt, England, and France. He had three personal meetings in London with Jordan's King Hussein to hammer out the terms of a possible settlement and the framework of a peace conference where such a settlement, or an interim solution, might be agreed upon between an Israeli and a "Jordanian-Palestinian" delegation. Clandestine meetings between Israeli leaders and King Hussein had taken place before, always accompanied by elaborate exchanges of presents—guns for the King, Bedouin swords for the Israelis. (On one occasion Hussein flew his own helicopter to a government guesthouse near Tel-Aviv and on another he presented Abba Eban with a gold-plated fountain pen for "signing our future peace.") But nothing politically substantial ever emerged from these meetings.

The King had been assuring Peres all along that if he received a promise similar to the one given Sadat before his famous flight to Jerusalem—namely, that Israel would withdraw from all former Jordanian territories it had occupied in 1967, including Muslim holy places in the Old City of Jerusalem—he, too, would be ready to come to Jerusalem and openly sign a peace treaty. The King's position, according to aides of Peres, was that if Israel was not yet ready, or able, to commit itself to full withdrawal he needed effective international backing—an "umbrella," as he put it, that would be held up by moderate Arab states (e.g., Egypt, Morocco) and the permanent members of the Security Council. In order to agree to any compromise—political or territorial, interim or permanent—that might be worked out between the sides, he needed an international "imprimatur," the King is said to have told Peres, to protect himself against Yasir Arafat and extremists of the Palestine Liberation Organization, with whom he had recently had an ugly quarrel.

Peres felt that this was an opportunity Israel should not miss. He was further encouraged by recent statements by the King to the effect that it was unrealistic to expect Israel to withdraw all the way to the pre-1967 boundaries, and that Jerusalem should remain united as a city, though presumably under two sovereignties. Peres was equally impressed by the King's apparent readiness to agree to a series of interim settlements in the form of partial withdrawals, or possibly joint Jordanian-Israeli administration of the occupied territories. The main obstacle was the King's insistence that while negotiations between the two sides would be direct, any unresolved differences must be referred to the five permanent members of the United Nations Security Council. This Peres would not accept; the two sides must reach their compromises between them, with no pressure from the great powers, two of which (Russia and China) were far from neutral on issues at stake, and even refused to maintain diplomatic relations with Israel.

At a secret meeting in London on April 11, which, it is said, lasted for more than seven hours, a breakthrough was apparently reached. The King, prodded by Prime Minister Margaret Thatcher of Britain, agreed that the proposed international conference would not impose any solutions or veto any agreements reached between the Jordanian-Palestinian delegation and Israel. The United States, which was on the record as supporting free nego-tiations between the two sides, would in any event have vetoed an imposed settlement. Peres was highly encouraged by these results. Whether the Russians would play the game or were preparing to spoil it was not clear at that stage. It was thought likely that at least China might be induced to take a role as an "umbrella" power. Some of the current restrictions on Jewish emigration from the Soviet Union might be relaxed.

Peres and his aides spoke ecstatically of "a historic breakthrough." The Palestine Liberation Organization would be kept out of the peace process at least for the time being, seeing that it was still unwilling to recognize Israel's right to exist. But there were hopeful indications that a number of prominent Palestinians on the occupied West Bank, with the tacit approval of Arafat, might join the Jordanian delegation and participate in formal peace talks: mayors and former mayors, a well-known lawyer, and a promi-nent publisher. Even if the most crucial points of a possible agreement were to remain undecided—final borders, Jewish settlements, demilitarized areas, the future of Jerusalem—Peres believed in the need to finally break the status quo and begin a new "dynamic." A written agreement—of a type that in the surrealist language of diplomacy is called a "non-paper"—was drawn up at the April meeting, on an "ad referendum" basis. Peres took it home with him to obtain the agreement of his right-wing partners in the coalition. He hoped that in one form or another such agreement would be forthcoming, perhaps through defection to his side of one or two of the more moderate Likud ministers. This had happened before, and had enabled Peres to force Cabinet agreement on withdrawal from Lebanon. To protect his flanks within his own party, Peres had been careful to take former Prime Minister Rabin, now Defense Minister, with him to London, to wit-ness and endorse his agreement with the King. But his optimism was unfounded: Peres had grossly overestimated his leverage with the hardlin-ers in Likud. Prime Minister Shamir had been fully aware of and noncom-mittal about the long-drawn-out negotiations with the King. Peres had hoped to threaten Shamir with a government crisis and, possibly, new elec-tions on the issue of "peace" or "no peace," which Peres felt sure he would win. But he had underestimated Shamir's talent as a tactician and political survivor. It has been said of Shamir that he has turned political immobility into an art. He is a man of considerable charm of the kind usually called Central European, but his unassuming figure, short and thickset, comes with a pair of piercing, hard eyes, which are the true index to his uncompromising nature. Shamir gave Peres a public dressing-down such as Peres had never received in his long career as a public servant and politician. He told Peres—and the press—that he would never agree to an international conference; that such a conference would be an invitation to pressure to abandon "Judea and Samaria," and even from Jerusalem. The fact that Hussein had not been criticized in the Arab world for his meeting with Peres—not even by Syria or the PLO—confirmed Shamir in his fears that Peres was planning a "sellout," in the words of one Shamir aide. In the Cabinet, Shamir was stronger than Peres: Peres needed a majority, Shamir needed only a deadlock. The agreement with the King of Jordan was not even put to a vote.

To preempt Peres's call for new elections, Shamir quickly struck a bargain with Shas, an ultra-Orthodox splinter group in the Knesset. In return for denying Peres the two or three votes he needed in order to call new elections, Shamir promised Shas increased funds for Orthodox institutions, and also, within two months, new religious legislation on converted Jews. Conversions to Judaism by Reform and Conservative rabbis in America and elsewhere outside Israel have until now been recognized under the Israeli Law of Return, which grants automatic citizenship to Jewish immigrants; under the new legislation that Shamir promised Shas, only conversions confirmed by Orthodox rabbis would be valid. (The name of this game is power: the ever-recurring question "Who is a Jew?"—which has bedevilled Israeli public life since 1948—is really a question about who is a rabbi.) To Shamir's dismay, his first attempt, earlier this month, to push through the promised legislation invalidating Reform and Conservative conversions narrowly missed the majority he needed. The two big parties were deadlocked on this subject, too. But Shamir was bound to try again to uphold his deal with Shas and save his government.

Peres was asked by an interviewer whether the ground could not have been prepared more thoroughly behind the scenes. No, a weary Peres answered, nothing can be done behind the scenes in Israel. In Israel you are always "on-stage." He did not want to arouse the slightest suspicion that he might be electioneering. Shamir humiliated Peres further by informing Hussein, and the rest of the world, that the Foreign Minister represented only himself, and not the Israeli government. Peres complained that he had also been let down by the Americans. The history of the Egyptian-Israeli peace process had clearly proved that no breakthrough could be achieved without active American involvement, but President Reagan and Secretary of State Shultz had been oddly reserved about, if not downright uninterested in, the idea of the international conference as it had been worked out by Peres and King Hussein. At Shamir's instigation, Shultz cancelled a planned trip to the Middle East; he was also said to have been irritated by the way Peres had handled the Pollard spy affair—in which Jonathan Jay Pollard, a former analyst for the United States Navy, and a Jew, pleaded guilty to selling American intelligence secrets to Israel. (The Israeli government lamely apologized, claiming that the recruitment of Pollard was a "rogue"operation. Hardly anybody in Washington or Jerusalem took this explanation seriously.)

The United States did not, of course, publicly oppose an initiative ostensibly advocated by both Israel and Jordan in the interests of peace. It was above all reluctant to become involved in an internal Israeli squabble. Reagan and Shultz were also hesitant to give the Russians a role to play in the Middle East—as though "they had not already been there for more than thirty years. The deadlock remained. It was reflected in a May editorial in the English-language *Jerusalem Post*. Alluding to a statement made by General Moshe Dayan immediately following the Six-Day War ("We are waiting for King Hussein to telephone"), the *Post* remarked upon the "historic irony that when King Hussein, after all these years, seemed ready to lift the phone, Israel's line was out of order and Washington's engaged."

Peres has since been cutting a rather pathetic figure, rushing from one European capital to another espousing his agreement with Hussein, but followed everywhere by Shamir's disparaging assertion that he is acting without authority, that he is just electioneering, just "power hungry." Peres is not under "house arrest," Shamir quipped on one occasion, but he ought not to be regarded by the outside world as an *interlocuteur valable*. Probably never before has a foreign minister wandered around the world as Peres has in recent weeks without a mandate from his government and in pursuit of a policy that his own Prime Minister was almost daily disavowing, publicly, in the strongest of terms. What Peres might have been telling Francois Mitterrand, Hosni Mubarak, Helmut Kohl, and others in these rather trying circumstances for a foreign minister is not known. He may believe that the international conference may still take place as a result of an improvement in U.S.-Soviet relations. Coming out of a meeting, recently, with Mubarak in Geneva, he announced once again that 1987 will be the "year of peace."

At the same time, Peres has almost studiously avoided taking his campaign to the people of Israel. He took a great risk but did not prepare for the aftermath. His reluctance to campaign for his plan within Israel as he did abroad was diversely interpreted. Moderates saw it as a personality flaw. Hardliners said that it proved he was afraid to present his case to the people because he might lose it. He himself complained that his own party was not giving him the support he deserved. Peres was further handicapped by Hussein; his position would have been easier if the King had not been so cagey, if he had come out of the royal closet instead of insisting on clandestine meetings, and on denying—albeit with a broad, knowing smile— that they had taken place at all. Sadat had not been as secretive; with his keen eye for the psychological dimension of the Arab-Israeli conflict, Sadat was a master of political theater and grand dramatic *gestes*, which visibly accelerated the Egyptian-Israeli process. By contrast, King Hussein, an authoritarian ruler, seems impervious to the psychological nuances that move politics and influence people in a democracy like Israel. He has done little if anything to make Peres's domestic position any easier. It also did not help Peres when Hussein invited Austria's President Kurt Waldheim, of all people, to pay a state visit to Jordan. That, a writer in the *Post* commented, could be another nail in the coffin of the peace conference.

❀

Peres has faced his discomfiture with a kind of grim, grinding resoluteness. He has never been a charismatic leader. He is an intellectual, an avid reader, a loner, and what the French call *un triste*. (The best photograph of him I know shows him with his head lowered so that his shoulders are level with his ears, and his chin resting on the backs of his hands.) His rise through the ranks of the Labor Party apparatus was slow. For some curious, never clearly defined reason, he has continued to suffer a "credibility" problem, and his political enemies have exploited it with vicious and, as far as is known, totally unfounded accusations. Since his return to power in 1984, he had been looking for the opportunity to bring distinction to his leadership, but when the chance of the great breakthrough, the lever to a possible peace, presented itself he seemed oddly quiet, inactive, and, to some observers, without inner conviction. On the eve of a Peres tour to three European capitals, Yoel Marcus, a columnist for *Ha'aretz*, Israel's leading independent daily, reminded him that it was more important to convince Israelis of the importance of an international conference than it was to convince Thatcher, Kohl, and Mitterrand. "When Churchill believed in something, he spoke out forcefully, he fought for his belief, he did not take a public-opinion poll," a Jerusalem history professor remarked in May.

Public-opinion polls commissioned by the Labor Party in May showed that some 60 percent of the Israeli public supported the international conference. Still, the campaign for peace—and new elections—did not warm up. The failure may have been caused at least in part by the aftereffects of the Pollard spy scandal. The affair cast a discrediting shadow on leading politicians of both parties, but Peres took a special beating. While the Knesset subcommittee for intelligence and security services, under the chairmanship of Eban, was conducting its secret hearings on the affair, Peres, annoyed by leaks, publicly called Eban a "pompous peacock." Eban responded that Peres might soon discover a new species—"a peacock with a sting in its tail." In its final report on the affair, the subcommittee tended to blame Peres more than others. Other ministers were also blamed for the way they had handled (or conveniently overlooked) the sordid business, but Peres, the subcommittee pointed out, had been Prime Minister at the time. Because he was "first among equals," it charged, his responsibility for what had been called—but was not—a "rogue" operation was greater. Peres' public prestige was not enhanced by this report, or by the subsequent squabbles between him and committee members. He tried to defend himself, rather lamely according to some, by saying that in England there were spy scandals, too, but no one had tried to blame Mrs. Thatcher. "Any three odd people, randomly picked on a Tel-Aviv street, would have conducted the Pollard Affair with more good sense" than Peres, Rabin, and Shamir did, the columnist B. Michael wrote in *Ha'aretz*. The newspaper had up to this point wholeheartedly supported Peres in his efforts to reach an accommodation with Jordan; after the publication of the Eban report, it asked for his resignation, and for the resignations of three other ministers—Shamir, Rabin, and Minister without Portfolio Moshe Arens. All four were held politically responsible for hiring Pollard and, subsequently, for the coverup.

The Israeli involvement in the Iran-Contra affair compounded the trouble, according to Israeli journalists reporting from the United States. "The problem is not whether the U.S. administration respects Israel—after all, our own government has become a joke recently," the head of a major Jewish organization in America was quoted by Zvi Barel, the *Ha'aretz* correspondent in Washington, as saying not long ago. What worried this American Jewish leader was that with the recent spate of scandals in Israel "the American public gains a too intimate familiarity with Israel." Israel, which was seen in the past more or less as a nation of supermen, now looks slightly "ridiculous." The American press has begun to report on Israeli affairs in much the same way that "the Israeli press does."

With one scandal following another in recent months, most ordinary Israelis can no longer tell the scandals apart. Watergate kept America busy for years; the Iran-Contra affair threatens to do the same. But in Israel there have recently been two or three scandals in a week. While the Pollard scandal was still riding high, the government almost collapsed over the international peace conference. It was threatened again when Shamir claimed that Peres was a "madman." Then came allegations of torture and revelations of extensive forgeries by agents of the Shin Bet, Israel's equivalent of the FBI, who for years had perjured themselves in order to secure convictions of suspected Arab terrorists. The Prime Minister quickly reassured the perjured agents and reportedly promised them immunity from prosecution. Another tremendous uproar arose when the government made a decision that in effect would charge Israeli Arab students almost 50 percent more in college-tuition fees than Israeli Jews are charged. (The outcry caused its reversal.) Relatively simple, albeit important, decisions, such as the appointment of ambassadors to the United States and Egypt, were delayed for months because the two major parties that make up the National Unity government could not agree on the candidates. In a series of dubious horse trades, which did little to enhance politics in the public view, small splinter parties in the Knesset were able to make the most of the current deadlock between the Labor Party and Likud. In some instances, the small parties settled for public funds for this or that project. In others, political figures were bribed away from minority parties by the inducement of safe seats on the list of a major party to secure their reelection.

The decline of parliamentary action is a direct result of the grand coalition between the two big parties, which essentially eliminates a lively, effective opposition. Ministers and members of the Knesset very often address a hundred or more empty seats. The discrediting of specific politicians—and perhaps of politics itself—has reached such a point in recent months that fears have been voiced that the system as such is on the verge of being discredited. That such fears are not entirely empty in a country of immigrants, many of whom come from authoritarian societies, is corroborated by the results of public-opinion polls, especially among young people, which point to a lack of or a decline in democratic values. There has been an acerbic debate here for many years over whether the reputed decline in democratic values does not derive mainly from the fact that since the war of 1967 Israel has in effect been a "dual" society (the polite term used to avoid the impolite "apartheid"): three and a half million Israelis enjoy full civil and political rights under the rule of law and one and a third million Palestinians within the same borders live under arbitrary military rule, with few civil rights and no political rights whatsoever, no right of free speech, of free assembly and political association, no right to travel freely or settle wherever they wish within Israeli territory, as Israelis can. Palestinians may go abroad only with permission from the military administration; they are not free to return home if they have stayed away for more than the allotted time, and are, in effect, expelled. The fact that the President of Israel bowed to right-wing and religious demonstrators by commuting the sentences of some of the Jewish terrorists, including those who had been serving life terms for murder and those who had been sentenced to shorter terms for attempting to blow up the mosques on the Jerusalem Temple Mount has been cited as an instance of "tribal justice"— one law for Jewish terrorists and another for Arabs. The extreme right and fundamentalist sectors of public opinion in Israel adhere to a theory of rights bestowed upon the Jewish people "divinely" in the entire Land of Israel within its never clearly defined Biblical boundaries. But the theories of democracy and of divine rights do not easily coexist. Democratic theory historically grew as a protest against divine right. The reemergence, in whatever form, of a divine-rights principle in a modern democracy undermines that democracy. Professor Dan Horowitz, a political scientist and sociologist at the Hebrew University of Jerusalem, is one of several academics who have warned in recent years of the fascist potential within Israeli society; its base, he says, is in the growing partnership of "tribal nationalism, religious fanaticism, and political populism."

The courts still function admirably to uphold the rule of law. But the political paralysis is imposing undue, and perhaps dangerous, burdens upon the courts. In a recent series of articles, Amnon Rubinstein, a former Tel-Aviv University professor of constitutional law and, until last May, when he resigned in protest, Minister of Communications in the Shamir-Peres government, warned against this danger. The courts cannot substitute for ineffective or opportunistic legislatures and executives, Rubinstein declared. The Supreme Court, especially, has been pushed into making what would normally be executive or legislative decisions, in the vacuum created by the paralysis of the two branches. It was the Supreme Court, acting upon the plea of a citizen, that decided there should be television on the Sabbath, and it was the Supreme Court that ordered the Orthodox Minister of the Interior to introduce daylight-saving time. (He had been reluctant to change the time in deference to Orthodox fears that Saturday-night buses would begin to run in Jerusalem before actual Sabbath sundown.) It was the Supreme Court that finally decided that newly formed political parties are entitled to public financing, that gasoline stations could remain open on Saturdays, that there was one definition of Jewishness, the Orthodox definition, but that converts to Reform Judaism can be registered in Israel as Jews.

Similarly, there has been a proliferation in recent years of "judicial inquiry commissions." They are called upon to perform what the executive or the legislature are unwilling to do. Such commissions are usually headed by a Supreme Court Justice. One such commission brought about the resignation of a chief of staff (General David Elazar), after the Yom Kippur War, and another the resignation of a Defense Minister (Ariel Sharon), after the Sabra and Shatilla massacres. When the Pollard spy scandal burst, there were demands for a judicial commission to establish the personal and political responsibility for it. It was as though there were no Knesset.

The missing link between authority and responsibility has nowhere been so clearly evidenced as in the reactions of those most politically involved in the Pollard affair and its aftermath. Shamir's first response to the public outcry for a thorough investigation was that there was nothing to investigate. Those who should know all the facts know them, he said, and those who should not know need not. When the Eban subcommittee published its report criticizing the comportment of Peres and Rabin, Peres again attacked Eban personally, accusing him of "disloyalty" to the party that had given him his Knesset seat. Peres told Eban bluntly that he was not an almighty judge but was serving on the Knesset Foreign Relations and Defense Committee as a representative of the party. Rabin said of Eban what, in colloquial Hebrew, is tantamount to "He can go hang himself." Eban was forced to defend himself at a meeting of the Party central committee which was convened expressly to censure him. These events could well mark the end of this civilized but lonely man in Israeli politics.

Shamir, Peres, and Rabin all dismissed the Eban report as just an opinion, of no particular consequence. They preferred to accept the conclusions of another team (a prominent lawyer and a retired general), which they themselves had appointed and which had in effect exonerated them by attributing "responsibility" for any mistakes that might have been made to the *entire* Cabinet. Only one Cabinet minister, Ezer Weizman, pointed out that ministers who had never heard of the spy operation in Washington before it became front-page news could hardly be held responsible. But if they *were* indeed responsible, he suggested, the entire Cabinet should resign. His proposal was made en passant, and was not put to a vote.

❋

I live in Jerusalem, where the Orthodox vote has always been higher than it has been in the rest of the country, although here, too, it is a minority. Only half a dozen or so restaurants have permits to open on the Sabbath in the Jewish part of Jerusalem, and some of those are occasionally stoned by ultra-Orthodox mobs, who also like to stone cars that approach their section of town. Needless to say, cinemas, theaters, and other places of entertainment are closed, and there is no public transportation. This spring, on the weekend following Independence Day, I drove by chance through Israel's coastal plain, the area in which more than 70 percent of the country's population lives. The Sabbath in Haifa and Tel-Aviv today is much as it is in any European or North American city. Theaters, restaurants, movie houses, public libraries, and swimming pools remain open. The buses are operating. Beaches and football stadiums are crowded. It is in Tel-Aviv and Haifa that an essential characteristic of modern Israel immediately becomes apparent: *the deepening gulf between the legal Israel and the real Israel.*

The real Israel is a predominantly secular, easygoing Mediterranean country. The legal Israel is centered around Jerusalem. The real Israel is centered in Tel-Aviv and the Cities of the Plain. But, even though the four or five religious splinter groups never win more than 12 or 13 percent of the seats in the Knesset, the legal Israel is a country increasingly under the sway of ultra-Orthodox national legislation—especially in those areas which cannot be circumvented by local law, as can the opening or closing of restaurants and movie houses. There are many reasons for this situation— partly cultural and psychological and partly political. The Zionist pioneers, through the 1940s, were by and large secular—or, at least, anti-Orthodox. In his seminal text *Der Judenstaat*, the father of modern Zionism, Theodor Herzl, deliberately spoke of a "Judenstaat"—a country for Jews, not of a Jewish state. The early Zionist pioneers believed they were creating a new "Hebrew" nation on the ancestral soil. They assumed that their version of secular nationalism and humanist socialism would be an effective substitute for the Orthodox Judaism of their fathers, against which or against whom they had rebelled. In the Tel-Aviv public school that I attended, in the 1930s and 1940s, an effort was made to shape our identities on the basis of the revived Hebrew language, of the Bible as literature, and of our teachers' Zionist interpretation of Jewish history: the diaspora was doomed, the future of the Jewish people was here. Jewish history, especially after the Holocaust, caught up with these simplifications and with the attempt to define Jewish nationality in purely secular terms; the composition of the

Israeli population was radically changed with the mass immigration of Jews from Afro-Asian countries, who had little or none of the ideological background of the early pioneers.

There has been, in a sense, a Freudian return of the repressed. But the uniquely Orthodox terms in which this return has been *legally* defined—the refusal to separate synagogue and state, the exclusion of all Conservative, Reform, and Reconstructionist forms of Jewish observance—are due, for the most part, to *political* manipulation. Israel's electoral system gives small religious groups a vastly disproportionate power to push through their laws. The fact that in day-to-day life there is such an enormous difference between the *real* Israel and the *legal* Israel explains why the splinter groups, whose power would be severely curtailed under electoral reform, have so far vehemently opposed it. But the fact that there is such a deep gulf may also be an indication that in this area, as in others, the story is not yet finished.

9

Intifada: The Palestinian Uprising, I

Thirteen weeks after the start of the popular uprising in the West Bank and the Gaza Strip—which right-wing Israeli politicians and a part of the local press still insist on calling the "unrest," the "events," the "discrepancies," the "disorders" in the territories—it is safe to make at least one sweeping generalization. The status quo, which Likud politicians have long regarded as the best of all possible worlds, is shattered forever.

Twenty years of shortsighted Israeli policies lie battered in the streets of the West Bank, Gaza, and East Jerusalem. The writing was on the wall for years, but most Israelis never bothered to read it. Some were distracted by real or imaginary security concerns. The disorienting abstractions of national and international political rhetoric and the ceaseless talk of a nonexistent "peace process," even among the sensitive, produced a numbness. Self-deception became a prerequisite for survival. Many overlooked the simple fact that since 1967 Israel has not been able to win a war. Other Israelis were blinded by nationalist and religious rhetoric and by the apparent ease and low maintenance costs of a military occupation that for more than two decades has held 1.5 million Palestinians as pawns, or bargaining chips, and as a source of cheap menial labor, while denying them the most basic human rights.

The pawns have now risen to manifest their frustration, their bitterness, and their political will, with a vengeance and determination that surprised everybody in Israel, including themselves and their "leaders" and "spokesmen" in the headquarters of the Palestine Liberation Organization in distant Tunis. The actual uprising appears to have been entirely spontaneous. A bad traffic accident in the Gaza Strip gave rise to wild rumors blaming the Israeli security services for the deaths that took place. The protest demonstrations quickly spilled over to the West Bank. In retrospect it is not surprising that the lid first blew off in Gaza, where the situation is at its most nightmarish. Into this narrow strip of land only some 10 kilometers wide and 36 kilometers long, where the population density is already among the highest in the world, the Israelis have introduced 2,000 Jewish settlers. They live on public or confiscated land in resort-like enclaves surrounded by wretched refugee camps.

In Gaza the social problems seem even more overwhelming than the political ones. The Palestinians living in the strip have been stateless since 1948. Neither Egypt before 1967 nor Israel after 1967 were ready formally to annex the area for fear of burdening themselves with an immense social problem. (The current population of 633,000 is estimated to reach one million by 2004.) The bitterness, hopelessness, and frustration, especially in the refugee camps, are compounded by the results of forty-one years of repression—until 1967 by the Egyptians and since 1967 by the Israeli Army. In Gaza the uprising was marked by strong Islamic fundamentalist feelings reminiscent of those expressed in the Iranian revolts of a decade ago. The revolts is not only against the traditional leadership in the strip but also against the conditions in which young people feel permanently trapped.

In Gaza as in the West Bank, the uprising was a children's crusade. I was led by a few thousand teen-agers and even younger boys and girls, armed with nothing but stones and slingshots and occasional Molotov bottles. Within a few weeks they seem to have achieved more for the Palestinian cause (though not necessarily for the PLO) than Yasir Arafat and his prosperous supporters or terrorists have in thirty years.

One result of the uprising is that Israeli politics and society will never be the same again. The surprise and the resultant trauma recall the shock of the 1973 Yom Kippur War. The uprising and the continuing difficulties in suppressing it to "restore order" provide a lesson in the limits of power. Israelis have long had a problem with the uses of power. Zionism was intended to give defenseless Jews a measure of power to determine their fate. Ever since, Zionists have philosophized about power. After the Holocaust it became a Zionist article of faith that "powerlessness" had been the main cause for the destruction of European Jewry. As a result, Israeli attitudes toward power have consistently been complex and sometimes neurotically contradictory, marked by a curious inability to make the needed distinction between power and violence.

The military victory of 1967, which was not translated into political results, i.e., peace, served only to confuse the issue further. Because Israel in 1967 conquered the territories while defending itself against a foreign threat, Israelis came out of that war still feeling weak when in reality they were strong, the dominant military power in the region. They might have been "generous victors" after 1967 and reached a kind of peace with the Palestinians in the occupied territories and with the Arab countries. But being human, and having been insecure for so many years, they desired absolute security, the kind that they could have only if the Arabs felt thoroughly insecure. The late Israeli historian Jacob Talmon used to warn against "the obsessive desires" awakened by the war of 1967; they constituted, he argued, a dangerous departure from what Freud had called the reality principle.

Talmon's warnings were proven tragically right during the Israeli intervention in Lebanon, which is still not over, and most recently again in the West Bank and Gaza. Power displays a strange impotence when, as in the case of Israel, it exceeds its defensive role and becomes violence. In 1967 it took the Israeli Army a day to take Gaza and fewer than three days to seize the entire West Bank. The same army—at least three times as strong now and equipped with the latest, most sophisticated weapons—has so far been unable to quell the riots in these territories and pacify a turbulent population.

The present uprising is the result of an astounding lack of foresight, imagination, and political empathy on the part of successive Israeli political leaders. They have allowed a situation to develop in the territories that was hopeless from the start and that could be sustained over the years only by force and more force. Political mistakes were compounded by the inadequacy and slovenliness of a military administration in the territories that in the beginning was quite liberal but that deteriorated and was increasingly corrupted over the years by neglect, by low pay, and by unlimited, or arbitrary, power. Men sometimes admit mistakes. Bureaucracies almost never do. They make their errors legitimate by administering them, later on.

2

More than ninety Palestinians have died so far. Most were shot; twenty-one are said to have died by asphyxiation by tear gas (including three babies less than seven months old, a boy of twelve, and one man a hundred years old).

Seven are said to have died as a result of beatings (including one fourteen-year-old boy and a man aged sixty). Hundreds have been wounded and beaten up by truncheon-wielding troops who follow orders that are at best confused and at worst downright brutal. But the riots continue and are now in their fourth month. The hospitals in Gaza and elsewhere are filled with youngsters suffering from broken arms or legs, or both. The demonstrators so far are convinced of their "successes." The resulting euphoria has produced remarkable acts of daring and that high level of social discipline—even without real leaders—which has often been observed in so-called revolutionary moments. Food and other necessities are often shared.

The riots seem carefully timed to break out in one locality and then another. This suggests central planning. Palestinian medical teams regularly tour the turbulent areas and look after wounded people who are afraid to enter hospitals for fear of being arrested. There are plenty of firearms in the occupied territories and it could not have been hard for the rioters to lay hands on them. Yet despite the widespread revolutionary fervor, in three months of uprising the rioters have not fired a single shot. They are said to obey the strict orders of the committees. A surgeon in charge of the intensive care unit at Tel Hashomer Medical Center near Tel-Aviv, Dr. Raphael Wolden (Shimon Peres's son-in-law, as it happens), told the press that he was treating a painfully wounded youth, seventeen years old, who had just been brought in, and who, when asked for his name, groaned only, "Jihad, jihad."

Thousands of Palestinians have been arrested, hundreds of thousands more have been intimidated and placed under prolonged house arrest in the recurrent curfews imposed upon villages, refugee camps, and entire cities. But the uprising, which authorities expected to quell within a few days, continues into its fourth month. Curfews often mean disconnected telephones and cuts in the supply of electricity. Men are hauled out of their houses in the middle of the night and made to stand in the village square until morning, and there are many similar acts of collective punishment. And yet the rioting continues. The press no longer reports each riot in detail, but speaks generally of rising or abating waves of violence or unrest. A typical newscast from the government-controlled radio the other day ran: "Two rioters were shot yesterday in the Shata refugee camp in Gaza. . . . Nevertheless in the Gaza strip yesterday there was relative quiet."

Even when there is no curfew in Gaza, Nablus, Bethlehem, or East Jerusalem, Palestinian cities seem deserted. Inhabitants shut themselves in; stores are closed, except at certain hours, which are determined by secret local committees so that people can buy food and other necessities. The government has tried to cut the flow of PLO funds from abroad that support the strikes by Palestinian merchants. But the commercial strikes continue as before, undeterred by tough fiscal and administrative countermeasures.

The demonstrators continue to march through the debris and the black smoke of burning tires, past shuttered stores, chanting slogans, waving flags. Little boys run ahead firing slingshots at the troops summoned to disperse them. The troops—many are reservists—look clumsy by comparison. They move slowly, with their heavy equipment, their walkie-talkies, M-16 rifles in one hand and truncheons in the other. Helicopters hover overhead dropping tear gas from the air. Between twenty and forty thousand troops are said to be engaged in the West Bank, Gaza, and Jerusalem. When they are not dispersing demonstrations or chasing boys through the narrow alleys of the Nablus casbah or the refugee camps, where the sewers run open between the ramshackle huts, in an air thick with the hatreds and resentments from tragedies suffered forty years ago and since sustained, the soldiers concentrate on keeping the main highways open and on protecting some one hundred Israeli settlements established in the territories since their occupation in 1967.

They cannot be everywhere. Almost every night Palestinian villagers and inmates of refugee camps roll out more rocks and boulders onto secondary roads to block access to their villages or camps. They hang up Palestinian flags, sing songs, and declare their villages or camps "liberated Palestinian territory." Then the army moves in again—too often with entirely gratuitous brutality, shattering furniture, slashing tires, smashing window panes and solar heating panels. Bulldozers arrive and clear away the rocks. A few youths are taken aside and brutally beaten. Others are arrested. Panic-stricken mothers scream and army officers plead with old men (who protest their impotence) to maintain calm. A week later the same scene occurs once again.

At first there was some concern in army circles that soldiers—especially civilians on reserve duty—would resent doing "dirty police work" and even refuse to obey orders. For this reason only regular troops or fresh recruits were used (many of them no older than the Palestinian youngsters who were stoning them). The concern proved unjustified. In the short run, the individual reaction of soldiers stoned or cursed may well be hawkish and brutal. In the long run, their reaction as citizens is dovish (as it was in Lebanon) and in favor of "getting rid of these territories." Paradoxically, the riots have lent a human dimension to the Palestinian cause; before the riots it was an evil abstraction. Now one can see particular men and women and children rioting for their rights. One lieutenant colonel was recently quoted in the daily *Davar* as saying: "When I read about Waldheim in the papers I worry how the future will interpret what I am doing in the territories today."

3

The so-called civil administration in the territories (a misnomer on both the West Bank and Gaza, it is a branch of the military and is run by army officers) is on the verge of collapse because of the voluntary or forced resignations or absenteeism of locally recruited Palestinians who work for it. Other collaborators with the Israeli occupation regime are under constant threat. One was publicly lynched by a mob. Since the beginning of the uprising there has been little if any evidence of the much-heralded efficacy of the Israeli secret services. In the past they were adept at infiltrating terrorist cells and quickly extracting vital information from arrested suspects. But they overlooked or misjudged the tension that was mounting in the West Bank, in Gaza, and even in "reunited" Jerusalem throughout most of the last year.

The uprising itself could have been forecast years ago by even the dumbest observer who toured the West Bank or the Gaza Strip. And yet the security services were fooled by the relative scarcity or inefficacy of overt terrorist acts. Months before the actual uprising the growing tension was more than evident in the rising number of unconnected local outbursts of spontaneous violence. More and more cars were stoned. Several Israelis were knifed as they walked through the Arab quarter in Jerusalem, etc. The security services are only slightly more effective now, even though the uprising is already being institutionalized here and there through secret "guidance committees" that have been set up in villages and neighborhoods. There seem to be at least a dozen major committees. Despite house searches and more than two thousand arrests the military authorities have not yet been able to apprehend a single member. Their identity is not known. They may be more or less radical than Arafat; they certainly control the field better than Arafat and his cohorts in the PLO ever did.

Clearly a new leadership class is growing underground. It still pays lip service to the PLO bureaucracy abroad, but the true extent of its dependence on the PLO is not known. The PLO is now trying to coordinate these committees from afar through the direct-dialing international telephone. But from all I have heard, the PLO is not, or not yet, controlling events. Nor apparently is the uprising controlled by well-known local Palestinians identified with the PLO, such as the *Al Fajr* editor Hanna Siniora or the Gaza lawyer Fayez Abu Rahma, who both met with Secretary Shultz last month in Washington and are constantly being interviewed by the international press. The futility of some of the current Israeli political debate is nowhere better illustrated than in the argument over whether it is "legitimate" to negotiate with Siniora and Abu Rahma or whether they should be jailed as supporters of the PLO. Whoever leads the uprising—perhaps no one does—is not likely to let Siniora, Abu Rahma, and the other traditional leaders benefit from it.

"Israel is now learning a very simple truth, which should have been known to us from the days of confronting the British army in Palestine in 1945–47," Shlomo Avineri, a professor at the Hebrew University of Jerusalem and a former director general of the Israeli foreign ministry, wrote the other day. "An army can beat an army, but an army cannot beat a people." Historians have known this for a long time, but "military men and politicians (and too many of Israel's politicians are former military men)" apparently don't grasp it. They are good at calculating guns, airplanes, tanks, and missiles. "What cannot be counted—like a people's will—just does not appear in their quantified map of the world."

4

The man in charge of the policy of "force, power, beatings"—all of which have shown little result so far—is that quintessential man of quantified thought, Defense Minister Yitzhak Rabin. He is a former military man with little if any interest in ideas, and no known deep convictions. He has been telling the Palestinians in recent weeks that rioting will get them nothing. He may he right, but his admonition might have been more effective if something tangible had been offered them during the twenty-one years of creeping annexation. It was always too early or too late to address their needs or, alternatively, to reach an accommodation with Jordan. In 1967, as chief of staff of the victorious Israeli Army, Rabin was regarded as symbolizing the tremendous achievement of gaining so much territory as a bargaining chip for peace. Today he is the living symbol of how that opportunity was missed.

In 1968 Rabin aroused the anger of the right wing by announcing that it would not be a disaster if, once there was peace and after the withdrawal of the Israeli Army, Israelis would have to apply for Arab visas in order to visit Hebron. Later he became a supporter of "territorial compromise," the partition of the occupied West Bank between Israel and Jordan, with East (Arab) Jerusalem remaining in Israeli hands. The partition project was first put forward by Yigal Allon, another former military man and Rabin's political mentor. Allon's plan, first formulated a few weeks after the 1967 war, envisaged the intensive settlement and annexation by Israel of a strip of land on the west bank of the Jordan. This was seen as a kind of barricade against invasion. Most of the rest of the West Bank would come under Jordanian control.

Since no agreement was reached, that strip, at first narrow and relatively short, continued to widen under the former Labor government until (in the latest version of Allon's plan, prior to his death in 1980) it included most of the occupied West Bank, with the exception of a few enclaves heavily settled by Palestinians around Nablus and Ramallah. The plan, in its several versions, was repeatedly offered to King Hussein of Jordan in secret meetings over the years by Golda Meir, Abba Eban, Moshe Dayan, Yitzhak Rabin, and Shimon Peres. It was always rejected. Hussein told his Israeli interlocutors, including only last April Rabin himself: "I am ready to make peace with Israel but only in return for Israeli withdrawal to the pre-1967 lines. I shall not survive if I settle for less. For anything less than complete withdrawal you must deal with the PLO."

Like most of his colleagues in the cabinet, notably Prime Minister Shamir but not, apparently, Foreign Minister Shimon Peres, Rabin at first misread the uprising and, seemingly unconcerned, left for a visit to the U.S. When Rabin returned almost two weeks later the uprising was in full swing. Suggesting that it was fomented by foreign agents, including those of Iran, he promised to put an end to it within a few days. Ten days later he surmised that perhaps a few weeks more would be necessary to restore law and order. Early in January he corrected this estimate to a few months, but assured his listeners that order would most definitely be restored. A week later he reversed himself and confessed that things would probably never return to what they had been before December. The uprising, he now said, was a new kind of war and Israel would have to live with it for the foreseeable future. With each subsequent statement he seemed angrier, pounding the table with his fist in response to irritating questions from reporters.

At the same time Rabin repeated his conviction that military measures would never resolve the problem, that there was only a political solution. Remarkably, despite the events of the past three months, the Palestinians are not a key it. The only solution, he announced in early March, is an agreement with Jordan that would leave some 500,000 Palestinians on the West Bank under Israeli rule in an Israel that would be expanded around Jerusalem

and along the Jordan River. In an exchange recently shown on Israeli television between Rabin and a Palestinian father in Gaza, who shouted that innocent children including his own were being hideously beaten by the troops
and that "this cannot go on, what shall we do, what shall we do?" Rabin said:
"*You* talk with Hussein! *You* talk with the Syrians! Then we all sit down at
the table and find a very easy solution." The Palestinian looked very puzzled
at this advice, and Rabin walked away, surrounded by bodyguards, aides, pho-
tographers, and sound men. A Palestinian in Nablus interviewed on the same
day remarked: "The Israelis deserve better leaders and the Palestinians too."
Shamir said a few days before that first and most important there was a need
reinstill fear in the hearts of the Palestinians. Another Labor minister, known
for his hawkish views, was reliably quoted as saying that at the root of the
crisis was the Palestinians' euphoria. "Before we get anywhere we must wipe
those smirks off their lips."

5

The end of the status quo is nowhere so painful and so dramatic as in Jerusalem. Twenty-one years after "reunification" (the neat euphemism given
after the Six Day War to the conquest of East Jerusalem by the Israeli
Army) Jerusalem has in a sense again become a divided city. It was never,
of course, as united as was claimed. Palestinians and Israelis continued to
live and work apart from each other, in separate quarters, much as though
the city were still divided by mine fields and barbed wire, with two distinctly separate downtown districts, two business centers, two transportation systems, two electric power grids.

Whatever interaction and coexistence had been worked out came to an
end when the Palestinian population in East Jerusalem joined the uprising in
December. There are now, in effect, No-Go areas in Jerusalem, as in Belfast.
Arabs are reluctant to enter the Jewish quarters and most Israelis dare not
enter the Arab quarters. A private security company in West Jerusalem is
now offering businessmen and others "safe" rides to East Jerusalem and the
occupied territories in specially equipped cars with armed escorts. The commercial strike in East Jerusalem, announced in leaflets by a secret coordination committee in December, has been meticulously observed for more than
two months now—longer than anywhere in the West Bank or Gaza—
despite harsh countermeasures by the authorities. Christian Arabs living in
Jerusalem have in the past rarely participated in Palestinian protests—
church leaders were known for their good personal relationships and coop-

eration with Mayor Teddy Kollek. Arab Christians now openly identify with the uprising. The leaders of the Christian churches in Jerusalem recently published a joint statement in support of the Palestinian struggle, calling upon their congregations to take part.

East Jerusalem, including much of the Old City within the medieval walls, is a ghost town these days. Heavily armed troops patrol the deserted streets. Some neighborhoods have taken on the air of a war zone. Newsmen follow their beats in cars clearly marked PRESS or TELEVISION as in Nicaragua and Honduras. To avoid being stoned by their own people Palestinian drivers prominently display keffiyehs around their necks. Curfews (unheard-of in Jerusalem since 1967) have been imposed on certain turbulent quarters (A-Tur on the Mount of Olives and Antha, the biblical Anathot, birthplace of the prophet Jeremiah). In December the authorities ordered all schools in East Jerusalem shut. They have remained closed ever since. After thousands of Palestinian Jerusalemites tore up their Israeli identity cards in what was described as a collective act of destruction, the minister of social welfare curtailed the automatic transfer of social security payments into their bank accounts. He announced that Arab beneficiaries must now present themselves in person each month and show they are still in possession of an identity card. Israeli buses and cars continue to be stoned or fire-bombed almost daily as they drive through or along the edge of the Arab sectors. Though it is possible to reach the Western Wall by a roundabout route, the great plaza facing the wall, which attracted thousands of visitors daily before the riots, has been almost deserted in recent weeks.

When the first great riot erupted in December, Mayor Teddy Kollek was overheard telling a friend in a broken voice: "My life-work is ruined." No other man in the past twenty years has done as much as Kollek to keep Jerusalem united; few men have worked harder for coexistence. Few have tried as much as he did to break the walls of hatred and suspicion that divide Jews and Arabs in Jerusalem. His power unfortunately never extended *beyond* the municipality to national politics. Criticizing the conventional Israeli view of Jerusalem as an Israeli nationalist icon, he said in 1985 that "in order to preserve peace and justice in Jerusalem we must go beyond the conventional formulas of national sovereignty, beyond the fears and prejudices that drive nations into wars, and search for new forms of freedom and of political organization." He too never got around to working out the new formulas that would go beyond conventional sovereignty.

Nor would it have made much difference if he had, since the powers of mayors in Israel are notoriously narrow. Kollek cannot move a bus stop from one street corner to the next in Jerusalem without authorization from the minister of transport. He proposed at one point to divide the city into semi-autonomous boroughs, Arab and Jewish, with the post of president of the Greater Jerusalem Council rotating among the national and religious communities. The scheme was vetoed by the central government and Kollek was savagely attacked by right-wingers as an "Arab lover." Kollek then requested a former Supreme Court justice to prepare a draft constitution for the borough system. The draft was shelved as soon as it was finished.

Kollek was recently seen on television talking to a Jewish woman in East Talpiot, a new suburb built after 1967 beyond the old demarcation line. "I am scared," the woman said. "I am also scared," Kollek replied. He looked tired and depressed and older than his seventy-six years. "Coexistence in Jerusalem," he said, "is dead."

In November Kollek and the municipal councilors will stand for office in separate elections. Kollek's own election as mayor is assured. Elections to the council, however, are not direct but proportional, on the basis of party lists. If Kollek loses his narrow majority in the City Council, as he well may, since it was the Arab vote that gave him his narrow edge and the Arabs are very likely to boycott the next elections, Kollek will be powerless after November 1988.

6

Thirteen weeks after the uprising began, Israel is a changed country. Issues that most people thought could be put off for another five or ten years suddenly have an unprecedented urgency. Secretary of State George Shultz went into action last month as a result of the Reagan administration's unexpected shift from tacit support for the Likud's "do-nothing-Israel-knows-best-what's-good-for-it" policy to active sponsorship of what until very recently was still almost anathema in Washington—an international peace conference with the participation of the five permanent members of the UN Security Council and "the parties involved in the Israeli-Arab conflict." (This is a new formula: it does not exclude the PLO if the PLO will accept Security Council resolutions 242 and 338 and renounced violence and terrorism.)

The Shultz initiative has not so far produced results, but it continues, and it seems to be developing a dynamic of its own which some Israeli observers warn—and others hope—could lead in the not-too-distant future to some kind of imposed settlement. Always low-key, without the histrionics of Kissinger, Shultz seems almost reluctantly to have gone further toward a peace negotiation than virtually anyone would have expected. In a few weeks of intensive diplomacy, he has launched a negotiation formula tied to a tight timetable that no one so far has dared to reject, although King Hussein wants it changed here and there and Prime Minister Shamir has made it clear there is much about it he doesn't like. The game being played has been described by the London *Economist* as a bicycle race, where the trick is to pedal as slowly as you can but without toppling over, in the hope that the other cyclists will fall first. It is still possible that no one will. Only Arafat has not mounted a bicycle—only he has rejected the Shultz initiative so far. (Arafat has never missed the chance to lose an opportunity.) President Mubarak of Egypt has welcomed the Shultz initiative. King Hussein of Jordan has seen "many positive elements" in it. Shimon Peres has accepted it wholeheartedly. Even Shamir on his recent visit to Washington, where he had gone to sound out Reagan and *inter alia* launch his upcoming election campaign, has carefully avoided saying "no." And even a clearcut no by Shamir could not have been a last word. Israel's position in Washington is not what it used to be. It is likely to become even more delicate after the U.S. presidential election.

The Shultz initiative is the fifth American attempt to make peace in the Middle East since the 1967 war. Two initiatives were successful (Henry Kissinger's in 1975 and Jimmy Carter's in 1978—both led to the 1979 Egyptian-Israeli peace treaty). Two initiatives failed (William Rogers's in 1970 and Reagan's in 1982); both envisaged considerable territorial concessions by Israel in return for peace. Both were scuttled at a very early stage, at Israel's instigation, by the powerful Jewish lobby in Washington. The Shultz initiative is the first U.S. peace effort in the Middle East that seemed from its outset to be supported by some important members and organizations of the American Jewish community. In years past, these organizations often acted as a pro-Israeli lobby in America; but during the past few weeks some of the most important among them have emerged as, in effect, a pro-American pressure group in Jerusalem, asking Shamir to accept the Shultz plan, urging him to trade peace for territory. Even Morris Abram, on behalf of the presidents of some forty Jewish organizations in the U.S., while publicly defending Israel, is reported to have warned Shamir privately that the tide was turning against Israel in the U.S.

In the meantime, as the uprising in the territories continues, the spiraling effect of riot and repression leads both sides to resort to more and more extreme measures. The leaders of the uprising, whoever they are, are trying to bring the uprising to a new peak. They have successfully enforced mass resignations of policemen and civilian government employees in the territories—with chaotic results. And the Israeli authorities are responding with harsher and more indiscriminate punitive measures: power and telephone lines have been cut to entire villages, and travel has been banned between the West Bank and the Gaza Strip. Both sides are constantly adding fuel to the fires of resentment. In this struggle between unequals, most observers expect the Palestinians to wear out first, though this may take time and many lives. As harder and harder repressive measures are applied in the territories, Israel's international image is tarnished too. Israeli exports to the European Common Market countries are now said to be in real jeopardy.

The gulf dividing Peres and Shamir has widened as a result of the latter's futile attempt in Washington to talk Reagan and Shultz out of the initiative. Both Shamir and Peres are likely to bolt the coalition government any minute now and call for elections. With the scheduled Israeli elections only months away in any event, political calculations rather than acts of statesmanship have been uppermost in the minds of Peres and Shamir, as in the minds of their allies and rivals within their own parties.

After his visit to Washington Shamir's men proudly proclaimed his successes there: even though he had stood up to Shultz and Reagan, the alliance between the two countries is as solid as ever. Peres countered by saying that Israel's problems were not with the U.S. administration but with U.S. public opinion and the U.S. Jewish community. Peres, who ever since his secret meeting with King Hussein in London in April last year has been calling for an international conference, claimed that Shamir's obstructionism had cost Israel a year. If the international conference had taken place last summer, perhaps the uprising would not have broken out. Moreover, the terms now proposed by Shultz with their tight timetable, Peres complained, were tougher than those he had agreed on with Hussein last April. In his heart Peres may well be praying for a solution imposed by the big powers. In early March he told a closed meeting that 1988 in some ways resembled 1948—the year Israel was founded. In the strained silence that followed he added that, as in 1948, in 1988 "Israel's fate will be decided."

10

Intifada: The Palestinian Uprising, II

The Palestinian uprising in the territories occupied by Israel in the 1967 war continues. The declared aim of the uprising, so far, is the early establishment of a Palestinian state. This is still anathema to the parties represented in the Israeli parliament, with the exception of a few back-benchers within Labor and the mini-parties further on the left. And yet, to many observers here, in the universities, in the press, even in the Intelligence community and in the Foreign and in the Defense Ministries, the occupation—now in its twenty-second year—is no longer a practical option either. A new situation seems to be evolving—in the territories, where chaos and civil disobedience have caused the near collapse of the Israeli administration and in the radically changed international climate on the issue of Palestinian rights, which climaxed in the decision last month by the United States to enter into a "substantive dialogue" with the PLO When the uprising broke out, more than a year ago, it was directed in the first place against the Israeli authorities, which for years had treated the inhabitants of Gaza and the West Bank as bargaining chips in a "peace process" that never materialized, denying them the most basic human and political rights. At the same time, the insurrection was a protest against the more extreme elements within the PLO who, one often heard Palestinian intellectuals in the territories say, had merely compounded Palestinian suffering by their sterility, their indiscriminate international terror, and their refusal of all compromise.

By and large, the Palestinians under occupation, including those openly identified with the various factions of the PLO, had always been more conciliatory than those of the Palestinian diaspora. Prominent supporters of the PLO in East Jerusalem, such as Sari Nusseibeh, Hanna Siniora, and Faisal Husseini (often said to be the chief PLO figure in the territories and at this moment under administrative arrest) had publicly endorsed the "two state solution" and had recognized Israel's "right to exist" long before Yasir Arafat finally did so in Geneva in 1988. Arafat was prodded to do so by the American, European, Egyptian, and Saudi-Arabian governments. But on the West Bank, in the Gaza Strip, and in East-Jerusalem most people I have spoken to recently are sure that it was pressure from Palestinians in the territories that finally pushed Arafat to moderate his stand.

Conditions for an uprising in the territories had ripened for years but like most historic turning points, it was triggered—in December 1987—by a freak accident: A fatal traffic collision in Gaza gave rise to wild riots. Rumors soon circulated that it had been caused by agents of the Israeli security service in retaliation for the stabbing of an Israeli the previous week. Wild demonstrations, led by teenagers armed mostly with slingshots and stones, soon spread from the squalid refugee camps of Gaza to the relatively affluent bourgeois urban centers of the West Bank. The three university towns there, Bethlehem, Ramallah, and Nablus, have long been hotbeds of Palestinian national fervor and unrest. The disturbances have since developed into an organized, apparently well-disciplined popular movement run by clandestine local committees strategically coordinated from abroad. In the beginning, they could not have embraced more than a few hundred frustrated, disorganized youngsters. Everything the authorities have since done—in a spiraling cycle of rioting and repression—has tended only to make it a true mass phenomenon.

Hardly a day passes without bloody clashes between Israeli troops and demonstrating Palestinian youngsters. Hardly a day passes without stones or fire-bombs being thrown at army vehicles or at Israeli settlers' cars passing through the West Bank or East Jerusalem. In East Jerusalem alone , according to official police figures published in *Ha'aretz*, during two weeks in December no less than seventeen fire-bombs were thrown on passing buses and police cars. Nadav Shragai, the newspaper's correspondent in Jerusalem wrote that the city, which after 1967 was said to be "reunited" was coming apart at the seams. The average number of violent incidents in East-Jerusalem alone during the past year was "ten a day, three-hundred a month." The situation is worse in the West Bank and very much worse in the Gaza Strip where much of the violence nowadays is guided less by the PLO than by Islamic fanatics. The world seems to have grown used to it. The international press no longer covers many of the clashes. The Israeli press, except when there are fatal casualties, by and large relegates them to the back pages. Most violent clashes are never reported at all. Scenes of protest and repression recur nevertheless almost daily. Demonstrators continue to wave Palestinian flags (a serious offense in the occupied territories), yelling *Falastin Falastin*, or *Rotzim Medina* (Hebrew for "We want a state").

Many of the demonstrators were born after the Israeli occupation began twenty-two years ago and speak more or less fluent Hebrew. The troops—many only a few years older than the rioters—fall on them with truncheons and clubs. The demonstrators aim stones at them with slingshots and occasionally petrol-bombs as well. The troops reply with tear-gas grenades and plastic or live bullets from M-16 automatic rifles. In Nablus and Gaza the walls are frequently covered with Palestinian slogans, disfiguring lichenous growths that cover entire housefronts. The authorities are picking up Palestinians at random in the streets and forcing them to paint the offensive slogans over with white paint. Overnight the slogans are there again. "FOR A FREE PALESTINE," "PLO," "VICTORY IS NEAR." After Arafat's announcement in Geneva that he recognized Israel's "right to exist" the grafitti confronting Israeli soldiers in Ramallah one morning, when I was there, said, in *Hebrew*: "WHAT MORE DO YOU WANT US TO SAY! A tax strike has been in effect in the territories for more than a year. The clandestine leadership has imposed a partial commercial strike. Its rules (businesses to remain open only from 9 A.M. to 12.30 P.M.) are meticulously observed. East Jerusalem and Bethlehem, which are normally overcrowded at this time of the year with Christmas tourists and pilgrims, have been ghost towns for months. The mass resignation of most Palestinian policeman, tax-collectors, and other local employees has left the territories without a police force (crime is said to be rampant) and the Israeli civil administration without manpower and running funds. Government operated social services have collapsed. Palestinian patients are no longer referred, as in the past, to Israeli hospitals. Villagers continue to block access roads. The more remote villages are declared "liberated Palestinian territory." The army usually arrives after a few hours, or days, and is pelted with stones and curses. Severe collective punishments are then imposed, including military orders that forbid farmers to harvest their fields. Mass arrests are made. Telephones and electricity lines are cut off, sometimes for weeks. Men and boys are forced to clear

away the roadblocks and climb high-tension electric poles to remove
Palestinian flags hung up there. The punishment has all been in vain so far.

※

Time and again during the past year the authorities have predicted the
imminent end of the uprising. Time and again events have been proving
them wrong. There have been ups and downs. The *intifada* (literally "resur-
gence" or the "throwing off") as the Palestinians call their uprising, has
continued as before. Most Palestinians insist that it is much more than
"demonstrations." It is said to breed a new "self-awareness," a sense of solidarity and a breaking down of old barriers of class, sex, and age never
before seen here on such a scale. Scope and severity of the punishments
have increased all the time. But the uprising continues. Its imprint upon
Israeli society differs from place to place. For the 80,000 Israeli settlers in
the West Bank and in the Gaza strip daily life has become a nightmare.
Many moved there in response to government-sponsored publicity cam-
paigns promising the good life at prices considerably lower than in Israel
proper. They now feel cheated and betrayed by a government and by an
army all too lenient, in their eyes, toward the rebels, and incapable of ensur-
ing the safety of their children on their school bus. The settlers are constantly threatening to form militias and engage in "punitive actions."

The *intifada* is uppermost in the minds of people in and about Jerusalem.
Jerusalem is a mixed city of some 350,000 Israelis and 150,000 Palestinians.
An invisible wall has risen once again between the two parts of the city.
There is a "geography of fear" here, as in Belfast. Few Israelis cross into East
Jerusalem. The Western Wall, in the heart of the Old City, is often deserted,
even on Sabbaths and holidays. In the bitter words of Teddy Kollek, the lib-
eral mayor, coexistence in the city has died or, at least, collapsed.

Elsewhere, in Israel, few people seem bothered by the uprising. As far as
most Israelis are concerned it takes places on a different planet. Most Israelis
do not go near the occupied territories, anyway. To the few who do newspaper ads offer automatic rifles, digital car telephones, and crash- or bulletproof plexiglass car windows at discount prices. Settlers in the territories who
commute every day to and from their jobs in Israel often travel in convoys.
Public buses to their new settlements are routinely escorted by jeeploads of
armed troops. When firebombs are thrown, the troops usually shoot to kill.
When suspected perpetrators are caught, dead or alive, army sappers move in
within hours and blow up the family home as the TV cameras roll. The innocent relatives, the children and women who are left roofless, ululate and wail.

The dynamiting of homes is done under a still valid British emergency regulation promulgated in 1946 to put down Jewish terrorists. As a result, 105 private homes have been demolished and 45 have been sealed so far by military order; 32 suspected ringleaders of the uprising have been deported to Lebanon; the same fate now awaits 27 more. Like actors in a recurrent tragedy—a tragedy, however, in which no catharsis is ever in the offering—the young rebels and the soldiers alternate on center stage. The former continue to demonstrate and to riot; the latter continue to move in after them, a bit flat footed, sweating profusely in their heavy gear, armed to the teeth, and put them down.

It is rarely for long. Some of the mass refugee camps in the Gaza Strip were under curfew last year for a total of 135 days. The city of Nablus, with its 120,000 inhabitants the largest on the West Bank, was under curfew for a total of 72 days. Villages nearby were under what is called "intermittent military closure" for months in order to pressure the inhabitants to surrender wanted suspects. One curfew imposed last year on the refugee camp of Gelasun, near Ramallah, lasted for forty consecutive days. The curfews, the mass arrests, the economic hardship, the collapse of public services, the intimidations, the beatings, the gunfire and the deportations, have been of no avail so far. Some 20,000 Palestinians have been imprisoned during 1988 for various lengths of time in connection with the uprising. Of these, approximately 5,600 are still detained—most of them without trial—in various jails and in a specially built prison camp in the Negev desert. (It has been estimated that on the average, out of every five Palestinian males over the age of fifteen in the territories, an average of two have been imprisoned for political reasons during the past ten years). The number of Palestinians shot dead during the past year can only be estimated. According to an official Israeli army spokesmen last November, the number of Palestinians killed during the first year of the uprising was 234. A few days later the deputy Chief of Staff of the Israeli army spoke of 301 dead. According to the Associated Press the true figure at that time was 318. According to *Al Haq*, a Palestinian human rights monitoring group at Ramallah, and an affiliate of the International Commission of Jurists in Geneva, 410 Palestinians have been killed by Israeli troops during the first year of the uprising and more than 20,000 wounded. During the same period two Israeli soldiers, two Israeli women and three children were killed by the rioters; 402 Israeli civilians and 730 soldiers were wounded, almost all of them by stones.

With the exception of isolated protests, public opinion in Israel has not so far been aroused by the brutalities that are reported almost daily in the press, nor by the demolition of homes one sees regularly on television or by any of the other forms of collective punishment meted out almost daily. With hundreds of Palestinians shot dead by the troops and a more than reasonable suspicion that at least some were the result of criminal acts, a reporter for the local newsweekly *Koteret Roshit* recently claimed that according to army sources only one soldier, a recent immigrant from Ethiopia, has so far been found guilty of manslaughter but was set free for "mental" reasons. Only two newspapers *Ha'aretz* and the *Jerusalem Post* have a policy of identifying by their names Palestinians shot dead. In the other (mass-circulation) newspapers and on the government-controlled television and radio Palestinian casualties are usually referred to anonymously as "Arabs" or "locals." News editors on the state-controlled radio and television are under orders to refer, if possible, to "riots" and "disorders" only. The words "uprising" or "intifada" are avoided. Television reporters are not allowed to initiate interviews with Palestinians in the territories to hear their side of the argument. When the PLO National Council recently met in Algiers, news editors of Israel Television succumbed to a request by the Defense Ministry not to broadcast any parts of Yasir Arafat's speech declaring the establishment of a "state of Palestine." Since Palestinians on the West Bank could have seen and heard the speech on Jordan Television, which is received throughout the territory, the army cut off West Bank electricity that night. Some Israelis console themselves with the thought that in the neighboring Arab countries a similar popular uprising would have been dealt with much more harshly. Many seem able to live with the excesses, crudities, and downright atrocities they hear and read about daily. Most seem to assume the outrages affect only Palestinians in the territories and will never become the norm in Israel proper. A. B. Yehoshua, one of Israel's finest novelists, was so upset last fall with this complacency, he told an interviewer that he was now able to understand how so many Germans could say after the Second World War that they had never seen or heard of the concentration camps. The statement struck a nerve and elicited a storm of protests.

Beaten, teargassed, and shot at for more than a year the protesters have nevertheless not yet become discouraged. Though they have not, or not yet, achieved anything tangible on the ground, and perhaps never will, the uprising goes on. Last December was the bloodiest month so far with 31 killed and more than 400 wounded, according to unofficial figures reported at year's end in *The Jerusalem Post*. Some of the dead last year were children under ten and men over seventy years old. There have also been reports of pregnant women who aborted and babies who died of asphyxiation, the result of being too directly exposed to tear gas grenades fired into closed rooms. Hardly a day passes without complaints of savage behavior by the troops, of fifteen-year-old boys being thrown off speeding army cars, of heads being knocked against steel shutters, of the beating of innocent bystanders or, during the frequent house-to-house searches, of the wanton smashing of furniture, TV sets, solar heaters, and window panes.

The complaints are almost invariably dismissed by the authorities as exaggerations or "isolated exceptions to proper military norms." The uprising inevitably upsets routine army training schedules, and is known to have caused problems of morale among younger conscripts. Fifty-four soldiers have received jail sentences since the beginning of the uprising for refusing to serve in the occupied territories (an unusually high figure for Israel where conscientious objection, except during the Lebanon war, has been almost unknown). The real number of conscientious objectors is said to be considerably higher since many manage to evade service in the territories thanks to sympathetic commanding officers. Reservists too are now liable to be called up for periods of up to 60 days annually and serve as day and night patrols in the debris-strewn streets of Gaza or Nablus. The number of soldiers now on duty in the West Bank is said to be more than three times the number needed in 1967 to conquer it during the Six Day War.

Given the enormous imbalance of forces the failure so far to put down the uprising is remarkable and the subject of some speculation. Ariel Sharon, who lost his job as Defense Minister in 1982 after the massacres at Sabra and Shatilla, has been claiming all along that the disturbances could be put down in a matter of days, but that the present Defense Minister, Yitzhak Rabin, is too inept or too scared or too "pro Arab" to do so. Other right wing politicians have suggested demolishing entire villages, even towns, and deporting the inhabitants to Lebanon or Jordan. A main reason why the government has not so far resorted to even harsher methods of repression is generally thought to be a fear of further antagonizing Israel's friends abroad, especially in the United States.

But fear of adverse reactions in the United States is not the only reason why tanks and machine guns have not been brought in so far, or why 32 and not 3,000 suspected militants have been deported, as Sharon might have done. Another reason is the mood of the army. Senior officers are said to be extremely unhappy with the army's new role as a riot police force in the territories. They have been actively lobbying the press and the Knesset to press their point of view on anyone ready to listen. The present General Staff is said to be uncommonly full of dovish generals. The officer now commanding all Israeli troops on the West Bank, General Amram Mitzna, happens to be the same man who in 1982 resigned his military post as head of Israel's War College, in protest against the war in Lebanon. In a closed meeting on the West Bank General Mitzna was recently accosted by angry orthodox settlers who accused him of "failing" to put down the uprising. According to a report in *Ha'aretz* he answered that it was "impossible" to put the uprising down. The army was not at fault, he said. Israel as a whole was at fault in not foreseeing for twenty years that the situation in the territories could not continue.

Several senior officers are of the opinion that retention of the entire West Bank is no longer as essential for Israel's defense as it might have been in the past. According to this view, modern electronic surveillance methods and weapons technologies make withdrawal from most of the West Bank strategically and tactically feasible. The army sees its role as training for the defense of Israel's frontiers and airspace; this you don't do by spending more and more time bashing teenagers in the streets of Gaza. The upper echelons of the army are said to feel that in the absence of some political breakthrough the *intifada* is here to stay. A senior officer recently described the *intifada* as a deeply entrenched "state of mind." Anyone who thinks that the old status quo can be restored, he added, "just doesn't know what he is talking about." He added that in his opinion there is no purely military solution; there can be only a political solution to it.

Defense Minister Rabin said the same publicly, even as he bullishly insisted, that as a matter of principle the rioters must be "taught a lesson" and force must be met with "force, power, beatings." Brigadier-General Ephraim Sneh, who until recently headed the Civil Administration on the West Bank, reflected a widespread view within the upper levels of the army when he told governors of the Jerusalem Foundation that in the *intifada* the Palestinians have discovered the power of their weakness and the Israelis the weakness of their strength. And the army chief of staff, General Dan Shomron, told a Knesset committee last fall that the long-range effects on the Palestinians in the territories of the present military measures may well turn out more dangerous for Israel than the very uprising these measures are meant to suppress.

❋

In the middle of all this, 2.3 million Israelis (79 percent of all eligible voters) went to the polls and decided, well—nothing. It was not for any lack of choice. The elections took place at a high point in the rebellion. Foreign Minister Shimon Peres insisted all along that the uprising might have been prevented if Prime Minister Shamir had not vetoed an agreement with

King Hussein of Jordan in April 1987 to attend a UN-sponsored peace conference together with a "Jordanian-Palestinian" delegation. Shamir's veto, Peres charged, had "murdered" the peace process. Much of the election campaign was over the question of remaining in the occupied territories or of withdrawing from at least some parts. Labor campaigned for withdrawals in return for peace. Likud campaigned for the retention of all the territories for reasons of national defense (the pre-1967 borders invited aggression) and of historical manifest destiny (the territories are part of the land God is said to have promised the Jews in the Bronze Age). The most Likud was ready to offer the Palestinian population of approximately 1.5 million was the limited municipal autonomy they have been rejecting for years. Labor reasoning was both negative (the high birth rates among Palestinians may soon give them a majority within "Greater Israel") and positive (Israel will not in the long run be able to remain a Jewish as well as a democratic state). Labor recruited an impressive array of well-known defense experts as well as a number of retired generals who tried to assure the public on television that the West Bank and Gaza were not vital for the country's defense. Even in the absence of peace Israel was said to be strong enough to defend itself against any serious danger from that direction.

Despite the usual caveats and equivocations the choice put to the voters by the two parties was unmistakable. As in 1984, the great territorial controversy that has divided the country for so many years was again left undecided. The three dramatic events which during the previous year had changed the entire picture—the uprising in the territories, the decision by King Hussein of Jordan to relinquish his claims on the West Bank, the peace offensive of the PLO—did not really move Israeli opinion at all. It remained basically what it had been before. A third of the seats in parliament went to Labor and a third to Likud. The rest fell to a dozen or so right-wing, left-wing, and religious mini-parties. The election returns illuminated the difficulty so many Israelis—only two generations away from the Nazi Holocaust—still have in internalizing the country's military strength. There is a dramatic contradiction between the image so many Israelis have of themselves and the image of Israel shared by most foreign observers and a good number of Israeli generals and defense experts. The former have a tendency to see (or have been manipulated to see) Israel as a weak, highly vulnerable state every day facing the possibility of another Holocaust. The latter see Israel as a powerful country, defended by one of the world's best, most effective armies, an air force and tank corps equal—some say superior—to those of England or France and in possession of its own tactical and strategic nuclear weapons, medium-range missiles and a sophisticated space programs.

The election returns reflected once again a basic defect within the Israeli political system, precipitating a feeling of intense constitutional crisis. The Israeli parliament is perhaps the only one in the democratic world today which is 100 percent proportional. The entire country is one constituency. Within that constituency the vote is for party lists who are assigned a number of seats in the Knesset in proportion to the votes they receive. The system has never accorded any party a clear majority and so has always lead to the establishment of inherently instable coalition governments. The air of constitutional crisis was compounded this time by the unexpected success at the polls of the fundamentalist, orthodox, and ultra-orthodox parties. They increased their strength by almost a third, gaining 18 seats in the house (15 percent of the total). The increase came in large part from slum areas and development towns inhabited by immigrants from Arab countries who in the past had voted Labor or Likud.

The new fundamentalist vote was successfully solicited among others by the voodoo-like invocations of "miracle" wielding hassidic rabbis. One of them was described by his fanatic following as no less than the "messiah still in disguise." The new Sephardi fundamentalist party *Shas* campaigned under the slogan "One Sephardi women who kisses the Torah is superior to 40 (presumably) Ashkenazi professors who teach that man is descended from the ape." The success of *Shas* at at the polls suggested that one reason for the growth of religious fundamentalism in Israel was similar to that often given for the rise of fundamentalist Islam in the neighbouring Arab countries: a growing disillusion with politics. The conventional political poles of Left and Right are found wanting. Neither appears capable of resolving crucial political and economic problems. The current vocabulary of ethnic resentment and ethnic self-assertion in Israel seemed to have stimulated this process. Thirty years after the end of mass immigration to Israel the newcomers and their offspring feel free of the political Tamanny Halls that had held them captive for so long. Their independent impact now affects the political culture as never before. The latest election results made one think that in some ways Israel is on the way to becoming a Third World country. Shiva Naipaul once observed that becoming part of the Third World was, to some degree, a psychological process, a quasi religious conversion. In Israel these days one senses this process. It is a state of mind and it seems to spread like an an infection.

After fifty-two days of outlandish intrigues and elaborate plots by the two major parties to outfox each other, yet another grand national coalition was finally formed by the two arch-foes with Yitzhak Shamir as Prime Minister and Shimon Peres as Minister of Finance. The establishment of this new coalition reflected a new—perhaps balancing—power in public Israeli life: the power of the American Jewish community. Until quite recently, American Jews had, by and large, supported every Israeli government or policy. In the aftermath of the November elections this was no longer so. Both Likud and Labor could have formed narrow, if unstable governments of their own. Both parties made clear that this was their first choice. Both were more than fed up with the joint cabinet of 1984–1988. The religious parties were ready to join either in a narrow coalition depending on who was the highest bidder. Their central demand was that the famous Law of Return be amended in a way that would have delegitimized all but Orthodox Jews, in particular converts to Reform or Conservative Judaism. Shamir was already committed in writing to push the proposed amendment through the Knesset and Peres was on the verge of doing the same. They were stopped short by a storm of protests among Jews in the United States. Planeloads of prominent American Jews descended on Jerusalem, dignitaries of all sorts representing every possible organization, major donors, fundraisers, rabbis, lay leaders, and spokesmen on behalf of the powerful Jewish-Israeli lobby in Washington.

All gave dire warnings that Israel would cause itself irreparable harm if the amendment were passed. Nothing remotely like this had ever happened before. Major contributors to the United Jewish Appeal and investors in Israel Government Bonds threatened to stop, or at least, seriously cut their annual commitments. They were joined by the Israeli ambassador in Washington who reported to Jerusalem that Israel risked alienating its closest friends and supporters not only within the Jewish community but in Congress as well. The unprecedented vehemence of these protests and threats made the formation of another grand coalition almost inevitable. For the first time in Israel's history American Jews had openly and successfully intervened in Israeli political life. A columnist in *Ha'aretz* mocked that "Max and Morris" had dictated the shape of the new Israeli government (a reference to Max Fischer, past chairman and Morris Abram, current chairman of the Conference of Presidents of American Jewish Organizations, both of whom had rushed to Jerusalem to protest). Another columnist in the same paper predicted—perhaps a little wishfully—that the intervention will not stop there but will encourage American Jews from now on to try influence Israeli decisions on territories and peace talks as well.

The sudden American decision to open talks with the PLO strengthened Peres's and Shamir's hands against opponents within their own parties. The American decision had taken everyone by surprise. It enabled Shamir and Peres to argue that this was clearly no moment to antagonize Israel's mainstay in the United States. Joining forces once again seemed the only alternative to mortally offending American Jews. Peres was accused of betraying his voters by agreeing to form another government with those he had just called "murderers of peace." He defended himself by saying that far from betraying anybody he was merely trying to save Likud from its worst impulses. In the former grand coalition the two major parties had cancelled each other out on most questions relating to peace or war. The new grand coalition was almost a clone of the old. What new peace initiatives, if any, could emerge from this government was anybody's guess. With regard to the latest Palestinian moves it left nothing to guesswork. Shamir dismissed Arafat's renunciation of terror as "a monumental lie" and his recognition of Israel as a "diabolic scheme" to destroy Israel in stages. Peres's rejection was less dramatic but equally firm. A few Labor backbenchers dissented and argued in favor of negotiations with the PLO So did prominent voices in the press, in the arts and in the academic community. But these were minority views of no immediate political consequence. The novelist Amos Oz said that far from being a threat to Israel, Arafat's recognition was a great Israeli victory. Mordechai Gazit, a retired general and former head of Israel army intelligence announced that if he were Prime Minister he would immediately invite Arafat to come to Jerusalem for talks, as Sadat had in 1977.

The new government's official "Guidelines" made clear that for the time being this was a mere pipedream. They reiterated Peres's and Shamir's absolute refusal to deal with the PLO or permit the establishment of a Palestinian state. Jordan was declared the only legitimate partner for negotiations. The only concession to the Palestinians in the territories was an offer to "participate in the determination of their future." It was certain to be rejected in this form. Shamir and Peres did hold out a vague possibility of elections in the territories but on condition that the uprising first come to an end. It sounded like the classic fusion of illusion and tragedy well-known since Algeria. During a rebellion negotiation is always thought of as appeasement to be avoided at all cost. But as soon as order is restored there is no need any more to deal, and so on and so on until it is too late.

11

Peace Now

Edward Gibbon said of Jerusalem, a city surrounded by a formidable medieval wall, that she derived her reputation from the number and importance of her "memorable sieges." Gibbon was not the first, or the last, to wonder how in the common discourse of three religions Jerusalem ever became the proverbial City of Peace. For much of her long history she has been a city of contention and strife. The historic core, the so-called Old City, with its holy places, its renowned synagogues, churches, mosques, and covered bazaars filled with religious and patriotic kitsch, is today surrounded by a modern city of some 150,000 Palestinians and 300,000 Israelis. The grim medieval walls—lovingly restored by the Israeli municipality after the 1967 war, when the Old City was taken by Israel—bristle with battlements, bastions, and escarps and special troops armed with submachine guns and walkie-talkies forever on the lookout for Palestinian terrorists.

This unlikely site was the scene recently of an event that astounded many who attended it. It was a pleasant Saturday afternoon between Hannukah and New Year. Yet another peace initiative had just run aground in the seemingly never shifting sands of the Near East. But here, for an hour or so, some thirty thousand Israelis and Palestinians, held hands and formed a human chain almost three miles long all around the Old City walls, chanting: WE WANT PEACE! WE WANT PEACE! In her long history of religious and communal

strife Jerusalem had never seen anything like it. It was the largest demonstration in the history of the city, the first ever jointly attended, by Palestinians and Israelis. Jerusalem in recent years has become a city with "no-go
areas" like Belfast. Mutual fears and hatreds between Arabs and Jews have
never been more salient than in the two and a half years since the outbreak
of the Palestinian uprising. It was staggering to see thousands of them suddenly joining hands in a common cause. The weather, as in one of those old
fashioned novels where the mood in the sky is supposed to reflect the mood
on earth, was unusually fine for the time of year.

The surrounding hills and valleys—they are still known by their ancient
ghostly names, Hill of Evil Counsel, Hill of Offense, Hell's Valley—gleamed
in the winter sun. The ramparts stood out sharply in the soft light as in an
etching. Behind them rose the domes and towers of the Old City where the
sanctities overlap and all extremes of creed and nationality intersect but
never meet. ("Jerusalem" wrote the tenth-century Arab geographer Muqad-
dasi, "is a golden basin filled with scorpions"). Everywhere around the ramparts, Palestinians and Israelis, holding hands, were singing WE SHALL LIVE IN
PEACE. There were people of all classes, all ages, children and old couples with
little olive branches pinned to their lapels; there were students and professors from the Hebrew University at Jerusalem and from the Palestinian university at Bir Zeit, Muslim ulemas, Reform rabbis, and priests of the Greek
and Syrian Orthodox church as well as a few hundred Italian, Dutch, and
French tourists who had traveled to Jerusalem especially for the occasion in
chartered aircraft. Colored balloons floated in the sunlit air inscribed 1990:
TIME FOR PEACE in Hebrew and Arabic. Teenagers donned white T-shirts with
stickers saying SHALOM and SALAAM. Some held up placards calling for peace
between two states for two independent peoples. Loudspeakers mounted on
trucks played Israeli and Palestinian folk music.

In a city haunted like few others by its past, poisoned by demons of
nationalist and religious extremism, the joint peace demonstration was an
unexpected, almost unbelievable, sight. The police force in the city had been
nearly doubled for the occasion. For a week or so before the joint demonstration right wing Israeli politicians had been clamoring that it was "sub-
versive," even financed and organized by terrorist organizations abroad.
The government had also taken a dim view of the demonstration but had
been unable or unwilling to outlaw it. Armed policemen were posed every
ten or twenty yards along the human chain facing the participants. The
demonstration remained orderly and calm until, toward the end, Arab
teenagers outside Herod's Gate at the northeastern corner of the Old City
started a commotion, shouting "Palestinian nationalist slogans," according

to the police. The police had been on edge throughout and, according to reports later in the local press, openly hostile towards the participants.

A report later in the week in *Ha'aretz*, noted that the police build-up had been "offensive, not defensive from the start." The policemen had not been issued with shields, as is common in a riot situation, but with guns and pistols. When the teenagers started shouting "nationalist Palestinian slogans" the police overreacted. They intervened massively with tear gas and water canons and wooden clubs not only against the shouting teenagers but against a much wider segment in the human chain. At one point along the north-wall I saw policemen firing rubber bullets at a crowd of middle aged men and women singing "We Want Peace." Elsewhere around the Old City the human chain continued in blissful ignorance of what was happening between Herod's and Damascus Gate, where two or three thousand people were trapped in clouds of tear gas between mounted police wielding wooden clubs. Some thirty people were left wounded. A Italian woman who was watching the commotion through the window in the hall of a nearby hotel lost an eye, the result, apparently, of glass shattered by plastic bullets or by a water cannon. Another Italian, a deputy of the European parliament was later quoted on television as saying that if that was how the police treated foreign visitors it was easy to imagine how brutal they might be with their own.

❋

The human chain around the Old City was the brainchild of a mainstream Israeli civic body called Peace Now. It is not the only extraparliamentarian protest movement in Israel today; there are at least two dozen others. But it is the oldest and by far the largest with roots in traditional elite groups of Israeli society. Founded in 1978, it is still without any formal membership or professional staff. Its main strongholds are in the universities, the arts, the kibbutzim, the media, the army reserves, and in the middle and upper middle classes of European origin in the big cities. The movement was launched a few months after President Sadat's dramatic visit to Jerusalem. Its indirect trigger was an open letter to Prime Minister Menachem Begin signed by some 350 reserve officers in the Israeli army and air force. All were men still serving annual stints of up to six weeks in the reserves, often in elite combat units; a few were bearers of the highest decorations for bravery in action. In their letter they warned the Prime Minister against establishing more Israeli settlements in the territories occupied in the 1967 war since that might undermine the historic opportunity to resolve the century-long armed conflict between Jews and Arabs, opened by Sadat's initiative. The signatories told the Prime Minister they preferred a smaller Israel at peace with its neighbors to a "Greater Israel" at permanent war. They wanted him to know that any other policy would arouse in them, citizen-soldiers serving in the army reserves, "doubts as to the justice of our cause . . . Real security can be achieved only in peace. The real strength of the Israeli army grows out of the citizen-soldiers' identification with state policy."

The appeal was meant to be a one-time effort. Quickly dubbed in the press as the "officers' letter" it scandalized a country traditionally conformist in matters of military security. The signatories were immediately attacked by pro-government figures as "traitors" (by Interior Minister Joseph Burg) as "primitives" (by Moshe Arens, today Israel's foreign minister) and as "paid" hirelings of the CIA (by Roni Millo, today Minister of Labor and Social Welfare). Simcha Ehrlich, Begin's Finance Minister accused the signatories of planning a "coup d'état." One Knesset member charged them with spreading a "peace disease" in the body politic. Dr Eldad Scheib, a well-known right-wing intellectual and translator of Nietzsche's *Thus Spake Zarathustra* decried what he called the fashionable addiction to "Nowism," a mark of narcissist decadence, he said, since true pleasure invariably grew out of "delaying" satisfaction. Former foreign minister Abba Eban and former premier Golda Meir, on the other hand, applauded the officers for their letter.

Out of the resultant debate a mass movement grew almost inadvertently—without offices or officeholders and without a single paid official—a vocal, often highly visible, extraparliamentary body, and a remarkable capacity to arouse public opinion. Prime Minister Begin on one occasion confessed that when the peace negotiations at Camp David with President Sadat broke down, as they often did, he would remember the peace demonstrators back home. Thousands had accompanied him to the airport on his way to America with placards that read: "Go in peace, and come back with peace." "They were often on my mind," he once said. Although launched by a group of young reserve officers—all were males in their twenties or early thirties—Peace Now quickly attracted both older and younger men and women—soon there would be more women than men—professionals, students and university people, members of kibbutzim, people in the mass media and the arts. It was supported entirely by member contributions, a "single issue" movement—the issue was Peace. Its activists believed that after four Arab Israeli wars peace was within reach not only with Egypt but with Jordan and the Palestinians as well; the price was a readiness for withdrawal from territories occupied in the 1967 war.

Tens of thousands attended the first Peace Now rallies and protest marches. The peak was in 1982 when a Peace Now sponsored mass meeting outside the Tel-Aviv town hall to protest the massacre at Sabra and Shatilla brought out nearly 400,000. Every ninth Israeli was there. The government had been refusing to appoint an inquiry commission to investigate the massacre on the grounds that, as Prime Minister Begin put it, when "goyim kill goyim" Jews should not be held responsible. After the mass rally the government relented. An official commission found Defense Minister Ariel Sharon indirectly responsible. Sharon was forced to resign.

Peace Now was founded in Jerusalem, and is still centered in Jerusalem because its main activists happen to live there. This is probably no accident. Unlike Tel-Aviv, Israel's largest city on the Mediterranean coast, Jerusalem is a mixed Israeli-Palestinian city and in the very eye of the storm. In the coastal plain the majority of Israelis still live almost unaffected by the Arab-Israeli conflict. In Jerusalem it is impossible to avoid it. For months during the bloody aftermath of the invasion of Lebanon Peace Now militants maintained a permanent vigil outside Begin's official residence on Balfour Street to protest the continuing bloodshed and demand the immediate withdrawal of Israeli forces. Each day they held up large wooden boards inscribed with the number of Israeli casualties to date. The number grew. Several times a day Begin passed by that placard. It was impossible to ignore it. Soon after the number passed the five hundred mark Begin resigned. He has never explained his decision but the persistence of the vigilantes with their morbid signs is often cited as a factor that may have contributed to it. (Begin, in self imposed house-arrest since 1983 and apparently in a state of deep depression, has remained behind shuttered windows ever since, refusing to leave his house, meet with, or talk on the telephone to, anybody except closest relatives and friends).

Extraparliamentary movements usually have short lifespans. The relative longevity of Peace Now has often been commented on. It may reflect a deeper malaise in a country where "consensus" has been a political fetish for years: Abba Eban once defined consensus as that which "many people say in chorus but do not believe as individuals." The resort to extraparliamentary action on the left as well as on the right may be the result of a flaw within a political system that never produces clear-cut majorities and where the main issues are discussed in double-talk because the two main parties are tempted to share the spoils of power within wall to wall national coalitions. Extraparliamentary protests movements have emerged on the far right as well but remain smaller. According to a recent study by Professor S. Lehman-Wilzig of Bar Ilan University near Tel-Aviv, there has been a fivefold rise in the number of demonstrations in Israel since 1960. The great increase is due to a feeling that "there are no other means for a citizen to express his opinions to the authorities."

❋

The most trying days for Peace Now came soon after the Lebanon war when one of its leading activists, a young graduate student named Emil Grunzweig, was killed by a right-wing fanatic who had thrown a hand grenade into an anti-war demonstration in Jerusalem. The murderer was apprehended and received a life sentence. "We always knew there was a price to pay," Tsali Reshef, today a Jerusalem corporation lawyer, who had helped draft the original "officers letter" in 1977, told me. "But we did not think it was lives." After Grunzweig's death Peace Now grew more radical. The polite, almost diffident style of the original "officers' letter" gave way to bolder protests. The demonstrators now protested the indiscriminate bombing of targets in Lebanon from the air. Peace Now had always opposed the establishment of more Israeli settlements in the occupied West Bank and the Gaza Strip; it now addressed itself increasingly to the growing violation of human rights in the territories. Peace Now demonstrators protested the practice of administrative detention without trial and the imposition of collective punishments—the most extreme being the demolition of the homes of suspects even before trial. "Don't be complacent! Don't stand aside!" Israelis were urged in their leaflets and posters protesting human rights violations.

"Demolition of family homes is a barbaric punishment," Professor Galia Golan, a Hebrew University sovietologist and veteran Peace Now activist told me. "Administrative detention without trial is just as bad," she added."You are taken out of your bed in the middle of the night. They throw a hood over your head and lead you away. Then they throw you into an over-crowded cell for practically indefinite periods without being charged, without trial, without even being told what you are accused of." Before the PLO recognized Israel and renounced terror in 1988 Peace Now had generally voiced support for the rights of the Palestinian people to a "national existence." After 1988, it called on Israel to "talk peace with the PLO now" and agree to the establishment of a Palestinian state next to Israel. Close to 100,000 demonstrators attended the rally in Tel-Aviv where this appeal was launched. "Let's change course now" said a recent Peace Now appeal for which it was soliciting signatures all over Israel. "The violent events in the territories prove that only a political settlement (with the

Palestinians) will free us from the vicious circle of violence—the result of our continued domination over one and a half million Palestinians. Let us act now before it is too late."

Last fall Peace Now militants staged another vigil outside Prime Minister Shamir's home to protest the daily death toll in the occupied territories. It stood there for several months. Once again, as in 1983, a large placard was displayed with the current number of Palestinians shot dead by Israeli troops in the occupied territories. (At year's end the number of Palestinians killed by Israeli troops since the beginning of the intifada was 609 , according to the Israeli Information Center for Human Rights in the Occupied Territories, including 136 children. Forty were under the age of twelve.

"In the West Bank and in Gaza, Israel finds itself in the situation of a classical colonial power," Avishai Margalit, a philosophy professor at the Hebrew University of Jerusalem and a member of the current Peace Now leadership group told me. "We must make peace with the Palestinians and get out of there as soon as possible." On the day before we met, Prime Minister Shamir had declared that he was ready to talk to anybody, even to the devil, but not to the men of the PLO. "Peace you negotiate with enemies," Margalit said, "otherwise there would be no need for it. Rather than question the legitimacy of the P.L.O we should put its sincerity to the test."

Among Peace Now's main spokesmen during the past ten years have been some of the country's best known writers (Amos Oz, A. B. Yehoshua), a former air force general, a retired army brigadier, leading actors and actresses (one was Hanna Meron, herself the victim, in 1970, of a Palestinian terrorist attack on the passengers of an Israeli airliner at Munich airport), a former Director General of the Foreign Ministry, a president of the National Academy and of the Weizmann Institute of Science. The movement has attracted prominent university professors, including the economists Michael Bruno, the current governor of the Bank of Israel and Yoram Ben Porath at present rector of the Hebrew University. Ben Porath wrote several of Peace Now's best known pamphlets and slogans. Abba Eban, the former foreign minister, has helped raise funds for Peace Now in the United States. A few years ago Eban and a group of European and Israeli parliamentarians nominated Peace Now for the Nobel Prize. "Peace Now has made a difference," Eban told me recently. "They help retain a measure of sanity in this country . . . they have stepped in, vigorously, where Labor [Eban's own party] tended to fail because of short-sightedness and indecision. Labor leaders resemble Hamlet," Eban said, "except in the felicity of their language." They were like Molière's Don Juan who promised marriage to five or six women and had to avoid being pinned down by any of them. They followed "the drumbeat of political opportunism rather than the voice of conscience."

When Peace Now first came into being its establishment was warmly greeted in the United States by Nobel Prize winners Saul Bellow and Kenneth Arrow, among others. In the United States and in several European countries there are now supporting chapters of Peace Now. I recently spoke to Mark Rosenblum, a political scientist at Brooklyn College who coordinates some twenty Friends of Peace Now chapters in the United States and Canada. "In our publications," he said, "we tell Jewish community leaders in America that they can serve Israel better by criticizing than by not criticizing her." When the first chapters were set up in America, according to Rosenblum, he received so many threats from Jewish Defense League militants and other fanatics he felt constrained for a time to open his mail with a screening device. Rosenblum cited recent polls that seem to indicate that among American Jewish leaders 80 percent now favor Israeli withdrawal from occupied territories in return for peace, 60 percent support negotiations with the PLO, and 51 percent, the establishment of a Palestinian state.

When Allen Ginsberg toured Israel in 1988, on a visit sponsored by the U.S. State Department, he was asked again and again to read his 1974 poem "Jaweh and Allah Battle," and he finally read it a Peace Now rally in Tel-Aviv, attended by some 80,000 people. The poem, written soon after the Yom Kippur war, still encapsulated much of the current tragedy and madness

Jaweh with Atom Bomb
Allah cuts throats of infidels . . .

HITLER AND STALIN SENT ME HERE!
WEIZMANN & BENGURION SENT ME HERE!
NASSER AND SADAT SENT ME HERE!
ARAFAT SENT ME HERE! MESSIAH SENT ME HERE!
Buchenwald sent me here! Vietnam sent me here!
Mylai sent me here! Lidice sent me here!
My mother sent me here!
I WAS BORN HERE IN ISRAEL, Arab
circumcised, my father had a coffee shop in Jerusalem One day the
soldiers came & told me to walk down road
    my hands up walk away leave my house business forever!

JAWEH AND ALLAH SENT ME HERE!

❋

Peace Now has grown more radical in recent years but it is still not a protest movement in the American mode during the Vienam war. It opposes the government but its activists don't burn draft cards or national flags. They insist they are patriots. They have not until now advocated draft dodging, though one of the leaders, the historian Mordechai Bar On, a colonel in the army reserve and a former Knesset deputy, now says he "understands" and even "sympathizes" with reservists and recruits who go to prison rather than serve in the occupied territories shooting children who throw stones at them. The number of reservists sentenced to prison for refusing to serve in the occupied territories reached one hundred early in March, including one who received five consecutive prison sentences continuing to refuse his call-up order. He was not an "intellectual" like most of the others but a masseur. After his fifth conviction the army relented and posted him to guard duty outside Jerusalem. Many of these refuseniks were affiliated with another Israeli protest movement named Yesh Gvul (a Hebrew pun that means both "enough is enough" and "there is a border here"). Yesh Gvul offers legal aid and some financial assistance through a pacifist foundation based in Berkeley, California. Yesh Gvul recently induced Amnesty International to recognize as "prisoners of conscience" not only convinced pacifists but also those imprisoned for "selective" or "partial" refusal to serve in an army.

As Amnesty International now puts it, one's reasons for objecting to conscription can be other than total pacifism. Political reasons to refuse service in a particular conflict, or in a particular place, are equally legitimate, according to Amnesty International. The relatively low number of soldiers who have gone to jail for refusing to serve in the occupied territories, has been cited by official spokesmen as proof that the phenomenon of "selective refusal" is insignificant. The real number of refuseniks, however, is widely thought to be much higher. A study published recently in the Tel-Aviv daily Yediot Aharonot highlighted what it called the "grey refusal," which never reaches the courts and public knowledge. For every convicted refusenik, said the paper, there are ten "grey refuseniks" who avoid reserve duty in the territories in tacit connivance with sympathetic commanding officers. For every "grey refusenik," said the paper, there are still another ten who manage the same result by feigning illness or going abroad for a few days, to nearby Cyprus or Egypt, in anticipation of the expected arrival of their call-up. As the Palestinian uprising entered its third year, the mood among young recruits might also be gauged by a sudden rise in the number of suicides. Twice as many recruits killed themselves in 1989 than in 1988. I asked a well known Peace Now veteran if he planned to do his annual stint as a reservist in a paratrooper brigade. He shrugged: "Do I have a choice?"

"In the territories?"

"It's only been once so far. Let's hope it won't be again."

"And if you are called up again?"

"I'll try and argue them out of it. But I don't think I'd refuse. I don't believe refusing to go serves our cause. I'll certainly refuse to obey orders that are manifestly illegal—that's my duty under the prevailing law. I'll try and behave like a Mensch."

Yesh Gvul and other more radical dissident groups often mock and occasionally criticize Peace Now activists for continuing to serve in the territories. During the Lebanon war Yesh Gvul sometimes reviled the men of Peace Now for feeling they must first march into Beirut as good disciplined soldiers before they come out to demonstrate outside Begin's home against war. During that war, Simon Avidan, a retired general and a legendary figure during Israel's war of independence, said he was proud of the draft dodgers who followed the call of conscience: "Our soldiers are not like German soldiers who were told to obey blindly."

The issue still dominates the debate between the various protest groups. "We will not at this stage advocate draft dodging" said Bar-On, who himself served in Lebanon during the 1982 war. Bar-On was fifty-four years old at the time. He had been assigned to accompany prominent foreign politicians and columnists to the Lebanese front. "I gave them the official line about that war," Bar-On told me. "Then I would tell them what I myself thought about it." Perhaps only in the Israeli army would a well-known peacenik like Bar-On be assigned such a task. When the fact became public, the hawkish chairman of the Knesset Foreign Affair and Defense Commitee criticized the Chief of Staff for allowing such a man "to poison the atmosphere." But Bar-On was not removed from his post. Bar-On said that Peace Now's position on refusal to serve was political not moral. "We are taken seriously by army leaders, by politicians and by a large segment of public opinion precisely because we remain within the system. If we lose that credibility we'll cease being politically effective. We want to be effective. Its our raison d'être. Also we still believe in the rule of law. We don't want to undermine the rule of law in this country where too many fanatics don't believe in it. We still believe that in the end the political system will gravitate into our camp." After a brief pause Bar-On mused: "If I knew that tomorrow two thousand reservists would publicly refuse service in the territories—and stand trial for it—I might change my mind. Two thousand open refuseniks might mean the end of the occupation. Right now, advocating refusal would not only be wrong it would be counterproductive."

Avishai Margalit, the Hebrew University philosophy professor, put the same idea this way: "Israel is a curious country—half super-modern, half sorely backward—a tribe rather than a state, a *mishpoche*. We are part of that tribe. We are not a passing bunch of aesthetes or beautiful souls—we are rooted in this odd society. Army service here is often like a primitive tribal initiation rite. It is a main socializing agent. Where else would you see entire families accompanying their children to the draft board? Or visiting them once a week at the base with food parcels and fresh underwear? Our main strength at the moment is in the army: among young recruits and reservists. Not that it's not important to be moral witnesses too. It's very important. But our task is different from that of, say, Vaclav Havel in Czechoslovakia. If we haven't yet moved public opinion as much as we would have liked this doesn't mean we will not be more successful tomorrow."

Nor has Peace Now yet practiced "confrontation tactics" as protest movements have done elsewhere. The demonstrations are as a rule coordinated with the police. The placards at their most recent demonstrations have said of the PLO: "Don't jail them! Talk to them." Peace Now has tried hard, with mixed results so far, to de-demonize the Palestinians whom Begin once called "two legged animals." An American professor attending a Peace Now rally last year noted with surprise that the demonstrators, who advocated talks with the PLO were waving national flags. His surprise grew even more as they concluded their rally singing the national anthem. (When the eighteen-year-old son of a leading Peace Now activist was recently dropped from one of the more rigid army officers courses for a minor disciplinary offense—he had neglected to shave—his mother moved heaven and earth among all her high ranking political and military acquaintances to get him readmitted. The incident threw a light on Peace Now's curious position both within and without the Israeli power elite: a strength as well as a weakness.)

※

In the 1920s the founders of modern Israel were pioneers of the social-democratic ethic of equality between the sexes. Sixty and seventy years later Israel was steeped in conservative, macho, or religiously motivated bias, dramatically deviating from contemporary American or European practice. Women's equality has been one of the great myths of the Israeli image-making industry. The militarization of society and public life as a result of the continuous state of war has strongly contributed to the erosion of the status of women. In the upper echelons of business and government the premium has been put on military background. Women, though they serve in the army in supporting noncombat posts, mostly as subordinate clerks and social workers, have found it increasingly difficult over he years to break into the political system or get top jobs in business. In the cabinet there are now five ex-generals but not a single woman. The number of women in parliament has eroded from 15 percent before independence to 5.8 percent today—an all-time low. The salary differential between men and women in the public sector, according to Naomi Chazan, a political science professor at Hebrw University, has grown in the past decade from 22 to 29 percent. Only males, combat soldiers, and certified military heroes signed the original "officers' letter" or appeared on the speakers platform during mass rallies. Peace as well as war was a man's game. Yuli Tamir, today a Tel-Aviv university sociologist, served two and a half years as a lieutenant in the army intelligence corps, much of it in an electronic listening post close to the Suez Canal before and during the Yom Kippur war. She was one of the founders of Peace Now in 1978 and participated in the formulation of the "officers' letter" but was not permitted to sign it. "The men thought it would be absolutely terrible if a woman signed it too," Tamir remembered the other day with a smile. "They were sure a woman's name would fatally weaken its political and moral impact."

The political vernacular of the hawkish right has been similarly dominated by male sexual imagery. It still is: dire warnings against the "castration" of the state through "withdrawal" or the "amputation" of parts; exhortations to remember that what does not grow, "shrinks." In the extraparliamentary peace movements, however, women have recently become rather dominant. Women militants were responsible for pushing Peace Now further towards the radical left in recent months. The preeminence of women in Israeli peace groups has been seen by some as proof of the burden imposed on women by the wars. The Israeli Civil Rights Movement was also founded by a woman a few years ago; she is now one of the few women members of the Knesset. Many more women than men are now voting in support of compromise and talks with the PLO, according to Professor Chasan.

The Palestinian uprising in the territories has further pushed women to greater involvement in radical peace groups. The uprising is no longer an impersonal battle between armies and machines; it has added an intimate, human dimension to the conflict. A dozen or so militant women's groups clamoring for peace have sprung up as a result and can now be encountered regularly in the streets and squares of the main cities. David Shipler, in a book rich in insights entitled *Arab and Jew: Wounded Spirits in a Promised Land* a few years ago warned the parties to this conflict that they "will not find peace in treaties or in victories. They wil find it, if at all, by looking into each others eyes."

This is what one new group, the Women Network, is trying to encourage. The Network is a coalition of several nonpolitical women's service organizations. It is has established encounter groups for Palestinian and Israeli women to meet and discuss the need for mutual recognition of one another's human rights. The police recently tried to prevent the Women's Network from holding a joint demonstration of Palestinian and Israeli women in Jerusalem on the grounds that it might lead to civic unrest, as the "human chain" had done a few weeks before. Lawyers for the Network appealed to the Supreme Court and won. Another group are the so-called Women in Black. They too practice a kind of "anti-politics," that is, their declared wish is to be guided by moral principle and a concern for human rights rather than political opportunism. Every Friday afternoon, rain or shine, groups of women dressed entirely in black gather for one hour at busy intersections in twenty Israeli cities and towns. Theirs is the longest regularly sustained protest activity so far. The solemn vigils have become regular features of the urban scene every Friday afternoon. In their somber dignity the women in black are reminiscent of the Buenos Aires Mothers of the Plaza. Their lament is marked by a silent, timeless eloquence. The black clothing, they explain, symbolizes the tragedy of both peoples, Israeli and Palestinian. Quietly, on the little placards they hold, they call for an end to the mutual bloodshed, an end to the killing of children and for peace talks with the Palestinian—only to be heckled and occasionally spat on by burly men as "whores" and "Arab fuckers."

❋

Much of the argument today between Palestinians and Israelis is over the compounded results of five wars (and many bloody skirmishes in between) rather than over any past grievances. To preach moderation and compromise in the heated atmosphere generated by those wars—that is the problem the protest groups face. None claims it has found satisfactory answers. Democracies are notorious for a tendency to obey the feelings rather than the mind. Their inborn nature often makes it difficult for them, after a hard-won war, to conclude a peace. Generous victors are rare. The difficulties of Peace Now and of other protest groups are compounded by the absence so far of similar groupings in the neighboring Arab states. Janet Aviad, an American-born sociologist and Peace Now's national treasurer, told me she is often tired and fed up. "This activity can really get you down," she said. "I am down anyway. I have a nineteen year old boy in the army!" She confessed she was often very pessimistic but only for the immediate future. "In the long run I am hopeful. Perhaps it's irrational. Sometimes I think this issue will be decided in the streets of Jerusalem and Tel-Aviv. I believe in the unexpected. Would you have expected what has happened this past year all over the world, from Eastern Europe to South Africa? Nothing was foreseen here either: not the war of 1967, when we won the territories that we should now trade for peace, nor that of 1973. Neither Sadat's journey to Jerusalem nor the PLO's volte face in 1988."

Aviad and other Peace Now activists still meet regularly with government ministers to plead their cause. The Hebrew University philosopher Avishai Margalit a few months ago visited Defense Minister Yitzhak Rabin in his office. Rabin is known in his Labor party as a hardliner. The discussion apparently became heated. Rabin was irritated. At one point he turned to Margalit and snapped: "Who are you to tell us what to do? How many votes does Peace Now have?"

Margalit, according to a witness, replied: "Maybe we don't have the votes. We do have the historians. They will have the last word in the future when today's disorders will be tidied up into books." The remark was perhaps a little elitist. Rabin, according to this source, seemed taken aback.

12

Letter from Alexandria

In the Greco-Roman Museum of Alexandria last April, an Egyptian acquaintance and I were admiring a marble head said to be that of Cleopatra. The chin, the forehead, the lips etched in unmistakable curves of power, the severe expression discredited the conventional notion of Cleopatra's great beauty. We were discussing this when a guard suddenly rushed in and ordered us to leave. The museum was closing, he said. It was a few minutes before eleven on a Friday morning. My acquaintance, an architect named Abdul Rahman, was surprised. "What on earth has happened?" Rahman demanded, perhaps a little too sharply. "We have only just come in."

The guard pointed to his wristwatch, and said that the museum was closing because the employees were entitled to attend Friday prayers. "It is their right," he added.

"Since when?" asked Rahman, a Muslim, who had not been to the museum for some time. By now, the head guard had joined us, having shepherded a few tourists from a nearby room, where the chief attraction was the mummy of a crocodile stretched out on a wooden bed.

"For some years," the head guard said. "I'm surprised that you did not know." He added that he was very sorry for the inconvenience—we should have been told earlier—and he assured us that if we cared to come back at 2 P.M. our tickets would be revalidated.

I said that I very much wanted to return. The museum was small but was filled with interesting works, including a roomful of exquisitely painted Hellenistic figurines that reflect daily life and fashion under the Ptolemies; they alone would have been well worth a trip to Alexandria. The museum was built in 1895, by Italian architects, along vaguely classical lines. The founders and first patrons were rich cotton barons—Alexandria has long been the center for Egypt's cotton trade—and other members of the city's then very sizable European community, comprising Greek, Italian, French, British, Spanish, and Maltese landowners, bankers, shipping agents and other commercéants, doctors, and hoteliers. (Before President Gamal Abdel Nasser mortgaged most of Egyptian cotton production to the Soviet Union, in the late 1950s, cotton was the main cash crop of Alexandria. A third of all the arable land in Egypt was given over to it, and Alexandria supplied between 6 and 8 percent of the world's needs.) "One of the first directors of this museum was an Italian named Breccia," Rahman said as we walked toward the exit. "His niece married my great-uncle. Alexandria was cosmopolitan then. Alexandrians of a certain class were open-minded. Many spoke four or five languages fluently. The city was not Greek or Italian, Arab or Egyptian. It was a hybrid. We would not have been turned out on a Friday morning then. Even under Nasser this would not have happened. "Nasser was xenophobic—he threw out the foreigners and ruined the economy—but he did not force religion on you."

As we walked down the museum steps, squinting in the bright sun, we noticed that the small square outside had undergone a dramatic change. An hour earlier, it had been clogged with traffic. Cars and carts had barely moved through clouds of dust and exhaust fumes. Now it was a peaceful expanse laid out with prayer mats. Parts of it were shaded against the sun by canvas sheets tied with ropes to impromptu masts. Three or four hundred men were crouched on the ground, waiting for a prayer service to begin. It was not the only improvised open-air mosque in Alexandria that morning. In the crowded downtown area, straw mats were laid out in empty lots and in narrow spaces between houses. Here and there, entire streets were blocked—rather provocatively, Rahman complained—and men bowed in prayer between the crumbling, peeling facades of former palatial homes that now serve as nationalized local banks and Egyptian government offices.

"This is how things are in today's Egypt," Rahman said. "Not enough mosques." Things had changed sinced the nineteenth century, when, in his now classic "An Account of the Manners and Customs of the Modern Egyptians," Edward Lane had noted that the great mosques of Egypt were rarely crowded, and even on Fridays were only partly filled. "Hundreds of mosques have been built in recent years," Rahman said, "but there are still not nearly enough." Or else there are too many Egyptians. One recent estimate is 52 million—more than double the population in 1960. Most government efforts to curtail population growth have been relatively unsuccessful. If the growth continues at the present rate, of a million a year, there will be 64 million Egyptians by the end of the century. The more the population grows, the stronger seems the Islamic revival. "It all started under Sadat," said Rahman. Anwar Sadat used to say that he was the Islamic President, of an Islamic people, in an Islamic land. At other times, he would ridicule the fundamentalists as a gang of fools or would attack them as a seditious minority of Communists, masking their true faces behind pious beards. Shortly before his death, he tried to stem the fundamentalist tide by ordering mass arrests. Since his assassination, by Islamic fanatics, the fundamentalists' influence has continued to grow, at all levels—notably in the universities and among the professions. The fundamentalists now control the major student unions. Three major professional associations—the engineers,' the doctors,' and the pharmacists'—are dominated by them. The fundamentalists are said to be especially strong in the city of Alexandria. As early as 1980, fundamentalist students at Alexandria University demanded that the sexes be separated in classrooms and cafeterias. Their demand was granted. I was told that at a recent mass rally at the university the fundamentalists protested the teaching of all foreign languages. Incredibly, even in the faculties of science and medicine there are hundreds of bearded male and veiled female students, whose religion forbids the males a glimpse of a naked female body. A concert on campus was recently cancelled under pressure from fundamentalist professors and students, who claimed that music—all music—was pagan debauchery. The fundamentalists claim that modern Egypt is corrupt—a huge whorehouse. Its public institutions are paralyzed by embezzlers. The only cure for these evils, they say, is a return to the pristine purity of Islam, and a halt to modern education, to industrialization, and to Westernization, with its dangerous byproducts of moral lassitude and permissiveness.

We drove back from the museum along the Corniche, Alexandria's magnificent sea esplanade. The beaches here still bear names that were given them in a different era—Stanley, Camp de César, Glymenopoulo, Sporting, San Stefano, Cleopatra, Côte d'Azur. Today, women are expected to wear extremely modest bathing suits. "Many of the women go into the water fully clothed," Rahman said. We stopped at a café on Stanley Beach. A few missile boats were moored in the bay. Behind us rose a long wall of high apartment buildings—the summer homes of rich Cairenes, empty at this time of the year. It is common to find little mosques in the basements of many of the new luxury establishments. (Mosques are exempt from taxation; having a mosque in the basement protects the builders from the taxman as well as from any fundamentalists who might riot against ostentatious luxury and "materialism.") Immediately behind the new apartment houses, wooden shacks and other slum dwellings lined narrow, labyrinthine unpaved lines. Half-naked children played in the dust. Some looked less than ten years old, but their faces seemed to reflect twenty years of misery and deprivation. "You think *this* is poverty?" said Rahman. "They are relatively well-off. The *really* poor live in the garbage dumps and the mud hovels in the outskirts." He remembered Stanley Beach from his childhood, when there was nothing here but the luxurious villas of the cotton pashas, standing far apart in the fields.

A waiter came and we ordered beer. He hesitated for a moment, then launched into a long explanation, which Rahman translated. The waiter was saying that until a short time ago beer was still served at this café. It was a well-known establishment—actors and writers from Cairo stopped here during the summer months. The waiter himself was absolutely in favor of serving every patron what he wanted; it was wrong to compel anyone to observe religious customs against his will. But he was only a waiter. The café's owner, he said, had recently made a pilgrimage to Mecca, and while there he had vowed never again to serve alcohol in his café. "We are becoming fewer and fewer," Rahman said.

❈

Of the ancient Greek Alexandria little survives but the name; the Arabs call it Iskandariyah. Other than Pompey's Pillar (erroneously so called by the Crusaders—it was erected in honor of the Emperor Diocletian), which E. M. Forster thought an "imposing but ungraceful object," and a charming Roman amphitheatre, there are few archeological remains. Precisely because there is so little to see, I found Forster's "Alexandria: A History and a Guide," extraordinarily evocative. It was published in 1922 by the Alexandria branch of an English printer. Long unavailable, it has recently been reissued, in England by Michael Haag, Ltd., and in the United States by the Oxford University Press.

Alexandria was the New York of the ancient world; it was the first world city, enormously rich—"the greatest emporium in the inhabited world," Strabo claimed. Like Manhattan, it was bordered by water and its streets were laid out in unvarying straight lines intersected by stately avenues. It, too, was the meeting and melting point of diverse races, languages, cultures, and religions, and was the city with the largest Jewish population in the world. The Diaspora started here long before the fall of Jerusalem. In Alexandria, the legend of Egypt was recast in a fusion of Eastern mysticism with the clear, cool reason of Hellas; of Jerusalem with Athens.

For more than three centuries, Alexandria was the most learned place on earth. Here man first surmised that the earth was round and revolved around the sun. The great library is reported to have contained 400,000 scrolls. It no longer existed in 641, when the Arab conqueror Amr took Alexandria. The city yielded to Amr almost without a struggle—perhaps because it "had no soul," as Forster thought, or perhaps because of the decadence of which the name "Alexandria" has often been emblematic. At that time, according to a contemporary chronicle, Alexandria still had 4,000 palaces, 4,000 baths, 400 theaters, and 40,000 poll-tax-paying Jews. There are too many fours in this account for us to take the numbers literally, but the city was undoubtedly populous. Under the Arabs, it declined. Napoleon found only a simple fishing village here. The modern city was built in the nineteenth century, by European entrepreneurs, who controlled most of Egypt's industry and commerce and were exempt from taxation and from Egyptian law.

All this, and much more, is in Forster's book—a minor classic, which continues to be of great practical use. Forster constructs an immense "ghost city." He takes us wandering through the modern streets, imagining the ancient avenues. He allows us to look at old maps and urges us to study the texts of ancient or modern authors, among them Shakespeare, Dryden, Callimachus, and Plutarch. During the First World War, Forster had spent three years in Alexandria as a medical orderly. He struck up a friendship with Constantine Cavafy, "the great Greek poet who so poignantly conveys the civilisation of his chosen city." For Cavafy, Alexandria was a city of anti-heroes: ambiguous, indolent, decadent, forever fin-de-siècle. The first English translation of one of Cavafy's best-known poems, "The God Abandons Antony," first appeared in Forster's book, sandwiched between its two halves, the "History" and the "Guide." The former evokes, in the form of a pageant, and at times whimsically, the city's main epochs. It is full of fine character sketches and takes pains to offend nearly all national and religious susceptibilities. Throughout, the novelist's eye is alive to texture and to the telling detail. The book begins with the towering figure of the Macedonian conqueror who founded the city, and ends with the British occupation of Egypt in 1882, an event that Forster deplored. In between, there are short sections on the strange dynasty of the Ptolemies (their incestuous marriages constituted "pride of race carried to an extreme degree"), on the librarians of Alexandria, on the poets, the astronomers and the Church fathers (like Gibbon, Forster regarded Christianity as a major catastrophe), on Amr (a "sensitive and generous soul," yet Islam "swept the city physically and spiritually into the sea"), and on Napoleon ("The expedition failed but its memory remained with him: he had touched the East, the nursery of kings"). Forster's theme is the eclectic blending of cultures. In Alexandria, the proto-cosmopolis, the eyes strained away from Africa to Greece, Italy, and France.

❀

One afternoon, a local acquaintance drove me out to the quarter of old Alexandria called Bacos, where Gamal Abdel Nasser was born, the son of a local postmaster who lived on an unpaved street. Most streets here are unpaved or are full of potholes, and the cars plow through dust. Open sewers run through some of the alleys. Outside a mosque, a radical mullah was addressing a large crowd. He was speaking through a megaphone about holy Islam and wicked Europe and America, about evil Communists and Jews, about justice, revolution, purity, corruption, sin, and redemption. The crowd, of several thousand, squatted on the ground, following the sermon with rapt attention. From time to time, backs were bowed in prayers that were like military drills. The crowd was hushed. There was something remarkable about the hush. The discipline was nearly absolute. In Egypt people rarely form a queue and, though good natured, are always rather disorderly, shouting, and jostling one another. At this meeting, they answered the mullah's entreaties with clockwork precision. I was told that there had been a food riot here the week before and the police had made several arrests. There were no police in sight that afternoon. After an hour or so, the mullah disappeared inside the mosque, and the crowd dispersed in perfect order. "He has changed my life," one of the worshippers told my acquaintance. The worshipper looked transported.

In each section of the "History," Forster refers the reader to specific pages in the "Guide." The reader moves back and forth constantly between past and present, between the ephemeral and the concrete. Thus, in the section on Arianism—a theological doctrine that produced a violent debate in Alexandria in the fourth century (is Christ of a substance like but inferior to that of God the Father, as Arius held, or of the same substance, which was Athanasius's view?)—he sends the reader to the "Guide" to look at a picture of the Council of Nicaea, which declared Arianism anathema. And in the section on Alexander he bids the reader find Alexander's portrait on a magnificent coin in the Greco-Roman Museum, and then go to a busy street corner in downtown Alexandria where Alexander is said to have been buried in a glass sarcophagus, under what is now a modern mosque. Michael Haag, in his footnotes to this edition of Forster's book, leads the reader from here to the nearby Rue Sharm el Sheikh, the former Rue Lepsius. Forster knew it well. On the second floor of No. 10, in what is now the Pension Amir, a seedy little boarding house, Cavafy lived for twenty-five years before his death in 1933—the period of his poetic maturity. Here, in 1907, Haag writes, "the literary apotheosis of Alexandria began." Downstairs was a brothel. Opposite was a hospital. Around the corner was a Greek Orthodox church. Cavafy used to say, "Where could I live better? Below, the brothel caters to the flesh. And there is the church which forgives sin. And there is the hospital where we die."

The little streets in this part of the city, which is almost completely run-down, housed most of the baroque characters in Lawrence Durrell's *Alexandria Quartet*: Justine, the classical Jewess of neurology; the timid schoolteacher Darley; the rich Copt Nessim; and Clea and Balthazar. (The last character seems to have been based on Cavafy: he has a similar penchant for the Hellenistic past, and for degrading homosexual affairs.) A note in *Justine* assures the reader that the characters are invented but that "the city is real." I now wonder about that. When I reread the "Quartet," in Alexandria, it seemed perilously close to a conventional Victorian fantasy of the East as a place of exotic escape and sexual license, and of Alexandria as an incestuous, androgynous Eden, where, as Durrell wrote in "Justine," the "sexual provender" at hand was "staggering in its variety and profusion,"and where there were "more than five sexes," whatever that means. (The English language could not tell them apart, he wrote; apparently, "only demotic Greek" could.) For Durrell, Alexandria was a backdrop: "clangs of the trams shuddering in their metal veins as they pierce the iodine-colored *meidan* of Mazarita," and "streets that run back from the docks . . . breathing into each others' mouths, keeling over." Or, more lurid, "shuttered balconies swarming with rats, and old women whose hair is full of the blood of ticks." One has to see Alexandria to realize that in the "Quartet" Durrell drew an inner landscape—his own.

In Forster's day and in Durrell's day, as throughout the second half of the nineteenth century, Alexandria was often described as a "European" city, more akin to Marseilles or Genoa than to nearby Cairo. How this myth was born should make a fascinating chapter in the archeology of knowledge.

The ratio of Egyptians to Europeans was always at least four to one, but in the eyes of many European travelers the Arabs of Alexandria tended to disappear. In 1844, Thackeray landed at Alexandria ready to yield to the mysteries of the East. He had braced himself overnight with "the help of a cigar and a moonlight contemplation on deck," only to find a city more like Portsmouth, he thought—full of clean-shaven, buxom merchants, as trim and fat as those on the Paris Bourse, and of polite European places of resort, where one got ices and the French papers. Flaubert stopped at Alexandria in 1850 on his way to Jerusalem (which he thought revolting). He wrote, *"Alexandrie . . . est presque un pays européen, tant il y a d'européens"* ("Alexandria is almost a European country, there are so many Europeans").

There could not have been more than two thousand Europeans in Alexandria at that time—most of them Greeks and Italians—in a population of sixty or eighty thousand Egyptians, Syrians, Libyans, and Sudanese. For Cavafy, Alexandria was a mythical land populated almost exclusively by ancient and modern Greeks. The Europeans' wealth and importance were undoubtedly huge, and out of all proportion to their numbers. Their engineers had laid out the heart of the modern city (the present downtown area) along European lines, with parks, some of which have since disappeared, and with a fine sea promenade and a central square, the Place des Consuls, which still exist. The square was later renamed Place Mohammed Ali, after the Albanian founder of modern Egypt. Most Alexandrians have never used either name. They still call it Menshieh, after a police station that once stood there.

At the end of the nineteenth century, Alexandria was virtually a British port, according to James Morris in *Pax Britannica: The Climax of an Empire*. The green Egyptian flag flew over the harbor, but the harbor was run by British officers in tarbooshes. Most of the steamer traffic that was cleared there was British. The trains were British and the trams always looked freshly painted. The telephone service, which today is highly erratic, had been installed by the Swiss and was then the envy of visiting Europeans. In 1905, the "brilliant narrowness" of Rue Chérif Pasha (today a warren of shabby shops selling drygoods and badly made shoes) reminded Ronald Storrs, a young Englishman, of London's Bond Street. Forster gently mocked the promenade of "eternally well-dressed people," presumably European or Levantine, driving back and forth on the Rue Rosette, the ancient Canopic road, lined with smart shops selling Parisian clothes; in ancient days, it had had marble colonnades along it, connecting the two gates at opposite ends of the city—the Gate of the Sun and the Gate of the Moon.

❋

The total population of Alexandria at the end of the First World War, when Forster completed his stay there, is generally given as about half a million. Estimates of the number of European nationals among that half million vary greatly—from 80,000 to 150,000. Perhaps as many as two-thirds of the Europeans were second- and third-generation Greek immigrants, with the rest Italians, French, British, Maltese, Romanians, Spaniards, Germans, Hungarians, and White Russians. Some were an impressive combination, among them Captain Jorge y Nelken-Waldberg, the author of "Mes Mémoires en Egypte," which is a mine of anecdotal information on fin-de-siècle Egypt. Waldberg was a Romanian with a Swedish-Spanish name, United States citizenship, and a commission in the Argentine Army, who edited the local French newspaper. He was born Jewish, but was a dignitary of the Alexandria Greek Orthodox Church.

Most Alexandrian Jews were of Levantine origin—the Baron de Menasce, for example (ennobled by the Austrian Kaiser after he paid a visit to the Near East), or the clans of Abdallah Levi and Ibrahim Valensi Pasha. Joseph de Picciotto Bey was a member of the Egyptian Senate. Contrary to a widespread myth, fewer than half the Jews were foreign nationals; the rest were Egyptian citizens or were stateless.

Although the richest foreigners were cotton brokers, landowners, shipping agents, importers of machinery, and hoteliers, there were many foreign artisans and small shopkeepers, too. The expatriates were often extremely patriotic about their "old countries." Rudolf Hess, Hitler's deputy, was born in Alexandria, and so was Giuseppe Ungaretti, the Italian poet of the First World War. During the First Balkan War of 1912–13, the Greek community of Alexandria presented the old country with two fully equipped battleships. Other Alexandrian Greeks financed the construction of the huge Athens stadium, covered entirely in marble. The Comédie Francaise performed regularly in Alexandria. In addition, Alexandria boasted a symphony orchestra and an opera house. In the gracious little theater of Zizinia (today a cinema), there were nightly performances, during the season, of such operas as "Tosca," "La Bohème," and "Lohengrin" (the severest form of Wagner then acceptable south of Naples).

The various foreign communities lived on terms of cordial antipathy. Intermarriage was rare except at the very highest or the very lowest social levels. Cavafy probably never entered an Egyptian home in his life, according to Robert Liddell, his biographer, and spoke Greek with a faint English accent. He spoke almost no Arabic. Very few Europeans spoke Arabic, and when they did, I was once told by an Alexandrian woman now living in Athens, it was "only in the imperative." Life in Alexandria, she recalled, was easy and, above all, comfortable. She remembered households where four or more servants were employed merely to do the ironing.

Several former Alexandrians have published memoirs or autobiographical novels in recent years. All stress the identity crisis that marked their sheltered but schizophrenic adolescence in Alexandria before the Second World War. They spoke French at home, and yet they were not French. They went to an English school (the posh Victoria College of Alexandria was patterned after Eton), and yet they were not English. Rachel Maccabi, a former Alexandrian who published a memoir a few years ago in Israel, entitled "Mizraim Sheli" ("My Egypt"), recalls her youth in an upper-middle-class villa (today the Banque de Misr) on the Rue Rosette, surrounded by Sudanese manservants, Egyptian parlor maids, Italian cooks, a chauffeur, and an English nanny. There were endless bridge parties, annual trips by luxury liner to Europe, and an overwhelming bourgeois ennui, which she finally escaped, in 1938, by running away to a kibbutz in what was then Palestine. The author's mother, "like all ladies, young and old," would travel to Cairo once a year to visit with the queen, who was as European as her visitors. (She was a great-granddaughter of one of Napoleon's generals.) The author's father, an engineer, was a native of Cairo but a Hungarian citizen, and would pay a similar annual visit to King Fuad I. "He too was a masqueraded Egyptian," Maccabi writes of the King. "The kingdom of Egypt was for them a profitable business." Families like the Maccabis, though they had lived in Egypt for generations, were almost totally isolated, socially and culturally, from their Egyptian environment. Directly opposite the Maccabi house, a few steps led up "a narrow, dark passageway to a seedy Arab quarter," she writes. "It is odd, but I never climbed those steps." The Arabs of Alexandria were "faceless men, dark-skinned, dim-eyed," crouched on low stools or on the ground, and "women with veiled faces." Throughout this moving, tense text the reader has a feeling that a time bomb is ticking away. It explodes unexpectedly. The author describes "an elderly man of great dignity" who had been a servant in the house for twenty-five years. He becomes an accomplice in the brutal assassination of her father.

Alexandria at that time was the "summer capital" of Egypt. The King, his entire court, and his ministers and under-secretaries moved to Alexandria for the whole summer, along with the diplomatic corps and "society." Suites of rooms were taken for offices in the cavernous Hotel San Stefano, which still stands but is very run-down. The King lived in one of two enormous palaces by the sea or on one of several yachts, entertaining rich foreigners and being entertained by them. He often said that after him the only kings left would be the king of England and the kings in a deck of cards. His jewelry collection included more than twenty thousand pieces. The revolution of 1952 put an end to all that and hastened the departure—or expulsion—of practically the entire foreign community. English and French residents were expelled in 1957, following the Suez war, and their property was confiscated. A few years later, most Greeks and Italians were forced out, too. Today, there are fewer than 10,000 Europeans left in the city. According to a spokesman for the local Greek Consulate, several former owners of nationalized property have in recent years received some compensation under the terms of an Egyptian-Greek treaty. Much bitterness remains, he said.

The Nasser revolution is today widely regarded in Egypt as an almost total failure. Nasser and his men ranted and raved about socialism and nationalism, but ultimately they lacked the discipline and the skills to sustain their vision. The disenchantment with the Nasser era comes through strongly in contemporary Egyptian literature. In "The Man Who Lost His Shadow," and in several other books, Naguib Mahfouz, Egypt's most distinguished living novelist, attacks Nasser's military adventurism and the brutality of his secret police. The expulsion of the foreigners is still seen as just—or, at least, as inevitable. In "Miramar," a novel by Mahfouz that was first published in 1967, there is this dialogue between Amer, an Egyptian of the ancien régime, and the Greek woman Mariana, who has remained behind after the exodus and runs a small pension by the sea:

> "Monsieur Amer, I don't know how you can say there's no place like Alexandria. It's all changed. The streets nowadays are infested with *canaille*."
> "My dear, it had to be claimed by its people." I try to comfort her and she retorts sharply.
> "But *we* created it."

One morning in Alexandria, I visited Isaac de Picciotto, the seventy-five-year-old president of the Jewish community. He showed me around the great synagogue, a stately Italianate building restored in 1872. It is practically abandoned now. There are no services except on days when a bus brings Israeli tourists on a visit. A sixth-generation Alexandrian, de Picciotto is an Italian citizen of North African origin, fluent in French, Italian, Hebrew, and Arabic. He owns a small shop that sells electrical appliances. He told me that of the ancient Jewish community of Alexandria only fifty old men and twelve old women are left. No one younger than sixty-five remains. "In

1948, we were more than twenty thousand," he said solemnly, as though reciting a well-known text. "Within a few years, we'll all be gone."

After a moment's silence, he said quietly that the so-called pluralist societies of the eastern Mediterranean have collapsed everywhere, and not only in Alexandria. Cyprus has fallen apart into two states, one Muslim-Turkish and the other Christian-Greek. Lebanon has completely disintegrated in the continuing war among its several ethnic, religious, and political groups. The recent Palestinian uprising raises serious doubts that Jews and Muslims could have successfully coexisted even in a pre-1967 Israel.

❋

The population of Alexandria is about five times as large today as it was in 1948. It was estimated at 4.5 million earlier this year, almost entirely indigenous. "European" Alexandria has gone to seed, as it were, reflowering as an almost purely Egyptian, or African, city. In the downtown area, an old English hotel is still named Cecil, but it belongs to a nationalized holding company. The signs over formerly Greek cafés still say "Pastroudis," "Baudrot," "Delice," but the owners and the clientele are Egyptians. At the Atheneion, old-fashioned fans turn slowly under a magnificent Art Nouveau ceiling. An elderly waiter pointed to a marble-topped table in the far corner and said that Cavafy used to sit there with his friends in the twenties. He remembered the poet distinctly, he said, and he went on to tell me that he had started work at this café as an eight-year-old boy, refilling glasses with ice water from a pitcher. He assured me that even though he was a Muslim, a native of Tanta, in the Nile Delta, "in my heart I became a Greek," and he said, "I can recite their poetry. I have worked with them most of my life."

Place Mohammed Ali, the great square, was renamed Midan al-Tahrir (Liberation Square) under Nasser, who held big rallies there. At Midan el Tahrir, he lashed out at "Egypt's enemies" and once narrowly escaped being assassinated by an Islamic fanatic. There he informed the West that it could go drown itself in the sea. There he proclaimed the nationalization of the Suez Canal, telling a delirious crowd, "The Canal will be run by Egyptians, Egyptians, Egyptians! Do you hear me? By Egyptians!"

An equestrian statue of Mohammed Ali stands in the center of the square. It is an impressive piece of French heroic sculpture, but its transfer to this spot in 1880 aroused hostility among Muslims, and to this day it bears no inscription. It is disfigured from time to time by Muslim fundamentalists protesting this violation of the Koran's injunction against figurative art.

There are new, high-rise office buildings nearby, and traffic policemen in smart white uniforms, but the United States consul-general in Alexandria drives through the city in a bulletproof limousine when he is on official business. In the harbor, which was once one of the busiest ports in the Mediterranean, there is relatively little life—only four or five boats daily, according to the lists published in the local papers. The city is teeming with recent arrivals from poor rural areas in the south who are in search of work. A third of Egypt's industry is said to be situated in and around Alexandria. Much of it is very recent. The sky above the city is darkened and the air is fouled by the chimneys of the foundries, asphalt works, paper and cotton mills, refineries, and food-processing plants in the vicinity. In just the past three years, more than $2.5 billion have been invested here in new chemical works, a new textile plant, and a huge new iron-and-steel complex on a new, four-lane road to Alamein.

The strains of excessive population growth are showing everywhere. The built-up area runs along the seashore for many miles. It begins at the Bay of Abukir (where the French fleet was defeated by Nelson in the so-called Battle of the Nile) and ends thirty miles west, in the tourist resort of Agami. Slums have sprung up in and between the old garden suburbs. The homes of the rich and super-rich are often closely ringed by unspeakable poverty. This proximity of wealth and wretchedness is a main feature of life in Alexandria today. In the twenties, the rich lived more sheltered lives along the sea, in great villas surrounded by parks, in an imaginary Europe. Of some two thousand grand villas that existed here thirty or forty years ago, fewer than two hundred still stand, according to a recent report in the Cairo daily *El Goumhouryia*. A number of them, in a state of almost complete dilapidation, can be seen along the Corniche. The sight of these ruins, and of the disintegrating stucco on the walls everywhere in the city, adds to a general air of exhaustion. The city is served (if that is the right word) by a municipal infrastructure built years ago for a fraction of its present population. Telephones, water pipes, electric-power lines often break down under the pressure. Recently, a main sewer burst in Ibrahimiya, a middle-class quarter formerly occupied by Greeks. The sewer stood open for days, threatening the water supply, while municipal workers searched in vain for the exact points of leakage. After two weeks, they had not yet found them. The charts of the original construction could not be located in the cobwebbed chaos of the city archives.

The Army is the mainstay of the present Egyptian regime. "Abolish the emergency laws and all hell will break loose," a United States diplomat said to me. (The emergency laws allow the President and his Interior Ministry to make administrative arrests and to control political activity.) President Hosni Mubarak's regime takes good care of the Army. On the Corniche, a neat little city of high-rise apartments, rented exclusively to Army officers, at liberally subsidized rates, has sprung up during the last two years. A friend drove me west past them one day to the former royal palace of Ras el Tin, from which King Farouk, with 204 trunks and a plentiful supply of champagne, embarked on his yacht after his abdication in 1952. His last words to the rebellious officers were "Your task will be difficult. It is not easy to govern Egypt." Those words were prophetic. General Mohammed Naguib, the first President of the new republic, failed to keep his job under pressure from Nasser, and was placed under house arrest, from which he was supposedly freed in 1960. Anwar Sadat was assassinated.

The palace, now a museum, is sometimes used to receive foreign dignitaries. It is known for its miles of gilded corridors, for its unsurpassed collection of high-kitsch furniture, paintings, and chandeliers, for its kitsch gothic and marble, for its ebony cigar holders studded with rubies, and for a secret room without windows, where the royal jewels were kept. Some of those jewels are now on public display, including a rattle studded with heavy diamonds which Farouk's father played with as a baby.

�֍

We drove past Ras el Tin and past the dock area and the busy new industrial zones along the road to the Western Desert and Alamein. It was at Alamein—then only a lonely railroad post in the narrow space between the sea and the Qattara Depression—that, as Churchill wrote, "the Hinge of Fate" turned in 1942, and the German advance on Egypt was finally repelled. Many people think of Alamein as being far out in the Western Desert, and are amazed to see that it is less than fifty miles from the suburbs of Alexandria. The new road to Alamein is now lined with summer resorts. A strategic highway, it runs 250 miles farther, to the Libyan border, which has been closed for years as a result of the near state of war between the two countries. At Alamein, the desert is still littered with blown-out tanks and armored troop carriers. The dunes are crisscrossed by miles of barbed wire. Little red signs warn you against unexploded mines.

There are also three large memorials at Alamein: a British and Commonwealth war cemetery, a German monument, and an Italian monument. Each fascinates as political architecture often does—as an index, not necessarily conscious, of national temperament. Great flower beds—a magnificent, if slightly incongruous, sight in this harsh desert landscape—cover the British memorial, where 8,182 casualties (815 unidentified) are buried under simple tombstones of uniform size but with individual inscriptions ("David McGuney—he was a great lover to his wife Tony").

The German memorial is a huge stone structure several miles down the road. From a distance, it looks like a bunker; close up, it feels like a medieval castle. It terrorizes through sheer size. Narrow shooting slots are cut in massive walls for invisible warriors. The British monument is, essentially, a cemetery; it commemorates the individual human. The German monument, by contrast, celebrates the collective. It is known in German as a *Totenburg* (castle of the dead). "Hier Ruhen Deutsche Soldaten" ("Here lie German soldiers"). There are many coats of arms. An octagonal central hall is open to the sky. In the stagnant air, the desert sun reflects blindingly off a bright stone floor. Under the floor are buried the ashes of over 4,200 Germans, in one common grave. The monument was designed in the late fifties by Robert Tischler, a German architect who pioneered this style in the thirties, even before the Third Reich. He built the first of the Nazis' *Totenburgen* during the Second World War. (Tischler's career as chief designer of *Totenburgen* for German soldiers continued uninterrupted after 1945.) A plaque says, "Let Their Death Be A Heritage And A Warning." The visitors' book is filled with didacticisms: "Nie wieder Krieg, Frieden Über Alles" ("Never again war, peace above all"); "Pray for peace." Also this: *"S'il y avait un Suisse comme Dieu tout cela n' aurait pas passé—g.h. Genève"* ("If God were Swiss, all this would not have happened"). There was no one about but the Egyptian guard, who closed the heavy gates behind us. He said that thousands of Germans come here every summer on their way to the bathing resorts of Sidi Abd el Rahman and Mersa Matruh. Only the day before, there had been two busloads. They left behind little flags and a few dried flowers in the visitors' book.

Beyond the German memorial, the shoreline runs farther west, and the flat, pale-blue sea merges with a pale-blue sky at an almost imperceptible horizon. The Italian memorial stands nearby on a low hill. It rises, cathedral-like, in pure-white stone and Carrara marble. Inside, on both sides of an altar, the walls commemorate 1,300 missing Italian soldiers. "Ignoti a Noi—Noti a Dio" ("Unknown to us—known to God"), says the inscription. Then comes an almost Dantesque line: "Giacciono In Luogo Sconosciuto nel Deserto" ("They lie in an unknown place in the desert"). An arrow points east: "Alessandria III km." Underneath, this reminder: "Mancarono la Fortuna non il Valore" ("They lacked good fortune, not valor").

Egyptians are well known for irony and self-deprecating humor. My friend ridiculed the pompous ceremoniousness of the nearby Egyptian military museum, built under Nasser, in 1965, as a monument to "the art of war." He mocked its careful "neutrality" between the Nazis and the British in the Battle of Alamein, and the indiscriminate respect shown Hitler and Churchill, Rommel and Montgomery—a heroic portrait of one matched by an equally heroic portrait of the other. Military museums are often tedious affairs—uniforms upon uniforms—as though what is important about so many dead were the uniform in which they died. Such museums usually emphasize not the horror but the chivalry of armies and wars, and this one is no exception. Many tourists come here, according to a young corporal who took us around. Many Germans come, he said, but Egyptian Army cadets come also. "They come to learn." Learn what? "To fight," said the guide. "Rommel was a perfect gentleman. Montgomery and he had the greatest respect for each other."

When we returned to Alexandria, in the late afternoon, the streets were deserted. It was the holy month of Ramadan. Most people had rushed home for the *iftar*, the breaking of the fast that lasts from sunrise to sunset. An eerie silence hung over streets that are usually congested with cars and swarming with people. Foreigners who have lived here for years say that the fast of Ramadan has never been so stringently and visibly observed, or so publicly honored, as in recent years. Television and radio broadcasts are interrupted five times a day for prayers. Alcohol is banned everywhere except in the big international hotels. Most restaurants are closed.

In other Muslim countries, Ramadan is traditionally an austere month. But in Egypt—and this is the other side of the coin of Muslim revival— every evening, the moment the fast ends, there is an explosion of gluttony and conspicuous consumption. During the *iftar* proper, the streets are empty. A short time afterward, the dense human mass flows back out, many people still eating sweets and nuts, and the stores reopen. They stay open, brightly lit, long past midnight, and are crowded with shoppers, as they never are during the day. Sales of food, clothing, and children's toys are higher during Ramadan than in any other month of the year: In the Cairo papers this year, columnists complained that Ramadan's lofty principles and sublime goals of austerity and introspection were being undermined.

In the little squares surrounding the main mosques of Cairo and Alexandria, the atmosphere this year was that of a carnival—something rarely encountered in other Sunni Muslim countries of the Middle East, and unthinkable among the ascetic Shiites of Iraq and Iran, who tend to self-flagellation during the holy month. Soon after *iftar* one evening in Alexandria, I encountered a dancing bear outside Abu 'al-Abbas, the main mosque. There were amateur theatricals, and spun-sugar stands for children. A well-known singer was giving a free, open-air concert. There was a carrousel. A Sufi danced and danced. Men swallowed fire or swords, and young marksmen lined up to shoot moving ducks and win puppets and honeyed cakes. The carnival was still going strong at 2 A.M., an hour before the *sohour*—the predawn meal before the beginning of the fast—when drum-beaters started to circulate among the celebrators, chanting "*Isha Ya Naym. Wahhid el Dayim. Ramadan Gana*" ("Awake from sleep. Praise God. Ramadan is here").

In the hall of the old Cecil Hotel, where I stayed, and where the walls are still hung with autographs of long-forgotten European opera singers, English lords, and Austro-Hungarian grand dukes, the myths spun by foreigners were stripped away at this early hour. The elevator man had left his ornate cage and was partaking of *sohour* with the night porter, the cook, and the cashier. Their small round table, among dusty ported palms and great mirrors framed in faded gold, was loaded with loaves of brown peasant pita, little glasses of black tea, and a large common plate of *ful* (fava beans) in oil and onions. Outside, across the wide Corniche, the sea roared. The stars hung in the sky, large and luminous, as when Berenice, the Ptolemaic queen, lost a lock of her hair, and Conon, the court astronomer, was constrained to name a constellation after it. The stars' chill, ghostly light was clearly visible in the dark.

13

A Crisis in the Gulf

There was a time when people here would say "things are likely to get worse before they get better but they'll finally get better and there will be peace." I was standing in line at a local schoolhouse to be issued a gasmask when I heard a man behind tell his wife: "Things here go only from worse to worst." With Saddam Hussein's threats to exterminate Israel with chemical and biological weapons, reality here seems grim enough to border on the dystopian. The conventional wisdom has long been that the Arab-Israel conflict no longer lends itself to a "military" solution. In the absence of any discernable effort to negotiate a political settlement, many people here now have a sinking feeling of being at the mercy of blind forces.

The center does not hold; the mad fringes flow into the resultant vacuum. The Palestinian uprising on the West Bank and in the Gaza strip seems more and more controlled by Muslim fanatics. Many intellectuals on the West Bank and in East Jerusalem were until very recently known for their moderation. They would frequent seminars on peace-making and talk of the need to arrive at a "historical compromise" with Israel. The same people now ally themselves with Saddam Hussein, who they say is fighting the have's in the interest of the have nots. Saddam's pictures are all over Nablus, Ramallah and East Jerusalem. Palestinian newspapers in East Jerusalem do not speak of an Iraqi invasion of Kuwait but of the "deployment" of Iraqi forces there. I asked a Palestinian journalist in East Jerusalem how, he thought, this identification with Iraq could help the cause of Palestinian self-determination. He said: "Most probably, it will do no good at all. It may even cause harm. But Israel refuses to talk to us and has left us no other choice."

In Israel too, events drift and get out of hand. National policy seems too often governed by impulse, not by sovereign will; by momentary mood, by the lowest common denominator, and by the obsessive desires of fanatics on the extreme right. The late Israeli historian Jacob Talmon used to warn against "obsessive desires" rampant in Israeli public life which constituted, he argued, a departure from what Freud called the reality principle. The predominance of local politics over foreign policy considerations—always strong here—has never been so powerful. Prime Minister Shamir's right-wing coalition is very narrow and often seems manipulated by the extreme fringe. During the past year Shamir has felt constrained to scuttle his own peace plan, which called for elections in the occupied territories and Israeli-Palestinians talks. In recent months he precipited, almost deliberately, a crisis with the United States only because it appeared easier in the short run to offend President Bush or Secretary Baker appeared easier than to offend half a dozen fundamentalist Knesset members who make up his narrow parliamentary majority.

The feeling of being at the mercy of blind forces is especially salient in the mixed city of Jerusalem where the spiraling effects of terror and repression have caused the last vestiges of Palestinian Israeli coexistence to break down almost completely. The "holy city" now leads a weird and violent existence. Hardly a day passes without a riot or a stoning, without cars torched, fire bombs thrown, attempted lynchings, and the stabbing of an Israeli by a Palestinian (or vice versa). After each massacre municipal cleaning machines, marked CITY OF PEACE in three languages, appear on the scene to wash the blood from the tarmac in time for the next file of pious pilgrims to pass by fingering their rosaries and muttering solemn prayers.

The mixture of nationalism and religion in Jerusalem—much like that of Cyprus or Northern Ireland—now comes with threats and counterthreats of nuclear or biological Armageddons. In the spooky clutter of holy places sacred to more than one religion, fanatics are hatching plots and counterplots and there is no telling where the next blow will fall. Housefronts in the Old City are smeared with graffiti screaming DEATH TO ARABS or ALLAH AKHBAR—SLAUGHTER THE JEWS. Others hail SADDAM HUSSEIN THE GREAT ARAB. Clouds of tear-gas hang overhead between towers and domes in what used to be called

Jerusalem the golden,
with milk and honey blest,
Beneath thy contemplation,
Sink heart and voice oppressed.

❋

The city is haunted by demons of fear, superstition, tribalism, and vengeance. The three year old Palestinian uprising has hit the Palestinian quarters of Jerusalem as hard and perhaps harder than cities in the occupied West Bank. Despite overwhelming displays of force by riot police and special troops, the violence now often spills across the old demarcation line, into Israeli residential areas. Panic breeds panic. One outrage generates another one. The stakes get higher all the time.

This was vividly shown in the tragic sequence of events that began recently with the announcement by a minuscule group of Jewish fanatics and publicity hunters that they intended to lay the foundation stone for the "Third Temple" within *al-Haram al-Sharif*, the Muslims' sacred enclosure on the ancient Jewish Temple Mount. (Of the Second Temple only the Western Wall now remains. It was destroyed by the Romans in 70 A.D.) The fanatics numbered only a handful. They had tried the same stunt several times before in the past but were always stopped by the police and prevented from entering the *haram*. They were stopped again but this time an angry mob of about three thousand Muslims had gathered in the *haram* before, listening to incendiary speeches by the imams and waving Palestinian flags and chanting slogans. At one point they began to throw down stones upon Jewish worshippers at the Western Wall below. Police officers on the spot panicked. They may also have been affected by considerations of tribal vanity and "face." They made a clumsy attempt to storm the *haram* and failed. Then they made a second attempt, accompanied by indiscriminate automatic firing. Seventeen Muslims were shot dead, more than one hundred were left wounded.

The political fallout from the killings in the *haram* were disastrous. For the first time in many years the United States joined in two consecutive condemnations of Israel in the United Nations Security Council. The Jordanian border which had been quiet for many years, with trade and tourists going back and forth, suddenly flared up with sporadic shooting and attempts at armed infiltrations. Jordan was said to be gripped by "fundamentalist fever" as a result of the Temple Mount killings and the Gulf crisis. Several armed infiltrators crossed the border with religious amulets and copies of the Koran. They were discovered to be regular Jordanian National Guardsmen determined to take private revenge for the massacre in the *haram*. Israeli intelligence experts concluded that the Jordanian government was finding it increasingly difficult, if not impossible, to control fundamentalist elements within its own army. There was talk, suddenly, of Jordan becoming "another Lebanon"; and of Israel's need to seize more land in the east, across the Jordanian border—a new "security zone" similar to the zone Israel now holds in the north, across the Lebanese border.

The repercussions on the local scene gave rise to even greater concerns. Week after week, some young Palestinian ran amok in the streets here with a kitchen knife in his hand, wounding or killing Israeli civilians, including women and children as well as security personnel. The stabbings were followed by savage riots. Infuriated Israelis, hungry for revenge, roamed the streets in search of Arabs to beat up and possibly kill. The dark underside of Israeli life which the political establishment has tended to ignore or belittle even if, on occasion, it has exploited it electorally, came into sharp view. The quasi-official funeral in Jerusalem of Meir Kahane, the nastiest racist rabble-rouser this country has ever seen, who was murdered in New York, magnified it for all the world to see. In his lifetime Kahane never attracted more than two or three hundred people to one of his meetings. His funeral was attended by a wild mob estimated at fifteen to twenty thousand people many of whom called for avenging Kahane's death in "rivers of Arab blood." Some cried" "Leftist Jews will also have to die" and "Let's go from here to liberate the Temple Mount." After the funeral thousands of mourners rampaged through the night beating up Arabs wherever they could find them. A Jerusalem woman I know—of German-Jewish origin—who witnessed the riot later said she never imagined there was so much hatred in the community. She said it reminded her of the *Volkswut* that produced the infamous *Kristallnacht* in Germany on November 9, 1938. Oddly, the riot in Jerusalem took place on exactly the fifty-second anniversary of that awful night. Later that same night, the mob tried to storm Television House. Rioters yelled that Israeli television news was controlled by the PLO. I heard one scream: "Kill the Arabs" and another: "Gas them! Gas them! Like they gassed Jews during the Holocaust!" Four Arabs and four policemen were wounded, one seriously.

Kahane's politics had been an amalgam of racism, pornography, and religion. His slogan was "I say what others think." He would show up at meetings accompanied by a young thug armed with an automatic rifle and said to be Trotsky's great grandson, spreading fear and hatred wherever he went. A few years ago he was suspected of planning to blow up the Muslim mosques on the Temple Mount and put under administrative arrest for six months. His rhetoric completely dehumanized all Arabs. He saw them as the Nazis had seen Jews, as a cancer, as rats and viruses to be mercilessly crushed. The Arab-Israel struggle was between an elected and an inferior people. Liberal Jews were "filthy traitors." He demanded heavy jail sentences for Arabs that defiled Jewish blood by having sexual intercourse with Jews. The funeral of this man was attended by two cabinet ministers, two deputy ministers, and by the Chief Sephardic Rabbi who urged the mourners to "follow in Kahane's ways." (The same Chief Rabbi a few years ago pronounced himself in favor of evicting the infidels from the Temple Mount). The Knesset that had once passed a law making it impossible for Kahane to run for office because of his racism met in special session to commemorate his death. He was criticized by some Knesset members and hailed by others as a "saint" like Anne Frank, who had also been killed only because he was Jewish. At the end the Speaker asked everyone to stand and thirty Knesset members did so to honor his memory with a minute of silence. Kahane did not invent Kahanism. Tom Segev, a columnist in *Ha'aretz* wrote after the funeral that there was always a fringe element of Kahanism in Zionism, as there is in any nationalism.

The events that shook Baka, a quiet residential quarter in South-Jerusalem, during the same week were another case in point. In Baka, a few days after the disaster in the *haram*, a young Arab construction worker employed by an Israeli contractor on a nearby building site suddenly ran through the quiet tree lined streets yelling "Allah Akhbar!" He stabbed a young woman soldier and two men to death with a big knife. He was taking revenge, he later said, for the desecration of the *haram*. Baka is an interesting cross-section of communities in Jerusalem. It is a respectable middle-class section today. In the early fifties a few hundred poor immigrants from Marocco and Iraq, and refugees from the ancient Jewish quarter of the Old City (at that time under Jordanian occupation), settled here in abandoned Arab homes and in new public-built apartment houses. Many others, more affluent, moved in since, mostly of European origin—university people, professionals, successful young businessmen, Western immigrants. Baka was long considered a model community where people of different income levels and ethnic groups were successfully cooperating in local self-government and in joint social and educational projects.

Barely fifteen minutes after the killings, a hundred or so rioting residents were stoning passing cars as well as the Baka home of a well-known Peace Now activist, a physics professor at the Hebrew University, who was accused by the rioters of "hiding the murderer" in his living room, even though the murderer was still lying wounded in the street. The rioters then turned against the police, yelling DEATH TO ARABS (and, incidently, death to the "media" and to all "leftist Arab-loving Jews," too). The common assumption that Israelis of European origin are "doves" and go to Peace Now demonstrations while those of Afro-Asian origin are "hawks" and vote for Likud is, of course, a stereotype; it has gained so much credence recently because it it contains a measure of truth. After the riot a Hebrew university professor and a resident of Baka was quoted in the press as saying: "I am scared. I saw for the first time that a lynching is possible here."

During the next two weeks there were eleven more stabbings in Jerusalem—all, allegedly, in revenge for the massacre in the *haram* and four nasty riots by Jews. The riots were directed against Arabs as much as against Israeli moderates and media people of all political shades who were said to rejoice each time they could write about or photograph a dead Jew.

A few days after the killings in Baka I attended a memorial meeting there. Some five hundred people crowded into an open square outside the local school. The speakers stood under a large sign saying Death to Arabs. A rabbi intoned a prayer in which he invoked God's vengeance on the wicked for the innocent blood spilled. Professor Yuval Neeman, the Minister of Science in Shamir's government called for the introduction of the death penalty; any Arab, irrespective of his age, who throws one stone at a Jew should be expelled immediately from the country together with his entire family, their home must be destroyed or turned over to new Jewish immigrants from Russia. If need be, entire Arab villages must be "erased," he said, if one of the inhabitants was engaged in terrorist activity. Approximately a third of the audience applauded these words. The rest listened in silence. A Likud Knesset member spoke next and accused the government of bending to U.S pressure. He complained that government was "abandoning the Jewish population" to Palestinian terror; stronger measures were needed.

❁

The city now often resembles an armed camp. Both sides are back in their own primordial worlds. Business centers, pedestrian zones, and the main squares in both parts of the city swarm with heavily armed special troops at all hours of the day. The Palestinian sector is patrolled by armored troop carriers and teen-aged soldiers wearing steel helmets and bullet or knife-proof flak-jackets. They walk in twos and threes, slowly through the Arab streets, in their heavy gear, with their walkie talkies, their truncheons, their M-16 rifles, a bit clumsy, perspiring in the sun, and visibly self-conscious; and it is difficult to say who is more afraid, they or the Palestinians. Many old houses in Jerusalem have water tanks on their roofs, a leftover from the days of the British mandate when the water supply was irregular and every household maintained a reservoir against possible shortages. Last month's bills from the city water department included a printed warning to make sure the reservoirs were tightly closed against possible attempts to poison the water.

One moment you feel you are in some macabre science-fiction world, with talk of high-tech warfare, Iraqi threats and Israeli counterthreats of chemical, biological, and possibly nuclear extinction; and in the next, you are back in tribal wars of times gone by waged with sticks and stones and knives and poisoned wells. Nobody in his right mind would have imagined, only a short time ago, that it should come to this. The effects on public morale are considerable. The intense hatred is new. Several generations of young Israelis went to war in the past, grim and determined, but without hatred. Now there is disdain, too, and the kind of racism that is apparent when bystanders try to stop a lynching and scream at the assailants: "He is not an Arab—don't hit him." In the past, morale here was vigorous and full of optimism. Israel was a country, perhaps the only country, where in wartime people would say "I am lucky to be here" and in peace "I wish to God I wasn't" and then stay on just the same. Israelis today are a people of spasms and upheavals. The country is polarized as never before. On the one hand, you have the infantile, often macabre thinking of religious and nationalist fanatics in whose eyes even Prime Minister Shamir is a weakling, subservient to the Americans; on the other, there is a barely contained panic that Shamir may be leading this country not only to a rift with the United States, but possibly to another terrible war.

❀

Shamir was seventy-five a few weeks ago. In a rare personal interview he said that throughout his long and stormy life as an underground leader before 1948 and later as a Mossad official and as a politician, he had always put his trust in "goddess luck." She had rarely let him down, he implied. He is a man of few words and short simple sentences but when he speaks of the Land, the homeland, in his grinding bass voice, the deep almost Wagnerian sound resonates through his small frame. His unassuming figure, short, muscular, and stocky, combines with a pair of hard grey eyes to convey an impression of bullish determination, tenacity, and resolve. Diplomatic immobilism has been the hallmark of his tenure as Prime Minister, but at the price of kindling and rekindling again and again the fires of the *intifada* and of growing international isolation. He continues to say that he will not yield a single centimeter of the Land, not even for what they call peace, "the land is ours and only ours" and the peace they offer is not peace, it's a fraud. A Palestinian state on the West Bank and in the Gaza Strip would would be the beginning of the end of the Israeli state, a first step toward its dismemberment. Local and foreign character analysts have long speculated on the complicated make up of his personality. He may be a *simplificateur terrible* or a shrewd judge of the prevailing power balance.

His predecessor as party leader and Prime Minister, Menahem Begin, was a man of vivid historical imagination who devoured history books and biographies of great men. Begin was sometimes swayed by speculations on what future historians would say about him. Shamir is not. He has few intellectual interests. As far as is known he reads only newspapers and intelligence reports. Begin had an oversized ego. Several foreign statesmen, including President Bush, are said to have made attempts to massage Shamir's ego; he is said to have none at all.

Nothing is known of his long-term strategy, if he has one, vis-à-vis the Palestinians. In his birthday interview he confessed an admiration for the courage and will power of Mao Zedong. He recalled that as a young man in Poland before the Second World War, he had possessed a weakness for the romantic Polish nationalists and freedom fighters of the nineteenth century. They had realized their national aspirations! "I recited by heart entire poems by Adam Mickiewicz," he said. The interviewer did ask how and where the Palestinians might one day realize their national aspirations. There is some speculation here that Shamir hopes the days of King Hussein on the throne of Jordan might be numbered (one of the king's private planes is said to be standing always ready at Amman airport for takeoff at a moment's notice). If Hussein falls, the Palestinians could take over Jordan, with Yasir Arafat as President. Perhaps Shamir expects to negotiate a compromise settlement with him there. But these are mere speculations. I once asked one of his aides if Shamir really believed that the Palestinians will be for ever content to live as disenfranchised citizens in a Jewish state. He said: "No, he doesn't. He wants to leave this thorny problem to his successors. Otherwise they will be so bored."

Shamir's is said to be concerned that after the resolution of the current Gulf crisis, the United States, in order to consolidate its new strategic partnership with Egypt, Saudi Arabia, and Syria, will force Israel out of the

West Bank. The opposition in Israel may be praying for just that. Alarming as an imposed Arab-Israel settlement may look to the advocates of Likud, it may yet turn out less of a danger to Israel than the present threat from an undefeated Saddam Hussein.

In the current Gulf crisis Israel is complying with a request by the United States to keep a most uncharacteristic "low profile." Behind the scenes there is a lot of back and forth. Is there or is there not military coordination between Israel and the United States? There have been so many speculations—and so many leaks—on this issue it is now a major item of public information, or disinformation, in the psychological warfare between the parties. According to some reports, there is so little coordination with the U.S. that Israel might be ready to mount a preventive attack on Iraq without even giving the U.S. prior warning; according to others, coordination is so complete Israel has even agreed to passively absorb an Iraqi first blow just to allay any suspicion that Israel provoked war.

In the present Gulf crisis Israel, in effect, became one of Saddam Hussein's hostages: Months before the Iraqi invasion of Kuwait, Saddam Hussein had threatened to wipe out "half of Israel" if Israel attacked Iraq. After the invasion, he announced that he would attack Israel if America attacked him or even if the economic sanctions began to hurt.

Israel has answered Saddam's threats with dire warnings of its own. Not a week has passed since the beginning of the Gulf crisis without such warnings by Shamir, or his Defense Minister Moshe Arens. Israel has often been described as keeping a nuclear arsenal ready in the cellar. Since the beginning of the Gulf crisis, the words Shamir used on more than one occasion were that if Iraq attacked the price Israel would make her pay will be *ayom wenora* (terrible and awful). They have been understood as a veiled threat of nuclear retaliation. Shamir has repeated them so often that one local expert on nuclear strategy, professor Yair Evron of Tel-Aviv University, has warned that such utterances by the Prime Minister might actually "legitimize" the use of nuclear weapons.

During the first weeks of the Gulf crisis Shamir's warnings were thought to be intended mainly for domestic consumption, to calm the local population. "It now seems they are carefully premeditated and are said with cold dispassion," Zev Shiff, the military editor of *Ha'aretz* recently wrote. "I suggest that Shamir's words be taken with utmost seriousness . . . his government, more than any former Israeli government, is unlikely to ignore any assault. The present Shamir government is more extremist than the Begin government that invaded Lebanon. . . . [it] tends to take extremist positions, to react strongly and to pay less attention to the consequences."

Uzi Benziman, a columnist in the same paper, wrote that under previous administrations a special committee of "wise men" had advised the government on nuclear issues and had coined the formula "Israel will not be the first to introduce nuclear weapons in the area." Benziman wondered whether this was still Israel's position. He asked: "Who are the wise men that are advising Shamir? Declarations of an escalating nature, by the Prime Minister, connoting a possible use of nuclear weapons—have they been carefully thought out and to which end?" Benziman reported that Shamir's aides continued to refuse answers to these questions.

14

Another War

Now that the Gulf War is past and Saddam Hussein's military machine—so demonized, so feared, but in retrospect so over-rated—has crumbled, people here ponder the meaning of this horrendous and chastening episode. Israeli armed forces stayed out of the war but it was the first since 1948 that hit the civilian population and caused much physical damage in the hinterland. Millions of civilians awoke to an acute sense of their vulnerability.

Israel has been through six full-fledged wars in its short life and many bloody skirmishes in between. This was, perhaps, the most political war Israel has ever been involved in. For the first time an international coalition led by the United States delivered a devastating blow against one of its most trenchant, powerful enemies. Wars are always situational ironies and produce unexpected results. In this war, not only the United States but also arch-enemies like Syria and Saudi Arabia were participating, however peripherally, in the defense of Israel against Iraqi missiles.

Now that it is over and people here have been told to dismantle their sealed rooms and pack away their gas masks, the place is once again full of political uncertainties. People wonder what the future will bring. Some are grim and angry. Many are worn out by the endless tension and disgusted by a banal, uninspiring government and by an often equally unappealing opposition. But living as they do under a curiously obtuse electoral system, at the mercy of self-indulgent party machines and unaccountable extortionist fringe groups, they are incapable of translating their disaffection politically. Speculations and wild rumors abound. Israel has always been a country of spasms and upheavals, moving in fits from one crisis to the next. Undoubtedly, many Israelis now would be glad to see the vaunted New World Order that President George Bush has spoken of materialize out of the thick air and as soon as possible. But I suspect few really believe they will. "A New Order, that's something you believe in only once in your life," I heard a middle-aged Jerusalemite man say the other day. "Never twice!."

The Gulf war was far away and at the same time very near. Every other night, or so, the sky was lit by sudden, obscene glares as the Scud missiles came in and Patriot missiles rose to disarm or deflect them and the combined debris crashed into populated residential areas. Late one night, in Jerusalem, moments after the air raid sirens had sounded and an army spokesman on the radio instructed us to put on our gas masks, I happened to look out of the bedroom window. The sky was starless and pitch black. There was a sudden flash of yellowish light. A heavy boom, like distant thunder, made the window panes vibrate. We soon learned that a missile had crashed 25 miles from here into a Tel-Aviv garden suburb, leveling half a dozen one-family houses and damaging seventy-five others but fortunately killing no one and wounding only five. During the next few days, even Jerusalem, which was never hit during the war, was a half dead city. People were scared and clung to their gas masks day and night. During the day traffic was sparse. At night it was practically nonexistent.

The missile attacks stunned and traumatized many people. Tens of thousands fled the greater Tel-Aviv area before nightfall each evening. The sirens wailed on into the small hours of the morning, and people across the nation put on their gas masks and staggered from their beds, into rooms haphazardly—and most probably insufficiently—sealed with nylon sheets and masking tape against poison gas and deadly microbes. The stationing, early in the war, of American Patriot missile batteries on the outskirts of the main cities calmed the deep sense of insecurity, but only temporarily. However "smart," the Patriots did not render the Scuds harmless while still in the stratosphere or far enough from populated urban centers, to prevent massive damage.

Defense Minister Moshe Arens went to Washington to try to convince President Bush that Israel should be allowed to retaliate and that for this purpose a corridor be cleared for Israeli bombers through Saudi Arabian air-space. He was being overly dramatic when he said in Washington that the damage in Tel-Aviv was "worse than anything seen in the West since

World War Two." Yet it was bad enough. A Scud missile may be clumsy and imprecise. But as it crashes into a built-up area at a speed several times that of sound the effect of only one can be devastating. I walked through some of the areas in and around Tel-Aviv that were hit by Scuds. They looked as though they had suffered a serious earthquake. The blasts reached far and wide. Roofs were ripped out, floors caved in, walls and balconies collapsed and, of course, windows and shutters were smashed within a radius of half a mile. Deep craters indicated the point of impact.

Nearly 9,000 damaged homes—some 120 totally destroyed—were reported in the Tel-Aviv metropolitan area alone. Miraculously, only one person died; according to an army spokesman, 239 were wounded, and 705 others were treated for light injuries. The Scuds were reported to have caused fourteen more "indirect" deaths, through heart failure or suffocation by people who in their haste had not unplugged their gas masks properly. The extent of moral and psychological damage was the subject of much public discussion. Israel is known for its abundance of mental health services and psychological first aid stations. All worked around the clock during the emergency, and were reportedly flooded with requests for help by anxiety-ridden people. After walking past a row of rickety old houses in South Tel-Aviv that had been badly hit by an Iraqi missile, a well-known literary critic and Tel-Aviv University professor named Dan Meron generalized bitterly on the "fragility and flimsiness" of the moth-and rust-eaten homes of Tel-Aviv, as though made only of "sawdust and glue." Other cities conveyed a sense of strength even in ruins, he wrote. Those of Tel-Aviv were only "tents of whitewash and mildewed plywood, sun-roasted and rotten from the rain." The crumbling lot, he suggested in a widely discussed article in *Ha'aretz*, reflected the wretchedness of the nation's "pasteboard" military and political strategists too, Israel's best and brightest, exposing their shallowness, their self-importance, and their dubious military and political scenarios.

Opposition leaders chastised the government for scuttling the peace process last year thus enabling Saddam Hussein to make political capital out of the unresolved Palestinian issue. Had Israel started peace talks with Jordan and the Palestinians before the Gulf crisis erupted, Israel might even have become a full-fledged partner in the anti-Iraq coalition, instead of remaining the leper that the others were trying to avoid. The government's answer was that by identifying so whole-heartedly with the "Butcher of Bagdad" the Palestinians were showing their true colors. Had Israel withdrawn from occupied territories or allowed the establishment of a Palestinian state, government spokesmen argued, that state could have allied itself with Iraq and allowed more accurate and even more devastating short-range missiles to be launched from its territory with not even the current four or five minutes warning time. Right-wing radicals urged the government to defy the United States and intervene in the war anyway. The endless stream of assertions by ex-generals that retaliation against Iraq was inevitable, and by politicians that it was imminent, multiplied the tensions generated by sleepless nights and left the country in a nerve-wracked holding pattern. Many people complained of chronic headaches and insomnia and of obsessive urges to smoke or overeat. There were other complaints as well. One morning I overheard a conversation between two women at a Jerusalem bus stop.

"You have slimmed," said one. "Are you on a diet?"

"No dear, it's the situation."

❀

Political pressure in favor of an independent attack on Iraq mounted all the time. One member of parliament announced that he had been assured by a "top psychiatrist" that if Israel did not not strike immediately at Iraq the national morale would completely "collapse." Public opinion polls showed rather that most people approved of the government's decision to stay out of the war and allow the Americans to reduce the Iraqi war-machine to ashes. To protect his flank, Prime Minister Yitzhak Shamir pushed his cabinet further to the right—under cover of the war—by taking in a new minister notorious for his support of the expulsion of all Palestinians from the occupied West Bank and Gaza Strip. But Shamir successfully resisted all demands that Israel intervene independently. Some top army and air force commanders kept telling him that Israel might do a better job than the United States in eliminated the missile launching pads in western Iraq. What Israel would do that America and her allies could not was never publicly spelled out. One heard vague complaints that U.S. Air Force pilots were too busy elsewhere to bother about missile launchers in western Iraq; that Israeli pilots might have been ready to take greater risks. According to one source the interventionists proposed to parachute Israeli commando troops into western Iraq. At one point in the debate, former Defense Minister Yitzhak Rabin sardonically observed that if the destruction of missile sites in distant Iraq were so easy why were they having such a hard time taking out Palestinian katyusha rocket launchers in nearby southern Lebanon.

Chief among the politicians pushing for retaliation against Iraq was Housing Minister Ariel Sharon. With his heavy frame, Sharon has recently come to look more and more like a figure in a Botero painting. Sharon made it a habit during the war to tour neighborhoods hit by Scud missiles. In his booming voice, he would tell the now homeless that the government had not given them the protection they deserved. Gideon Samet, a columnist in *Ha'aretz* accused Sharon of "scavenging in the ruins." Inside the cabinet Sharon pushed for a massive Israeli retaliatory strike against Iraq. He maintained that if Israel did not strike out, she would lose her "credibility" and her power to deter future attacks. Every Arab state would feel free to attack her with impunity. Sharon proposed sending a strong tank column through Jordanian territory into western Iraq. In the cabinet the Prime Minister refused to put Sharon's proposals to the vote. When, later on during the ground war, tens of thousands of Iraqi soldiers surrendered without a fight to the advancing allies , the joke among militant Israelis was that the Iraqi and Israeli army had one thing in common: neither participated in the fighting.

United States airplanes operating from Turkish bases continued to bomb Scud missile launching sites in western Iraq. But the number of mobile missile launchers seems to have been grossly underestimated by American and Israeli intelligence. Many were hiding out in the dunes, and Iraqi missiles continued to fall on Israel until the last days of the war. The country sometimes appeared almost paralyzed as a result. During the first few days of the war the government itself asked people to stay home. Later on, it was unable to bring the country back to any kind of normalcy. During daylight, Tel-Avivians tried to continue in their usual hectic but nervous pace. On the streets people walked to their daily chores carrying gas masks and antropin injectors (against nerve gas). Cafes and restaurants were deserted. Schools were shut down. The university called off examinations and closed a week before the end of the winter term. Buses stopped running after dark. Tel-Aviv promotes itself as a "City Without Pause." Before the war it was not uncommon to encounter serious traffic jams in Tel-Aviv at 3 A.M. During the Gulf War, the streets emptied as soon as it grew dark. The city seemed at times like a Palestinian town in the occupied territories under military curfew. The all-night cafés and restaurants and bars remained shut. Many people did not go to work. Many more or less closed themselves into their homes for the duration of the war. When a day or two passed without a missile attack the tension mounted almost palpably. People were irritable and quick-tempered. Missile attacks came late at night. People were aroused from their uneasy sleep and complained in the morning of "Saddam Hussein jet-lag."

Entire apartment blocks in more affluent North Tel-Aviv were said to have been almost totally evacuated as thousands moved out of town to stay with relatives and friends, or in kibbutz guest-houses, out in the country. The rich with their families and Filipina nannies settled into five-star tourist hotels in Jerusalem that had been practically deserted since the Gulf crisis broke out. Others went farther south. One hotel operator in the Red Sea resort of Eilat was quoted as saying: "First Saddam Hussein chased away our tourists. Now he he is bringing them back."

Although they had been, in a general way, warned against such a war, Israelis were unprepared for it when it came. Conventional bomb-proof air-raid shelters were few and in most cases too far apart to enable people to reach them safely in the four or five minutes it took from the time they were aroused from their beds until the missiles fell. Public shelters were in a bad state of repair. They had been built decades before to provide protection against conventional bombs dropped from relatively slow flying aircraft that could be detected in time by radar. In this war missiles were shot into space from fixed or mobile launchers more than 500 kilometers away and came down on their targets with lightening speed.

It was a war unlike any other Israelis had known. Its imagery, strategy, geography, and weaponry were different and more surrealist than anything the country had been used to in the past. Its alleged purpose was to terrorize Israel into widening the Gulf war into an Arab-Israel war, thereby, presumably, breaking up the American-led alliance. Its implied threat was the use of poison gas. Poison gas has been widely employed before against troops and sporadically against civilians in Third World countries; but this was probably the first time an entire nation was on the alert against a possible attack by nerve and mustard gas. It was possibly the first time an entire nation on a single command put on gas masks—clumsy, elephantine, rubber contraptions—and unpacked the little gauze pads, sodium bi-carbonate, special cleansing powders, and antropin injectors. When the air-raid sirens sounded just about everybody donned their gas masks until they were told on the radio to remove them, some 45 minutes later. Babies were locked into cumbersome contraptions that looked like transparent tents or incubators. Small children were made to put on see-through helmets with battery operated air-pumps. After schools reopened, a million school-children went about every morning carrying gas masks to class. In class they were drilled to throw themselves on the floor in the case of an attack and if necessary give themselves antropin injections in the thigh. At home children were told of warheads carrying bacteria of plague or cholera. Five-year-olds learned to ask after an attack whether it had been "conventional" or "chemical." No one can say what the effects of all this will be on the young or how it was connected to the faceless "Arab" they hear of or to the Palestinians they may see every day and whom they will have to live close to for the rest of their lives. That the experience tainted the children somehow is probable. "In the land of the Jews," Novelist David Grossman wrote a few days after the war broke out, "long before children learn the facts of life we must tell them the facts of death."

The revelations in the German press that German manufacturers had sold Iraq mustard-gas technology and that German engineers may have helped Iraq to increase the range of Soviet Scud missiles—enough to reach southern Israel from western Iraq—unleashed a wave of protests in Israel and Germany. Survivors of Nazi concentration camps associated the German involvement in Iraq with their worst memories of World War Two. A veritable storm of breast-beating German visitors, headed by Foreign Minister Genscher and Bundestag president Rita Sussmuth descended on Jerusalem and Tel-Aviv. In a fit of bad conscience visiting German mayors handed out lavish gifts to Israeli cities and Genscher awarded grants totalling $900 million, mostly to buy submarines and other war machinery in Germany. Halfway through the war there were so many prominent German politicians in Israel ("more or less in a state of stress") that, according to the reporter of the Hamburg newsweekly *Der Spiegel*, the King David Hotel in Jerusalem seemed "almost like the Bundestag."

It is not difficult to imagine the emotional charge and power of the word "gas" in Israel, poison gas made in Germany or manufactured under German license, as the gas in Iraq's arsenal was thought to be. Israeli school children learn about the gas chambers of Auschwitz much as children in Japan learn about Hiroshima. Before and during the Gulf war the Iraqi leader threatened to "incinerate half of Israel." He spoke of an Islamic *fin de siècle* Armageddon, a "Mother of All Battles." During the last three or four days of the war, the looming likelihood and fear of a chemical or biological attack on Israel as a final spasm of Iraqi defiance cast an apocalyptic spell. It was widely believed that in the event of a chemical or biological strike Israel would retaliate with nuclear weapons. General Dan Shomron, the Israeli chief of staff, escalated the standard formula ("Israel will not be the first to introduce nuclear weapons") saying Israel would not be the first to "use" them. Two weeks after the war began U. S. Defense Secretary Richard Cheney warned Iraq openly of such a possibility. We will probably never know if these threats actually deterred Iraq from using chemical or biological weapons or whether Iraq had been bluffing or incapable of using them. Uzi Benziman, a columnist in *Ha'aretz* wondered what the long-range consequences of this verbal escalation might be and if the Shamir government had seriously taken into consideration the larger dynamic involved in the launching of such threats. Benziman had raised such questions even earlier. It was characteristic of the public apathy on this issue that at war's end he was still the only journalist who raised probing questions on this issue in an otherwise discordant press.

❋

Throughout all the somber threats and counterthreats, immigrants from the Soviet Union continued to arrive in Israel. They came in by special El Al charters; all other airlines had suspended flights to Tel-Aviv due to the war. Even as the missiles were falling during the first four weeks, some 15,000 Soviet immigrants landed at the Tel-Aviv airport. Though twice as many had arrived in December, the number of those arriving during the war was still remarkably high; it was high enough to illustrate the continuing eagerness of Russian Jews to become Israelis, or their desperate desire to get out of the Soviet Union, even to a place where upon landing the first thing they were given was a gas mask. One planeload of Russian immigrants approached the airport in the middle of a missile attack and was turned back in midair. It flew back to Budapest where the passengers disembarked for the night. When it turned round next morning, according to a newspaper report, no one had dropped out and those on the second flight had been joined by an additional forty. On television one saw immigrants kissing the tarmac as they stepped off the plane. One said "I thank God for being here, for you being here, for us being here." Another, asked by a television reporter if he was not afraid of Scud missiles, smiled broadly and said in a thick accent: "No, things made in Russia don't work." It was noted that a surprisingly high number of Russians were bringing in poodles and other thoroughbred dogs, presumably to sell in Israel. One immigrant offered the explanation that "grand-pianos are more cumbersome to transport and, frankly, there isn't anything else to buy nowadays in Moscow."

Continuing immigration was a boost to morale. But as missiles continued to fall the proud self-image of an Israel protected by a tough citizen army adept at practicing the biblical doctrine of an "eye for an eye" was overshadowed in the eyes of many by an older image of the helpless Jew huddling for protection. Nor was the sight—albeit welcome—of United States soldiers manning Patriot missile batteries on the outskirts of Tel-Aviv, Haifa, and Jerusalem any less sobering. Ever since Moshe Dayan had announced, on the eve of the 1967 war, that he did not want American soldiers to fight Israel's wars, Israel has been proud of its self-sufficiency, at least on the battlefield. The Americans were supposed to leave as soon as

Israeli crews were trained to operate the batteries themselves. But even on a temporary basis the presence of American troops was a blow to self-esteem and established military doctrine. Nevertheless, a few imaginative spirits saw something hopeful in all this. They hoped that the presence of American troops in Israel was a precedent which would pave the way to an American-Israel defense treaty, which might give Israel the courage to relinquish occupied territories. Others expressed a faint hope that people who had been locked into their sealed rooms so often for so long would feel more empathy in the future for Palestinians in the occupied territories who are routinely locked into their homes for weeks on end during the frequent curfews imposed by Israeli army commanders. In Haifa one night, just as the novelist A. B. Yehoshua and his family were putting on gas masks, they heard on the radio that at this very moment people in Riad and Bahrain were doing the same. Yehoshua described his sense of wonder at "this strange community of fate with Saudis and Bahrainis, devout Moslems, with a fine per capita income." The stereotype of "a one dimensional Arab world, monolytic and menacing," he wrote, "has been destroyed." Yehoshua believes that Israel should withdraw from the West Bank and allow the Palestinians to establish a demilitarized state there. Israel's claim for the West Bank is political mysticism, he says. "We are a spoiled Western society . . . [but] we perpetuate a religious-metaphysical myth from 2000 years ago . . . They don't go together. If you want a modern, Western lifestyle, with all of its luxuries, then you have to let go of the metaphysical myths. You can't live both ways at the same time."

Inevitably, there was humor too and a spate of excellent satire on television. And, scary as some of the missiles were, especially during the multiple bombardments of the first week, the fireworks in the sky attracted many watchers. Thousands climbed the flat roofs of Tel-Aviv during alerts to watch the missiles shoot in and call a radio station to describe what they had seen. Teenagers painted their gas masks in psychedelic colors. "Designer" bags for gas masks were on sale at every supermarket. Many bore inscriptions such as "Love" or "We'll get over this too" Despite a ban on public gatherings several symphony orchestras continued to play for smaller audiences in the afternoons. And in Jerusalem, once, the air-raid sirens sounded while Isaac Stern was performing Mozart's violin concerto No 3. Stern and the orchestra withdrew to their sealed dressing rooms. Most people in the audience put on gas masks. But after a few minutes, the alert still on, Stern returned to the stage without a mask and played a Bach adagio to a charmed but still largely masked audience. There was also a wave of jokes of the gallows-humor variety. They accentuated the general sense of gloom, which continued well into the postwar period. The war was widely seen as a fore-taste of what Israel might face in the future. Next time there might be many more missiles, more accurate and more powerful.

There was a widespread awareness that only a fluke, an "incredible piece of luck," in the words of a Civil Defense spokesman, had kept the casualty rate as low as it was. The Scuds that hit low-density suburbs might have hit high-density areas, schools, hospitals, high rise apartment houses. Masses of people might have been killed, as in SaudiArabia, where an Iraqi Scud hit an American barracks and killed twenty-eight soldiers. Apart from chemical and biological warheads, the greatest concern of the Civil Defense authorities was of mass casualties by conventional means. There was a concern that existing emergency services would not be enough to cope with the results of dozens of missiles crashing simultaneously into urban areas, necessitating the evacuation tens of thousands or even hundreds of thousands of people from their homes.

❋

The Palestinians in the occupied territories supported Saddam Hussein but they were probably the last who "wanted" a war in the Gulf which they feared might spread to neighboring Jordan. Their leaders hoped to exploit the Gulf crisis politically but short of a war that might serve the Israelis as a pretext to expel thousands of Palestinian militants. Jordanian television is seen on the West Bank and Yasir Arafat was frequently on it embracing and kissing the Iraqi leader. He too may have hoped that there would be no war. He should have known better. He did not—thus confirming once more the old adage that the Palestinian leadership never misses a chance to spoil its case or lose an opportunity.

"If the PLO had remained, like Jordan, on the sidelines," a senior American diplomat in Israel told me, "they would have survived the war unharmed. Had the PLO remained neutral it might have been able to negotiate after the war from a position of strength. Had it joined the American led Egyptian-Saudi-Syrian coalition it might have established a Palestinian state on the West Bank and Gaza within a year or two." But Arafat sided with Saddam Hussein. Halfway through the war he declared "These are days of glory and pride and steadfastness of our Arab nation . . . The real aim of the treacherous American aggression is not to enforce compliance with UN resolutions but to destroy Palestine and the Arab nation . . . (and make place for) three million Russian Jews in a Greater Israel (stretching) from the Nile to the Euphrates." Yassar Abed-Rabbo a member of the PLO executive, well-known to Israeli liberals and academics from recent international encounters and seminars where he had assured them that the PLO was opposed to all violence, was quoted as saying that Bush's real aim was not the liberation of Kuwait but rather to ensure Israeli hegemony in the Middle East and the continued terrorization of the Palestinians. "The Israelis," he predicted, "will be taught a bloody lesson in this war."

Once again, as so often in the past, one watched with awe and incomprehension the self-destructive nature of Palestinian politics. A few academics and at least one prominent Palestinian leader in East Jerusalem confided to American or Israeli acquaintances a fear that support for Iraq might prove disastrous to the Palestinian cause. None ever said so publicly. If this reflected the weakness or short-sightedness of the local Palestinian leadership it was also true that this leadership had been decimated over the years by imprisonments and expulsions at the hand of the Israeli occupation authorities. Outspoken Palestinians also live in fear of being assassinated by nationalist or Islamic fanatics.

Palestinian support for Saddam Hussein was nurtured by grief and by rage, grief over the failure and weakness of generations of Palestinians, rage at Israel and at America, the demon thought to have made Israel's humiliation of the Palestinians possible. The rage was was a kind of poor man's revenge. The weak may not be able to defeat the strong but they can drive them nuts. A few weeks before the war, on a day when the walls of East Jerusalem were covered with pro-Iraqi and pro PLO grafitti and Palestinian newspapers were filled with expressions of sympathy for Saddam Hussein, I asked a Palestinian militant in what manner such identification with Iraq could possibly help the cause of Palestinian self-determination. He said, "Israel refuses to talk to us and has left us no other choice." He was aware, he added, that Saddam Hussein was "a bloody tyrant," and even "guilty of genocide." He readily granted that Saddam Hussein probably did not care for the Palestinian cause and was merely exploiting it to undermine the anti-Iraq alliance. But Saddam Hussein was breaking the ground rules in the Middle East which for Palestinians had become unbearable. "I don't idolize Saddam," he insisted but in the crisis Saddam Hussein had generated, he saw a potential to change the status quo in Palestine." Another Palestinian, a professor at the university of Bir Zeit, which the military government closed three years ago at the beginning of the *intifada*, said: "What have we to lose? Most of our leaders are in jail. Those who are not in jail are refused permission to go abroad. Those who are not abroad are under house arrest. Our cities are shut by curfews. People cannot work. Tens of thousands on the West Bank have lost their livelihood." When I visited him the professor had just finished holding an illegal seminar in his living room for some of his students. "I am trying my best to keep them intellectually alive," he said.

Two days before the Gulf war *A Nahar*, the pro-Jordanian Palestinian daily paper published in East Jerusalem, defied the Israeli military press censor and printed a long paean to Saddam Hussein on its front page. The homage, rendered in heavy handed sarcasm, was in the form of a free verse poem. Here is a free translation of some of the lines:

Kill him! For being the
Arab nations' hope and symbol!
Kill him! For battling
the desert tribes of Arabia,
for not worshipping almighty dollar,
for not bowing down to America!
Kill him! For battling to unite all Arabs
and give them a forbidden power.
Go ahead and kill him
for defending honor
which America trampled.
For singing freedom's song
that Brittain stifled
Russia buried
and Europe renounced.
Kill him! For being tough and rebellious
like Harun al Rashid, Saladin and Nebuchadnezzar.
Kill him! For rejecting half solutions.
There is no half honor
and no half jihad.
Kill him! For telling the world:
Give us liberty
or let us die like men.

When the first missiles fell on Tel-Aviv Israeli newspapers reported that Palestinians were "dancing on the rooftops" for joy. The phrase has since become a political and journalistic common place. For more than a month I have been looking for someone who saw with his own eyes the "dancing on the rooftops." I have found no one and have come to suspect that this might be one of those myths of war that capture the imagination of peoples because they conform to deeply ingrained prejudices in the political culture, like the rape of the nuns in Belgium during the first world war. Myth is often "history" people assume they already "know" somehow. The lights of Tel-Aviv are clearly visible from many Palestinian villages in the Judean and Samarian foothills and certainly Palestinians did climb their roofs to watch the fireworks generated by the flying Scud and Patriot missiles. But so did thousands of Tel-Aviv residents. The myth may have originated in a common journalistic cliché, or in its opposite, as in "the day taxes were raised there was no dancing in the streets." True or false, the "dancing on the rooftops" has become a key phrase in the arguments used now against withdrawal from occupied territories. There is no doubt that many Palestinians welcomed the destruction caused in Tel-Aviv by Iraqi missiles. Many undoubtedly sung the jingle "*Ya Saddam, ya habib/Udrub, udrub Tel Abib.*" (O Saddam, dear fellow/ beat, beat Tel-Aviv). After a Scud missile hit the posh Tel-Aviv garden suburb where Defense Minister Moshe Arens lives, a Palestinian lawyer from Ramallah whom I met in East Jerusalem, said to me: "God bless Saddam Hussein. Finally we have a man who fights back and brings the *intifada*, like a boomerang, to the streets of Tel-Aviv. Tel-Aviv is now as deserted as Ramallah. No cinema and no concerts." One evening in Jerusalem I heard Yassar Abed-Rabbo of the PLO say on Jordanian television "The missiles on Tel-Aviv emphasize the link between Kuwait and Palestine." Immediately afterward Jordanian television showed a documentary about American atrocities against Iraqi children "seekers of truth, justice, equality and peace." An Iraqi soldier, making the V sign, cried out in Arabic: "See you in Jerusalem!"

East Jerusalem and the West Bank were alive with rumors of American defeats in the Gulf, and other odd tales. One old lady assured an acquaintance of mine that during the night she had seen an Iraqi missile flying over Jerusalem. It had hovered for a moment above al-Haram-al Sharif, from where Muhammad had climbed to heaven on a ladder of light; after tipping its wings in a salute to the holy mosques it had continued on its way to Tel-Aviv.

Faisal Husseini, son of a famous Palestinian guerrilla leader who died in the 1948 civil war between Palestinian Jews and Palestinian Arabs has often been described as the PLO's chief representative in the occupied territories and as a possible successor to Yasir Arafat. He heads a research institute in East Jerusalem and is frequently interviewed by local and international journalists. During the first week of the war, Israel radio quoted a statement he had made on BBC radio deploring the bombardment of innocent civilians in Tel-Aviv. He was reported to have received so many threats to his life from Palestinian extremists that he issued a firm denial, claiming that the broadcast was an Israeli attempt to distort his words for propaganda purposes. A few days later he elaborated on it and explained to a reporter for the Israeli mass circulation tabloid *Yediot Ahronot*: "I don't want to see Bagdad destroyed. I don't want to see Tel-Aviv destroyed. I want us to finish this war so we can start building a Palestinian state alongside (and at peace with) Israel." Dr. Sari Nusseibeh, another well known PLO supporter, published an article in an East Jerusalem paper entitled "Saddam smashes the Six Day War myth." Soon afterward, he was accused of being an Iraqi spy and put under administrative arrest. On the eve of the Muslim feast of al Isra and al Miraj to celebrate Muhammad's ascent to heaven from Jerusalem, Baghdad radio announced a special "holiday gift" from president Saddam Hussein to the valiant Palestinian people. That night two missiles were launched against the Tel-Aviv metropolitan area.

When the ground war began and as it became obvious that Iraq would suffer a devastating military defeat, Palestinian militants with whom I spoke began to sound slightly occult, insisting that on the contrary, as he was losing the war Saddam Hussein was actually winning it. Dr Mahdi Abdul Hady, a former high official in the Jordanian government who now heads a Palestinian think tank in East Jerusalem, told me: "The Western mind will say, incorrectly, that Saddam committed suicide. The Arab mind will say he died a martyr. Saddam will become a shining legend. He will bring about another pan-Arab awakening."

The East Jerusalem press never reported the full extent of the Iraqi army defeat in the field, nor did Jordanian Television. On Jordanian television one never saw the long lines of haggard, starving Iraqi soldiers surrendering to the allied troops or the wrecks of the destroyed Iraqi war machinery littering the desert. Many Palestinians took their cue from Jordanian prime minister Mudar Badran who told parliament there was no rout but a well organized and orderly redeployment of Iraqi armed forces. According to reports in the East Jerusalem press the war ended in a standoff and was even a kind of victory for Iraq which had been able to withstand a treacherous attack by nearly the whole world. I asked a Palestinian editor why they were not reporting the whole truth. "What is truth?" he said bitterly "The Palestinians have been betrayed by most Arab governments and humiliated by Israel for a generation . . . for us truth is what gives strength and hope to face a hard future." The "General United Command of the Intifada" in a leaflet distributed after the war claimed that the "firm stand of the Iraqi army compelled the aggressors, headed by the criminal Bush, to call a cease fire.

There was a tendency in some quarters to interpret Iraq's defeat in near eschatological terms. Jonathan Kuttab, a prominent civil rights lawyer in

East Jerusalem, and a Christian told me that after the Iraqi defeat he had gone back to watch the entire CNN interview with Saddam Hussein. "For the first time in my life I felt I could relate to Islam. He seemed like a prophet. His message sounded almost like liberation theology."

I asked Kuttab what that message was. "Saddam took a position in the name of Islam to confront Western duplicity, materialism and corruption," he said "Saddam spoke of social equality and the evils of Saudi consumerism. Arab intellectuals with their borrowed Western ideas—capitalism or Marxism—have no roots in Arab society. Islam does. I am a Christian but as an Arab I now recognize my Islamic roots. Secular Arab nationalism died in this war. Saddam Hussein's message, in two simple words was: *Allahu Akhbar*. God is great, god is greater than Bush, stronger than his devastating bombs, stronger than the Israeli occupation of our Land. Israel and America should be worried. Saddam's victory will be obvious to everyone in five years from now."

✺

For many years, the Arab-Israel conflict has been like a classic Greek tragedy: the clash is not between good and evil but between two rights, two kinds of justice. After each act the curtain falls on a stage littered with corpses. In the words of the Israeli historian Meron Benvenisti, after the fifth or sixth act the spectators cry: Wait a minute! Where is the catharsis in this tragedy? But the catharsis never comes. The play only gets worse and worse. A few days ago, at the end of the most recent act in that play, Secretary of State James Baker entered the stage here amidst speculation that he might actually, at long last, like some *deus ex machina*, begin to make peace, between Israel and the Arab states and between Israel and the Palestinians.

He was on the penultimate leg of a tour of the Middle East and one of his main purposes was to pry both sides, Israelis and Palestinians, out of their mutual claustrophilia. The defeat of Saddam Hussein, the weakened position of Yasir Arafat, the success of Egypt (which had made peace with Israel) to regain its position of leadership in the Arab world, the near brush with chemical and nuclear weapons of destruction, the growing, crushing economic cost of war—were seen as propitious opening conditions for political, military, and economic settlements. In addition, the Machiavellian "reversal of alliances" during the recent war may have opened possibilities never before seen. As an amateur psychiatrist in Jerusalem pointed out, it should not be difficult to reconcile two enemies as long as a third is available they may jointly hate.

Baker's initiative elicited new hopes in some and old fears in others. Baker did not come with a blueprint but, as he put it, with a number of "ideas." Peace might be attainable but in exchange for territory. On this issue Baker found Israelis as sharply divided as they have always been. Doves and hawks considered their views vindicated by the events of the late war. Doves argued that the missiles fired from such great distance rendered the old notion of "secure borders" obsolete. During the Gulf war, early warnings on missile attacks had come not from radar stations on the West Bank but from an American satellite broadcasting to Washingtom via a relay station in Australia. The best thing that could come from this war, according to the doves, was for Israel to gain a sense of its true size and strength. Hawks argued that strategic depth was still vital. Even if such depth gave no immediate protection against missiles, it was was still the only protection against ground attack. Even the mighty U.S. expeditionary force with its smart weapons and overwhelming air power had to wage a ground war to defeat Saddam Hussein. Israeli troops must remain where they are, they said, and the United States should block the rush by Saudi Arabia, Egypt, and Syria to acquire more armaments.

Ariel Sharon addressed an impassioned appeal to Baker as did Yossi Beilin, a Labor member of the Knesset and a former deputy minister of foreign affairs. Sharon urged Baker to bear in mind the devious mentality of the Arabs; they had not yet given up on their murderous designs. Rather than succumb to a "strange and obsessive preoccupation" with the Palestinian question, said Sharon, "Assad-led Syria's venemous fangs must be removed as well as those of Khaddafi's Lybia."

Beilin told Baker "If you meet someone in the Middle East who claims he understands the mentality of the Jews or the mentality of the Arabs, know that you are meeting someone who is against peace. In this area everyone understands the mentality of the other side but not his own." Several previous American peace initiatives had floundered on procedural wrangles. Beilin warned Baker, "if someone tells you that procedural questions are very serious—be aware of a trap. Procedure is the last resort of the enemy of peace."

"There will not be peace without Israeli withdrawal from most of the occupied territories which would eventually revert to Arab rule— Palestinian, Jordanian or joint Jordanian-Palestinian," Beilin wrote. "Evacuated areas would have to be demilitarized." Every peace proposal since 1967 had been based on this or on a similar version, "every Israeli politician knows this and this is the reason why some Israeli politicians during the last twenty-five years have supported such a settlement and why others topple every proposal on procedural grounds in order not be put on a spot and refuse reasonable offer of peace."

On the eve of Baker's arrival a man from the Gaza strip—often dubbed Israel's "Soweto"—knifed four Israeli women to death on a West-Jerusalem street, as a "message to James Baker," he told the police after his arrest. Astonishingly enough, he was a male nurse, trained to heal; he too cried out *Allahu Akhbar*! as he thrust a long kitchen knife in and out four times in a row. Palestinian leaders on the West Bank and in the Gaza Strip unanimously condemned the murderer as a psychopath but they remained divided on whether or not they should meet with Baker, in view of the United States treacherous attack on Iraq. After much back and forth, the moderates prevailed. Arafat authorized the meeting. A delegation of local Palestinian leaders headed by Faisal Husseini met with Baker in the U.S. consulate. Outside the consulate Israeli right-wingers protested their arrival with signs saying: "Baker go dance on the roof tops with Husseini." Baker apparently assured the Palestinian delegation that while the organization headed by Arafat may have suffered a serious setback as a result of its identification with Saddam Hussein, the need to resolve the Palestinian problem was more urgent now than ever before. He asked whether they are able to move without Arafat and the PLO. The Palestinians assured him that they could and would not. The PLO remained the one and only representative of the Palestinian people, they said. They appeared shocked when Baker told them that not one of the eight Arab leaders with whom he had spoken in Riad would talk with Arafat. Whether the local Palestinian leadership would be able from now on to be less dependent on Arafat and on the warring PLO factions in Tunis remained an open question.

The Israeli government sent Baker on a helicopter trip to underline Israel's need for strategic depth, on the Golan heights and at the famous ten miles "narrow waist" in Central Israel. Baker came back and told the Israeli leaders that, in his opinion, geography alone is no guarantee for security and security does not grow out of military force alone. He did not threaten and he did not press. He warned against missing a "historical opportunity." In his talks with eight Arab foreign ministers in Riad, he said, he had encountered important signs of change. There was "new thinking" and a willingness to move toward Israel but for that willingness to ripen Israel must indicate a readiness to trade territory for peace and show greater flexibility on the Palestinian issue. For the time being neither Palestinians nor Israelis were saying "no" to Baker. One Israeli diplomat said, admiringly, "Baker has started a Middle East contest: who will be the first to say no.

Israel certainly does not want to be the winner. For this reason the negotiations will go on . . . and on."

But if the key to any accord was territory, other observers here were wondering whether this present government, under Shamir, would ever be willing, and if willing, capable, to relinquish any. Past Israeli governments, almost as a rule, have succeeded in outliving several American secretaries of state and even administrations. Shamir may well hope to wear out the current one, as his predecessors have outworn and survived others. The peace for territory debate between Israel and the United States is not a new one. In one form or another it has been going on since 1967. Shamir and Baker had one long tete a tete meeting. There was speculation here that an Arab-Israeli peace conference chaired by the United States and the Soviet Union was discussed, along with a series of mutual Arab and Israeli humanitarian gestures. There might be a readiness in the future to cede some territory on the Golan heights in return for peace with Syria. But Syria was not likely to move without progress on the Palestinian issue. It was hard to see any movement on this issue, unless the Palestinians can be talked into being content, for a limited interim period, with some kind of limited autonomy rule. They were offered autonomy in 1978 and refused. A few Palestinians now admit in private that if they had accepted autonomy in 1978 the massive Israeli settlement program on the West Bank might not have taken place, and perhaps, by now they would have had an independent state. Admittedly, it's a very big "perhaps" and, anyway, the past cannot be undone and the Palestinians have not become less militant since. Israel in turn, will relinquish "historic" or "strategically important" territory only when enough people in power in Jerusalem begin to feel that the West Bank and Gaza are not military assets, nor religious or historic icons, but an unbearable burden.

15

A Visit with Arafat

Street names in Tunis are a nice mix of colonial French and Third World nationalism. The Avenue de France intersects the rue Gamal Abdul Nasser. Boulevard Raspail runs into rue Patrice Lumumba; Jaures into Paléstine. Driving up the rue Paléstine, lined with garages and hardware stores, one quickly reaches the wide belt of new ruins of Carthage. In Sidi Bou Said, the picturesque old fishermen's village, now a luxury resort, guides show you the house where Andre Gide lived and the sumptuous villa where in 1988, Khalil al Wasir (alias Abu Jihad, the PLO's minister of war) was assassinated by Israeli commandoes.

The nearby suburbs of al Manzah and al Manar are less chic; many streets are so new that they have only numbers, and some are not yet paved. But the lawns and flowering flame trees behind the high garden walls and *ferre forgé* iron gates are well tended. In their driveways one spots Mercedes and other luxury cars.

Into this wealthy, even bucolic world of middle-class and upper-middle-class comfort, the desk-bound guerrilla leaders and revolutionaries of the Palestine Liberation Organization withdrew, after their forced ouster from Beirut, in the early eighties, along with an army of body guards, bureaucrats, and butlers and a fortune variously estimated at one billion dollars. (The PLO fighting army of some twenty thousand men was not allowed into Tunisia;

they are said to be encamped in Libya and South Yemen). Yasir Arafat himself picked Tunisia for his new headquarters because of the relative political—though not military—freedom he was offered at the instigation of the French and the Greek governments, and of President Bourguiba's fervent wife, Vasilla, a long-time supporter of the Palestinian cause. A formal accord signed between the two sides spelled out the military restrictions. Other Arab countries at that time imposed more severe limitations on the PLO, and Syria was actually waging war against them.

A decade later, here at al Manzah and al Manar, the surviving guerrilla leaders are still around, each with his *chef de cabinet*, his fax machines and computers, his fleet of luxury cars fitted with cellular phones, grim-looking body guards, and burgeoning retinues of counselors, secretaries, valets, maids, chauffeurs, and cooks. Palestine is more than a thousand miles away. But the Japanese electronic company Sharp has custom-built an elaborate communication system enabling PLO members easy contact with their men throughout the Arab world.

There has been no lack of friction over the years with the Tunisian government. The authorities have clamped down whenever the Palestinians seemed to violate the original accord or threaten, by their very presence, the thriving Tunisian tourist industry. In 1985, after the Israeli air force bombed a PLO command post outside Hamam al Shat, north of the city of Tunis, in retaliation against a Palestinian terrorist attack on Israeli yachtsmen in Cyprus, the Tunisian government ordered Palestinian "military" personnel removed from Tunisia; the Palestinians could no longer launch terrorist attacks from Tunisian bases, or at least they hid them more carefully. By and large they have been allowed by a sympathetic regime to pursue their political cause. They remain under constant surveillance by the *mukhabarat*, the Tunisian secret police.

There is no central PLO administration building in Tunis. Offices are spread out in suburban villas, large and small, in al Manzah and al Manar, much like those of the FLN leaders in the fifties, but more comfortable and with the latest electronic gadgetry—revolutionary technology having impressively advanced since that time. It is the government of a phantom—some say a pantomime—state, elected by a phantom parliament from throughout the Palestinian diaspora (a parliament not unlike the Zionist congresses of old, and as ridden by rivalries and schisms). The leader is still Yasir Arafat, as he has been since 1969. The man who often proclaimed in the past that he didn't want peace, "We want war, victory. Peace for us means the destruction of Israel," has in the past four years, under U.S. pressure, recognized Israel's right to exist in peace and security and renounced terrorism. He insists he now favors a two-state solution—with Palestine and Israel living peacefully side by side. In Madrid and Washington he has been negotiating a peace settlement with Israel indirectly, through Palestinian delegates from the occupied territories. They fly in and out of Tunis constantly to receive instructions from him.

At sixty-four, he is a short, plump man, with oddly protruding eyes, wide hips, small hands, and veins that stand out on them like river systems. Recovering from head injuries incurred in an airplane crash, he is almost completely bald under the checked *kaffiyah* that he wears whenever a visitor or photographer is in sight. The trademark beard, now greying, is said to have been inspired by Fidel Castro.

Arafat's public image is still that of a romantic guerrilla fighter. He is always in uniform, never without a Smith & Wesson pistol on his hip. Yet he is first and foremost an accomplished politician, or, some would say, superb actor. No other third world figure has been so adept in the successful manipulation of the mass media. In the words of Edward Said, Arafat has put "the Palestinians as a group in circulation." Thomas L. Friedman, who first knew him in the squalor and relative obscurity of the Beirut Palestinian slums, wrote in *From Beirut to Jerusalem* (New York: Farrar, Straus, 1989) that he was the "Teflon guerrilla—nothing stuck to Yasir Arafat, not bullets, not criticism, not any particular political position; and most of all, not failure." And, as Friedman wrote, he succeeded almost single handedly in bringing the Palestinians out of the deserts of obscurity into prime time.

He has been an embarrassment for most Arab governments; at the same time he has managed to play them off against one another and extort sums of financial support. And he was able to keep together his loose band of warring politicians, gunmen, guerrillas, mullahs, Marxist intellectuals, and excited youngsters (mesmerized by the successes of the Algerian FLN, Fidel Castro and Baader-Meinhof) who, even before there was a Palestinian state were ready to tear it apart. He gave them a sense of cohesion. Even as a leader of hijackers and terrorists he achieved an international standing for his PLO that no other national independence movement or raw terrorist ever had since the days of Gandhi and Nehru in India or Nelson Mandela in South Africa.

For decades, every twist and turn in the rise and fortunes of the PLO and the inflection of every statement by Arafat was scrutinized internationally to prove one point, or its opposite. He was the first, and, as far as I can tell the only, leader of a national independence movement invited to address the United Nations or to open the embassy of his nonexistent state in dozens of foreign countries. He made it impossible to look at the Middle

East, and at Israel, without also seeing the Palestinians. The Kurds, the Basques, the radical wing of the IRA, the Angolans—to mention only a few—have never come anywhere near to such recognition or to the accumulation of billion-dollar investment portfolios, one large enough that the interest supports a great many military and civilian payrolls.

By what means Arafat and the PLO achieved all this is a question worthy of some discussion. No other guerrilla movement has ever forced itself with such ruthlessness and indiscriminate violence on uninvolved third parties as Palestinians have done since 1968. The Irish, the Kurds, the Armenians, the Afghans have never blown up or hijacked Swiss, American, German, French, or Belgian airplanes, or so randomly thrown bombs into foreign churches and air terminals that have killed and maimed innocent bystanders. Only the IRA and the Basque ETA can claim to compete with the PLO in these respects. The PLO's standing in Europe, and elsewhere, may also have benefited from lingering, perhaps unconscious, sentiments of anti-Semitism and at the same time from a sense of guilt over the fact that the Palestinians, who bore no responsibility for the crimes of anti-Semitism in Europe, were in the end punished for them.

The Cold War, and the oil crisis of 1973 greatly increased the international impact of the PLO. The romantic enthusiasm for the Palestinian cause, seemed part, paradoxically, of the Arab oil boom. In addition, the Communist block helped to provide the Palestinians with arms, safe havens, and political support. A generation of *Fatah* field officers was trained in Soviet army academies. The use of Semtex explosives was taught in Czech and East German army installations. Such unity within the ranks as Arafat was able to maintain (there were frequent schisms) came at the price of courting the lowest common denominator. Yasir Abd Rabuh, a member of the Executive who was active for years in Nayif Hawathme's Marxist Democratic Front for the Liberation of Palestine, told me that there were always many good reasons to criticize Arafat, but not even his loudest opponents within the movement had ever accused him of being "undemocratic." I understood this to mean that first and foremost he was always eager to maintain a consensus.

2

Arafat flies in and out of Tunis almost every day in his private jet. During my visit, he went abroad every other day; an aide told me he visited, among other destinations, Cairo, Amman, and Saudi Arabia. Almost as frequently in the air are the fifteen members of the PLO Executive Committee, who come directly under Arafat in the hierarchy and mostly reside in Tunis. A PLO staff of eight is on duty at the airport around the clock to facilitate arrivals and departures. "I practically live at the airport," one told me.

The executives head a dozen semi-ministerial departments charged with specific responsibilities: political—or foreign—affairs, administration, culture, finance, education, youth, propaganda, and welfare. The Israeli military government has never succeeded in blocking the transfer the transfer of PLO funds into the occupied West Bank and Gaza Strip. Through its subsidies, salaries, and welfare payments, the PLO is the second most important employer in Gaza and in the West Bank. According to a recent report in the Israeli newspaper *Ha'aretz*, citing Arab sources, the various PLO departments pay out 16,000 monthly pensions to the families of Palestinian convicts, detainees, and casualties of the Israeli army. In addition the organization pays salaries to 23,000 Palestinian teachers, youth leaders, welfare and hospital workers, and activists of professional and civic organizations in the West Bank and Gaza—lawyers, newspapermen, trade union activists, and the like.

It is easy to mock the vanity postage stamps and passports issued by other PLO Departments in Tunis that cannot be used to mail a letter or enter a foreign country. And yet the PLO is recognized by more than a hundred governments. It maintains embassies or diplomatic representations in ninety-two countries. On the surface, the twenty-seven year old Israeli taboo on negotiations with the PLO is being maintained, but top Israeli officials admit that by negotiating with the PLO militants in Easter Jerusalem, they are in fact dealing with Arafat. Nineteen foreign ambassadors resident in Tunis present their letters of accreditations to both Yasir Arafat and to the President of Tunisia.

The PLO's administrative staff has been steadily growing in recent years. Yasir Arafat is surrounded by advisers with staffs of their own. According to one adviser, Bassam Abu Sharif, Arafat's presidential office alone employs nearly one thousand people (excluding body guards). Arafat has his own foreign relations staff independent of that under Faruk Kadumi, head of the PLO foreign affairs department. The total number of PLO employees in Tunis is close to five thousand, Abu-Sharif told me. "You might say we are a medium sized state," he added with a wry smile. Arafat's press secretary Ra'ada Taha cites a lower figure; there are not more than 2,500 on the payroll, she maintains. Even if the number is only 2,000, it is difficult to imagine what they might all be doing. "You certainly qualify as a modern state, seeing that you already have a big, idle bureaucracy," a foreign visitor, in a light moment, recently told Arafat, who did not find it amusing. Because of a drastic cut in income, the PLO has been in serious financial difficulties recently.

The financial crisis is one of the results of the Gulf war during which Arafat and the PLO sided with Iraq, although Arafat now says that they had been "misunderstood." The lack of funds and the deadlocked peace talks with Israel are the two major concerns of the Palestinians I met in Tunis. The big shots around Arafat (though he himself only very rarely) have often been criticized for their ostentatious life styles, in Tunis and abroad, their lavish expense accounts, elegant clothes, cars, servants, and villas. They have been accused of travelling only first class and reserving only the best suites in deluxe hotels. Arafat furiously stormed out of a Fatah central committee meeting recently after being accused of financial mismanagement and of allowing some of his closest aides to dip into PLO funds to finance private business ventures.

Against the background of such criticism, the sudden shortfall of available funds has hit the PLO fairly hard. Income from its own investments has always been supplemented by lavish subsidies from Arab governments and by the proceeds of a special surtax levied on the salaries of Palestinian workers by the governments of the Gulf Emirates and Saudi Arabia. In the aftermath of the Gulf war, the Emirates and Saudi Arabia ceased all or most of their direct aid to the PLO. They also blocked the tax money withheld from salaried Palestinians; much of it came anyway from Kuwait where most Palestinians had been expelled after the war. According to Bassam Abu Sharif, Kuwait owes the PLO close to $300 million.

Early last May the London Arabic weekly *Alwast* claimed that the PLO has had to cut its administrative budget by more than half, from $320 to $140 million annually. The paper did not supply details. It quoted a PLO diplomat saying the budget of PLO "embassies" and "diplomatic representations" worldwide was cut by 30 percent. Ahmed Kria, head of the the PLO Economic Department was quoted in the weekly as saying that salaries had been cut by 18 percent and that there were difficulties in financing the Palestinian delegation to the peace talks in Washington. Bassam Abu Sharif denies some of these reports but confirms that his own salary was cut by 34 percent. There were reports in mid June of violent riots by Fatah soldiers in Lybia protesting the non=payment of their salaries.

The release of blocked accounts in the Emirates and the resumption of direct financial aid from Saudi Arabia, I was told, had been one of the conditions the PLO tried to impose before it agreed to allow the Palestinian delegates from the occupied territories to return to the Washington peace talks. The attempt failed. The Saudis were ready to resume payments but insisted on channeling them directly to Palestinian institutions in the occupied territories, thereby sidestepping the PLO. Under heavy pressure from the Arab countries the PLO gave in and agreed to allow the resumption of the peace talks in Washington anyway.

At this point, suddenly, the West Bank and Gaza delegates, in the egotistic isolation of their despair, balked. They still claimed that the PLO was their leader. But as the talks resumed they went beyond the agreed timetables and made new demands—a statement of principle on the nature of the final settlement and the future status of Jerusalem. This caused the last round of talks to end in deadlock. It became obvious that Arafat and the PLO in Tunis were more moderate and accommodating than PLO militants in the occupied territories, who in the aftermath of the *intifada* had forced the moderate line on Arafat in the first place. The Israelis had always insisted that the opposite was true.

A Western diplomat in Tunis says that for several years now, a sense of being "respectable" and "established" has settled over this odd community of unrequited but materially comfortable revolutionaries. Several are still in their late forties and early fifties but becoming pot-bellied and grey. According to a western diplomat who has known them for years, several fear that time may be running out for them. They seek a breakthrough in their lifetimes. Of the so-called "generation of revenge"—the original five founders of Fatah (Literally "Conquest"— Reversed acronym for Palestine National Liberation Movement), the leading group within the PLO—only Arafat, Faruk Kadumi and Khalid al Hassan survive.

Kadumi is known as the leading hardliner within the ruling group. In 1988 he voted in favor of recognizing and negotiating with Israel but at the same time called for a continued "armed struggle. We cannot abandon the military struggle against Israel despite the recent peace efforts" (Quoted in Guy Bechor, PLO Lexicon, Israeli Ministry Publishing House, Tel-Aviv, 1991).

Hassan is the main ideologist of Fatah, hence also of the PLO. He was the first prominent leader to dare to say publicly that the Palestinians were only inviting their own disaster by spurning all diplomatic means. He once told an interviewer: "I never held a gun in my hands, even during the worst of times." Hassan was the main architect of the breakthrough resolution by the PLO National Council in 1988 endorsing the two-state solution and UN Security Council Resolutions 224 and 338. (In the PLO National Covenant of 1964 the partition resolution of 1947 had been declared null and void. UN Resolution 224 (1967) calls for Israeli withdrawal from territories occupied in the Six Day war and for the right of every state in the area to live in peace within "secure and recognized" borders free from threats and acts of force. The P.L.O had always rejected this resolution because it contained no reference to the Palestinian People and referred only to the need for a "just settlement of the refugee problem. Resolution 338(1973) called for negotiations between "the parties concerned" to establish a "just and durable peace in the Middle East.") Only a short time earlier, American requests that the PLO unequivocally endorse these resolution to enable the beginning of a dialogue with the United States had been dismissed by Palestinian spokesmen as "breathtaking arrogance" and "unheard of demands." Hassan convinced the national council to change its mind. He is a rich businessman now, a major importer of Japanese electronic goods to the Gulf Emirates.

Arafat too, in a sense, has settled down. He once lived out of a suitcase, and in Beirut, for security reasons, was constantly on the run, rarely sleeping more than a night or two under the same roof. He now has a permanent home in Tunis. He used to tell reporters that he had no time for women ("I am married to the Palestinian revolution"). At sixty-two, he married a young Christian Palestinian woman, more than thirty years his junior, the daughter of a well-to-do banker now living in Paris. The marriage was kept secret for some time until it was leaked, probably by the Mossad, to the Israeli daily Ha'aretz.

Arafat's working habits have also changed. Partly because he kept such irregular hours and partly as a public relations trick, he kept reporters on hand waiting for weeks to interview him. Distinguished columnists, who would hardly put up with such antics from their own president, hung around hotel rooms for days or even weeks waiting for a phone call that would order them, sometimes at 3 A.M., to be ready within minutes for the coveted interview. Nowadays you call Arafat's office from abroad and are given a reasonable date well beforehand. Such little differences should not be overrated but they give you some sense of the man. Arafat now has permanent living quarters upstairs from his office in al Manzah. It is a spacious comfortable place, with several guest rooms, where his new mother-in-law stays on one of her frequent visits to Tunis.

3

A few hours after my arrival in Tunis, Arafat's press secretary, Ra'ada Taha met me and two other Israeli journalists in the lobby of our hotel and drove us in her little car to Arafat's headquarters. The two others were Zvi Barel, deputy editor of *Ha'aretz* and Danny Rubinstein, that paper's Arab affairs columnist. Taha's name sounded familiar to Rubinstein and she immediately agreed that it might be. Yes, her father Aly Taha had been the commander of a spectacular, but abortive attempt in 1972 to hijack a Sabena airliner at Tel-Aviv airport. He was shot dead by Israeli soldiers. She had been a little girl then and since graduated from an American university. After a short ride through the dark suburban streets, the car stopped at a brightly illuminated villa surrounded by a high wall. A dozen men armed with automatic rifles lolled about or leaned against the garden wall. A Tunisian sentry stood watch in a wooden booth. Behind the garden gate there were more armed men muttering welcome, welcome, while they carefully fingered through our trouser legs and crotches, and whisked electronic metal detectors up and down our backs and chests.

Inside, in the lobby of what looked like a fairly large two-story home, a circular staircase led upstairs to the private rooms. The ground floor was all offices. Telephones were ringing simultaneously in several rooms. On the walls, everywhere, hung large poster-sized photographs of Arafat: Arafat shouldering a gun or riding in an open command car, inspecting the troops, caressing a child; Arafat with the pope; Arafat with Abu Jihad, the Number Two man in the PLO mysteriously gunned down on the eve of the Gulf war.

After we stood around for a few minutes a dark-stained door was thrown open and we entered Arafat's office. We found ourselves in a long, large room. At one end was Arafat's oval-shaped desk; the wall behind it was entirely covered by a giant photograph of Jerusalem, the Mosque of Omar in foreground and all the Israeli buildings behind and along the horizon smoothly blotted out. At the other far end of the room, under a another large portrait of Arafat, a television set was tuned to CNN. When he looks up from his desk Arafat sees himself inside a large gold frame on the other side of the room.

He stood by his desk, his pistol on his hip, with his arms broadly stretched out towards Danny Rubinstein, calling out, "Danny, Danny! I read everything you write! Everything! Truly! It's on my desk here the same morning." The large room was thronged with Arafat's aides and advisers. He was the smallest among them. He was also the only one, including even the guards outside, wearing a uniform. It was a well-pressed, tailor-made affair in dark green cloth decorated with several colored insignia. Under a red-gold-white Palestinian badge on his shoulder, he had a special pocket on his left arm holding two ballpoints and a Cross pen.

His short stature is surprising if you have seen him only on television. The face, fleshy yet with narrow cheekbones, and with the thin stubbles of a beard—said to be five days old—was framed by the checked scarf and matching headgear knotted on his mid forehead. He smoothes the folded end over his right shoulder as he moves and you see again that the headgear is a gimmick of his own making, part of the show that has made his face one of the best known in the world. The large bulging eyes with their dilated pupils fixate upon you with a shining stare when he speaks, but the most striking thing about his face are the lips, the lower one so thick it looks as though he has been stung by a bee and so red you might think he uses lipstick.

We settled along a large horseshoe-shaped table facing his desk. Arafat began in a soft voice. While he spoke, often searching for words, he paused to smile, the long coquettish smile of one used to being adored. War images from Bosnia Herzogovina glimmered on the TV facing his desk. He asked solemnly: "Are you ready to make the decisive step—peace with the Palestinians? Because we are ready. We offer total peace in return for total withdrawal."

He added that he would prefer a complete settlement immediately. He was sure that we would as well, if only we were as familiar as he was with the details of the Palestinian tragedy. Still, he could not realistically imagine it would happen in a single stage. An interim autonomy in Gaza first would be a possibility, but on condition it was in the context of an interim self-government somewhere on the West Bank too, perhaps in Jericho. Otherwise he could be accused of abandoning the West Bank. And there would have to be a corridor connecting Gaza and the West Bank, like that to Berlin before 1989, but internationally guaranteed. Gaza was Israel's Soweto, Arafat said, but despite the widespread chaos and misery there and the lack of a local economic infrastructure, he was perfectly capable of taking over there and keeping it calm. "Remember," he added pointedly, "I governed Lebanon for ten years!" (An aide corrected him: "Controlled Lebanon!" He repeated:"I controlled Lebanon for ten years. Things were more difficult there than in Gaza.")

He complained that from the very beginning of the current peace talks, the Israeli side has been trying to stall and delay while building settlements at the same time in the occupied territories. "We, on the other hand, proved our good faith by going to Madrid despite Shamir's bad terms. Give me another example in history," he raised his voice, "where one side allowed the other to dictate who his representatives at a negotiation must be. We agreed even to this because we desire peace"

He spoke slowly, in halting English, in a peculiar, at times moving combination of outrage and irony, although his silences were clumsily composed. At one point, when he was complaining about the harshness of the Israeli occupation regime and Barel, interjecting, remarked "yes, but it forges you as a nation," Arafat snapped, "Thank you! Thank you!" Later he rebuked us for "not following the details of the Palestinian tragedy! It is a problem even for Palestinians to bury their dead! I spent days to find a place to bury a Palestinian who had died in Moscow recently. It took me ten days to finally find one in Jordan." He can be ludicrous: "Why are Israeli leaders spoiling Judaism? It's such a pity!" Or coy: he claimed that unlike Rabin he even has a solution for Jerusalem, but he preferred not to reveal it at this time. Why? "Why not?" he snapped. And: Rabin has only one opposition. I have half a dozen. Arab, Muslim and Christian. Don't you know my Christian opposition? It's Dr Habash and the Copt Patriarch of Egypt, Shinoda."

Television, oddly enough, serves Arafat badly. It often merely highlights one or two aspects of his more jarring clownish features. In person and in context, he appears much more serious, with a keen mind and with a certain appealing charm, struggling for words, repeating himself constantly to remind us of the intensity and extent of the Palestinian tragedy. That he may have contributed to that tragedy hardly occurs to him; in this he is not different from other politicians.

He is not an easy man to talk to. Even as he spoke his aides surrounded him in clusters, interrupting him constantly with scribbled notes with who knows what suggestions and information, and he would often snap curt orders at them to bring him this or that paper. As I recall the conversation something was occasionally slightly off. Figures, dates, historical facts did not always tally, or so it seemed to me. Even the framed pictures on the wall hung at random, too high or too low. I wasn't sure if I had read something about this being a Palestinian characteristic in one of Edward Said's books.

For two or three hours we covered many of the current controversies and tactics of both sides and a good bit of history, as Israelis and Palestinians often do when they meet, and of course we kept turning in endless circles. On both sides history and memory have become political and conflated with power. Palestinians and Israelis both feel they are victims; none was ever the aggressor. Israelis always complain of Palestinian terror, but even if there had never been any Palestinian terror there would still be serious problems between the two peoples. It is always difficult to understand the nationalism of others. Israeli and Palestinian identity occupies the same territorial and psychological space; each side lives in fear that by granting the other's identity (or rights) it is undermining its own.

Arafat assured us that he had instructed his delegates to achieve a "break-through" at the current round of autonomy talks. But, we must remember, he could not simply issue orders. "I am not a dictator. I am proud of our democracy. I have no right to ignore their feelings . . . Here," he pointed a finger at his press secretary. "Take Ra'ada, she is a hawk! She argues with me a lot!" Still, risks had to be taken by both sides. The greatest risk would be that the peace talks grind to a halt. The result would be the "Balkanization of the Middle East, total chaos and fanaticism everywhere."

I asked him if he didn't occasionally regret that it had taken the PLO so long to recognize Israel and to be ready for peace. Abba Eban once said that the PLO never lost a chance to miss an opportunity. Under the pressure of wars and terror Israel had perhaps moved too much to the right, established too many facts on the ground, more than three hundred thousand settlers in the territories and East Jerusalem. Why was he so late?

Arafat's reaction to this was: "I don't agree we were late . . . " He was interrupted by one of his aides, the Palestinian poet Mahmoud Darwish, who cried: "So what if we were late in the past! What about our future!"

"As victims we had a right to hesitate," Arafat continued. Yes, timing was all important in politics but the truth, as he sees it, was different. In 1969, he insisted, the PLO had offered the Israelis a joint "secular, democratic, pluralistic state." But weren't Jews born abroad or after 1917 in Palestine to be excluded from this settlement? No, because a year later the PLO offered a binational state similar to Belgium. He recited a long list of further oppor-tunities, which, as he put it, were missed by the Israelis, from the PLO's readiness in 1974 to participate at the Geneva conference to its acceptance in 1977 of the Brezhniev-Mitterand peace plan. But, he maintained, Golda Meir kept cynically asking, who are the Palestinians? I am a Palestinian. "We were not late. We were giving signals. You should have read them." He had offered his hand in 1968 but Israel had rejected it. He was now offering it again. "I offer you a peace of the brave. Don't reject it. . . . I offered my hand in 1968 but you rejected it."

I wondered aloud if instead of accepting the autonomy plan today as an interim solution for Gaza and the West Bank, he had accepted it in when it was first postulated in 1978 in the Israeli-Egyptian peace treaty—wasn't that one great opportunity he had missed? Wouldn't he have had a Pales-tinian state by now? There were hardly any Jewish settlers on the West Bank at that time. Instead he had declared war on that treaty, After all, the thirteen American colonies had begun with less, and became the United

States. Arafat looked up sharply. "For your information," he said, stressing every syllable. "Nothing official was ever offered *me*."

So it went. At one A.M. we were invited upstairs to the private quarters where Suha Arafat joined us at a table set for a late supper. Arafat, beaming in his oft-acclaimed role as attentive host, and with the pistol still at his hip, handed us our plates and ladled in the chicken soup and broke off hunks of white cheese and halva for us to savor. He himself follows a strict regimen—low fat ricotta cheese, whole wheat crackers, rice, eggs, raw carrots, and cucumbers—nothing spicy—and drinks only mineral water. He devoured the halva in large chunks. He does not smoke. Elsewhere among the Palestinian leaders and notables in Tunis, whiskey flows freely and we were nearly always sitting in clouds of cigarette smoke.

4

As I go over the notes I took after meetings with Arafat and the other Palestinian leaders in Tunis I find myself ambling back to when I first met some of them. There was Suha, Arafat's wife, whom I had first met twelve years ago, a teenager in her parents' house in Ramallah. Her mother—Raimonda Tawil—was one of the first West Bank Palestinians who advocated a *compromesso storico* between Palestinians and Israelis long before that term became fashionable among Palestinians. And there was Mahmoud Darwish, often referred to as the Palestinian national poet, a man close to Arafat and a member of the PLO's governing Executive Committee. He is an Israeli Palestinian who crossed the lines in 1971 to become Arafat's head cultural spokesman in Beirut. His remarkable poetry echoes the frustration, the despair, the unrelieved intensity of the Palestinian exile:

> Where should we go after the last frontiers,
> Where should the birds fly after the last sky?
> But I am the exile
> Seal me with your eyes.
> Take me wherever you are.
> Take me whatever you are—
> Restore to me the color of face
> And the warmth of body
> The light of heart and eye
> The salt of bread and rhythm
> The taste of earth . . . The Mother land

I first met Darwish as a student at Hebrew University in Jerusalem where he was a communist militant agitating for the establishment of a Palestinian state. I remember a heated debate between him and other Israeli students. He favored a Palestinian state next to Israel sharply reduced in size to the frontiers of the original 1947 U.N. partition resolution. Meeting Darwish after so many years in Arafat's office, Rubinstein, speaking Hebrew asked teasingly: "Mahmoud, what the hell are you doing here? Why don't you come home?"

"I'll be back within two years at the latest. It depends on these negotiations." What about communism, Rubinstein asked. "Oh," said Darwish and laughed, "that was when I was a boy. Now its different." Darwish created a stir a few years ago when, in response to Rabin's order to "break the bones" of stone-throwing Palestinian boys, he published a crude poem calling on the Jews to get out and take their dead with them. He defended himself at the time saying he had been mistranslated, and that the early Zionist poets had written worse things about their persecutors. His position, as he explained it to me, is that in propaganda the victim is allowed everything.

Another acquaintance was Akram Hania, a forty year old newspaperman from East Jerusalem and former editor of the East Jerusalem pro-Fatah daily *Elshaab*. I used to call on him at his office in East Jerusalem to discuss politics. Once I ran into him in the Members' restaurant in the Knesset where, I believe, he had come to talk to Abba Eban, at that time chairman of the foreign relations committee. In 1986, after losing a complicated legal battle against the Israeli military authorities, he was expelled to Tunis via Algeria. His expulsion came not as the result of any terrorist involvement but for engaging in purely political activity, which for Palestinians in the occupied territory was illegal at that time. He too is now on Arafat's staff.

Finally there was Bassam Abu Sharif, a brilliant man who lost an eye, his hearing in one ear, three fingers on his left hand and one on the right as a result of an Israeli explosive charge he received in the mail one day in Beirut in 1970, probably because of his involvement in the hijacking of three American airliners to an abandoned airfield in Jordan. (At that time he was one of George Habash's lieutenants.) In 1986 he quit Habash after an angry argument and came out for coexistence with Israel. He announced that Israel's aim was "lasting peace" and this should also be the aim of the Palestinians).

We had dinner one long night in his fine villa in Tunis and he assured us that the squabbling in Washington over fine points of language and international law was just eyewash, "I can tell you authoritatively that the breakthrough has already been achieved. You can quote me. I can't tell you the details. But I know what I am talking about." He also said, "We must all help Rabin. You can quote me on that too. He is a man of Peace. We understand now that he has a problem with his constituency. We don't do enough to help him overcome it." The PLO, he said, should try and help to secure the release of Israeli prisoners of war held in Lebanon and in the removal of the Arab boycott.

The United States is regarded by Arafat and his lieutenants as the magic Archimedean factor, outside the direct Arab-Israeli sphere, that will produce miracles. They have a paranoid concept of the grandiose power of Jews in U.S. and elsewhere in the world. Maybe they are still, with all their sophistication, a people of declarations. Asked to give his assessment of Rabin, Arafat said, "He is not a de Gaulle. Let him be at least a De Clerk." When I quoted this remark later to Bassam abu Sherif, he replied in a sarcastic tone, "Well, the old man is no de Gaulle either."

On the whole I found the mood in Tunis much more optimistic than in Jerusalem. Everywhere we went, we encountered the same expectant intimacy and display of pleasure at meeting Israelis. I was struck by a kind of shorthand between the Israeli newsmen and the Palestinian officials. There were frequent exchanges of jokes and knowing glances in what seemed a tacit understanding that what was being said was not entirely what was meant. I have never encountered the same semi-conspiratorial intimacy between Israelis and Egyptians. I was unprepared for the optimism. I would often wonder whether this optimism reflected the true state of affairs or a kind of wishful thinking, a sense of weakness, a fear of being left behind by the new Islamic forces at work among Palestinians. The *intifada* was an uprising not only against Israeli oppression, but also against the sterility of PLO rhetoric and terror. For Arafat's PLO, diplomacy now means cooperating with the inevitable; and for Israel—the breaking of a twenty-seven-year-old destructive taboo.

16

Peacemakers

In September 1993, a few days after Yizhak Rabin and Yasir Arafat shook hands on the White House lawn, it became known that two obscure freelance Israeli peaceniks had played a large part in making that event possible. A sarcastic European diplomat in Washington remarked that, while the United States had done little to bring about this breakthrough, the two Israelis had inadvertently given Bill Clinton his first spectacular moment in foreign affairs.

They were an odd pair in the world of high-level diplomacy: an eccentric, bearded forty-nine-year-old man named Yair Hirschfeld who is a lecturer in Middle East history at a minor Israeli university and looks something like a cross between Allen Ginsberg and Karl Marx, and a former student of his named Ron Pundik, who had just received his doctorate and was looking for a permanent position.

In Jerusalem, where bureaucrats are no more inclined to share glory with others than are bureaucrats elsewhere, a Foreign Ministry official remarked snidely that Hirschfeld and Pundik were merely "accidental tourists in history." Another government official was more generous. "Bureaucracies are too clumsy," he said. "They rarely lend themselves to starting something big. For this you need a couple of nuts." Hirschfeld and Pundik were outsiders, he said, committed to the idea of a Palestinian-Israeli compromise—

a goal for which they had striven at a time when consecutive Israeli governments had made such an attitude almost tantamount to treason. "They
were determined not to let any given 'reality' stand in their way," the official went on. "So in the end they succeeded where the striped-pants diplomats had failed."

In 1992, on their own time and at first on their own money, they had
started illicit talks with a prominent PLO official named Ahmed Suleiman
Karia, who is Arafat's director of finances and is better know by his *nom de
guerre*, Abu Ala. Hirschfeld and Pundik had only the vaguest commitment
from Yossi Beilin, Israel's newly elected Deputy Foreign Minister: they
would send him a report and he would read it, but he did not advise them.
And they had no understanding at all with Rabin or Shimon Peres. If their
initiative became public, Beilin warned, he would deny all knowledge of it.

After the June 1992 elections in Israel, which the Labor Party had won
narrowly, Jan Egeland, Norway's Deputy Foreign Minister, asked Beilin if
he would like Norway to arrange a meeting between him and some high
representative of the PLO. Beilin told him that this was completely out of
the question. He wasn't ready to commit political suicide. But, he told
Egland, he had a friend, Yair Hirschfeld, who had an independent mind and
was not in the government and was meeting with militant Palestinians all
the time. Egeland said he liked working with outsiders. His offer had been
a wild shot in the blue. He didn't at the time expect anything substantial to
come out of couple of informal meetings. There had been several others in
the past which had produced nothing.

Beilin recently said about Hirschfeld: "I admired his passion, his energy
and his learning. In this little country he is one of those people—many of
them in the academy—who in the past twenty years have raked their minds
to find ways that will bring Palestinians and Israelis together. Hirschfeld
could never have functioned within a government bureaucracy. He is too
unconventional." At the time of Egeland's meeting with Beilin, the Israeli
government still banned all contacts with the PLO and believed that it must
circumvent and isolate Arafat and his organization by working out a deal in
the occupied West Bank and Gaza with local Palestinian leaders of its own
choosing. Beilin never cleared his understanding with Egeland or Hirschfeld, vague it was, with his direct superiors, Peres and Rabin. Peres was
known as a hawk. He was so ambivalent about all Palestinians, Abba Eban
once said, that for years Peres had resembled Hamlet on this issue, except
in the felicity of his language, and his main aim had been to arrive at an
accommodation with Jordan at the expense of Palestinian national aspirations. Rabin, for his part, continued to blame the PLO, and Arafat person-

ally, for the deadlock. In December of 1992—a month before Hirschfeld and Pundik began their secret talks with Abu Ala in Norway—Rabin had thrown some 400 Palestinian militants across the Lebanese border onto a snow-covered hill. One result of this act was that the U.S.-sponsored peace talks in Washington were indefinitely suspended.

Hirschfeld was an old hand at illicit Palestinian-Israeli contacts. He liked to quote the warning attributed to an early Zionist leader that if you don't take care of politics you'll get into trouble since politics will take care of you. Some fifteen years earlier, Hirschfeld had come to know the late Austrian chancellor Bruno Kreisky, who was a Jew and and a Social Democrat. Kreisky was obsessed with the need to solve the "Palestinian problem," which he considered the heart of the Israeli-Arab conflict. He was bitterly critical of the leaders of the Israeli Labor Party at the time, Golda Meir and Yitzhak Rabin, for refusing to see things his way. Kreisky was the first European head of government who received Arafat in Vienna as a state visitor and believed that Arafat was ready for a "historical compromise" with Israel. Hirschfeld was deeply affected by Kreisky's thinking. He had emigrated to Israel in 1967, and had spent much of his free time getting to know Palestinians in the occupied territories. Some became his close friends. "We liked him," a Palestinian militant at Bir Zeit university recently said about Hirschfeld. "He spent so much time with us it almost seemed he was neglecting his academic career. In his late forties he was still not even an assistant professor. Sometimes he was the starry-eyed idealist; sometimes he talked tough. But it was easier to talk to him than to other Israelis. He wasn't condescending as many often were—even those who claimed they were 'doves.'" Hirschfeld struck them as a man who wished to resolve problems. "He didn't repeat all the old slogans. Perhaps he even didn't know them."

In the fall of 1992, Hirschfeld had been involved in a study, financed by the European Economic Community, of economic conditions in the occupied West Bank and the Gaza Strip. He was routinely meeting with Palestinian activists in East Jerusalem and Ramallah and was promoting "the typical fair dream of an academic—economic development as a basis for political compromise." He smiled as he said this, during a visit I paid him at his rambling house in the country north of Haifa, where he lives with his wife, Ruth, four children, a cat, and a dog. The two elder daughters currently serve in the Army. Hirschfeld had just come home and was kicking off his sneakers and changing into a pair of rumpled jeans. "I was there at Peace Now demonstration but I also believed that one must do more than protest," he said. One thing he could do was meet and reason with senior representatives of the PLO even though that was against the law at the time. Hirschfeld chuckled as he spoke about breaking the law. In the Austro-Hungarian Army, he said, there was a special medal, the Maria Theresa. It was given to officers who won a battle even though they were breaching military discipline. "If you broke discipline in the Austro-Hungarian Army, you had two choices: get the Maria Theresa medal or be shot."

One afternoon, he told me he and Pundik were talking with Hanan Ashrawi, the Palestinian spokeswoman at the peace talks sponsored by the United States, who had just returned from Washington. Hirschfeld mentioned that he was off to London to attend a university seminar. Ashrawi suggested that he might want to talk to Abu Ala, the PLO's "chief economic planner," who would be in London at the same time and who was interested, she said, in the "links between peace and economic development." Hirschfeld did not commit himself at the time, but he did give Ashrawi his phone number in London.

In London, a few weeks later, Hirschfeld apparently thought about it again. A friend of Egeland's, a Norwegian sociologist named Terje Rod Larsen whom he had met before in Jerusalem, happened to be in town, and he too spoke to Hirschfeld about that same Abu Ala. Larsen and his wife, Mona Juul, would come to play critical roles in the future talks—less as mediators, perhaps, than as father and mother confessors. Larsen was the head of the Norwegian Institute of Applied Sciences, in Oslo (known as FAFO). His wife, Mona Juul, was was a senior Norwegian diplomat, well-prepared to play a role in Middle East peacemaking. Her first foreign posting had been in Cairo. Larsen told Hirschfeld that Abu Ala was a serious man close to Arafat. Hirschfeld agreed to a meeting. Larsen volunteered to arrange it. Over breakfast the next day, he told Hirschfeld that if the meeting should go well and if he and Abu Ala should decide to continue their dialogue, FAFO and—he felt sure—the Norwegian government were ready to offer them full facilities in Norway under conditions of utmost secrecy.

Hirschfeld and Abu Ala first came together in the breakfast room of Larsen's hotel in Central London. The circumstances were reminiscent of a B movie: minutes before Abu Ala and an aide entered the room, Larsen slipped out of his chair and disappeared. Abu Ala and Hirschfeld carried on alone. Abu Ala is a white-haired, whimsical-looking man in his mid-fifties. He later said that his initial meeting with Hirschfeld went very well. "We clicked personally." Hirschfeld was one of the first Israelis he had ever met, and he liked Hirschfeld's informality and sense of humor. Hirschfeld told me that Abu Ala did not tell him anything he couldn't have heard before, from other Palestinians. "Some of what he said was objectionable. But I liked his tone," Hirschfeld said. "It was like in opera. What counted was the music. The librettos of most operas are often lousy anyway."

The two men agreed to meet again later in the day. Beilin happened to be in London that day. "A crazy coincidence," Hirschfeld now admits, stroking his beard. "I know you won't believe it! I swear it was total coincidence! My wife, who is superstitious about these things, says that that same day was full of many other miracles and wonders too. Those I won't talk about! But the fact is, I hadn't told Beilin that I was going to meet the PLO big shot. It could have embarrassed him.

Hirschfeld went to see Beilin in his London hotel and told him that the meeting with Abu Ala had gone very well."

"What was his reaction?," I asked.

"Ask him."

"Did he tell you not to meet Abu Ala again?"

"I'm an independent man. He can't tell me what to do."

"He encouraged you?"

"I'm not sure. No, not really."

Hirschfeld met with Abu Ala again that night, in the cafe of the Ritz Hotel, where the Palestinian was staying. Abu Ala said that he would be interested in broad bilateral talks with Israeli officials. Hirschfeld said that he was not an official but that the search for common ground between Israelis and Palestinians had been a singular pursuit of his during the past ten years. He could speak only for himself but added that he knew a few people in the new Labor government and might try to act as a channel to them. He could not promise anything, and the Israeli government was not aware of this meeting. The government was opposed to all deals with the PLO, he went on, and if their meetings should continue in Norway and become public knowledge the government would deny any connection with him.

Abu Ala seemed uncertain but was nevertheless intrigued. He and Hirschfeld agreed to an exploratory meeting in Norway after which they would decide whether or not to proceed. They wouldn't negotiate. They would feel each other out. They would "brainstorm," as Hirschfeld put it. He called Pundik in Tel-Aviv to tell him the news. "I think we have something running." Pundik, who had lost his older brother in the Yom Kippur war, had like Hirschfeld shown up regularly in recent years in anti-government Peace Now rallies. When Hirschfeld called to tell him about Abu Ala, Pundik replied: "Let's do it."

❃

Thus started an adventure—some would say an intrigue—that would last late into the summer. The two peaceniks threw themselves into it with relish. Their exploits throw an interesting light on one of the most surprising *voltes faces* of recent diplomatic history and on the role of two independent players to help cause it.

In retrospect, of course, the proceedings in Norway now seem more sophisticated and more shrewdly thought out than they really were—an impression that does not do justice to the true nature of the talks, which were propelled by impulse, contingency, improvisation, and coincidence. Peres himself, with remarkable self-irony, alluded to this when he said afterward: "History is such a clown! It makes all of us look like fools."

In contrast to this version is the conspiratorial one, which postulates two-faced politicians who publicly mouth one policy but secretly follow another. They cunningly interpose a couple of independent intellectuals to circumvent the sterility of a public bureaucracy shackled by the tabus they themselves had imposed on it. The conspiratorial version is scarcely convincing in view of the facts as we now know them. In the territories a popular uprising was in full swing. The new government vainly tried to reassert itself with a brutality rarely if ever evinced by its right-wing predecessors. The new government's guidelines for the stalemated peace talks in Washington remained, by and large, what they had been under the old: No Palestinian state; negotiations only with local Palestinian notables personally acceptable to the Israeli government; no political concessions to these notables except within the framework of a very limited autonomy regime; within that autonomy, only an administrative, not a legislative central Palestinian body; above all no recognition of and no talks with the PLO

Foreign Minister Peres was not aware of Hirschfeld's first meetings with Abu Ala in Norway. Rabin, for his part, may have learned of the secret meetings from a report by the Mossad, which is said to have planted a spy, Adnan Yassin, in the Tunis headquarters of the PLO (Yassin was recently arrested). Yassin allegedly tapped the telephones of Arafat's closest aides, including, presumably, Abu Ala's. Rabin did not believe that anything could come of direct contacts with Arafat. He may have considered them at best a nuisance or, at worst, another ill-conceived maneuver by his old rival Peres. Rabin, in his 1978 memoirs, had described Peres as a "venomous," and as an "indefatigable intrigant," who "worked evil" everywhere.

Rabin's public position during the months leading up to the accord later became the subject of much speculation in the Israeli press. Was Rabin lying when he said Israel would never deal with the PLO? Had he changed his mind? If he had, when? Some said he had been dragged into the deal by Peres, who, in turn, had been dragged into it by Beilin. Others invoked A. J. P. Taylor's remark that the greatest acts of statesmanship were made by people who did not know what they were doing. Still others cited Abba Eban, who had often clashed with Rabin in the past. "It isn't that governments are constitutionally incapable of arriving at the right decision; the trouble with governments is that they usually do so only as a matter of last resort."

The first of the brainstorming sessions in Norway began on January 21, 1993, two days after the Knesset, against the express wishes of Rabin, abrogated the law forbidding contact with the PLO. Larsen's research institute, FAFO, was the host. Mona Juul acted as liaison to the Norwegian Foreign Ministry, which was paying the bill. As a cover, the participants agreed to pretend that the meeting was a "seminar" to consider the results of a FAFO field study on living standards in the occupied territories. Though the two sides had agreed in principle to a meeting, endless international phone calls to Tunis and Israel, and vice versa, had been necessary to make it finally happen. They gave Larsen some idea of the difficulties that would face them when real issues were to be discussed. Pundik says, "All these calls, often half a dozen a day, went through my private phone or fax machine and at my expense. My wife had a shock when she saw the first bill."

Finally everything was set. Abu Ala arrived at the meeting with two aides, a political adviser in the PLO Tunis administration named Hassan Assfur who was a native of Gaza, and an economist named Maher al Kurd, a graduate of the American University of Cairo who spoke fluent English. Hirschfeld arrived with Pundik. Because nobody in Israel was paying their expenses, FAFO paid their airfare; the expenses of Abu Ala's and his aides were paid by the PLO.

Larsen and Juul gave careful thought to the choice of a suitable site. It had to be secluded, tranquil, and inviting. "We did not want to place them around a table in a square conference room," Juul told me. "We wanted them to feel easy in a pleasant house." They found one some sixty miles east of Oslo, in Sarpsborg: an industrialist friend of theirs owned a country home there and he would let them have it without asking too many questions. Borregaard Manor House, surrounded by forests and lakes, was an austere-looking white neoclassic country-house that in the Middle Ages had been the hunting lodge of a Norwegian king. The rooms were cozy, with large fireplaces and simple furnishings. The participants were to sleep under the same roof and take all their meals together. The bar was well-stocked. The cooks specialized in hearty Norwegian fare. Seating arrangements around the dinner table were carefully planned to ensure conviviality and ease. The staff was told that a couple of professors were writing a book together and might talk for hours and order coffee and sandwiches at four A.M. but otherwise they must not be disturbed.

Since the meeting had to be top secret, only a handful of Norwegians were told about it. The participants were shunted through the airport by a special route and were driven separately to Borregaard in inconspicuous rented cars. The person charged with their comings and goings was Evan Aas, a young man then at FAFO, who happened to be the trainer of the Norwegian women's speed-skating team. He said later "Skaters do everything on edge and the whole peace process was on edge because if one had done one false step it would have failed."

Larsen felt he had to pay at least some lip-service to the supposed "subject" of the seminar. Hirschfeld said later with a wicked smile "It was the funniest seminar I ever attended." Three Palestinians and two Israelis having to sit for a whole morning and listen to papers on sliding wage-scales and rising cost-of-living-indices when, Hirschfeld said, "they had really come to talk about other things." At lunch the first day they were joined by Jan Egeland. The presence of the Norwegian Deputy Foreign Minister lent a certain formal aura to the gathering and endowed the two Israelis with a status that might have been premature at this early stage. Egeland was certainly taking a risk. Pundik said later he had felt a little "kooky" all day: "Who was I? What exactly was I doing there? Whom was I representing."

After lunch Egeland drove back to Oslo and the Palestinians and the Israelis secluded themselves in a side room. Larsen and Juul patiently waited for many hours outside, checking from time to time to see that they had enough coffee and enough of whatever else they might need. The opening music was encouraging. The participants solemnly agreed they must never recite the past. Abu Ala set the precedent for this by gently reprimanding one of his aides, who started quoting past United Nations resolutions which he claimed Israel had ignored. "Let us not compete about who was right and who was wrong in the past," Abu Ala said. "And let us not compete about who can be more clever in the present. Let us see what we can do in the future." Later on, whenever somebody referred to past history he would be told that he was out of order. "It became a kind of a joke," Pundik says.

The first brainstorming session lasted some eight hours with one or two brief breaks for meals and short walks outside. The atmosphere was intense. Larsen remembers that one of the participants rushed out to the bathroom to throw up. But the five men soon came to know one another better, and their sympathetic hosts as well. Both sides made a serious effort to listen, Abu Ala later said.

Three weeks later, they reconvened at Borregaard Manor. Both sides must have talked things over with people at home." We reported to Beilin," Pundik says. "We did not ask for instructions and he did not offer us any. He urged us to continue."

At one point the discussants played at changing sides. The Israelis tried to represent the Palestinian case as best they could, and the Palestinians the Israeli. "Abu Ala was ready to play such a game?" I asked Larsen. He said admiringly: "There is no game he isn't capable of playing." Hirschfeld now had the useful idea of trying to work out, in very broad outlines, a common program. It took the form of a Joint Declaration of Principles, which in its main outline presaged much of the future accord. At this early stage they still thought it could be shunted to the deadlocked Washington talks and formally approved there. The joint paper envisaged free elections in the occupied territories and the gradual establishment of an interim autonomous regime there, at first in Gaza, later elsewhere in the territories; it enunciated a number "guidelines" for the launching of a new "Marshall plan" which would make peace palatable to the Palestinians—especially to those in the miserable Gaza Strip.

"Agreement was not reached on all issues on all issues particularly not on (a) jurisdiction over territory, (b) Jerusalem, and (c) arbitration," Hirschfeld wrote to Beilin in a private memorandum. "However the Palestinians stated clearly they knew they had to make further concessions and expressed willingness in case U.S. mediation (at the Washington peace talks) would enable them to legitimize such concessions on their side. . . . They expressed great interest in proceeding as quickly as possible and they specifically asked us to encourage the Americans to discuss the outlines of the proposed agreement already at the forthcoming visit of Warren Christopher [to the area]."

To Beilin, this was unexpected news. The principle of "gradualism"— staged withdrawal of Israeli forces and gradual autonomy for Palestinians—was Hirschfeld's idea, and it was something new. It meant that during the first two or three years the process of Israeli withdrawal could be halted or even reversed. The great surprise was that the Palestinians had accepted it. There had been no built-in gradualist in the original autonomy plan agreed to by Israel, Egypt, and the United States at Camp David in 1978. Beilin must have asked himself why this news was brought to him by two amateurs rather than by the professionals at the deadlocked Washington talks. However, that first draft, was still not enough for an accommodation. It was too ambiguous regarding Jerusalem; and there was nothing in it on borders, settlements, or security. But it was not "an anonymous letter to be put aside without answering," Beilin remembers.

He took the draft to Foreign Minister Peres who learned only then of the informal negotiating channel in Norway. Peres was surprised; then he was skeptical. But he thought there was little risk in letting the two freelance negotiators continue. He liked the idea of a new "Marshal plan"; he had been preaching a similar theme for years. Peres now told Rabin that two friends of Beilins', "two *meshugoim*"—crackpots—had decided to sound out the PLO. Rabin was even more skeptical, but he was also opening up to new suggestions. His government was in trouble. Before the elections, he had promised a deal with the local Palestinians within six months to a year. In this he had failed. The situation had since gone from bad to worse. In the territories, the pro-Iranian, Islamic fundamentalists of Hamas, an organization opposed to peace, were gaining at the expense of Arafat's more moderate faction, Al Fatah. Rabin had just received a report on this from the General Security Service, Israel's FBI. Violence was mounting in the territories and in Israel proper. Peres assured Rabin they were not committing themselves to anything. Hirschfeld and Pundik could always be disowned as eccentric academics. The government would not be hurt. Rabin pondered this suggestion from his old arch-rival. Amos Oz, the novelist, later said that Peres and Rabin were like two elderly women in an old-age home who were constantly quarreling but who realized that to cross a street they had to hold hands.

❀

Five more informal meetings took place between February and May, usually over long weekends at Borregard Manor and other secluded country places. The main task of the negotiators was to convince themselves that the other side was serious. Abu Ala had understandable doubts about Hirschfeld and Pundik. At one point, he told Larsen that unless the Israelis sent someone official to negotiate he would not attend further meetings. "Hirschfeld and Pundik are very nice," he told Larsen. "But who are they?" He was well aware of the internal Israeli debate. "Are they speaking for themselves? For Beilin (about whom Rabin was constantly making disparaging remarks in public)? For Peres? For Rabin? Larsen took it upon himself to reassure Abu Ala he was not wasting his time—"Beilin had told me so on the telephone."

In early April, a moment came when Abu Ala told Larsen, "I don't believe this any more. Go and see Beilin personally." Larsen flew to Israel and saw Beilin, who assured him that Hirschfeld was now authorized to conduct "pre-negotiations." The two sides continued to exchange ideas and improve the original draft. The two Israeli amateurs were still more or less on their own—no committee back home was preparing position papers for them—and as the talks got more serious Pundik was beginning to wonder how soon they would be kicked out to make place for official negotiators.

The Israelis, for their part, had their doubts about Abu Ala. They asked for proof that he was speaking for Arafat. "We'd never had any contacts with the PLO before," Beilin said later. "We didn't really know what it stood for." They had only the raw data that usually goes into intelligence reports, shorn of any personal experiential quality. "We knew the propaganda. We did not know the truth. Hirschfeld was the first Israeli who found out for us what was more important and what was less important for them. Where were their red lines? Where could they give? Where could we? Hirschfeld's personality functioned very well in this context." That was his and Pundik's main contribution: they prepared the practical and the psychological ground that enabled the professionals to join them after the seventh meeting, early in May. By then, they had reached a point that led Peres to propose flying to Norway himself to conduct the talks. Rabin thought that this was going too far. It was decided to send Uri Savir, the newly appointed Director General of the Foreign Ministry and, later, Yoel Singer, a legal expert, to Norway. Both men were known for their dovish views. Both were new faces at the top level of the Israeli foreign service. But Israel would "upgrade" the talks only on condition that everything remain secret.

Earlier in the year, the Norwegians informed the United States of the secret contacts. In March the Americans were given a copy of the first draft of the joint declaration worked out by Hirschfeld, Pundik and Abu Ala. Although American officials were sympathetic, Mona Juul told me, "they didn't believe we could pull it off. They weren't all that . . . " She smiled. "I don't want to be impolite, so we stopped telling them. We felt why should we bother. And they didn't ask any questions." In May, the Norwegian Foreign Minister gave Warren Christopher a full report on what had been agreed so far. Christopher is said to have had "great trouble" getting his mind around the idea that Norway might succeed where Washington could not. But he encouraged the Norwegians to go on.

❋

I spent a few days in Oslo recently interviewing some of the people who had been involved in this enterprise. Oslo is one of the smallest, prettiest capitals of Western Europe. For a few hours each day while I was there, the shingled rooftops and spires in the old city were cast in the golden light of a late autumn sun. The city is magnificently laid out between the fiord and the surrounding mountains. Traffic is sparse. There is a clean, cozy, provincial slightly fairy-tale atmosphere about Oslo: the king still takes an occasional walk in town, and his small palace stands on a low hill in a park, surrounded by an old university, a theater, a museum, and a few old-fashioned hotels and restaurants where waiters will point out to you Nansen's and Knut Hamsen's favorite tables. Upon meeting so many sympathetic people of good will, I was tempted to think that if central casting were to look for a couple of peacemakers between nasty enemies it would find them there. The intimacy of the place suggests a large family. The Norwegian popular press has played up the roles during the secret peace talks of strategically placed wives. Marianne Heiberg, the wife of the Foreign Minister, had done research at Larsen's institute. Holst himself is a friend of the Larsens. The Holsts' four year old son, Edward, was said to have broken the ice when at one informal party he climbed on the knees of both Abu Ala and Savir. "It wasn't a soap opera, as it was presented in the Oslo press," Juul told me a bit angrily. Then she added with a smile: "But it was cozy."

In the Foreign Ministry I interviewed Jan Egeland. He is thirty-six years old and is not a civil servant but a political appointee. He and Juul had been classmates at Oslo University. Before his appointment in 1990 he worked for the International Red Cross in Geneva and for six years was a senior official at Amnesty International. "We have a fairly dynamic foreign policy practice," he said, "and we believe in strong cooperation with nongovernmental groups, solidarity, church, academic, and environmental groups—to stimulate human rights and peace talks. I don't know if other governments would have got involved with amateurs like Hirschfeld and Pundik. We have been active in this sense in Guatemala, in Africa, and in the Baltic countries. We like to experiment."

The Norwegian experiment with the two odd peaceniks surprised the whole world when it turned out a success. It did not surprise Egeland. He is the author of a book, published in 1988, titled *Impotent Superpower—Potent Small State—Potentials and Limitations of Human Rights Objectives and Foreign Policies of the United States and Norway*. In it Egeland tries to show that a small, rich, well-liked, nonthreatening country like Norway is considerably better placed than the United States, Britain, or France, to broker peace accords and human rights around the world. This is so, he claims, mainly because Norway, unlike the larger countries, cannot be suspected of hidden agendas, political or commercial. Nor can it be seen as imposing on or threatening anybody. The book had been Egeland's Ph.D. thesis. Upon reading it, one of his professors, who had been a little doubtful of its claims, challenged him to go into politics and prove it.

"I did," Egeland says. "And I remembered that we must not try to mediate. This was our strength. Both sides often spoke to Larsen, Juul, and me. They told us where they were. We acted as buffers for emotions that were often very very heavy. Larsen and Juul were often able to defuse tensions by a light remark. Or by an offer to discuss the issue with them or take a walk outside. But we never sat in on the actual discussions. We kept ourselves available at all times—outside. It wasn't easy. The discussions often lasted twenty hours in a row. The Palestinians liked to work all night and sleep three or four hours in the morning. Larsen and Juul were always there, to be helpful if they could, and if they couldn't, to be sympathetic and shut up and see that there was enough coffee. When they were asked they said what they thought. Nothing was volunteered."

It had been a serendipitous confluence of personalities, characters, timing, personal moods, and external circumstances. The Norwegians prodded gently. Pundik says, "Larsen was wonderful—ready to be a four-star general at one moment and at the next a corporal bringing in the coffee." Asfour, Abu Ala's aide says, "We all became a little Norwegian in the end." Shared meals (Hirschfeld claims he gained twenty five pounds), a convivial atmosphere in an inviting natural setting, secrecy—all played a role. Hirschfeld, a garrulous man, later said: "Keeping our mouths shut was one of the most difficult things." If the right people had not approached the right people on the other side at the right moment through the right third party this accord would have come about much later, if at all. The third, nonthreatening party was crucial; it was almost a case of "The wolf also shall dwell with the lamb, and the leopard shall lie down with the kid . . . and a *little child* shall lead them."

The arrival of the Israeli officials Savir and Singer changed the pace and context of the talks. Pundik half expected that as soon as the professionals arrived he and Hirschfeld would be kicked out, but Savir and Singer, wanting to preserve the informal atmosphere and make use of their insights, asked them to stay on. Legal details and technical minutae of implementation became the main subject matter. Security measures for the conferees became even more elaborate. "On one occasion Savir lived in our private flat," Larsen says. "it was too risky for him to check into a hotel where he might be recognized. I remember standing with him on our terrace late one night after his first meeting with Abu Ala. He nearly had tears in his eyes, and he said, 'I will use everything I have to persuade Rabin and Peres to let us continue this negotiation.' "

The talks usually began late Friday and continued, with almost no breaks for sleep, until early Monday morning. Savir could not stay longer. He was the powerful director of the Foreign Ministry with a full-time job to maintain at home. To reduce the initial tension, Larsen made a brave attempt to introduce the Israeli professionals to Abu Ala in a light tone met by laughter on all sides. Larsen said to him: "This is your enemy number 1," and "This is your enemy number 2." Savir later told an aide that Abu Ala didn't really look like an enemy at all. "The world always looks different when you remove the dark glasses you have been wearing all your life." Nevertheless, the negotiations became very tough. Both sides constantly issued ultimatums, caused interminable crises and kept threatening to go home. "Brinkmanship was their negotiation technique. It was outright war. They used every trick in the book, screaming, bluffing, taking risks. Fortunately a very strong relationship grew between Abu Ala and Savir— a passionate love-hate, almost," Larsen says. "They also have this same strange sense of humor." Both men told jokes all the time and talked about their families. At the low point of one crisis, Abu Ala announced he was resigning. Savir delivered an emotional speech that was full of bitter recriminations against them all for having failed and missed a unique opportunity. Then the two men went into seclusion and, as Hirschfeld says, "Humpty Dumpty was put together again." What turned the trick was an Israeli offer that the two sides announce they mutually recognize each other formally. This had been the major Palestinian objective since 1988 and the most difficult psychological block for the Israelis. Savir would later ask himself whether the secret Oslo negotiations would have been necessary if they had offered mutual recognition in the first place.

Then, in the early hours of August 20, came the formal initialing of an agreement. The same, somewhat bizarre B-movie atmosphere that had marked the beginning of the talks marked their formal end. To attend the signing, Peres flew to Oslo on a previously arranged visit. No one in his entourage—not even the Israeli ambassador in Oslo—knew the real reason for his trip. He stayed at the official guest house of the Norwegian government, an old villa behind the royal palace that had been built in the last century for a rich petroleum importer. Foreign Minister Holst gave a dinner there in Peres's honor. Meanwhile, in a suite on top of a nearby posh hotel, Savir and Abu Ala were still hammering out some last-minute problems with the wording. As the official dinner was nearing its end, Larsen and Juul convinced the other guests that Peres was tired and wanted to retire. The Israelis and Palestinian negotiators were then smuggled out of their hotel through the service entrance and driven in a van to the official guesthouse. "We tried to give the signing ceremony a little formality. At the same time we knew each other so well," Juul says. A famous old desk—Norway's secession from Sweden in 1905 was signed on it—was hauled upstairs to the salon. The papers were laid out on it. Abu Ala and Savir came in through separate doors and signed. Holst signed as a witness and Peres watched from the sidelines. The signers hailed the historic breakthrough. Peres said nothing. "All of us nearly cried," Juul says. "It was almost like living in a movie we had designed ourselves."

The scene was in fact recorded on video tape. "I have seen the film and it's rather nice," Juul says. The Palestinians wanted a copy, and so did several television companies." But the Israelis insisted that it be locked in a safe." No one knows why. Perhaps it reflected too much fraternizing. Hirschfeld, on his way home, stopped in Vienna, where his parents live. For the first time, he hinted to them that peace might be nearer than most people thought. His mother shook her head. "Son," she said, "You don't understand. Such things always take far more time."

For the veterans of the "Oslo channel," the glitzy public ceremony, three weeks later, on the White House lawn, came as an anticlimax. It lacked the passionate intimacy, intrigue and melodrama of the first. Hirschfeld and Pundik were treated shabbily by the government they had served. They were not invited to attend the Washington ceremony. When Peres was asked why they had been excluded, he said blandly, "Nurses and midwives were not invited." To this day, Pundik says, he hasn't even received a letter of acknowledgment. "So we took yet another independent initiative and flew to Washington on our own," Pundik says. There were still problems. Their names were, of course, not on the list of Israeli invitees. The White House did not know who they were. The Norwegians could not put their names on their list. In the end, a good soul in the Israeli Embassy in Washington succeeded in including their names on the list of prominent Americans invited by the White House to attend. Unrecognized in the large crowd, the two amateur peacemakers watched the ceremony. Abu Ala greeted them warmly.

17

Look Over Jordan

On a clear day, the outskirts of Amman are easily visible from any tall building in Jerusalem. Pink and rosy, they loom on the far horizon in the dry mountain air, above the frozen undulations of the desert, across the deep hollow of the Dead Sea. Like Jerusalem, Amman is perched on high at an altitude of about half a mile above sea level and the distance between the two cities, as the crow—perhaps one should say the hawk—flies, is little more than forty miles. The journey from one to the other takes only an hour and half—that is, if you are lucky enough to have the right permits and are traveling in a UN car.

It so happened that a few hours before I set out from Jerusalem for Amman, a Jewish fanatic named Baruch Goldstein had massacred thirty Palestinians in a Hebron mosque, caused the death of at least thirty others, and wounded more than a hundred. In doing so, he had derailed the ongoing peace talks and damaged, perhaps irreparably, the excruciatingly slow process of reconciliation between Palestinians and Israelis that was started in 1993 in Oslo and on the White House lawn. The process by which demonized enemies were becoming legitimate adversaries haggling over details of a historical compromise was blocked and perhaps reversed. The event showed once again how the sinister passion of one man could affect

Arab-Israeli affairs. Both sides were bracing themselves for the "counter massacre," which was widely held to be inevitable.

Even as we were leaving Jerusalem, wild riots were erupting all over the occupied territories. Clouds of tear gas were rising over the rooftops of the Old City. Driving down toward the Jordan Valley, the barren scenery of the Judean desert—gloomy, diaphanous, like a vision on the moon—reflected the bleak state of political affairs, as though custom-made by some supreme central caster. Above the vast desolate expanse of dead soil the sky was ablaze in a blinding glare. When we reached the border at midday there were only blacks and whites on the parched ground, as in the mind of a fanatic, no muted colors in between.

Barbed-wire fences crisscrossed the large expanse of dead soil at the border. Every ten yards or so little red triangles on both sides of the narrow road warned you to beware of mines. Unusually large Israeli flags—as though trying hard to make a point—flew over grim watchtowers and bunkers. The Jordanians don't recognize this as a border and fly none of their own flags. The actual crossing point was is a Bayley bridge, its freshly painted iron bars covered with wooden planks that shake and rattle underfoot. The Israelis still call it by its old name, Allenby Bridge, after the British field marshal who conquered Palestine in 1917. The Jordanians named it after their king, Hussein Bridge. Cars are not allowed to cross. My luggage was carried only to the middle of the bridge and there it was picked up by a Jordanian porter who carried it to the another car waiting on the other side. The atmosphere here is reminiscent of the Glienicke Bridge at Berlin where the spies where exchanged during the Cold War.

I had half expected the bridge to be closed, as it often is at times of unrest. Instead, we were seen through without much ado. The traffic on the bridge, scarce as it was, was said to be normal. Controls on both sides were quick and perfunctory. The scenery on the Jordanian side was a mirror image of that on the Israeli side. Away in the waste stood a few grizzled trees ashen from the dust. We entered a parched flat. Jordanian soldiers in green camouflage jackets waved us through a number of roadblocks and open gates. Wild ravines ran down from the near mountaintops. There was a turnoff and the steep road started climbing through the dust and gravel. The barren coasts and bitter waters of the Dead Sea were visible behind through the haze.

The fertile higher ground is reached much quicker here than on the other side. The road climbed in twists and turns. The soil darkened and turned green. We entered a modern superhighway and drove past orchards and Mediterraenan style pine forests and reached the high mountain plateau. Little villages, reminiscent of those in the West Bank, were set in similar hard-to-till stony fields growing olive, barley, and fig as well as small flocks of sheep. Then, barely half an hour after crossing the river, we reached the brand-new outer suburbs of Amman, full of imported tinted glass and other manifestations of conspicious affluence: marble-covered walls, two- or three-car garages, stylish shops, and tall TV antennas shaped like miniature Eiffel towers.

2

Amman takes its name from the biblical Ammon, a tribe very much in disfavor with the author of Deuteronomy (23:6). He cites God ordering Moses "Thou shalt not seek their peace nor their prosperity all thy days for ever." There is considerable prosperity in Amman today and, by and large, more peacefulness and civilized political stability than just about anywhere else in the region. From little more than a village, populated by 15,000 or 20,000 settled Bedouins and Circassians before the Second World War it has since grown to a city of two million. The dominant Western veneer is at odds with the usual image of a Middle Eastern capital. Except in the oldest part, Amman is tidy, clean, modern, with none of the dust, congestion, squalor, or noise of other Arab capitals. It is certainly more neat and tidy than anything you might see in Israel. The feel of the place is a blend of England and the Levant. Cyprus with its minarets and Olde English Pubs used to be like this when it was a colony forty years ago. The thirty-eighth anniversary of the "Arabization of the Jordanian Armed Forces" (i.e., the expulsion of the British general who ran them) was celebrated in Amman when I was there but the ghosts of Glubb Pasha and Alec Kirkbride, both chums of T. E.Lawrence and other Brits who virtually ran the place till 1955, still hover.

The modern city is built in stone, as in Jerusalem; the basic town plan was probably prepared by the same people. As in Jerusalem, the sunlit mountain air has an extraordinary quality: luminous and clear. There are hardly any trees and relatively few gardens, the result, apparently, of a growing water shortage. Built on fifteen or sixteen contiguous hills, named Jebel Amman, Jebel Hussein, Weibdeh, Shmeisani or Al Qusour (a hill taken up almost in its entirety by the royal compound), streets and sidewalks are wide and well-kept and seem to be scrubbed clean daily. The newest suburbs are often quite faceless because of their sameness. Mail is delivered to post office boxes since most streets have no names and houses are only rarely numbered.

Well-maintained cars cruise along broad avenues from one traffic circle to the next. Public monuments display inscriptions in beautiful script hailing Industry or God, King and Country, in that order. The avenues drop into deep ravines before they rise to climb another hill under a soaring overpass or go under it in a tiled tunnel. They are lined with handsome buildings, done in bright limestone, as in Jerusalem, but better maintained, and tall glass-and-concrete office blocks. Many international and Arab banks and corporations opened branch offices here after the destruction of Beirut in civil war. The universities and hospitals in Jordan are said to be the best in the Arab Middle East today.

The look of Amman and the economic achievements of modern Jordan seem surprising in view of the scant resources of a country with little natural wealth which has been crippled over the years by war and civil strife and the influx of hundreds of thousands of destitute Palestinian refugees. Only 6 percent of the land can be cultivated. For years the country was glibly dismissed as a mere extension of the desert, a backdrop to a Lawrence of Arabia movie, a postcolonial kingdom whose days were numbered. A comparison of conditions in Jordan with those on the West Bank, which until 1967 was under Jordanian rule, is illuminating. A professor at Amman university recalled for me that for a good meal or man's suit or a book one would have driven to East Jerusalem before 1967—"Amman at that time offered so little." It is a reflection on the Israeli military occupation of the West Bank that in almost every respect—urban culture, transport, sanitation, town planning, social institutions, cultural amenities, medical services, and education—the Israeli-occupied West Bank lags at least twenty-five years behind Jordan. "We are ahead of them in the physical quality of our lives," the professor says. "They are ahead of us in their dedication to democracy."

Jordan's elections in 1993 to a multiparty parliament were generally judged by local and foreign observers as free and fair. But Jordan remains an authoritarian state, a patriarchal system in which parliament is regularly scolded by the king. "There is a constitution," a Jordanian political scientist told me. "But the king can change it by making two phone calls, if he wishes." His power, which in the past depended on an army of loyal Bedouin soldiers, an efficient bureaucracy, and a well-organized secret police, has been considerably augmented in recent years by the widespread support of a population that appreciates the stability and relative freedom he offers them. "Republicanism is a dirty word in the Arab world today, seeing what abolishing monarchies has brought about in Egypt, Libya or in Iran," an Amman intellectual said. "Not even the Islamicists here favor a Republic."

The widespread facade of smartness and prosperity obscures serious continuing economic difficulties. What Jordanian experts call a "crisis"—particularly in employment and in the balance of payments—began in the mid-
eighties and reached a high point during the Gulf war. When Jordan refused
to condemn Iraq, Saudi Arabia suspended trade and aid and the profitable
transit business with Iraq was curtailed by allied sanctions. The Gulf war also
caused the sudden influx of some 300,000 Palestinian-Jordanians expelled
from Kuwait and 120,000 Iraqi refugees as well. Jordan was the only place
that would take them in. But the Gulf war also turned out to be a kind of
blessing, causing a large number of gifted and energetic people to return to
Jordan (many of whom had built homes for themselves in Amman before the
war) and the reinvestment of their capital at home. The growth rate last year
is said to have been 9 percent. The returning Palestinians also brought in
some 50,000, cars causing the first serious traffic jams in Amman's history.

3

I spent a week in Jordan, mostly in Amman, speaking with politicians and
academics. Most were astonished to meet an Israeli. In retrospect, I thought,
it was a good thing I had come at a time of palpable political tension, just
after the Hebron massacre. Before the massacre I might have encountered
too many polite pleasantries in a country long committed to maintaining
extensive, if clandestine, political exchanges with Israel at the highest level
as well as tacit military accords. Two or three people would not see me
(though none said so explicitly); everyone else, in and out of the government and in the royal palace (including several prominent Jordanians of
Palestinian origin) welcomed talking with an Israeli. [None suspected that
formal peace would be concluded with Israel within less than a year; nor did
I.] Everyone I spoke to said they hoped the Israeli government would now
finally clamp down hard on religious and right-wing fanatics. Nearly all
added that the loathsome massacre was one more reason why the peace talks
must not be abandoned, and why, on the contrary, all sides must redouble
their efforts to reconcile Palestinians and Israelis. "You are squeezing Arafat
too hard because you know he has no alternative," a Jordanian university
professor told me. "It's a great mistake. You did that to the late king Abdullah
(in 1950) and you know what happened to him!" (Abdullah was assassinated by a Palestinian nationalist).

Here and there in the downtown districts I saw pictures of the "libera-
tor" Saddam Hussein. On Jordanian tourist maps Israel is still a blank, like

the undiscovered lands populated by dragons on medieval maps. On the other hand, both Israeli television channels were on view in the rooms of the Intercontinental Hotel, Amman's best, though it is hard to imagine who among the guests at that hotel, mostly Gulf Arabs, might be interested in the news in Hebrew. Several people I spoke to said: "We must finally make peace," and at least two prominent figures in the king's public administration criticized him for going so slow on peace with Israel. "Sometimes he plays it too safe," one said. Practically all the Jordanians I talked to said they would like to visit Tel-Aviv or Jerusalem, which is two hours away by car; and they seemed excited at the prospect that they would soon be able to visit both cities.

Almost two thirds of the population of Amman is said to be of more or less recent Palestinian origin. One Palestinian academic in Amman, a former Fatah militant, said of the Hebron massacre: "A loathsome crime. But Jordanians ought to be the last to sound off self-righteously—they themselves massacred thousands of Palestinians in 1970." This was a minority view. There were mass demonstrations in Amman for three days in a row protesting the massacre; speaker after speaker denounced Arafat for negotiating with Israel and called for his downfall. A mixed crowd of between 6,000 and 10,000, including hundreds of veiled women from a Palestinian refugee camp on the outskirts of the city, shouted "No to peace, yes to holy war." They were led by Islamic fundamentalists and "leftist" politicians and union leaders who severely assailed Arafat and his peace-making strategy with Israel and demanded that all Arab parties, including Jordan and the PLO, withdraw immediately from the peace talks. One demonstration got rather violent and was dispersed by helicopters dropping tear-gas canisters from the air. This was shown only on foreign television. The tension in Amman continued the entire week. Riot police remained on guard at strategic points in the city. At the offices in Amman of Hamas, the terrorist Islamic Resistance Movement, a spokesman named Nazzal each day exhorted all Arab governments to renounce the peace process and "join hands to liberate Palestine through armed struggle." After a German tourist and an English tourist were stabbed in downtown Amman, several Western embassies called upon their nationals to avoid going out during the next few days.

King Hussein's first public reaction to the massacre was restrained. He announced that he was donating 100,000 Jordanian dinars ($160,000) to the families of the victims and visited the clubhouse of a Palestinian charitable organization to present his condolences. "How shrewd of the king," I heard one man say, "mark you, the emphasis was on *their* tragedy, not

Jordan's." In a speech to members of parliament (some of whom had called on Jordan to withdraw from the Arab-Israeli peace negotiations) the king admonished them saying "It is not our right to discuss these things." It was Jordan's role to exert "positive influence" on events and "control passion through reason." There were advantages in withdrawing from the talks, he said, but there were also disadvantages. He did not say what he would do, but whatever decision he took would be "in cooperation and coordination with our brethren in the Arab world." A remarkable article next morning in the semi-official *Jordan Times* by Rami G.Khouri added a note of optimism rare in the Arab press

> In historical terms the Hebron mosque progrom will probably turn out to be the decisive turning point that finally pushed Palestinians and Israelis, along with the other concerned Middle Eastern players, to resolve the Arab Israeli conflict through peaceful diplomacy . . . The most appropriate response that we can offer to the to the legacy of Baruch Goldstein and the military Zionism he personified is to refuse to play by his rules . . . through a negotiated disengagement and a peace accord that allows the Palestinians to exercise their national rights in their own land.

On the following day, Jordan joined her "Arab brethren," as the king promised, and suspended the peace talks with Israel. They were bogged down anyway because Jordan was waiting for Syria to make the first step and Syria was waiting for Israeli concessions on the Golan. "Jordan will never be the first to make peace. It cannot," one of Hussein's ministers told me. "The king has to be cautious. It's been the secret of his survival for forty years at the head of the most stable regime in the Middle East. Jordan's position—for strategic as well as for demographic reasons—is too vulnerable."

4

The king, who assumed power in 1953, has been so long in office he often seems older than he is. He was fifty-eight in November 1993. He has been in treatment for cancer of the urethra and according to knowledgeable sources in Amman he has anything from three to fifteen years to live. Israelis tend to speak of him condescendingly, ("the little king") but without rancor; they watch on Jordanian TV his elaborate and frequent public appearances in fanciful black uniforms braided in gold-and-red. During the early sixties Hussein realized, however reluctantly, that Israel was here to stay and that sooner or later the Arab states would have to make peace with it. He was the first Arab leader to do so. His relations with the PLO (which tried to topple him in 1970) have never run smoothly. The PLO has vilified him for years. I heard people in Amman say that the king despises Arafat, and yet for many years, in the soft, dignified calm tone that marks all his public utterances, he has employed his considerable prestige to muster international support for the Palestinians' cause and to show sympathy for their tragedy. In 1972 he tried to satisfy both Israel and the Palestinians by offering peace with Israel in return for Israeli withdrawal from the occupied West Bank (including East Jerusalem) and the establishment of a Palestinian-Jordanian confederation. Both Israel and the PLO rejected the offer.

No other Arab leader has had so many clandestine meetings with Israeli leaders. Hussein's first meeting with an Israeli emissary was held in 1963 in the home of his Jewish dentist in London, not far from the Israeli embassy residence in Northwest London. The most recent (with foreign minister Shimon Peres) took place in Amman on November 3, 1993 and is said to have lasted nine hours and to have resulted in a written memorandum. It contained a long list of possible joint economic projects that could be undertaken after a peace treaty were concluded, e.g. water desalination, shared electricity grids, joint ports and airports at Aqaba and Elath, agriculture in the Jordan valley, etc.

During the intervening thirty years there were at least two dozen meetings between the king and Israeli officials, mainly Labor leaders, including Abba Eban, Levi Eshkol, Golda Meir, Moshe Dayan, Yitzhak Rabin and others. Some took place in remote spots along the Israeli Jordanian frontier; others aboard motor launches in Red Sea waters off the coast of Aqaba or Elath. The king is a licensed pilot. On one occasion he flew his helicopter to Tel-Aviv where Rabin escorted him one night on a ride along Dizengoff where, in Abba Eban's words, "our Mediterranean culture is expressed in all its turbulent, neon-lit brashness but also in the patent civility and deep rooted peacefulness of the passing crowds." At these meetings the king and the Israelis exchanged rare daggers, pistols, Galil submachine-guns and other martial gifts, while they discussed the possibility of peace.

They could not agree on the terms. The king was ready to make peace if Israel withdrew from all occupied West Bank territories, including East Jerusalem (with a special regime in the Old City). Israel always insisted on considerable border rectifications and refused all compromise on Jerusalem. In the absence of an agreement on peace the two sides continued to meet regularly. They shared a common concern about Palestinian and Syrian aspirations. A kind of strategic alliance emerged on this basis, confirming Freud's view that it is easy to create bonds of love between two persons as long as they have a third one that they can hate. Israeli leaders were fascinated by Hussein's charm and humor. (At one of their meetings with Hussein in the mid seventies Rabin complained about a military agreement the king had just signed with President Assad of Syria. King Hussein replied: "Not everyone I go to bed with I marry"). Naphtali Lavie, Dayan's press secretary during the Yom Kippur war, claimed in his recent memoirs that ten days before the outbreak of war Hussein visited Golda Meir in Tel-Aviv and warned her of an impending Syrian-Egyptian attack. (The high military echelon in Israel, including Dayan, were not impressed and ignored the warning.)

Abba Eban has written that Hussein, not Sadat, was the pioneer of realism in the Arab perception of Israel. At a time when Dayan persisted in his bleak view that the Arab-Israel conflict was inherently irreconcilable, at least within the foreseeable future, Hussein gave Israeli moderates a feeling that it was not. He kept telling the Israelis he talked to that they could have peace or territories, but not both. At the same time, according to Eban, the king "seemed embarrassed by a feeling that we Israelis were expecting too much of him in proposing that he should take the burden of the first breakthrough to an Arab Israeli settlement." Hence, he always gave Israeli leaders "maximum courtesy and minimal commitment." He has bitterly complained that the history of the Arab Israel conflict was a "history of missed opportunities."

A prominent former Jordanian minister (of Palestinian origin) outlined to me three such missed opportunities between Israel and Jordan. The first was the rejection by Israel and the PLO of his 1972 offer to establish a Jordanian-Palestinian confederation—at peace with Israel—in return for Israeli withdrawal. The Arab-Israel conflict, he said, might thus have been peacefully resolved twenty years ago if that offer had been accepted—there were no Islamic fundamentalists then and hardly any militant Israeli settlers. Another missed opportunity, he added, resulted from "the king's own mistake—a terrible mistake, I am sure he is aware of it now—his refusal in 1978 to join the Camp David peace treaty between Israel and Egypt." The third missed opportunity, according to the same man, was in 1987, when the then Israeli Prime Minister Yitzhak Shamir vetoed an agreement worked out between Foreign Minister Peres and King Hussein at a secret meeting in London. That agreement stipulated the establishment of a Palestinian entity closely linked to Jordan.

After that failure, Jordan officially renounced its claim to the West Bank and withdrew from the field in favor of the PLO. I often thought, while I was in Jordan, of these and other missed opportunities, traveling (with some envy) through the tranquil countryside, encountering almost everywhere I went an orderly civilized way of life and stable government and a sophisticated political elite. Time and again the melancholy thought recurred that on several occasions an accord had perhaps been possible that would have saved many lives and might have proven more satisfactory and reliable than anything one might achieve today—but these opportunities were missed through shortsightedness if not downright folly.

The king's reluctance since 1987 to step forward again has often been deplored by Israeli leaders and Western statesmen who in the same breath have gone on to state that his caution was probably justified. Jordan is far less powerful than Egypt or Syria and Iraq nor is it as rich as Saudi Arabia and the Gulf states. Its continued existence depends to a large degree on the good will of the other Arab countries and of its two million Palestinian citizen. Their loyalty is by no means certain.

Israelis sometimes complain of the king's "hypocrisy"—his public support of Palestinian independence while he knows well that Israel will do everything to prevent it. Jordanian officials dismiss this change. They insist that Jordan must always steer a middle course—between Arabs and Israelis and between the Arabs themselves, as during the Gulf war. They complain that Israel and the United States ignore the constraints that limit Jordan's freedom of actions, constraints they themselves find frustrating. Soon after Rabin's spectacular handshake with Arafat last September in Washington a high Jordanian official asked Henry Siegmann of the American Jewish Congress, who was visiting Amman, "Whatever possessed Rabin to deal with Yasir Arafat?" "You did," Siegman responded. "For years you have been telling the Israelis that Jordan would not speak for the Palestinians. Israel must deal with the PLO. You left them no alternative."

Some of the king's advisers have urged him in recent months to adopt a "Jordan first" policy: forget the Palestinians, they have only caused us trouble! Concentrate only on strengthening Jordan! (Those who hold this view are sometimes referred to in Amman drawing rooms as "the Jordanian Likud"). The king occasionally gives some encouragement to these Jordan-firsters, perhaps as a buffer against Islamic fundamentalists, many of whom are Palestinians. Fewer Palestinians now hold top government positions than ever before. One, who still holds high office, told me: "I am beginning to feel like a second class citizen."

The king is said to live in constant fear that the United States or Israel would take him for granted. This was obvious in the aftermath of the Israel-Palestinian accord of September 1993. The king was furious that he had not been consulted on an issue of immediate concern to Jordan. He was concerned that the delicate balance achieved in recent years between the royal house and the Palestinians was in jeopardy. In the near panic of the first few hours, the Jordanians stopped all traffic on the bridges from the Occupied Territories into Jordan. The king told an interviewer he was so worried he had not slept all night. The official press warned that supreme national interests" of Jordan had been put in jeopardy.

Jordan was concerned that as a result of the Palestinian-Israeli accord, tens, or maybe hundreds of thousands Palestinians from the West Bank and Gaza might migrate to Jordan. These initial concerns appear to have since been allayed, or at least lessened. The exact nature of the assurances or reassurances offered the king by Rabin, Peres, and Arafat during their recent meetings is unknown. It is widely assumed that the Israelis have promised the king that everything possible will be done to prevent the projected Palestinian entity on the West Bank from subverting the Jordanian state. The bridges over the river Jordan will remain under Israeli control, at least during the interim period. Peres, indefatigably optimistic, returned from his last not-so-secret meeting with the king in Amman with a pronouncement that a peace treaty with Jordan was ready "the only thing that's missing is a pen." Then, nothing happened. The Jordanians even delayed holding a international investors conference in Amman to discuss joint Israeli-Jordanian development projects, an idea promoted also by President Clinton.

In the Oslo accord, the final status of the autonomous Palestinian region was left open, subject to negotiations in the future. For the long-term solution, Rabin and Peres have not, or not yet, given up hope that Jordan will play an important part in any long-term solution. This is still called the "Jordanian option," a phrase that Abba Eban once described as a most unhappy semantic device since it obscured the limitations of the Jordanian role under the competitive pressure of the Palestinian nationalist cause. "It also overestimates the stature of Amman within the Arab regional complex."

And yet, in Jerusalem the "option" is still alive. Rabin and Peres continue to proclaim their opposition to an independent Palestinian state. Prominent Labor politicians, the press, and of course, spokesmen for the opposition claim that these are convenient Machiavellian lies. But Rabin may well be telling the truth. Peres continues to drop hints that a fully independent Palestinian state can be established only in the Gaza Strip (to be developed, Peres has suggested, on the model of Singapore) while the long-term solution for the West Bank (with its 120,000 Israeli settlers that can no longer be displaced) will be a limited autonomy overseen jointly by

Gaza-Palestine, Jordan, and Israel. According to Peres the West Bank is settled by too many Israeli settlers and can no longer be partitioned. For
Jerusalem he contemplates a series of Muslim and Christian enclaves mod-
eled on the Vatican. Proposals in this spirit have been offered to Hussein in
the hope that he would endorse them. From all I could gather in Amman
there is little likelihood that he will.

5

One morning in Amman an officer came to take me to an interview with the
king's younger brother, Crown Prince Hassan Bin Talal. The royal compound occupies almost an entire hilltop, the only one in treeless Amman
that is wooded and overlooks the downtown district and the Roman amphi-
theater. Hassan is Hussein's appointed successor and close adviser. He lives
on the palace grounds with his Pakistani wife and four children in the elegant villa once occupied by the British resident. His office, next to the king's,
in the *diwan*—the court administration building—is patrolled by fierce-
looking Circassian guards wearing black uniforms out of *Boris Godunov*
and carrying silver-trimmed daggers.

The prince is an easy-going man. A certain informality prevails in his
office: a sign printed in English in the waiting room requests employees to
refer to the prince as the "employer," not as "fathead" or "gumshoe." On
the walls of his study are photographs of his family, leather-bound volumes
of the Koran, and a large painting of the mosques on the temple platform
of Jerusalem.

Unlike the king, who has married four times, Hassan is said to be a family man, and an intellectual of wide and varied interests. (He is also a skier,
a polo and squash player, and he has a black belt in karate.) Like his brother,
he is short in stature; he has a large head, and his deep booming voice and
loud laughter make him seem bigger than he is. He talks with machine-
gun-like rapidity in a clipped British accent with a touch of wry, self-effac-
ing wit, on the lookout for paradoxes and ironies, and with a weakness,
occasionally, for campus-speak. He is the author of several scholarly books,
including a polemic aimed at disproving the legitimacy of Israel's historic
and legal claim to Jerusalem and another on the inalienable right of Palestinians to self-determination—with or without links to Jordan.

The Hebron massacre was a very, very serious setback, he told me, for it
highlighted once again the great danger that the political might be sub-
sumed, as he put it, by the religious. Jordan had merely suspended the peace

talks with Israel, he stressed, not quit them. But it was too soon to say "how far off track" the massacre would take the peace process. "I honestly don't know anymore what that term—peace process—means." Originally he had hoped that 1994 would be "the threshold for peace." Even before the Hebron massacre he was no longer sure. Syria, Jordan, and Lebanon had their separate agendas. Israel was not tackling the concerns of all of them "with the kind of comprehensiveness we would like to see."

Moreover, the "nonvoting" chairman (i.e., the United States) was really little more than "a mailbox . . . impulsive here and there but with no toughness." He did not want to score points, the crown prince said, but there was more to making peace than the flip remarks of the sort Shimon Peres had been making in recent months (e.g., only a pen is missing to sign a peace treaty). Much more was missing, the crown prince insisted. "After twenty-six months of direct negotiations between Israel and Jordan all we were able to achieve in practical terms was an agreement on pest control in the Jordan Valley. . . . This we could have achieved in the Mixed Armistice Commission." At the same time, Israel has rejected so far even "the principle of discussing boundaries with Jordan simply because, as they say, they have diverse pressures within which prevent them from discussing boundaries. "Perhaps, he said, they "fear setting a precedent." (Apart from Jerusalem, the main border dispute between the two countries concerns no more than some 300 square kilometers (186 square miles) abutting the Negev that Israel seized in 1967 and has cultivated since.)

"We have been accused of waiting for a Syrian lead," the prince said. "But the fact is we have been asking for movement on the question of boundaries. But even the principle of discussing boundaries has not been accepted."

The Israelis, he said, were eager to discuss joint economic projects in the Jordan Valley and elsewhere. But a number of basic "concepts" had to be clarified first: among them were boundaries, Jerusalem, the fair distribution of water resources, and the future of refugees. Israel, he said, has unilaterally established its own *fait accompli* on each of these four issues.

"When I saw Mr. Peres in Washington I made this very clear to him. His opening lines were: this project and that project. I said to him, look, we didn't come here to discuss projects without a concept."

I asked the prince if he was aware that Mr. Peres's vision of peace was quite similar to his own: they were both stressing the importance of regional security and cooperation; both were constantly emphasizing economic interests (both speak of a "dimension") and the need to move beyond the narrow nationalisms of the past. Both were talking about the common man, what the prince called "anthropolitics." And both were accusing each other of ambiguity. "Couldn't these ambiguities be cleared up," I asked, "if the two sides got together more frequently?"

"Well, contacts are quite frequent," the crown prince said. "But readiness on the part of the political decisionmakers is lacking—I don't want to sound tough, I am not accusing anybody—there is a deadlock."

"Perhaps the principals should get together in an intensive way, I said, before another madman . . . "

"Believe me," Prince Hassan interceded, "we are in contact in an intensive manner in more than one way . . ."

"I realize that now," I said, "but it's also true these intensive contacts are rather far apart."

"We'll invite you the next time and you can shout at us both," said the crown prince, with a loud laugh.

"Peres is ready to meet you on a daily basis."

"It's not this meeting [with me] that is the reason for my concern but what's happening [when he meets] Rabin in Tel-Aviv," he answered, still laughing.

"Perhaps we should get King Hussein and Premier Rabin together more often—lock them up in a room until they find a solution, I said."

The prince mumbled something I took to mean this wouldn't be a bad idea. I said I hoped this should happen sooner than later, before another Jewish madman or an Arab madman upsets everything once again.

"There is major lasting damage control to be done now during the next few weeks," he said. "After that we must get back on track. Something meaningful will have to be done before the congressional and U.S. government summer recess. Otherwise, really, this will be a year of terrible backsliding into violence."

The United States was not doing everything it should, the prince said. "The structure of the peace talks of Madrid envisaged, effectively, that the third party, the sponsor, the United States, play a full role . . . Instead of saying what we shouldn't be discussing because it's too explosive, let them be creative from time to time and say what we could or should be discussing . . . After Hebron something more than charm is required . . . Washington always wants a gimmick. . . . Something more is needed—not along the lines of 'let's have another public handshake.' The key issues have to be addressed." These statements will come over very badly in print, the crown prince concluded. The trouble with the United States was that it always "rushes to claim credit for many things"—he was alluding to the White House ceremony in September 1993—but peacemaking "after all, is much more than that . . ."

18

The Politics of Memory

Among Israelis at the end of World War II there was, at first, a stunned silence about the revelations of the Holocaust: a mixture of awe and shame. Older people suffered from pangs of conscience and guilt at not having been able to do something to prevent the disaster or at least reduce its dimensions. There was also an inability, frequently noted, on the part of younger, native-born Israelis to deal sympathetically with Holocaust survivors. This was, at least partly, a result of standard Zionist education and propaganda. Generations of youngsters had been brought up to believe that the existence of the Diaspora was not only a catastrophe but also a disgrace. Jewish victims of Nazism were often thought to have gone "like cowardly sheep" to the slaughter. I remember a Hebrew textbook, widely used in Israeli high schools until at least the late Fifties, which included the following analysis of the Hebrew poet Bialik's great lament on the Kishinev pogrom of 1903: "This poem depicts the mean brutality of the assailants and the disgraceful shame and cowardice of the Jews of the Diaspora shtetl."

In this odd text, the words "disgraceful," "shame," and "cowardice" were key terms that pointed to the heart of Zionist education. In the shifting moods of remembrance and rejection, younger Israelis were at first torn between anger and shame at having such a cursed past. A number of leading politicians were haunted by anguish and feelings of guilt, which some of them could never resolve, that they might perhaps have done more to diminish, even marginally, the extent of the tragedy.

The first foreign minister, Moshe Sharret, was obsessed by such questions to the end of his life. He agonized for years over the case of Joel Brand, the controversial emissary who came out of Hungary in 1944 with Eichmann's offer to exchange Jewish lives for shipments of trucks. The British held Brand in a military prison in Aleppo. Sharret interrogated him there and came away convinced of Brand's honesty and of the need, not to accept Eichmann's offer, but to continue talking to and bluffing Eichmann in order to gain time. The Russians were, after all, advancing on Hungary. The British would not hear of it. The rescue of Jews was secondary in their eyes to the main task of defeating the Nazis. Moreover, the Russians were vehemently against any deal and deeply suspicious of a possible separate Anglo-American German peace. To the end of his life Sharret reproached himself for perhaps not having been dramatic enough in his desperate appeals, or too disciplined in his loyalty to the Western allies.

By the late fifties, the stunned silence about the Holocaust gave way to loquacious—often officially sponsored—national discussion of its effects. It became common to speak of the Holocaust as the central trauma affecting Israeli society. It would be impossible to exaggerate its effect on the process of nation building. Tocqueville observed that, as in the lives of men, the circumstances of the birth of nations deeply affect their development. At a time in Israel when much of the national ethos and much of the political idiom were being formed, the images that were cast upon the dark mirrors of the mind were those of a veritable hell. The early Zionists had intended Israel to be a safe haven for persecuted Jews, yet Israel had come into existence too late to save the dead millions. To this day there is a latent hysteria in Israeli life that springs directly from this source. It explains the paranoiac sense of isolation that has been a main characteristic of the Israeli temper since 1948. It accounts for the towering suspicions, the obsessive urge for self-reliance, the fear—which sometimes collapses into contempt—of outsiders, especially of Arabs, and lately of Palestinians. Standing behind each Arab or Palestinian, Israelis tend to see SS men determined to push them once again into gas chambers and crematoria.

Israelis of course are not the only people who live under the shadow of a traumatic past. In Europe, the self-image of, say, the Poles or the Irish is rooted in similar notions. The massacre of millions of Armenians provides perhaps the closest parallel. Hitler is said to have remarked: "Who remembers the Armenian massacres?"—so the Jews can be safely annihilated, too. But if others were also annihilated, the Jews thought that their case was different because (with the exception of the gypsies) they alone were singled out for extermination as a people, as an alleged "species." Generations of Israelis have been brought up on this somber tenet: Jews were singled out to die not because of their religion, or their politics, or because of what they did, but simply because they were there, they existed.

This message has been instilled in them for years and with far-reaching political, cultural, and religious consequences. Out of it grew a distinct political philosophy, a bleak, hard, pessimistic view of life. The late historian Jacob L. Talmon described this view, approvingly, as a "divine and creative madness which not only stills all fear and hesitation but also makes for clarity of vision in a landscape bathed in a lurid, distorting light." Talmon wrote these words in 1960. Before he died twenty years later, he had come to regret them. For, if the prevailing traumatic memory of the Nazi Holocaust had become more powerful and widespread over the years, it was now also manipulated by politicians and ideologues. The memory of the Nazi Holocaust became more salient in political life, paradoxically, after Israel's lightning victory over three powerful Arab states in 1967. Talmon's "divine and creative madness" had accounted for much of the daring and energy of the young state. But after 1967 it was also one of the causes for much of the narrow-mindedness and sanctified nationalistic egoism that came in the wake of the Six Day and the Yom Kippur wars—the paranoia, of "the entire world is against us" and the disregard of Palestinian rights and of international opinion.

The resultant intransigence was probably one of the reasons why peace with Egypt, which was a distinct possibility in 1971 or 1972, was achieved in 1978 only after the terrible bloodletting of the Yom Kippur War. I remember being present at a conversation in 1972 between Richard Crossman, a prominent British Labour politician, and a retired senior Israeli diplomat. Crossman, a long-time friend of Israel, complained bitterly of Israel's intransigence concerning Palestinian rights and especially that of the then prime minister, Golda Meir. The diplomat sadly nodded his assent. Then he tried to make Golda Meir's intransigence comprehensible to Crossman by evoking the memory of the Holocaust. "We're a traumatized people," he said. "Please understand!"

"Certainly," Crossman responded. "You certainly are a traumatized people! But you are a traumatized people with an atom bomb! Such people belong behind bars!"

After the Six Day War the difference between history and propaganda was often blurred. Most Israeli political leaders were caught up in their own contradictions. The same right of self-determination Israelis claimed for themselves they now denied to others—in the name of memory. While vehemently opposing any attempt to see the Nazi holocaust in historical or comparative perspective—insisting that it was absolutely incomparable and unique—they, for their part, could call the Arabs Nazis and Arafat another Hitler. In a well-known letter to Ronald Reagan during the Lebanese war, Menachem Begin wrote that when Israeli tanks were rolling into Beirut he felt as though he were breaking into Berlin to catch Hitler in his bunker. Nor was this rhetoric a speciality of Begin or of the Likud. Abba Eban, the most moderate of Labor politicians, described the pre-1967 frontiers—frontiers which had enabled Israel to crush three Arab armies in only six days—as "Auschwitz borders."

The original difficulty in confronting the memory of the Holocaust left an imprint on Israeli historiography too. During the first two decades the writing of Israel's history was handicapped by truisms derived from mainstream Zionist ideology. The result was a series of ideological and apologetic works aimed at proving the historic need for a Jewish state. They are acutely analyzed in *The Seventh Million, Israel, and the Holocaust*, an important study by Tom Segev, a leading Israeli scholar.(New York: Hill and Wang, 1993).

Segev points out that despite the pervasiveness of the subject in Israeli life most serious works by Jewish writers on Nazism were written by non-Israelis, and—perhaps because they did not fully conform with current formulas—only a handful of those were translated into Hebrew, nearly always belatedly. Raul Hilberg's monumental work on the Holocaust was never translated. Alan Bullock's book on Hitler came out in Hebrew only after a twenty-year delay, Joachim Fest's *Hitler* only in 1986—in Fest's case, the Israeli publisher saw fit to add a subtitle that contradicted the book's main thesis: "Portrait of a Non-Human." I mention these maneuvers and delays only as a characteristic of the tendency at that time to prefer simplistic versions to more nuanced ones. It took more than a generation to produce Israeli historians able to detach the history of the Holocaust from their own biographies.

The writing of history, we all know, is one way of ridding oneself of the crushing, often debilitating weight of the past; in Benedetto Croce's words, "it liberates us from history." The Israeli political class, however, was reluctant to free itself from clichés. The use of memory as a political instrument became more evident under the right-wing government that came to power in 1978. I am sometimes reminded of its rhetoric when I read the statements—full of affirmations that history equals destiny—that come out of the former Yugoslavia these days. Begin habitually described every major policy act of his government—in Lebanon or in the virtually annexed occupied territories—as a milestone in Israel's historic march "from Holocaust to redemption." He tried, through legal measures, to expropriate the Holocaust from historiography. A law passed in 1981 made it a criminal offense to deny the existence of the Holocaust, as though that event was no longer a matter for historians but was now, in Segev's words, a "doctrine" of national truth anchored in law, a state religion. (In principle the doctrine seems better protected under this law than religion. The maximum penalty for "gross violation of religious sentiment," including presumably denying there is a God, is one year in jail; the mandatory punishment for denying the Holocaust is five years. Both laws are essentially expressions of the political rhetoric. Nobody has ever been tried under either.) Political language is still filled with early clichés about the Holocaust. In 1991, General Ehud Barak, chief of staff of the Israeli army, with an entourage of adjutants and TV reporters, visited Auschwitz. As he stood by the ruins of the crematoria, he solemnly pronounced: "We came here fifty years too late."

By the same token, it was only very slowly that the way was opened in Israel for an understanding of the nature of the German Federal Republic: that it was a new beginning, and not such a bad one after all; that it was an open society and a fairly well-functioning democracy, a complex place, a place that didn't resemble a painting by Otto Dix or George Grosz but one, say, by Anselm Kiefer. On the German question, David Ben-Gurion was the great exception among politicians. He often contradicted the prevailing hostile view of West Germany by insisting that it was now a liberal democracy. He must have done so for reasons of state, but also because he was convinced that there was now "another" Germany. He did not get very far, even within his own party. And he failed to convince his successor. A revealing incident took place in 1966 at a state dinner in Konrad Adenauer's honor in Jerusalem at which I happened to be present. In his after-dinner speech Prime Minister Levi Eshkol, reading a prepared text, hailed Adenauer for his past and present record and then declared that "penance is impossible. . . . Israel seeks proof that Germany deserves to return to the family of nations." Adenauer put down his wine glass and told Eshkol that he was breaking off his visit; in his statement, he complained, Eshkol had denied his life's work.

Eshkol was flabbergasted. The guests at the table looked at one another with pained faces. Eshkol did not understand what had gone wrong. He tried to placate Adenauer: "But I praised you personally," he said. This seemed to make things worse. Adenauer announced that he was ordering his airplane to stand ready to take off early next morning. In the end

Adenauer did not cut short his visit. Diplomats of both sides huddled in the next room and found a reconciling formula. But the incident was telling. It was not just the slip of a speech writer, or the fatigue or absent-mindedness of a politician.

Levi Eshkol was a singularly humane, moderate, and conciliatory man. He was among the early, by now legendary, wave of pioneers who had set-tled in the country before the First World War and founded the first kib-butz. Unlike Begin or Shamir he had no personal experience of Nazism. But he was representative of Israelis of all ages and all ethnic origins for whom, long before, the Holocaust had become larger than a personal trauma. It had become one of three main pillars of collective identity; the other two being nationalism and religion. The Holocaust was an event many native Israelis felt they had experienced vicariously, as it were, irrespective of age, origin, or education. Even non-Jewish Israelis, including Arabs and Druze, share in the same feeling by a kind of osmosis.

In 1978, with the sharp turn to the right in Israeli politics, "remem-brance" was further institutionalized within the national ritual and the edu-cational system. The history of the Holocaust had always been taught in the schools as a part of the regular history curriculum. It now became a subject in citizenship classes and religion classes as well. The "lessons" and "values" of the Holocaust, its religious "meaning" were regularly discussed. As Eastern Europe opened up to Israeli tourism in the mid-eighties, Holocaust studies in the classroom were supplemented by government-subsidized school tours to Poland. Thousands of high-school students took part in these tours—called "Marches of the Living"—accompanied by former concentra-tion-camp inmates who acted as special guides. The students usually flew first to Warsaw and visited the site of the former ghetto. From there they would continue to Treblinka and Auschwitz, which was the high point. Singing Israeli songs, waving Israeli national flags, wearing T-shirts embla-zoned with big Stars of David and the inscription ISRAEL or ISRAEL LIVES, the young visitors would march through the Auschwitz *Stammlager* guided by a former inmate. At nearby Birkenau they would hoist their flags at the for-mer crematoria and intone a special prayer for the safety of soldiers in the Israeli army, wherever they might be. They then recited the *kaddish,* the traditional Jewish prayer to the dead.

Upon their return from Poland, some of the young participants in these tours told the press that on the site of the former extermination camp they had become "better" Zionists; they had become convinced that Israel must keep every square centimeter of Eretz Israel; territorial compromise was impossible. According to one of the guide books issued especially for the trips by a branch of the Israeli ministry of education, Auschwitz exemplified the immutable hatred for Jews, a hatred which has always existed and will always exist as long as there are Gentiles and Jews. Another text states:

> We stand, with bitter hearts and tearful eyes, by the crematoria in the extermination camp and mourn the terrible end of European Jewry. But even as we cry and mourn, our hearts fill with pride and happiness at the privilege we enjoy as citizens of the independent State of Israel. We answer and promise with all our hearts: long live the State of Israel for ever and ever.

The same textbook decries both current Polish anti-Semitism and the fact that even after the fall of communism, the Polish government recognizes the Palestinians' right of self-determination, as though the two were one and the same thing.

The atmosphere that pervaded these tours, and that they generate in turn, has been the subject of heavy criticism in recent years. The debate was opened a few years ago by a leading Israeli educator, Professor Yehuda Elkana of Tel-Aviv University, himself a survivor of Auschwitz. In an article published in *Ha'aretz*, entitled "The Need to Forget," Elkana protested the current uses of memory for political purposes. He warned of their possible political and psychological consequences:

> What are children to do with such memories? The somber injunction, Remember! may easily be interpreted as a call for blind hatred. It is possible that the world at large must remember.... But for ourselves, I see no greater educational task than to stand up for life, to build our future in this land without wallowing day in and day out in ghastly symbols, harrowing ceremonies, and somber lessons of the Holocaust.... The deepest political and social factor that motivates much of Israeli society in its relation with the Palestinians is a *profound* existential "Angst" fed by a particular interpretation of the lessons of the Holocaust and the readiness to believe that the whole world is against us, that we are the eternal victim.
>
> In this ancient belief, shared by many today, I see the tragic and paradoxical victory of Hitler. Two [Jewish] nations, metaphorically speaking, emerged from the ashes of Auschwitz: a minority who assert "this must never happen again" and a frightened and haunted majority who assert "this must never happen to us." If these are the only possible lessons, I for one have always held with the former. I

have seen the latter as catastrophic. History and collective memory are an inseparable part of any culture; but the past is not and must not be allowed to become the dominant element determining the future of society and the destiny of a people.

Elkana was savagely criticized for this view. Yet he was not alone, in recent years, in admonishing Israelis, in Carlyle's phrase, wisely to remember and wisely also to forget. Nietzsche's well-known argument comes to mind that life in any true sense is impossible without some forgetfulness. "There is a degree of sleeplessness, or rumination, of 'historical sense' that (in the victim at least) injures the living thing, be it a man, or a people, or a system of culture."

I have lived in Israel most of my life and have come to the conclusion that where there is so much traumatic memory, so much pain, so much memory innocently or deliberately mobilized for political purposes, a little forgetfulness might finally be in order. This should not be seen as a banal plea to "forgive and forget." Forgiveness has nothing to do with it. While remembrance is often a form of vengeance, it is also, paradoxically, the basis of reconciliation. What is needed, in my view, is a shift in emphasis and proportion, and a new equilibrium in Israeli political life between memory and hope.

For this purpose, too, the 1992 change of government in Israel was an important step forward. It was not only a matter of the government's being ready to conclude a historic peace agreement with the Palestinians, who are no longer seen by government officials as latter-day Nazis. The change also related specifically to the Holocaust. Shulamit Aloni, Rabin's first minister of education, argued along lines similar to those of Elkana. Before Rabin was forced by the ultra-religious bloc to remove her from the ministry, Aloni canceled all organized school tours to Auschwitz. She took the position that the state school system must not propagate so-called "values of the Holocaust." The very term, she said, made her shudder: the Holocaust had no values. Instead of curing wounds, Aloni suggested, Israelis were constantly tearing them open again. Instead of "administrating" the trauma Israelis should begin to cure it. How this can be done politically I do not know, except that our hope lies in the possibility that the vision of Yehuda Elkana will prevail.

19

Egypt's Iceberg

> Egypt resembles an iceberg, one eighth is above sea level.
> Seven eighths are submerged in the depths. One eighth of
> our lives takes place in the light of the twentieth century,
> seven eighths in medieval darkness. . . . In the nineteenth
> century we went through pangs of birth . . . but the renais-
> sance was stillborn, and when another embryo was formed
> in the womb (under Nasser) it was aborted.
>
> *Dr. Louis Awad, prominent Egyptian literary critic, 1969.*

By simply turning a corner in central Cairo, one enters a different world
and even a different time. A short distance behind the glossy steel-glass-
and-marble office-tower of *Al-Ahram*, the prestigious semiofficial Egyptian daily, another age, another Egypt begins.

Here is the sophisticated gadgetry of a great publishing house and
research center with its ultra-modern computers and automated printing
presses and its sophisticated executives, fluent in several languages, who
communicate with their secretaries—and perhaps also with the outside
world—by closed-circuit television. Luxury cars come and go and doormen
in dark suits behind high glass walls require all visitors to walk through
blinking metal detectors as in an airport.

And here, barely fifty yards away, begins the labyrinth of narrow unpaved lanes where millions live in seedy shacks and dark warrens above and
below, often without water, sewers, or electricity. Vast slum areas stretch far
into the distance. They are teeming with people. On crumbling walls fundamentalist graffiti proclaim the imminent victory of radical Islam to
whom Mubarak is a second Shah. "For every Shah there is an Ayatolah,'
"'Islam is the solution," "There is no God but God." On the broken up
pavement someone has just slaughtered a lamb and is cutting up its limbs
with a large saw. Barefoot kids wade in the dust. Used shoes are laid out for

sale in great heaps. Clouds of smoke, dust, and sewer water hang in the thick air between shacks of mud and corrugated iron.

Much of the top floor of the *Al Ahram* tower is taken up by an executive dining room, where top editors, columnists, politicians, and well-known Egyptian intellectuals gather for lunch. Since the days of Nasser and Sadat, intellectuals (including some who oppose the government) have had their offices in the building when, for political reasons, the semioffical *Al Ahram* would never print their articles. Through the large picture windows there is a fascinating view of Cairo, old and new. In the far distance, the pyramids float on pink-grey clouds of air pollution. Nearer, the city's latest skyscrapers soar against a background of seemingly endless slums. In the harsh light everything is bleak and grey and there is hardly a tree, or anything green, in sight.

I sat up there some time ago with one of Egypt's leading columnists of *Al Ahram*. He was furious that beer and other alcoholic drinks were now banned from the *Al Ahram* dining room as a concession to the Islamicists. He held forth, darkly, on the rise of fundamentalism, the "new barbarism," and on Egypt's seemingly irresolvable economic problems, a result partly of the ongoing population explosion, and partly of corruption in high places. Then he said that at the same time, Egypt boasted the best writers in the Middle East and some of the world's finest astronomers, physicists, and cardiologists. He gesticulated dramatically with his hand. Pointing to the near slums and to a complicated looking electronic device on a neighboring roof, he cried: "Here we are! One foot on the moon! The other stuck in the sewer!"

Egypt today is a somber country, frustrated, grim, and disillusioned. Intellectuals are cynical and pessimistic. Having squandered their credibility by siding with Marxism or Nasserism, quite a few are now trying to regain it by openly siding with the Islamicists. They preach an amalgam of religious fundamentalism, nationalist integralism, and xenophobia. In the hope of stemming the radical tide, the government is putting on more and more religious airs. The social programs of the fundamentalists are expanding despite the government's efforts to stop them. The crisis of the political system is reflected in their success. Some people speak of a state within a state. Estimates of what the Islamicists would gain if the government permitted them to participate in the elections vary between 40 and 60 percent. They have money, arms, and veterans trained trained by the CIA during the Afganistan war. They have active support groups in Saudi Arabia, in Europe, and in the United States. Some of their money comes from the United States, from Saudi Arabia, and the Sudan. Most Egyptian universities are controlled by militant Islamic groups. Islamicist teachers have massively infiltrated the high schools. They control the lawyers,' doctors' and engineers' syndicates, corporate bodies left over from Nasser's days. You see more bearded men in Cairo than ever before. In the poorer sections every other women wears the Islamic headdress.

The despondency is heightened by the continuing rash of terrorist bombings and assassination attempts. Hardly a day goes by without some report of armed clashes between government forces and fundamentalists with casualties on both sides. Some of these clashes, especially in Upper Egypt, seem to have degenerated into mutual vendettas, much as in Southern Italy a few years ago. The tourist industry has been crippled. Tourist revenue lost since 1992 has been estimated at more than $3 billion. In January 1995, when I was there (the peak of the tourist season), hotels in Cairo were said to be half empty and offering rooms at drasticaly reduced rates. The presence of militiamen carrying and bayonets in downtown Cairo was overwhelming. Riot policemen in special trucks were stationed on the main squares and outside the Egyptian Museum, where some of the pharaonic mummies are once again on display. (They had been removed under Sadat, allegedly for the patriotic reason that it was unseeming for Egypt's ancient kings to be so exposed.) At night, troops were patrolling the main bridges on the Nile. From the terrace of my room in the old Shepheard's hotel, overlooking the river, I would watch their trucks drive back and forth directing their searchlights at suspicious shadows.

The conventional wisdom here is that Egypt is not Algeria, because of its history, its geography, and several other important factors. "It can't happen here." Egyptians are Suni not Shiite Muslims. Other Arab communities may be "tribes with flags" but Egypt is a real nation with its own stable authentic identity. "The Islamic threat may not be marginal, but it is temporary," says the director of the semiofficial *Al Ahram Center for Political and Strategic Studies,* Abdel Monem Said Aly. "It is less significant than the conflict with Israel [was]." Peace with Israel will hopefully "release the funds needed to stem the Islamic tide."

The government refuses to engage moderate Islamicists in dialogue and expresses its displeasure when American diplomats do. "Americans and their Iranian complexes! Egypt is not Iran," said a senior Egyptian official. The government continues to dismiss the terrorists with contempt. In a recent interview published in the *The New Yorker* President Mubarak called them "belly dancers, drummers from the slums" in the pay of Iran and Sudan. They had nothing to do with Islam. "It's all a matter of money."

This is obviously not how the police see it, perhaps not even Mubarak himself. Human rights organizations claim that between 20,000 and 25,000

Islamic militants are currently in Egyptian jails. Many are the relatives of suspected terrorists behind bars as hostages. The attempt in 1994 on the life of Nobel Prize winning novelist Naguib Mahfouz, according to the liberal sociologist Saad Eddin Ibrahim, "showed that all prominent members of our society are under threat of assassination." The attack of Mahfouz came in the wake of similar assaults in 1993 on the lives of Prime Minister Atef Sidky, Interior Minister Hassan al Alfi, and Information Minister Sawfat al Sharif. According to Dr. Ibrahim the scope of terrorist attacks is not merely the government but society as a whole. Attacks on the Coptic Christian minority in Egypt "also increased, notably in Upper Egypt." Dr. Ibrahim heads the prestigious independent think-tank Ibn Khaldun Center, which promotes "democratic transformation" in Egypt and other Arab countries. Peace, human rights, women's rights, and minority rights are its main concern. In 1994, Dr. Ibrahim proposed an international conference in Cairo on minorities in the Middle East. Ibrahim's insistence that Egypt's Copts, their rights and lack of rights, be on the agenda of the conference raised such an outcry in the government press that he was forced to move the conference to Limassol. The conventional wisdom in Egypt is that Copts are not a minority and so, by definition, cannot lack rights.

❋

A widespread disillusion with conventional politics is a central feature of the country. There was a time, under Nasser, when Egyptians had looked left and a time, under Sadat, when they had looked right; now many look upward for salvation. They too will be disappointed as heaven will fail to produce manna. Fifteen years ago, when I first started going to Egypt in the wake of Sadat's pilgrimage to Jerusalem, there was still widespread hope that peace would release resources for development. Sadat promised a new age of prosperity. Millions cheered him in the streets upon his return from Jerusalem and Camp David. "Who is for peace? The soldiers themselves!" the popular journalist Anis Mansour, Sadat's semiofficial mouthpiece, wrote at that time. "The war has embittered everyone's life. The war has denied them home, street and livelihood. Whoever reaches for the telephone and does not get a line, or opens the faucet and the water does not come, or stands in the street for hours and waits for the bus which does not arrive, and when it does there is no space on it, not even on the steps; every young man who does not find work, and if he finds work does not find a home, and if he finds a home can't afford the rent, and hence can't marry—all of these do not want war. . . . Peace will bring prosperity for all."

Such hopes were already squashed during Sadat's lifetime. Sadat was assassinated by a fundamentalist army officer less for making peace with Israel, as is often thought, than for being a "corrupt" godless "pharaoh"; his "shamelessly" westernized wife was a "disgrace to Arabism and Islam." The assassin spoke at great length during his trial, haranguing Sadat and his ministers for their sins. It is said that he never once mentioned Israel. Vice President Hosni Mubrarak's subsequent rise to power was generally greeted in Egypt with satisfaction and relief. Mubarak was a former air-force officer known for his down to earth straightforward manner. He abolished the crude cult of personality that surrounded his predecessors. He released Sadat's political prisoners. He liberalized the press and parts of the political system. Next to Mubarak's own National Democratic Party, several opposition parties were allowed to participate in elections even though results were widely thought to be unrepresentative and manipulated. Several independent nongovernmental organizations were allowed to function, though at times precariously, and there were the modest beginnings of a civil society, including organizations that publicly militate against human rights violations in Egypt. They would have been unthinkable in the past. "We live in a pharaonic 'democracy,' " a well-known Egyptian journalist told me. "Mubarak runs an authoritarian, highly centralized regime. But he and his ministers are not unaffected by public opinion. In Nasser's time," he adds, "if you opposed the regime you were thrown into prison. Under Sadat, you lost your job. Under Mubarak you only get a telephone call. And maybe, you don't get a raise."

The first decade of Mubarak's rule saw a number of remarkable achievements. The most important was in birth control. Estimates vary and official figures are thought to be unreliable. But according to one United Nations expert, population growth in Egypt declined in the past fifteen years from 3.5 to 2.4. The population of Egypt is now expected to reach only 90 million by the year 2025, considerably fewer than the 120–140 million it might have reached had birth rates not dropped as they did. Military expenditure is also said to have dropped from 16 to 6 percent of GNP (it had been as high as 36 percent under Nasser). Thanks largely to United States and European aid, Cairo's infrastructure has vastly improved. In the early eighties the sewer system in central Cairo was on the verge of collapse. I remember a week early in 1983 when pipes in Giza and Mohandessin burst but could not immediately be repaired because the plans could not be found (there were insinuations that the British had taken them with them in 1952). Entire streets were flooded; people crossed on planks and bricks. The army was brought in to help. The papers claimed that the city was "floating on a lake of sewage."

Since then, sewage, water, electricity, and telephone systems in central Cairo have been overhauled. Public transportation, at least in Cairo, has also improved. One no longer sees thousands of people riding on the rooftops of buses and suburban trains, or hanging in clusters out of their open doors, as was common only ten years ago. There is a new French built metro. Numerous elevated roads have relieved some of the traffic jams.

At the same time, however, the economy began to stagnate under Mubarak's tired, uninspired rule. Cairo is full of jokes about Mubarak. He is the man who never ties his shoelaces, a reference to his hesitating, heavy gait and his reluctance to make clear-cut decisions precisely explained. In another joke, the guardian angel at the gate of paradise asks Mubarak to state his talents and capabilities. He answers "None." The guardian angel promptly says "Ah, you must be Mubarak." Mubarak is in his third term of office but has still not picked himself a vice president. The reason for this, according to another joke, is that throughout Egypt he could not find a man less bright than himself. Before the recent referendum on granting Mubarak a third presidential term a joke made the rounds about Clinton who presents Mubarak with a monkey and says: "I'll double your aid program if you make this monkey laugh and cry. Mubarak makes the monkey laugh and cry. "How on earth did you do this," Clinton wonders. "I told him that I am president," Mubarak says, "and the monkey laughed. So then I told him that I am angling for a third term, and he cried!" The cynicism about Hosni Mubarak was especially apparent after the official results of the referendum were made public. In a country where the vast majority of voters are not even registered, 84 percent were said to have participated in the referendum of which 96 percent voted "yes."

At a time when Egypt should have had an economy growing at 6 to 8 percent a year, as in the mid-seventies, merely to keep its head above water, growth is said have fallen in 1993 to between 1.5 and 2 percent, and to between zero to 1 percent in 1994. The per capita income fell from some $730 to $630 annually. During the same time the prices of basic foodstuffs rose sharply. The poor grew poorer and more numerous and the rich, at least in Cairo, visibly grew much richer, perhaps very much richer than before. The middle and lower middle classes were especially hit and were seeking solace—or expressing their rage—by joining the fundamentalists. Since the days of King Farouk and his collection of Rolls Royces and diamond-studded cravats, there has never been so much conspicuous spending in Cairo as there is today. The contrasts one encounters are staggering. In the narrow slum streets, the teeming crowds stoically part to allow long luxury cars, costing up to half a million dollars, pass through in the dust, their dark tinted windows carefully rolled up to make the air-conditioned interiors completely invisible from the outside. According to a report in a recent issue of *Al Ahram* some of the posh weddings one encounters nightly in five star hotels, cost up to $200,000. The new super-rich are widely rumored to be Mubarak's personal friends and relatives. Official corruption is said to have tripled since the days of Sadat whose sons and in-laws were also rumored to have amassed millions.

The private business community is no longer as marginalized by Egypt's power structure as it had been in the decades after Nasser's sequestration of private property, in the fifties and sixties. The business community has even been maintaining for some time its own, privately funded, research institute, the Middle East Research Institute, headed by a retired army general. The center, undoubtedly created with the government's blessings, is dedicated to the formulation of new national strategies divergent from, and hopefully more open minded than, those of the other, semiofficial research institute, the *Al Ahram* Center for Political and Strategic Studies, which was founded by Nasser after the 1967 war, and still staffed by many of former admirers. The latter still boycott Israel and will not visit it even though they write about it a lot. The new institute has attempted to help break this boycott. It encourages contacts with Israeli scholars and businessmen and recently hosted a number of round table meetings between visiting Israeli politicians and leading Egyptian intellectuals. For some of the latter—sixteen years after the peace treaty—those meetings were their first.

The private sector in industry, banking, commerce, and tourism has grown in recent years. But the economy, according to a World Bank expert, is still largely a "Soviet style command economy. There isn't a country in Eastern Europe today where 80–90 percent of GDP is still generated by the public sector."

It is not easy to unwind the results of forty years of socialism without a revolution. There is no question that Egyptian businessmen are enterprising, energetic, and hardworking. Egypt is a country where you can likely see two brothers-in-law hard at work in the middle of the night fixing their pick-up truck while a five-year-old boy is holding up the light for them. The problem is the system, the inert bureaucracy that stifles all initiative. The United States, which gives Egypt $2.3 billion in aid annually, and the World Bank have been urging Egypt for years to privatize public sector companies that remain afloat only because they are receiving large government subsidies. A growing number of technocrats within the government have been saying the same. But Mubarak insists on moving slowly. "Too slowly," says a Western diplomat, "especially in view of the likely reduction of Egypt's annual aid package from the United States. But concepts of economic risk are incomprehensible to Mubarak." His government is no longer "ideologically" committed to socialism but Mubarak is reluctant to push privatization for fear of its political consequences.

The government is pragmatic. In Egypt only some of the opposition parties follow "ideology." One of Mubarak's advocates told me he was correct in rejecting the demands of the World Bank: "The World Bank has caused more violent unrest in the Third World than did the late Soviet Union." Privatization inevitably means massive unemployment. Massive unemployment at a time of growing support for Islamic radicals could prove disastrous for the regime. There is no social safety net here to support the unemployed. The system itself is the only social safety net. The regime seems symbiotically linked with the bloated public sector and with the office-holders who are running it. Many are luminaries of the governing National Democratic Party. Not surprisingly, of 280 public companies earmarked three years ago for privatization only three have so far been privatized, Coca Cola, Pepsi Cola, and the Nasser Boiler Company. Yearnings for a "reformed Nasserism" are still rampant. An exchange in Naguib Mahfouz's novella *Miramar* illustrates why. One of Mahfouz's protagonists is furious at Nasser. A friend chastises him for this.

"What other regime was possible here instead? If you think seriously you'll understand there were only two possibilities, communists or Muslim Brothers. Which of the two would you prefer?" "None," he answered quickly." And I: "Exactly so. Let this be your consolation."

※

In Middle Eastern affairs too, Egypt has recently been in search of a new role. Ever since Sadat's dramatic flight to Jerusalem in 1977, Egypt has been a pioneer of peace. In the early eighties, it payed a price for this courage when it found itself ostracized and calumnized by the PLO and the Arab countries. During those years of isolation Egypt did not give up on its efforts to promote comprehensive Middle East peace. So successful has Egypt been in this task as *interlocuteur valable* that during the past three years it has practically worked itself out of its chosen role. Israel was induced to recognize the PLO. and sign a formal agreement. Egypt played a discreet but important role in encouraging this breakthrough. Morocco, Tunisia, and some of the Gulf sheikdoms followed suit. By the time Jordan came round and signed a peace treaty with Israel it did not even consult Cairo. Rabin had the courtesy to telephone Mubarak a few days before to inform him of what was about to happen. Hussein, Mubarak recently complained to an Israeli visitor, did not bother.

Some Egyptians now began to worry that Israeli entrepreneurs and Arab financiers with surplus capital might team up to conquer vast markets in Egypt and the rest of the Arab world. Egyptian pundits filled the columns of *Al Ahram* and other Cairo papers with dire warnings that, if not checked, Israel might eliminate Egypt's position as a "leading country" in the region and the dominant political, economic, and cultural power. The key word in this campaign, which in some way must have been encouraged by the government, was "hegemony." A quest for "hegemony" was behind Israel's loud talk of a "new Middle East." Egypt was called upon to reassert its role as a rival leader to defend itself from the "political and economic threat" emanating from Tel-Aviv. Privately, Egyptians were saying that Israel was effectively undermining Egypt's position in the region and harming its economy by encouraging Qatar, Oman, and other Gulf states to sell their oil to Europe via pipelines running through Israel instead of shipping it through the Suez Canal. Israel was driving wedges between the Arab brothers. In the new era of peace, the "co-existence" between Egypt and Israel would be a co-existence "in struggle," similar to that of France and Germany during the nineteenth century. This "rivalry" would determine the future of the region. According to Mohammed Sid-Ahmed in *Al Ahram* Israel arrogantly assumed it was the "only victor"; it interpreted "the land-for-peace formula as an exchange of land for a Middle East market."

The Israelis had, of course, provoked some of this by a lot of loose talk of their own. Almost 700 over-eager Israeli businessmen and politicians descended on Casablanca during a recent conference there on regional development, dictating its agenda, or so it seemed to the far fewer delegates from the Arab world. For some reason Rabin chose to pick this time to announce, cryptically, that Israel must once again prepare for a general Arab-Israeli war in the medium range of time. A memo prepared by the Israeli foreign ministry's planning department, leaked to *Ha'aretz* proposed "punishing Egypt" for its insistence that Israel sign the Nuclear Non-proliferation Treaty by depriving it of its role as Arab-Israeli peace broker and by inducing Washington congressmen to cut U.S. aid to Egypt. Peres quickly announced that the memo was simply a memo and did not reflect Israeli policy. Egyptian officials were sure it had been deliberately leaked. Foreign Minister Amr Moussa described its authors as "feeble minded."

In the angry press war that followed Peres was misquoted in the Egyptian media as saying that Egypt was the "donkey" that would push the stalled car of progress up the Middle East road. Peres did tell the Arabs that their policies had so far given them only misery. They could achieve prosperity but only in cooperation with Israel. Several Israeli economists were quick to question this obvious over-statement. Peres's repeated calls for a Common Market in the Middle East, on the model of the European Union, had been questionable from the beginning; the very comparison with Europe was dubious because of the vast difference between the near post-industrial economy of Israel and the Third World economy of its neighbors with per capita incomes only a tenth and less that of Israel. Peres also proposed that Israel be accepted as a member of the Arab league. This too was interpreted in Egypt as a "hegemonial" attempt to dominate the League just as it was celebrating its fiftieth anniversary. (Israelis would not have reacted more generously if Arafat had asked to be received as a member of the Executive of the World Zionist Organization).

The air was thick with suspicions on both sides. If Egypt had indeed asked the Gulf states to take a cautious attitude toward normalization of relations with Israel, as officials in Jerusalem were insinuating, it may have been another attempt to make them coordinate their moves; or it may have been another attempt to show that Egypt was still able to call the shots. Rabin, as if to disprove this, promptly flew to Oman on a state visit. The predictable reaction was a Syrian-Saudi-Egyptian summit meeting in Cairo seen by Israel as an attempt to slow the peace process.

Israeli and Egyptian insecurities mirrored one another. The idea of peace had always been interpreted differently by each side. It has long been obvious that neither side would fulfill the other's expectations. Egyptians underestimated Israeli fears. They were oblivious of the dynamics of emotions in a democratic mass society governed by coalition governments. Israelis have always had difficulty in realizing how deep a wound they had inflicted over the years in the Arab soul; the few who did sense it were tortured by guilt and, perhaps unconsciously, wanted the Palestinians to say that they are forgiven. This too was unlikely. According to a poll published in *Al Ahram*, 75 percent of Egyptians say they are against Israeli investments in Egypt, 71 percent refuse to buy Israeli goods, 53 percent are opposed to Israeli tourists visiting Egypt and would themselves never go to Israel.

Ali Salim, a well-known Egyptian playwright, did visit Israel last year and wrote a witty, sympathetic book about his tour which became an instant best-seller in Egypt. For this he was savagely attacked in both the pro-government and opposition press. He received so many threats that the police assigned body-guards to him around the clock.

When Sheikh Abdel Azuz bin Baz, the mufti of Saudi Arabia, issued a *fatwa* last fall sanctioning peace with Israel, *Al Ahram* reminded its readers that the same sheikh had also decreed that the earth was flat. Successive delegations of Israeli intellectuals visiting Cairo were shocked by the criticism they heard. Members of the Israeli Foreign Affairs Council who visited in December came back overwhelmed by Egyptian complaints of Israeli "hegemonial" designs. Their impression was that Egypt was worried about the "speed and direction of the peace process which might have an adverse effect on Egypt's standing in the region." President Weizman, on a state visit in Cairo, was so shocked by Egyptian talk of possible economic domination that he told an acquaintance that Egyptians seemed to believe the Protocols of Zion were true. Egyptian press comments on Israel grew so numerous, an innocent reader might have concluded the two countries were on the verge of rupture or even war. The truth, of course, is that Egypt's intellectual elite, has always had its reservations about the Israeli-Egyptian peace treaty of 1978. As a group they have been traditionally been pan-Arabist, Nasserist, or philo-communist. A good example is Mohammed Sid Ahmed, the brilliant leftist columnist of *Al Ahram*. He literally invented the Israeli-Arab peace in his seminal 1975 book *When the Guns Fall Silent*, the first of its kind in the Arab world. In this book he offered imaginative proposals on how to make peace safe for both sides, e.g., the building of industrial belts along the borders, in order to discourage acts of violence. When, three years later, peace was actually achieved at Camp David, Sid Ahmad changed his mind first because it was sponsored by the United States, not by the U.S. and the Soviet Union jointly, and secondly because it was a separate peace, rejected by the Palestinians and the other Arabs.

Almost two decades afterward, stereotypes abound. I often heard it said that Egypt had opened the door to peace but was Israel trying to push its way in? An Israeli diplomat in Cairo told me, in some shock, that a distinguished Egyptian lady had told him that Abraham had been an Arab. The remark was paradigmatic, in his view, of Egyptian attitudes in general. "Some of them even deny the Holocaust!" he complained. (*Schindler's List* was banned for reasons of "public morality"). "They see us through a prism which we will never change." Another woman asked him: "So you have decided to overrun us once again [as in 1967]—this time with your produce?" A second Israeli diplomat said: "In making peace they may have hoped to cut us down to our true size, as they saw it. Now they see they didn't and they are furious."

During a ten-day visit to Cairo I talked to some of the best-known Egyptian intellectuals. I came away, at times, feeling that many saw Israel as another Japan, a small island off the Arab subcontinent, racist and greedy, armed with nuclear weapons, ready now to overpower them. At one point I said "okay, if you are so concerned perhaps it would be better if there were to be no regional common market. Israel could seek its political and economic future within the European Union." The answer was, "If that's what they'll do it will only prove that they are colonialists and intruders. We always knew they don't want to integrate in the area." One writer told me "Israel takes Egypt for granted." Another insisted that "the mentality of Israel is the main problem." Samir Ragab, the distinguished publisher of the English language *Egyptian Gazette*, wrote on January 24, 1995:

"What kind of peace are they talking about and how can we build mutual trust in this climate?

"Frankly speaking, the Jews haven't and will not give up their wickedness which began in the days of the Prophet Moses and until the day of the resurrection."

"We breathe in the present but think in the past," Lutfi Kholi, the noted political essayist, told me. "The problem is that among my colleagues in the intellectual community many still oppose all normalization with Israel." According to Tahsin Basheer, a veteran diplomat, "Nobody is coming up with a new idea, everybody is turning in circles." Peres, with his high-flying plans for a Middle East common market was imaginative enough "but pointing to the stars without seeing the tips of one's fingers was not very practical either." In this atmosphere of suspicion and distrust the expiration in April 1995 of the Nuclear Nonproliferation Treaty added another nasty bone of contention. Egyptian public opinion was agitated about this for months. (It eventually was renewed.)

The United States was pressing for a renewal of this treaty for an indefinite period. Egypt announced it would not sign unless Israel also did. The United States feared that if Egypt does not sign other Afro-Asian countries might follow suit. Israel accused Egypt of raising this issue at the worst of all possible moments and for reasons of "prestige" and "hegemony." Egypt was outraged that Israel refused even discussions on the subject. "Whenever we mention it they jump up as if stung." Would Israel feel more secure if the [treaty] breaks down and the Arab countries develop or acquire their own nuclear arsenal? Mohammed Heikal, Egypt's best-known publicist and others were already calling on Egypt to develop its own nuclear bomb. Some Egyptians wondered why in Israel, a democratic country, there was not even public discussion on this theme.

Official spokesmen warned Israel it could not maintain a "monopoly on nuclear weapons." Field Marshal Mohamed Tantawi, Egypt's Defense Minister, said that a military imbalance "often leads to the adoption of policies that are not well calculated." Osama el Baz, President Mubarak's chief adviser on foreign affairs and national security spoke of a dangerous "strate-

gic imbalance." Everything would remain "lopsided" unless Israel dismantled its nuclear arsenal and signed the treaty. Ahmed Abdel-Halim, a retired
general and strategy expert of the privately funded Middle East Research
Institute told me he understood that Israel had "legitimate security concerns." It may well need a "last resort" protection by nuclear weapons. "We
could live with it when, as we were told, Israel had eight or ten nuclear warheads. But now we are told Israel has two hundred warheads! That we see as
a threat to impose their policies on Egypt and the entire region"

Rabin's rash talk of a "possible general war" added fuel to the fires. Israel
has never admitted that it possesses nuclear weapons. It defines its nuclear
policy as deliberately "ambiguous" yet it has leaked many hints over the
years that its potential nuclear capability was a last-ditch deterrent against
all-out attack. For this reason Israel has refused to sign a treaty before the
establishment of general peace in the region, to include Iraq and Iran.

There are real mental barriers and, when all is said and done, perhaps also
a true clash of interests. The art of statesmanship would be to keep it within
limits. One morning in Cairo I had a long talk with Osama el Baz, the
President's adviser. His high-ceilinged office is in a dusty old palace on the
banks of the Nile, resplendent in gilded wood carvings and faded cream walls.
He said that Egypt would sign the treaty even if Israel did not, but on one
condition: that Israel allow inspection of its sites and agreement was reached
on the timetable and on the modalities of disarmament at a future date. He
assured me that the nuclear issue was serious but "not a major contention
between the two countries. . . . I understand perfectly what Rabin can and
cannot do. . . . He is for peace. We do not want to weaken him and his government . . . Mubarak often asks us to understand Rabin's difficult problems
and concerns . . . Rabin has a heart . . . Mubarak and Rabin are very cosy."
Osama el Baz also said that the bad image of Israel in the semiofficial
Egyptian press was unjustified. He shrugged his slight shoulders: "We can't
do anything about that! There is freedom of the press in Egypt!" He assured
me that he and the president were convinced that Israel did not intend to
"dominate" the region. Peres was perhaps overly imaginative but wise.
Rabin was no fool. They knew well they would fail if they tried. The great
problem, as al Baz saw it, was the "perception" of Israel in Egyptian eyes. The
perception was bad. Israeli leaders were at least partly to blame for that. If the
"perception" was wrong, I asked el Baz, was the Egyptian government doing
anything to correct it? He himself had often made public statements to correct this erroneous perception even though "it isn't my proper domain." In
his public lectures, about once a week, the subject invariably came up. The
trouble was that the press was not always reporting his remarks in full.

20

Politics and Archaeology

A story is told of some early Zionist pioneers at Beit Alpha, a communal settlement in the Esdraelon Valley, founded in the early 1920s by young men and women belonging to the socialist youth movement *Hashomer Hatzair* (Young Guard). They subscribed to a bizarre fusion of utopian Marxism, Freudian psychoanalysis, and the then fashionable German *Jugendkultur*, with its romantic worship of nature, cult of eroticism, and disdain for bourgeois values. In December 1928, some of them were digging an irrigation channel and suddenly struck the brilliantly colored mosaic of a sixth-century Jewish synagogue. A first reaction was to keep the discovery secret and possibly cover it up again—a natural impulse, perhaps, that field archaeologists often encounter. Their main concern, after all, had been the digging of an irrigation channel. The unexpected discovery complicated this task and threatened to hold it up, perhaps indefinitely.

But there was more to it: an anti-religion attitude. The young kibbutzniks, full of the fervor of Russian revolutionism, had only a year or two earlier come out of Eastern Europe,—as the saying went at the time—"with no clothes, but with copies of *Das Capital* and Freud's *Interpretation of Dreams* in their knapsacks." A few were still teenagers. Many were in open rebellion against their Orthodox religious fathers. Some had actually run away from home to help build socialism, and the "new Jew," in the historic land of his forefathers: a utopian, psychic community in which their identity would be redefined and based on socialism and love. Religion was the opium of the people. For this reason alone, it might be best if the synagogue-mosaic were covered up again. Others argued that the mosaic was not necessarily a religious but rather a political, a Zionist monument. It was important, so the argument went, to uphold every archeological remnant that testified to the Jewish presence in the land, since time immemorial, and confirmed the legitimacy of the Zionist claim.

A debate ensued. The conservationist view prevailed over the iconoclastic. The story may be apocryphal but it sums up, as such stories sometimes do, the central facts of the case. A Jewish archaeologist, Eliezer Lipa Sukenik (the father of Yigael Yadin) was consulted. He proposed to conduct a scientific excavation of the site. It would be his first. Sukenik had been a high school teacher in Jerusalem in mathematics and geography who had gone on to study archaeology at the university of Berlin, at a time when the leading archaeologists and ethnologists at that university were obsessed with *Volk* and related ethnocentric prejudice. His great ambition then was the creation of a "Jewish archaeology." His view of history was narrowly Zionist, or if you like, Hegelian. He thought he recognized its spirit in Jewish longings for Zion throughout the ages. Jewish history during the past eighteen centuries was but an interval between the national independence lost in the first century and the national independence to be regained, hopefully, in the twentieth. He lectured the young kibbutzniks on Jewish history, modern archaeology, and on *memory*. Jews were a community of memory. In his enthusiasm for digging up remnants and relics of the glorious Jewish past he won over the majority of kibbutzniks who until that moment had been less interested in digging up the past than in building a utopian future. The site was solemnly excavated to much acclaim. A story in the *New York Times* reported that Jewish workers in Palestine were excavating "Jewish history in the Holy Land."

❈

It was probably no accident that the first recorded outbreak of a popular passion for Jewish archaeology occurred at a time of, relatively, low morale among the settlers owing to the economic crisis and the mounting Arab opposition to Jewish settlement. Among the more sensitive there might even have been something like nagging guilt at being intruders in a country now populated by another people that bitterly resented their arrival. For them, Sukenik's Jewish archaeology had a kind of cathartic effect. Word of Sukenik's dig at Beit Alpha spread quickly. Volunteers streamed to the site to work on the dig. A richly colored mosaic was uncovered in a state of remarkably good preservation. It included not only Hebrew inscriptions and common Jewish religious symbols but also a surprising representation of Helios, the pagan Greek sun god—highlighting the eclectic nature of Jewish religious worship at that time.

Contemporary reports stress the festive atmosphere among the participants at the dig. Reading these accounts today you get the feeling they were participating in a kind of communion. By digging up the hard ground they were retrieving memory—one is tempted to say—like checked baggage from a storage room.

Sukenik later recalled the event in glowing terms. "Suddenly people could see things that had never been so tangible before. . . . There was a feeling that this piece of ground, for which people had suffered so much, wasn't just any plot of land but a piece of earth where their forefathers had lived fifteen hundred to two thousand years ago. Their work in the present was cast in a different light. Their history was revealed to them and they saw it with their own eyes."

The enthusiasm at Beith Alpha, from all we know, was unprecedented in the checkered history of the Zionist enterprise. Earlier pioneers—in the first and second wave of immigration—had barely been moved by the charm of antique sites. They felt little need for buried proofs of the past to uphold their claims of in the present. Self-conscious of their historic roles, many of them were men of letters, inveterate diarists, polemicists, endlessly writing editorials, manifestoes, essays, and pamphlets. Yet, even though their first years in Israel coincided with the first great excavations of important biblical sites by Sir William Sellin, Sir Flinders Petrie, and R. A. S. Macalister, in their extensive writings there is hardly a word to suggest that any discoveries touched them even peripherally. The sudden outbreak of enthusiasm for Jewish archaeology at Beit Alpha in 1928 was unprecedented. It anticipated the fervor of future years and the political uses of archaeology in what was later hailed—or decried—as a "national syndrome": a popular craze for archaeology, a *bulmus* in Hebrew. *Bulmus* is an old Talmudic term. It denotes a fit, a rage, a craze, a mania, a ravenous hunger resulting from prolonged fasting.

Archaeology often converged with nationalism in the new nation states created in Europe after the World War I and in Latin America but perhaps nowhere did archaeology loom so large or for so long as in Israeli life until the early 1970s. In Czechoslovakia, Turkey, Finland, Poland, and the Baltic states archaeology was used politically to provide and occasionally fabricate material evidence of unbroken historical continuity. And let us not forget the Byzantine Queen Helena. Yigael Yadin called her, a little wistfully, perhaps, "the most successful archaeologist in history." Whatever she looked for she promptly found hundreds of years after the event: the stable where Mary had given birth to Christ, the twelve stations of the cross, Calvary, the true cross, the nails, the lancet, the Holy Sepulchre and so on and on. In our own time we have seen elaborate celebrations at Persepolis staged by the Shah, a few years before his fall, to commemorate the 2500th anniversary of "his" empire. In Iraq, Saddam Hussein proclaims himself a worthy successor of the ancient Babylonians. The Serbs venerate Kosovo. Like Masada it is not the site of a victory but of a defeat.

✳

Archaeological finds have inspired nearly all Israeli national symbols, from the State Seal to postage stamps to medals and coins. (Walter Benjamin claimed that postage stamps were the visiting cards left by governments in children's playrooms.) Since independence, Israeli coins have been stamped with motifs copied from first-century Jewish silver shekels. (Many years ago, I remember seeing in the shop window of an antique dealer on Allenby Road in Tel-Aviv a display that attracted some attention: a few modern Israeli coins were placed there in a row next to the ancient Jewish coins that had inspired them. It was obvious to anyone looking that the design and overall aesthetics of the ancient coins were considerably more accomplished than those of the modern). And I remember a television interview with Prime Minister Menachem Begin at the peak point of hyperinflation in Israel in 1980 when a pack of cigarettes cost thousands and cash registers could longer cope with so many digits and the economy was grinding to a halt because of a sudden drop in investments. Begin was expected to announce cuts in public spending, a wage-and-price freeze, and other anti-inflation measures. He didn't. He only proclaimed that the name of the monetary unit would be changed from the foreign name lira (i.e. livre, or "pound") to shekel, a Hebrew name of ancient renown. Its historic weight alone, as Begin put it, would make it one of the world's hard currencies at par with the American dollar.

How did all this come about? In the years of struggle leading up to the establishment of the new state and during its first two decades or so, the cult of archaeological relics was a determining factor in Israeli culture. It was widely thought to provide an immigrant society with a common culture. There was, of course, also a calculated effort at public relations aimed at Bible-oriented customers abroad. In a deeper sense, however, the apparent obsession with ancient Jewish sites and artifacts grew out of and served the feverish search for identity—a secular identity—which was characteristic of the period. The Dead Sea Scrolls thrilled *secular* Israelis; most orthodox Jews were indifferent to them. In the ethnocentric atmosphere of the early years there was a rush to identify Jewish sites and an overemphasis on digging them up and a tendency to expose to public view the Jewish strata of a site even where other layers may have been historically or artistically more significant or revealing. The task of archaeology was to prove a point about Jews in the Holy Land and not always, as it probably should have been, to explore material remains in order to determine the circumstances of ancient cultures and civilizations in a country where they have been so many and so varied. There was even a comic attempt, fortunately short-lived, by the then Director of Antiquities to impose a nationalistic nomenclature. He requested that the Iron Age be referred to henceforward as the Israelite Period, the Hellenistic as the Hasmonean, the Roman as the Mishnaic, and the Byzantine as the Talmudic periods.

In our own time, a new post-Zionist generation of younger archaeologists has come to question the patriotic oversell and single-mindedness of their predecessors, their arbitrary choice of terms and areas of study, their seeming haste occasionally to identify this or that site as unfailingly Jewish on the basis of partial or insufficient evidence. There is even a movement to discard the very term "Biblical archaeology" as a misleading and ethnocentric term. This is, perhaps, as it should be. And yet, mistakes in attribution are common in art, too. The big question we must always ask is: Was the mistake caused by ideology? Excessive claims are also made in physics too and in all other exact sciences. Oversell in science often stems from a need to raise money to support further research. In the philosophy of science it is common to distinguish between contexts of *discovery* and *justification*. We all have the right to pursue what we want to pursue and to explore and eventually dig it up—this is the "discovery." That we do so may be a personal or even a nationalistic choice or prejudice. But choosing a field of study as a result of personal interest or ideology is common and natural in every field and as such is not objectionable. The problem arises when the "justification," or proof of our discovery is prompted not by evidence but by ideology. I may decide to study the history of my own family rather than that of someone else. But I may present my grandmother as a Balkan princess only if I can provide exact and irrefutable proof.

To judge them on this basis, I should say, most Israeli archaeologists, even of the early period, come out rather well. They were digging not only for knowledge but also for the reassurance of roots, which they found in the Israelite ruins scattered throughout the country. They may have been prejudiced in their choice of study but not, in most cases, in the analysis of the results. They oversold their discoveries as other scientists do. The difference lay in the resonance of their work in the culture as a whole, and in the manner its results were heralded sensationally in the press and on television, adopted by patriotic fan clubs, and popularized and given subtexts by eager school teachers, nationalist historians, tour guides, Bible-nuts, youth leaders, and politicians. I am not saying that archaeologists themselves had nothing to do with this manipulation. I am suggesting that their role in it was minor in comparison to, say, the powerful lobby of elementary and high school Bible-teachers.

There were political and, I assume, psychological reasons why Israeli archaeology had at that time a distinctive, even chauvinistic, air. Several amateur archaeologists among the generals and the politicians imbued archaeological discoveries with a current "meaning." Moses Finley, reviewing Yadin's book on Masada in 1966, suggested that there was "a large and interesting book to be written about the politics of modern archaeology in which Masada will be a centerpiece." This has recently been done by Neal Silberman in his very revealing biography of Yadin *A Prophet From Amongst You—The Life of a "Soldier, Scholar and Mythmaker* (New York: Addison-Wesley, 1993).

As Silberman puts it, very succinctly, I think, under Yadin archaeology in Israel was not strictly an academic activity but "a tangible means of communion between the people and the land." The religious term communion is very well chosen here. Yadin himself often suggested that for young Israelis a "faith" in history and archaeology was a kind of "religion." Its high priests were school teachers, youth leaders, army education officers. They and the mass media combined to give archaeology—a certain kind of archaeology—a cultic aspect, and a prominence it never had, as far as I know, in another culture.

As Silberman writes, archaeological discoveries of ancient Jewish sites offered "poetic validation for modern Jewish settlement. Artifacts came to possess the power of sacred relics in a new cult of veneration for the ancestors." Now Yadin was a certainly a very serious scientist. In his archaeological digs he followed the strictest scientific rules. And he kept insisting that archaeology and politics must strictly be kept apart. Yet, as Silberman shows, there was always an extra-scientific message afterwards, in the oversell.

He notes Yadin's reluctance or inability to define precisely the modern significance of Masada, if there was one. This is only partly true. Yadin initiated the practice of swearing-in troops on the top of Masada. He attended these bizarre ceremonies himself. In one often quoted speech he told the young recruits during the ceremony:

"When Napoleon and his troops stood by the pyramids of Egypt he told them that four thousand years of history were looking down on them. What would he not have given to be able to say: Four thousand years of *your own* history look down on you. . . . The echo of your oath this night will resound throughout the encampments of our foes. Its significance is not less powerful that of all our defensive armaments."

In his 1957 book *The Message of the Scrolls* Yadin gave a special symbolic meaning to the date on which his late father had purchased the first of the Dead Sea scrolls: " . . . at the [very] moment of the creation of the state of Israel. It is as if these manuscripts had been waiting in caves for two thousand years, ever since the destruction of Israel's independence until the people of Israel returned to their home and regained their freedom. The symbolism is heightened by the fact that the first three scrolls were brought to my father for Israel on 29 November 1947—the very day the United Nations voted for the recreation of a Jewish state in Israel after two thousand years."

He had, when he spoke, the rare knack for drama that allows some men to endow dumb stones with the quality of speech. Speak they did in his hands, on his lecture tours through five continents where he did more for Israel than all its hack government propagandists put together; and, in Israel, on a highly successful TV quiz program on archaeology he hosted for two years every fortnight. After finding a series of ancient papyri in a Judean desert cave, including dispatches from Bar Kokhba, the fabled leader of the last Jewish uprising against the Romans in A.D. 120, he arranged for the entire government to assemble at President Ben Zvi's residence without, however, giving them prior notice of what he had unearthed. Cabinet ministers at that time were more docile, or less busy, than they are today. At one point during this meeting he turned to the President and announced: "Excellency, Mr. President of the State of Israel. I have the honor to present to you letters dispatched by the last president of the state of Israel: Bar Kokhba." The event, if I remember correctly, was broadcast live on radio.

✻

I remember hearing Yadin argue, on one private occasion, that he could not be held responsible for the immense publicity emanating from his digs; nor for the popular image of Masada which had registered so powerfully and on occasion incorrectly in the public mind ("the Masada complex"). It is also true that he never conducted an excavation in the occupied territories; or even in East Jerusalem, as he might have after 1967. Moreover, after 1967 he publicly decried the spreading worship of national and religious relics as an "idolatrous" practice. Judaism was an abstract religion, he claimed, not given to the worship of saints and dead stones. And he ridiculed those who in 1968 had forced their way into the Muslim mosque within the cave of the Makhpela at Hebron, where Abraham, Isaac, Jacob, and their spouses are supposed to be buried and had turned parts of the mosque into a Jewish synagogue. He mocked the entire idea and the worshippers too and stated that he did not see why they were making so much fuss over the tombs of a couple of Arab sheiks.

He demonstratively refused to attend the bizarre state funeral Prime Minister Begin staged before television cameras of obscure bones that had been found twenty years earlier in a Judean desert cave and were said to be the remains of Bar Kokhba's heroic soldiers who died in battle for Israel. By then Yadin was Begin's deputy prime minister. Begin insisted on staging the event as one of great contemporary relevance. The coffin containing the controversial bones (several were of women and children) was draped in flags and carried to a tomb on the shoulders of four generals. Yadin continued to protest against this kind of political theater; but his protests were in vain. The images he had helped to imprint on the nation's mind had taken on a life of their own.

In the 1950s, thousands of Israelis became ardent amateur archaeologists. Archaeology—by now a national cult—became a popular movement, as well as a sport of kings: politicians, socialites, top civil servants, famous army generals were known as ardent collectors. It was a cult quite unknown in this form in other countries: a national sport, almost—not a spectator sport but an active pastime. It turned into a movement that included tens of thousands of people in all walks of life, as perhaps fishing or hunting or bowling does elsewhere. In many a suburban private garden, flowerpots posed on florid ancient marble pedestals. In middle-class homes one could see sizeable archaeological collections assembled on bookshelves through purchase or illicit digging by enthusiastic amateurs.

Government attempts to curtail illegal digging in the interest of science and the public museums were half-hearted and generally futile. The best-known amateur archaeologist was general Moshe Dayan. His lifelong pursuit of archaeology nearly cost him his life in 1968 when a tunnel he was digging through a wet Philistine mound near Tel-Aviv collapsed and broke several of his ribs. He was asked in an interview what exactly had he been looking for underground. His answer was:

"The ancient Land of Israel. Everything that ancient Israel was. Those who lived here then . . . I sometimes feel I can literally enter their presence."

Dayan was a man of great personal magnetism. His life style was hedonistic. His military victories, his love of fast cars and money, his numerous mistresses and his enormous collection of ancient artifacts reflected the wide range of his interests and gifts. His fame vastly contributed to the popular macho appeal of archaeology as a bloodless field sport. His private collection was one of the world's largest hoards of ancient Near Eastern artifacts, some of which he had dug up with his own hands. The most dramatic items were sarcophagi and burial urns. Here was a man, the darling of local and foreign electronic media, the favorite star of all the Barbara Walterses of the world, who in the eyes of millions had come to symbolize the sabra, the new Jew, an ancient people's newly found vitality in modern times. Yet in the intimacy of his private home he lived in a morbid decor of burial urns, funeral plaques, death offerings, and sarcophagi.

In the fifties and sixties, the annual conventions of the Israel Exploration Society—a regular get-together of patriotic bible and geography-of-Israel teachers—were regularly attended by more than a thousand spectators. This was almost one per thousand of the total Jewish population at that time. (Imagine about 150,000 people attending a similar seminar in the United States.) Long before the cable car to Masada was built, scout leaders regularly led their young followers up the steep serpentine path to the top of Masada to spend a night there. Lit up by blazing torches, the dramatic nocturnal setting—much like Barbarossa's mountain—invited mythic interpretations. Gathering around campfires the youngsters recited the grisly tale of the mass suicide and intoned the well known refrain of Lamdan's poem "Masada Shall Not Fall Again." Masada, Hatzor, and Meggido—all excavated by Yadin and popularized with his marvelous gift of communication—were part and parcel of a young person's political education at that time.

So were the Dead Sea scrolls, displayed in a specially built "shrine" on the grounds of the Israel Museum in Jerusalem. Archaeology and nationalism were perfectly matched in the "Shrine of the Book," shaped like a chapel over a round altar where the main scroll was displayed like the relic of a saint. A ten-year-old schoolchild could easily read it. (Would a ten-year-old in Athens or Rome find it as easy to read ancient Greek or Latin inscriptions? In Greece and Italy, the language is no longer the same. In Jerusalem it is.) In an immigrant country, among a hybrid people from

more than a hundred countries of origin, all this effort reflected an obsessive search for common roots. It also promoted a kind of historical amnesia
which assured that events that had taken place two thousand years ago
were grasped more vividly than anything since then until the present.
Joshua Kenaz, one of Israel's foremost novelists, drew a vivid picture of this
in his fine novel *Hitganvut Yekhidim* (Individual Stealth). Here is Alon's
monologue a training sergeant haranguing a couple of *nebbish* recruits in
an army auxiliary unit:

> Imagine a shepherd of kibbutz Megiddo with his flock of sheep on the
> slope of an ancient mound. He suddenly discovers a tablet. It's
> inscribed in cuneiform letters. He passes this on to the archaeologists.
> They decipher it. They discover it's part of the epos of Gilgamesh.
> Someone wrote it 3500 years ago . . . D'you understand? . . . Here's a
> tale from ancient Babylon. It's suddenly discovered here. In the Land
> of Israel. Next to your house. In the yard outside they discover
> Herod's palace. In Nahal Hever near Ein Gedi they find a cave. Close
> to the remains of the Roman encampments there. A cave full of skele-
> tons. Womens' and children's bones. They all starved to death during
> the siege. Next to them shoes. Rags of clothes. Remains of foodstuff.
> And the big shard of a jar with Hebrew letters. As though waiting for
> us. For us to come and discover it. And now it all overflows and
> explodes. As the earth has saved it all just for us. As our roots. . . .
>
> It's amazing. It's not like reading about it in the bible. . . . These
> men . . . they were like Arik Sharon's guys . . . men who know every
> wadi and don't know what fear is . . .

But it wasn't all politics, of course. Archaeology was more than politics,
roots, or romantic yearnings for a distant barbaric past. There was an easy
attraction in archeology: unlike other outdoor sports, it combined fresh air
with bookish toil and adventure. In Tel-Aviv, where I grew up, we were
never more than fifteen minutes away from three or four known but not
yet fully excavated sites—Roman, Jewish or Hellenistic—each of them so
rich in all kinds of fantastic finds that we rarely returned from an outing
without a nice coin, or shining piece of wonderful blue Phoenician glass, or
an oil-lamp or the interesting fragment of one, or a potsherd or a lump of
sculptured marble.

As one grew older, one occasionally had a sense in Israel of living inside a
time machine. The millennium-spanning mixture of ancient and modern
history, the relentless intensity of daily life coupled with a notion, perhaps

not always quite conscious, of a problematic legitimacy—or at least a legitimacy widely contested and by one's nearest neighbors in the region—all that
was likely to reinforce a lifelong fascination with antiquities of all kinds. You
did not have to be an Israeli to share in it. Edmund Wilson who by inclina-
tion was a shrinker of myths succumbed to it very willingly, as his published
dairies In the Sixties clearly show.

Later on when the Old City of Jerusalem became accessible, the proximity of things there again induced a frame of mind conducive to allow the
historical warp. The forces of the past were so strong it sometimes seemed
the city failed to have a present. The extremes intersected but almost never
met. Everything was tight, crowded, old, ruined, and intertwined. Under a
stone parapet placed there by a British engineer after the first World War
lies a Mamluk doorway built over a Hasmonean tower standing on foundations from the time of the Judean kings. A Roman arch of the first century spans an early Jewish pavement that connects the apses of a Byzantine
church with the top of a Muslim mosque. The Western Wall, the Holy
Sepulchre, the Mosques on the ancient temple mount are within a stone's
throw of each other—no pun is intended here—I simply wish to emphasize
the oppressing proximity of things, the way they overhang and overlap.

A young person growing up in this milieu would frequently hear it said
that the present in Israel reflected the distant past (and vice versa). Ben
Gurion himself drew the analogy between Yoshua, conqueror of Canaan
"in storm" (to quote Tchernichovsky's famous poem) and General Yadin
himself. Such rhetoric highlighted the mirroring of past and present. It
stressed myths and symbols. We all turn history into myth and ritual and
into symbols that give meaning to life. This is why we celebrate birth. This
is why we have mourning rites and funerals. The rhetoric was convoluted
at times but it had its appeal and sometimes it almost caused the time zones
to overlap, as in those historic paintings in Italy or France where one sees
Dante holding hands with Virgil, or Charlemagne in animated conversation with Napoleon.

❋

Today, more than a century since the beginning of settlement, Israel is
often said to be the most excavated country in the world. Last year,
according to official figures, some 250 excavations took place within Israel
proper (plus more than fifty in the occupied territories). And yet archaeology no longer looms as large as it did in years past. It is no longer the
popular field sport it was two or three decades ago. The trend has been

noticeable for some years. The great stars are gone too. There has been a dramatic decline in public interest in archaeology. The army, for reasons of economy, I am told, no longer stages spectacular swearing-in ceremonies on Masada. Native Israelis—they are the overwhelming majority now—appear to have less need to search for roots; those who do turn rather to religion. The secular majority appears self-assured enough to accept a historical compromise with the Palestinians in a pragmatic mood of post-Zionist open mindedness.

During the past decade, a younger generation of archaeologists and historians has deconstructed the Masada myth of patriotic suicide into, at best—a calculated invention of the first-century historian Flavius Josephus and, at worst—a senseless mass hysteria, a kind of "Jewish Jonestown." (Oddly enough, this may well have been the view at the time of the Jewish religious establishment too. There isn't a word about Masada in rabbinical literature).

In a population almost six times larger than it was in 1952 the number of those attending the annual conventions of the Israel Exploration Society remains roughly the same it was then. University statistics indicate a parallel drop, relatively speaking, in the number of archaeology students and a truly dramatic decline in Jewish and Hebrew studies generally, from Talmud to Jewish history and Hebrew literature or language. At the Hebrew University—in the fifties the center of Jewish, Land-of-Israel and related studies—504 students registered in 1994 in the department of Japanese and Chinese studies. Only nineteen were in the Department of Talmud (one of them was Japanese).

Peace, if it comes, will accelerate this openness. Following the Oslo agreement between Israel and the PLO a first exchange of views on "archaeology" was marked by intransigence on both sides. Israel was ready to grant the Palestinians control only over "Muslim" or "Arab" archaeological sites on the West Bank; PLO representatives insisted on control of all sites, including Jewish ones, and furthermore demanded the restitution, among others, of the Dead Sea Scrolls (which were bought by Israelis in New York and elsewhere or seized during the 1967 war). They argued that the authors of the Dead Sea Scrolls, the Essenes, had been an "ancient Palestinian sect." Jesus Christ too is being claimed nowadays by Palestinian intellectuals as an "ancient Palestinian." Palestinian nationalism, which has so often in the past taken cues from Zionism, seems nowadays to be in need of archaeology to assist in nation building.

It may well be that both Israeli and Palestinian claims on archaeological sites are merely opening positions in what is bound to be a long-lasting negotiation. Except when it comes to Jerusalem, which is a hypersensitive subject for everyone, those claims are not likely to jeopardize a future settlement in the name of the past, however evocative or important the sites may be for the sense of identity on both sides.

We have all heard the old saying that archaeology thrives on ruins and war. There are more known ancient sites per square mile in Israel than in any other country. In Jerusalem alone—we know of some fifty major sieges, sacks, captures, and destructions during the past thirty centuries (three in this century alone)—at least ten more or less violent changes in the ruling religion. Jerusalem is a veritable outdoor Louvre of the history of warfare. A short time before his death W. H. Auden visited Jerusalem. I saw the poet standing one afternoon on the terrace of Mishkenot Shaanim, the municipal guest house, admiring the magnificent view of the Old City. Mayor Teddy Kollek was standing there too, they were all looking out across the valley of Hinnom and the battlements and tombs and the mayor said in a laconic tone that Jerusalem would be a beautiful place if it weren't for the wars, and the orthodox of all faiths, their squabbles and their riots. He said this, Auden recalled later, as one would say in London that it would be a lovely place except for the weather. Shortly after this in what may have been his last poem, Auden wrote that archaeology was proof that all school textbooks lied. There was no reason to be proud of history, Auden insisted, since it was made by the criminal in us.

21

The Demons of the Jews

After the assassination of Yitzhak Rabin at a peace rally in Tel Aviv, the country was for several weeks swept by waves of shame, shock, pain, guilt, remorse, and mutual accusations. Large crowds, of mostly young people, continued to gather at Rabin's graveside in the National Cemetary on Mount Herzl outside Jerusalem. Day in day out, thousands of memorial candles spelled out their sentiments on the ground, at the tombside, below the municipal building where Rabin was slain and outside his private home in north Tel Aviv.

The main question asked but not always answered was "why?" It dominated the op-ed pages. Talk shows on television and radio continued the debate from early in the morning late into each night. The left accused the right-wing parties of causing the catastrophe by the verbal violence they had used against the government during the past two years ("Rabin Murderer," "Rabin Traitor") which was toned down only after Rabin's death. Likud leaders complained that the left had originated this violent style during the Lebanon war. After the massacres at Sabra and Shatilla, Begin and Sharon too had been called murderers. The answer from the left was "Yes, but did we kill? The bullets in Israel are always shot from from right to left."

West Bank settlers claimed that the killer's act was born of the despair among patriotic Jews caused by the government's betrayal of the *Land—*

Eretz-Israel. The continuing debate echoed another battle—hopefully the last—in the long struggle over whether Israel is a civil-democratic or a tribal-messianic society.

The political class, sanctimonious as well as cynical, and with an eye on the May 1996 elections, was busy picking up the pieces. The country remained deeply divided between supporters and opponents of peace with Syria and the Palestinians in return for withdrawal from land occupied in 1967. Laborites were concerned that Peres might not be able to generate the same public support for peace as Rabin, the war hero, did. Likud leaders were on the defensive. They would not remain so for long. In other circumstances, their insistent calls for "unity" and "reconciliation" might have been uplifting; but at a time when so many Israelis felt they must stand up and be counted such calls appeared merely as cover-ups. The police investigation of the confessed murderer and his alleged accomplices brought into focus the seedy underworld of ruthless terrorists informally allied with fairly prominent rabbis, religious leaders, mystagogues, kabbalists, and other salvation-mongers. Everybody knew of, or suspected, the existence of this underworld before. For years its exponents had been talking their heads off to the local and foreign media. Yet in the past nobody had been ready to deal with them seriously—perhaps because they had mostly threatened only Arabs in the Occupied Territories. To the extent that a few had been prosecuted in the past, they had, as a rule, been treated leniently by the courts and with something like "understanding" for their motives. When sentenced to longer prison terms—as were those who murdered three students at Hebron university or crippled two Arab mayors or attempted to blow up the Dome of the Rock on the Temple Mount of Jerusalem—their sentences were commuted by the President and they were set free. According to a report submitted to the Attorney General, hundreds of suspected acts of aggression by settlers against Palestinians, remain unresolved.

The assassination highlighted once more the deep malaise that had afflicted the Orthodox synagogue in the aftermath of the Six Day War. Professor David Hartmann, himself an Orthodox rabbi and founding director of an institute in Jerusalem dedicated to reinterpreting the authoritarian tradition of *halacha* in a way compatible with democratic morality, said: "Rabin's killer was an innocent, straight kid who took his tradition seriously or too literally. In addition to hearing what secular secular politicians had to say about the peace process, from his Orthodox rabbis he heard the evocative language of religious dogmatism, always couched in absolute the terms, as articulated in the *halacha* by third-century rabbis under the radically different conditions of the barbaric Sassanite empire. The text became his identity. It encouraged hate and destruction. Amir was no aberration. He was wholly *within* the normative tradition that has survived crude and frozen through the ages to our own times. I am shocked at the irresponsibility of *halacha* teachers who afterward said: "We use this language but we never thought people are going to act on it. They should have known better."

"The assassin could think he was called upon by God to prevent another Holocaust. It came not as a revelation in the middle of the night. It was rather the culmination of a long process of indoctrination and so-called learning. The *halacha* is, of course, not as simple-minded as the killer may have thought. There are sufficient other (humane and pacifist) resources in the tradition to counterbalance the dogmatism. The tragedy is that a group of fanatical and politicized rabbis has in recent years become dominant over all other voices. They continue to block out all these alternative voices. In America too the majority of the orthodox community seems to have adopted the idea that returning the Land was endangering the Jewish future."

I asked Hartmann whether these American rabbis would justify the murder of Yitzhak Rabin.

"In some way," he said, "I am afraid, they would not only justify it. Some would [even] celebrate it. There is a deep disease in orthodoxy that wasn't there in the past."

❀

Like other national movements born in the second half of the last century, Zionism was originally a secular, even anticlerical movement. Its aim was to establish a safe haven for Jews in their ancient homeland, change social and occupational patterns, and resurrect the Hebrew language. The early Zionists bluntly dismissed the possibility of a theocracy. Steeped in the liberalism of nineteenth-century nationalism, Herzl wrote, "if faith keeps us united science makes us free." Elsewhere in the same book he promised to keep the theocrats in their temples, just as we shall confine our professional soldiers to their barracks. He underestimated not only the nationalism of the Arabs but also the latent forces of ethnocentrity released by the Zionist revival; and he overestimated the liberalism of Jews in an age of universal selfishness which—although of an apocalyptic frame of mind—he could not foresee in all its fearful brutality. The rise of "religious Zionism," especially after the Six Day War, complicated matters considerably. Once you mystify the Land in such a way as to make it the carrier of all your religious passion, as religious Zionists have done, especially since 1967, then it follows that someone who threatens this religious passion for the Land or is ready to give parts of it away—as Rabin and Peres were—becomes the enemy.

In this sense Rabin's murder was a "religious murder." Abraham Burg, the new chairman of the Jewish Agency, himself an Orthodox Jew (and one of the victims of a hand-grenade thrown in 1983 by a Jewish terrorist at a Peace Now parade), insisted on this from the start. Shortly after Rabin's murder by a student of Bar-Ilan, outside Tel Aviv, a religious university of some renown and a well-known citadel of right-wing sentiment—Burg lashed out at that institution calling it "Bar Ilan-Teheran." The killer was a 25-year-old fundamentalist named Yigal Amir. His avowed aim was to derail the peace process. He claimed that the agreement with the Palestinians contradicted sacred religious principle. Religious Zionism was nurtured for years by this mind set. Amir said in court that according to *halacha*, a Jew who like Rabin "gives over his people and his land to the enemy he must be killed. My whole life I have been studying the *halacha* and I have all the data." He held Rabin personally responsible for the killing of Jews by Palestinian terrorists. Their blood was on Rabin's hand, he charged. Rabin was their ally.

To say, as is often said in such cases, that the killer was a lunatic implies that he was incoherent. From what we know it is obvious that he was not. The graduate of a paramilitary yeshiva, at the time of the murder he was a third-year honor student at the law faculty of Bar Ilan. Bar Ilan first achieved some political notoriety in the early eighties when the campus rabbi, one Israel Hess, published a treatise entitled "Mitzvat genocide batorah," the mitzva (commandment) of genocide in the torah. All who declare war on "God's people" were declared "Amalekites." In defense, "God declares a counter-jihad," Hess wrote. In such a war the "Amalekites" must be wiped out, as in the Bible, down to their last woman and child. To reassure readers that this was not a purely historical matter he added: "The day will come when all of us will be summoned to conclude this holy war to destroy Amalek." Hess, according to a recent report in *Ha'aretz*, is still a lecturer at Bar Ilan. It is a university where until recently Kahanists could paste up racist posters (and such that showed Rabin washing the blood off his hands) with impunity but a student who hugged his girlfriend on campus risked being expelled.

Amir's teachers at this university described him as serious, sensitive, and intellectual; a brilliant young man, dedicated to his studies ("he spent the whole day at the library"). Amir's mother said, "His brilliance had been his undoing." (She sent a letter of condolence "to Mrs. Rabin and the entire People of Israel" printed out from her computer in unusually large letters—

an odd display of free floating anxiety, pain, detachment and alienation). On the day after the murder, one of Amir's teachers confessed on radio that he had lain awake all night wondering where he had gone too far. The university suspended all teaching for three days and held memorial and prayer meetings. A student who announced on the Internet "The witch is dead" was promptly kicked out of Bar Ilan. Nothing was heard of steps taken there to identify teachers who might have thought or taught the same.

Amir also attended an orthodox *kolel* (talmud seminar) affiliated to the university. Many of the students there, and some of the instructors, are known to be fanatical opponents of the peace process. When he was not taking courses in civil and company law and in computer studies, the assassin organized support groups for the settlements on the West Bank. Last year he falsely registered as a resident in one of these settlements. On that basis of such an address he was issued a permit to carry the pistol he used to kill Yitzhak Rabin.

He was not a loner who wanted his name to go down in history, like Lee Harvey Oswald. He was sociable, good-looking, and well-liked. He was the child of Orthodox immigrants from Yemen who had worked their way up to a measure of affluence and a position of prominence in the community. He lived with his parents in a lower-middle-class suburb outside Tel Aviv. The family is now described as " warm and loving." His mother runs a popular kindergarten. The killer was the proverbial nice boy next door. He was a locally born and bred killer, not a weird American doctor, like Baruch Goldstein—the doctor who killed thirty worshippers in a Hebron mosque— in search of a Wild West where whites were allowed to fire at Indians. Amir had done his military service in a crack army unit; later, the Jewish Agency sent him to Russia to give Hebrew lessons to Jews planning to emigrate to Israel. His language was a mix, typical of his class, of military and talmudic jargon. He was, in the words of the author Zev Chafetz, "as Israeli as hummus-pie. He was trained by his rabbis, and as far as I am concerned, he pulled the trigger for them."

He was sure he had wide support and he may have been right in thinking so. In his own eyes, the ultimate sanction for his act was *religious,* as it had been for nearly all other acts of terror perpetrated in recent years by Jews in Israel and in the occupied territories. Most have gone unpunished. In many cases, the perpetrators first consulted their rabbis, seeking what they called "spiritual authority." Some were ordained rabbis themselves. The names of these rabbinical consultants were freely bandied about in the press. The former Likud government refrained from investigating, let alone prosecuting, them.

✻

Another time or place could have produced a different Yigal Amir. He was born in 1970, into the triumphal, messianic fervor generated by the Six Day War, which the salvation mongers in some of the country's leading rabbinical seminaries, were widely interpreting as a *milchemet mitzva*, a kind of "holy war" or Jewish jihad, heralding the dawn of Redemption: the advent of a new chiliastic age, the End of Days. The "Land of Israel" was not a territorial but a theological-salvationist concept. The Jewish tradition known as *halacha* is a many-layered body of argument and counter-argument, exegesis and exegesis-of-exgesis. It is an inherently manipulable text. Since the rise of the self-styled messiah Sabbatai Zevi in the seventeenth century, that text had never been as evocatively, as successfully manipulated as it has been by radical right-wing Israeli rabbis, in the aftermath of the Six Day War. Judaism is a highly decentralized religion. The office of chief rabbi is purely administrative. The lack of a hierarchy allows all ordained (and some unordained) rabbis to pronounce so-called halachic rulings. Texts often contradict one another. Traditional exegists insist that any literal reading of such texts can be highly misleading; at the very least it would be highly controversial.

One such literal reading in recent years concerned the halachic injunction to settle "the Land" which some of the more radical exegists considered more binding than all others, including even the ten commandments. Among the more militant, this created a peculiar dilemma about democracy and rule of law. When "democracy" or secular state laws were seen as contradicting the metaphysic authority of *halacha*, democracy and state laws were anathematized as *memshelet sadon* ("reign of iniquity") and contravenable. "There are more important things than majority rule," the militants said, especially when, as in Israel at the time of Rabin's murder, the government's majority in the Knesset was narrow and was secured only thanks to Arab votes ("Hitler was also elected in democratic elections," I heard one religious militant say). Rabin's agreement with the PLO ceding parts of the Land to the Palestinians was seen as "delaying the messianic process."

Furthermore, by delivering the settlers of Judea and Samaria to the whims of Arafat ("another Hitler"), the government was like a Judenrat in Nazi-occupied Europe cooperating with the Gestapo. Rabin was shouted down as a Quisling. He was a collaborator with evil. His hands were dripping with Jewish blood, the blood of those killed by Hamas terrorists. Rabin was guilty of being what a halachic luminary in the third century, had called a *rodef* ("persecutor"), a crime punishable by death.

A few weeks before Rabin's death, twelve kabbalists gathered outside Rabin's official residence in Jerusalem intoning all sorts of ancient Jewish oaths, curses, and other tricks of voodoo designed to bring about Rabin's death. The weird invocation was reported in the press. By a strange coincidence, a short time afterward an international conference on "Magic and Magia in Judaism," sponsored by the Hebrew University, took place in Jerusalem. They could not have picked a more fitting venue. Moshe Idel, the most prominent Israeli scholar in this field after Gershom Scholem a professor of Jewish Thought, was one of the organizers of the conference. He informed the participants of the kabbalist invocation outside Rabin's home. It happened, he said, right here, "in the the heart of Jerusalem, in fairly normal times. No one in the religious world cried out to protest. Nobody said it's all nonsense. In other words, they believe that [these invocations of black magic] actually work. Perhaps some were sorry that it's done to a prime minister or a Jew—but nobody doubts that it works." The decline in rationality, Idel concluded, expresses itself in the "introduction of magic into politics."

A decade earlier, in an essay on the rise of Meir Kahane, Leon Wieseltier wrote that the Jews must attend to their demons as well as to their enemies. One by one the enemies have since fallen away. But the demons remain.

The police were convinced that Rabin's killer too had received some kind of support from a rabbinical authority for his lethal interpretation of *halacha*—in other words, a kind of rabbinic *fatwa*. They were believed to be on the trail of a man they say was a "spiritual adviser" to Amir and his accomplices. The police assumed that a believer like Amir would not have shot the prime minister without some rabbinical consent offered in the name of *halacha*. Prior to the act, he may have offered what is described as a "confession in synagogue." At this stage there are only speculations to whom. A prominent West Bank dissident, a rabbi named Yoel Bin-Nun issued a (belated) ultimatum to Amir's so-called "spiritual" advisers. They had issued halachic rulings, he claimed, that Rabin was indeed a *rodef* and deserved death. Bin-Nun announced that he knew their identity. Unless they immediately resigned their rabbinic posts he would reveal their names publicly. They were bound to be important, revered rabbinical authorities. He would fight them, Bin-Nun announced in the now fashionable style, if need be "unto death."

✳

At his arraignment in court, the killer boasted of his act. His short speech was articulate, concise, to the point and reflected his interpretation of *halacha*. This was the smaller part of his monologue detailing Rabin's halachic crimes. The rest echoed almost sentence by sentence remarks made in recent months by Likud leaders Benjamin Netanyahu, Uzi Landau, Ariel Sharon, or by spokesmen of the two smaller right-wing opposition parties, the ex-generals Eiytan and Zeevy.

Their personal vitriolic attacks on Rabin had produced the lowest point in Israeli political discourse since the foundation of the state. By a carefully concocted strategy, Rabin was heckled and roughly harangued almost everywhere he had gone in the what would prove to be the last six months of his life. Likud spokesmen openly confessed their aim was to break him psychologically, to break his self-confidence. At an outing of normally well behaved immigrants from the Anglo-Saxon countries organized by the right-wing *Jerusalem Post* he was met with shouts "here comes the bloody dog." Rabin was to have "no mandate." He was accused to have, indirectly, encouraged Palestinian terror. "You, Mr Prime Minister," Netanyahu said in the Knesset on April 18, 1994 will enter history as a prime minister who established "an army of Palestinian terrorists." And a few days later, at a press conference: "Rabin will be able to announce: I have founded the terrorist state of Palestine." A year later, after a passenger bus was blown up in Tel Aviv by a Palestinian suicide terrorist: "You Yitzhak Rabin, I accuse you of direct responsibility for stirring up Arab terror and for the horror of this massacre in Tel Aviv. You are guilty. This blood is on your head."

Israeli politics are habitually rough but no Israeli government had ever been as deliberately and systematically delegitimized by its opposition as Rabin's had been. He was stabbing the country in its back. He was always grovelling before foreign statesmen. He had no sense of national pride. Rabin was willing to withdraw to "Auschwitz borders." His effigy, dressed in a Nazi uniform or wearing a checked headdress à la Arafat, was prominently displayed at opposition rallies. Netanyahu himself addressed such a rally in downtown Jerusalem. Even as prominent rabbis, including two former chief rabbis, were calling on Israeli soldiers, in the name of *halacha*, to disobey any orders to evacuate parts of the West Bank, leading spokesmen of the opposition were saying that Rabin had "no mandate" for doing what he was doing. His majority in parliament was illegitimate, since it depended on "non-Jewish Knesset members" who received their orders from Arafat. Repeated warnings (by the police too) that this language might lead to attempts on the lives of Rabin and Peres were ignored. Sharon dismissed the warnings as "Stalinist" or as "provocations by the media." An American rabbi named Hecht announced on Israeli television that Rabin deserved to

die. He based this verdict on Maimonides. In another time, in another country, such threats might have led to criminal charges. Nowadays, they usually
lead only to another talk show. Netanyahu, even as he was mildly admonishing his followers for their manners, was, along with his allies, riding the
tigers they had unleashed.

With remarkable candor, a veteran politician of the National-Religious
party, observed in public: "It is an undeniable fact that nearly all violent
right-wing extremists in Israel today are wearing skull-caps and are graduates of religious educational institutions. We must ask ourselves where we
have gone wrong." In down-town Jerusalem, an old bearded man wearing
a yarmulke was seen carrying a sign that said: "I am ashamed." It remains
to be seen if Likud too will show any signs of remorse remotely resembling
those that now mark the Orthodox community.

Index

28 ~~DA~~ DAYS